Lecture Notes in Computer Science 7641

Commenced Publication in 1973
Founding and Former Series Editors:
Gerhard Goos, Juris Hartmanis, and Jan van Leeuwen

Brian Nielsen   Carsten Weise (Eds.)

Testing Software and Systems

24th IFIP WG 6.1 International Conference, ICTSS 2012
Aalborg, Denmark, November 19-21, 2012
Proceedings

Springer

Volume Editors

Brian Nielsen
Aalborg University
Department of Computer Science
Selma Lagerlöfs Vej 300, 9220, Aalborg, Denmark
E-mail: bnielsen@cs.aau.dk

Carsten Weise
IVU Traffic Technologies AG
Borchersstr. 20, 52072 Aachen, Germany
E-mail: realtimecarsten@googlemail.com

ISSN 0302-9743   e-ISSN 1611-3349
ISBN 978-3-642-34690-3   e-ISBN 978-3-642-34691-0
DOI 10.1007/978-3-642-34691-0
Springer Heidelberg Dordrecht London New York

Library of Congress Control Number: 2012950603

CR Subject Classification (1998): D.2.4-5, D.2.9, D.2.11, C.2.2, C.2.4, D.3.2, C.3, F.3.1, K.6.3-4

LNCS Sublibrary: SL 2 – Programming and Software Engineering

Typesetting: Camera-ready by author, data conversion by Scientific Publishing Services, Chennai, India

Printed on acid-free paper

Springer is part of Springer Science+Business Media (www.springer.com)

Preface

It is our pleasure and honor to present the proceedings of the 24th IFIP International Conference on Testing Software and Systems (ICTSS 2012), held during November 19–21, 2012, in Aalborg, Denmark.

Testing is the most important quality assurance technique for the (partial) verification of communication and software systems and their models. Yet, testing remains very challenging in the underlying theory, methods and tools, in industrial use, and in its systematic combined application with other verification techniques. This important topic deserves a persistent and dedicated forum to address the fundamental and practical problems of testing software and systems.

ICTSS is a series of international conferences that aims at being a forum for researcher, developers, and testers to advance, discuss, and learn about new approaches, concepts, theories, methodologies, tools, and experiences of testing software systems in different application domains, including communication protocols, services, distributed platforms, middleware, embedded- and cyber-physical-systems, and security infrastructures.

The previous instances of ICTSS were held in Paris, France (2011), and in Natal, Brazil (2010). The ICTSS conference series is the successor of previous (joint) conferences TestCom (the IFIP TC 6/WG 6.1 International Conference on Testing of Communicating Systems) and Fates (International Workshop on Formal Approaches to Testing of Software), that together form a traditional and important event on testing, validation, and specification of software and systems. The conferences have a long history: TestCom is an IFIP-sponsored series of international conferences, previously called International Workshop on Protocol Test Systems (IWPTS) and International Workshop on Testing of Communicating Systems (IWTCS). It is devoted to testing communicating systems, including testing of communication protocols, services, distributed platforms, and middleware. The previous events were held in Vancouver, Canada (1988); Berlin, Germany (1989); McLean, USA (1990); Leidschendam, The Netherlands (1991); Montreal, Canada (1992); Pau, France (1993); Tokyo, Japan (1994); Evry, France (1995); Darmstadt, Germany (1996); Cheju Island, South Korea (1997); Tomsk, Russia (1998); Budapest, Hungary (1999); Ottawa, Canada (2000); Berlin, Germany (2002); Sophia Antipolis, France (2003); Oxford, UK (2004); Montreal, Canada (2005); and New York, USA (2006). Fates, Formal Approaches to Testing of Software, is a series of workshops devoted to the use of formal methods in software testing. Previous events were held in Aalborg, Denmark (2001); Brno, Czech Republic (2002); Montreal, Canada (2003); Linz, Austria (2004); Edinburgh, UK (2005); and Seattle, USA (2006). From 2007 on, TestCom and Fates have been held jointly in Tallinn, Estonia (2007), Tokyo, Japan (2008), and Eindhoven, The Netherlands (2009).

This book contains the refereed proceedings of the 24th instance of the International Conference on Testing Software and Systems (ICTSS 2012). We received 48 submissions. Each submission was thoroughly reviewed by at least three Program Committee members or sub-reviewers. Based on the subsequent discussions, the Program Committee selected 16 contributions for presentation and publication. The accepted papers were revised based on the comments made by the reviewers. These revised papers are presented in this volume. The program also included two invited talks:

- Klaus Havelund, Jet Propulsion Laboratory - Laboratory for Reliable Software, USA: Requirements-Driven Log Analysis
- Frits Vaandrager, Radboud University Nijmegen, The Netherlands: Active Learning of Extended Finite State Machines

We would like to thank all authors for submitting to ICTSS. We also wish to thank the distinguished invited speakers for accepting our invitation and for submitting extended abstracts for the proceedings. We are grateful to the members of the Program Committee and other reviewers for their hard work that made this conference possible. We appreciate their competent handling of the submissions during the summer period.

We would also like to thank the local organizers, staff from the distributed and embedded systems research group at Aalborg University, for arranging and preparing for the conference. In particular, thanks to Rikke W. Uhrenholt for her professional and friendly administrative and practical support. We thank the providers of the EasyChair conference management system, which has been of great value, and the Springer LNCS team for their support. Finally, we gratefully acknowledge the financial support we received from the Centre for Embedded Software System.

September 2012   Brian Nielsen
                                                       Carsten Weise

Organization

ICTSS 2012 was organized by the department of Computer Science, Aalborg University and The Centre for Embedded Software Systems (CISS), Denmark.

Program Chairs

Brian Nielsen   Aalborg University, Denmark
Carsten Weise   IVU Traffic Technologies, Germany

Steering Committee

Rob Hierons   Brunel University, UK (Chair, Elected by IFIP WG)
Andreas Ulrich   Siemens AG, Germany (Elected by IFIP WG)
Ana R. Cavalli   Telecom SudParis, France (Elected by IFIP WG)
Paul Baker   Visa Corporate, UK (Rotating member, 2009–2012)
Manuel Núñez   University of Complutense de Madrid, Spain
                          (Rotating member 2009–2012)
Alexandre Petrenko   CRIM, Canada (Rotating member 2010–2013)
Burkhart Wolff   University of Paris-Sud, France (Rotating member,
                          2011–2014)
Fatiha Zaïdi   University of Paris-Sud, France (Rotating member,
                          2011–2014)

Program Committee

Bernhard K. Aichernig   Technical University of Graz, Austria
Paul Baker   Visa Corp., UK
Ana Cavalli   National Institute of Telecommunications, France
Antonia Bertolino   CNR, Italy
John Derrick   University of Sheffield, UK
Khaled El-Fakih   American University of Sharjah, UAE
Jens Grabowski   University of Göttingen, Germany
Wolfgang Grieskamp   Google, USA
Roland Groz   Grenoble Institute of Technology, France
Toru Hasegawa   KDDI R&D Labs, Japan
Klaus Havelund   Nasa Jet Propulsion Laboratory, USA
Rob Hierons   University of Brunel, UK
Teruo Higashino   University of Osaka, Japan
Thierry Jéron   IRISA Rennes, France
Ferhat Khendek   University of Concordia, Canada
Victor Kuliamin   Russain Academy of Sciences, Russia
Bruno Legeard   Smartesting, France

Stéphane Maag	Telecom Sud Paris, France
Karl Meinke	KTH Royal Institute of Technology, Sweden
Mercedes Merayo	University of Complutense de Madrid, Spain
Zoltán Micskei	Budapest University of Technology and Economics, Hungary
Manuel Núñez	University of Complutense de Madrid, Spain
Doron Peled	University of Bar-Ilan, Israel
Alexandre Petrenko	CRIM, Canada
Paul Pettersson	University of Mälardalerne, Sweden
Andrea Polini	University of Camerino, Italy
Geguang Pu	ECNU, China
Holger Schlingloff	Humboldt University Berlin, Germany
Paul Strooper	University of Queensland, Australia
Adenilso Simão	University of Sao Paulo, Brazil
Kenji Suzuki	Kennisbron Co. Ltd., Japan
Nikolai Tillmann	Microsoft Research, U.S.A
Andreas Ulrich	Siemens AG, Germany
Hasan Ural	University of Ottawa, Canada
Jüri Vain	Technical University of Tallinn, Estonia
Nicky Williams	CEA-List, France
Burkhart Wolff	University of Paris-Sud, France
Nina Yevtushenko	Tomsk State University, Russia
Fatiha Zaïdi	University of Paris-Sud, France
Jian Zhang	Chinese Academy of Science, China

Additional Reviewers

Marat Akhin
El-Hashemi Alikacem
Cesar Andres
Oscar Botero
Xiaoping Che
Alexandre David
Juhan-Peep Ernits
Maxim Gromov
Rene Rydhof Hansen
Siyuan Jiang
Jun Kato
Olga Kondratyeva
Natalia Kushik
Felipe Lalanne
Mounir Lallali
Shuhao Li
Philip Makedonski
Pramila Mouttappa
Fei Niu
Alberto Nunez
Thomas Rings
Ramsay Taylor
Khalifa Toumi

Sponsoring Institutions

The Centre for Embedded Software Systems (CISS), Denmark
Department of Computer Science, Aalborg University, Denmark
EU Artemis Project Combined Model-Based Test and Analysis (MBAT)
International Federation for Information Processing (IFIP)

Table of Contents

Requirements-Driven Log Analysis
(Extended Abstract)

Klaus Havelund*

Jet Propulsion Laboratory
California Institute of Technology
California, USA

1   Background

Imagine that you are tasked to help a project improve their testing effort. In a
realistic scenario it will quickly become clear, that having an impact is difficult.
First of all, it will likely be a challenge to suggest an alternative approach which
is significantly more automated and/or more effective than current practice. The
reality is that an average software system has a complex input/output behavior.
An automated testing approach will have to auto-generate test cases, each being
a pair (i, o) consisting of a test input i and an oracle o. The test input i has to
be somewhat meaningful, and the oracle o can be very complicated to compute.
Second, even in the case where some testing technology has been developed that
might improve current practice, it is then likely difficult to completely change the
current behavior of the testing team unless the technique is obviously superior
and does everything already done by existing technology.

So is there an easier way to incorporate formal methods-based approaches
than the full fledged test revolution? Fortunately the answer is affirmative. A
relatively simple approach is to benefit from possibly already existing logging
infrastructure, which after all is part of most systems put in production. A log is
a sequence of events, generated by special log recording statements, most often
manually inserted in the code by the programmers. An event can be considered
as a data record: a mapping from field names to values. We can analyze such
a log using formal methods, for example checking it against a formal specification. This separates running the system from analyzing its behavior. It is not
meant as an alternative to testing since it does not address the important input generation problem. However, it offers a solution which testing teams might
accept since it has low impact on the existing process. A single person might
be assigned to perform such log analysis, compared to the entire testing team
changing behavior.

Note that although logging often is manually programmed, it can be performed using automated code instrumentation, using for example aspect-oriented
programming. The point here, however, is that manual logging is often already

* Part of the work described in this publication was carried out at Jet Propulsion
Laboratory, California Institute of Technology, under a contract with the National
Aeronautics and Space Administration.

done by programmers, and we can try to benefit from this. Analyzing program executions using formal methods is also referred to as *runtime verification* (RV).

2   LogScope and TraceContract

At Jet Propulsion Laboratory (JPL) some positive, although still limited, success with this approach has been gained. Two different systems for analyzing logs against formal specifications have been developed and applied: LOGSCOPE and TRACECONTRACT. These systems in turn are inspired by previous work, most specifically RULER [6].

LOGSCOPE [3,8] checks logs against specifications written in a so-called *external DSL* - a stand-alone small Domain Specific Language with its own parser. It is based on a parameterized automaton formalism (conceptually a subset of RULER) with a second layer of temporal logic which is translated to the automaton level. The temporal logic formalism is very simple and intuitive to use. LOGSCOPE was used for a short period by the testing team for the MSL (Mars Science Laboratory) rover, also named Curiosity [12], which landed on Mars on August 5, 2012. LOGSCOPE was usable due to its simplicity and ease of adoption. The testing team was, however, shut down during a period due to an otherwise unrelated 2 year delay in the mission, and LOGSCOPE was not used when a new team was built later. The application of LOGSCOPE on MSL was reported in [3,8].

TRACECONTRACT [4,5] is a so-called *internal DSL* (an extension of an existing programming language), an API in the SCALA programming language, offering an interesting combination of data parameterized state machines and temporal logic. It is currently being tried out by the testing team on the SMAP project [13] at JPL (a future Earth orbiting satellite measuring soil moisture), and by the LADEE project [10] at NASA Ames Research Center (a future Moon orbiting satellite measuring dust in the lunar atmosphere). The attraction of TRACECONTRACT is the expressiveness of the logic, in large part caused by it being an extension of a high-level modern programming language. As such TRACECONTRACT represents the use of an advanced programming language for modeling, an interesting point in itself, as also pointed out in [9]. Furthermore, TRACECONTRACT has a very small implementation and is exceptionally easy to modify compared to LOGSCOPE. We shall discuss the two applications of TRACECONTRACT to SMAP and LADEE and compare to the previous application of LOGSCOPE to MSL.

3   Requirements Engineering and Logging

We shall furthermore discuss the possibility of relating requirements engineering to logging, and thereby log analysis. A natural thought is to formulate requirements as statements, even informal, involving concrete events (data records), and then enforce programmers to log such events. Requirements can consequently be converted into monitors and tested on the running system. As an example, consider the informal requirement:

Requirement *If a resource is granted to a task, the resource cannot be granted to some other task without being canceled first by the first task.*

We could formulate this requirement in terms of two formalized event types:

- *Grant(t,r)* : task *t* is granted the resource *r*.
- *Cancel(t,r)* : task *t* cancels (hands back) resource *r*.

The now semi-formal requirement becomes:

Requirement *If a resource is granted to a task with Grant(t,r), the resource cannot be granted to some other task with Grant(_,r) without being canceled first with Cancel(t,r) by the first task.*

Of course, a proper formalization will be more desirable, but even this informal statement in English over formal events can be useful for subsequent testing purposes. A monitor can for example later be programmed in a system such as TRACECONTRACT:

```
class GrantToOne extends Monitor[Event] {
  always {
    case Grant(t, r) =>
      watch {
        case Grant(_, 'r') => error
        case Cancel('t', 'r') => ok
      }
  }
}
```

A specific monitor, such as GrantToOne above, sub-classes the Monitor class, parameterized with the type of events. The Monitor class in turn offers a collection of methods for writing properties, such as **always** and **watch**, taking partial functions as argument, specified using pattern matching with SCALA's **case** statements. This monitor illustrates the mixture of SCALA and added DSL constructs.

4   Future Work

Beyond expressiveness and convenience of a logic, efficiency of monitoring is of main importance. The key problem in evaluating a set of monitors given an incoming event is to perform *efficient* matching of the event (and possibly other facts depending on the logic) against conditions in monitors. This becomes particularly challenging when events carry data parameters, as also heavily studied in state of the art systems [1,11]. We are investigating the combination of expressiveness and efficiency, with focus on expressiveness, as documented in [2]. The field of Artificial Intelligence (AI) has itself studied a problem very similar to the runtime verification problem, namely *rule-based production systems*, used for example to represent knowledge systems. We are specifically studying the RETE algorithm [7] for its relevance for the RV problem. This includes implementing it in the SCALA programming language, and visualizing its operation on data structures.

References

1. Allan, C., Avgustinov, P., Christensen, A.S., Hendren, L., Kuzins, S., Lhoták, O., de Moor, O., Sereni, D., Sittamplan, G., Tibble, J.: Adding trace matching with free variables to AspectJ. In: OOPSLA 2005. ACM Press (2005)
2. Barringer, H., Falcone, Y., Havelund, K., Reger, G., Rydeheard, D.: Quantified Event Automata: Towards Expressive and Efficient Runtime Monitors. In: Giannakopoulou, D., Méry, D. (eds.) FM 2012. LNCS, vol. 7436, pp. 68–84. Springer, Heidelberg (2012)
3. Barringer, H., Groce, A., Havelund, K., Smith, M.: Formal analysis of log files. Journal of Aerospace Computing, Information, and Communication 7(11), 365–390 (2010)
4. Barringer, H., Havelund, K.: TRACECONTRACT: A Scala DSL for Trace Analysis. In: Butler, M., Schulte, W. (eds.) FM 2011. LNCS, vol. 6664, pp. 57–72. Springer, Heidelberg (2011)
5. Barringer, H., Havelund, K., Kurklu, E., Morris, R.: Checking flight rules with TraceContract: Application of a Scala DSL for trace analysis. In: Scala Days 2011. Stanford University, California (2011)
6. Barringer, H., Rydeheard, D.E., Havelund, K.: Rule systems for run-time monitoring: from Eagle to RuleR. J. Log. Comput. 20(3), 675–706 (2010)
7. Forgy, C.: Rete: A fast algorithm for the many pattern/many object pattern match problem. Artificial Intelligence 19, 17–37 (1982)
8. Groce, A., Havelund, K., Smith, M.H.: From scripts to specifications: the evolution of a flight software testing effort. In: 32nd Int. Conference on Software Engineering (ICSE 2010), pp. 129–138. ACM SIG, Cape Town (2010)
9. Havelund, K.: Closing the gap between specification and programming: VDM^{++} and Scala. In: Korovina, M., Voronkov, A. (eds.) HOWARD-60: Higher-Order Workshop on Automated Runtime Verification and Debugging. EasyChair Proceedings, Manchester, UK, vol. 1 (December 2011)
10. LADEE: Lunar Atmosphere Dust Environment Explorer, http://www.nasa.gov/mission_pages/LADEE/main
11. Meredith, P., Jin, D., Griffith, D., Chen, F., Roşu, G.: An overview of the MOP runtime verification framework. Software Tools for Technology Transfer (STTT) 14(3), 249–289 (2012)
12. MSL: Mars Science Laboratory, http://mars.jpl.nasa.gov/msl
13. SMAP: Soil Moisture Active Passive, http://smap.jpl.nasa.gov

Active Learning
of Extended Finite State Machines

Frits Vaandrager*

Institute for Computing and Information Sciences, Radboud University Nijmegen,
P.O. Box 9010, 6500 GL Nijmegen
the Netherlands

Once they have high-level models of the behavior of software components, engineers can construct better software in less time. A key problem in practice, however, is the construction of models for existing software components, for which no or only limited documentation is available. In this talk, I will present an overview of recent work by my group — done in close collaboration with the Universities of Dortmund and Uppsala — in which we use machine learning to infer state diagram models of embedded controllers and network protocols fully automatically through observation and test, that is, through black box reverse engineering.

Starting from the well-known L^* algorithm of Angluin [6], our aim is to develop algorithms for active learning of richer classes of (extended) finite state machines. Abstraction is the key when learning behavioral models of realistic systems. Hence, in practical applications, researchers manually define abstractions which, depending on the history, map a large set of concrete events to a small set of abstract events that can be handled by automata learning tools. Our work, which builds on earlier results from concurrency theory and the theory of abstraction interpretation, shows how such abstractions can be constructed fully automatically for a restricted class of extended finite state machines in which one can test for equality of data parameters, but no operations on data are allowed [2,1]. Our approach uses counterexample-guided abstraction refinement (CEGAR): whenever the current abstraction is too coarse and induces nondeterministic behavior, the abstraction is refined automatically. In the talk, I will compare our approach with the related work of Howar et al [8,9] on register automata.

Using the LearnLib [11,10] tool from Dortmund in combination with Tomte [1], a prototype implementation of our CEGAR algorithm, we have succeeded to learn models of several realistic software components, such as the SIP protocol [3,1], the new biometric passport [5], banking cards, and printer controllers.

Once we have learned a model of a software component, we may use model checking technology to analyze this model and model-based testing to automatically infer test suites. This allows us to check, for instance, whether no new faults have been introduced in a modified version of the component (regression testing), whether an alternative implementation by some other vendor agrees with a reference implementation, or whether some communication protocol is

---

* Supported by STW project 11763 Integrating Testing And Learning of Interface Automata (ITALIA), http://www.italia.cs.ru.nl/

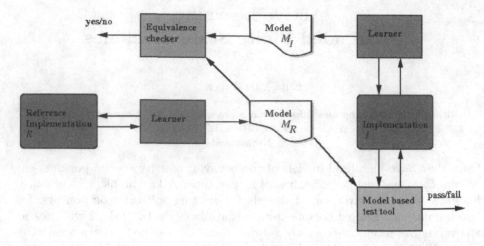

Fig. 1. Use of automata learning to establish conformance of implementations

secure. Using a well-known industrial case study from the verification literature, the bounded retransmission protocol [7], we show how active learning can
be used to establish the correctness of protocol implementation I relative to a
given reference implementation R. Using active learning, we learn a model M_R
of reference implementation R, which serves as input for a model based testing
tool that checks conformance of implementation I to M_R. In addition, we also
explore an alternative approach in which we learn a model M_I of implementation I, which is compared to model M_R using an equivalence checker. Our work
uses a unique combination of software tools for model construction (Uppaal),
active learning (LearnLib, Tomte), model-based testing (JTorX, TorXakis) and
verification (CADP, MRMC). We show how these tools can be used for learning these models, analyzing the obtained results, and improving the learning
performance [4].

References

1. Aarts, F., Heidarian, F., Kuppens, H., Olsen, P., Vaandrager, F.W.: Automata Learning through Counterexample Guided Abstraction Refinement. In:
   Giannakopoulou, D., Méry, D. (eds.) FM 2012. LNCS, vol. 7436, pp. 10–27.
   Springer, Heidelberg (2012)
2. Aarts, F., Heidarian, F., Vaandrager, F.W.: A Theory of History Dependent Abstractions for Learning Interface Automata. In: Koutny, M., Ulidowski, I. (eds.)
   CONCUR 2012. LNCS, vol. 7454, pp. 240–255. Springer, Heidelberg (2012)
3. Aarts, F., Jonsson, B., Uijen, J.: Generating Models of Infinite-State Commu-
   nication Protocols Using Regular Inference with Abstraction. In: Petrenko, A.,
   Simão, A., Maldonado, J.C. (eds.) ICTSS 2010. LNCS, vol. 6435, pp. 188–204.
   Springer, Heidelberg (2010)

4. Aarts, F., Kuppens, H., Tretmans, G.J., Vaandrager, F.W., Verwer, S.: Learning and testing the bounded retransmission protocol. In: Heinz, J., de la Higuera, C., Oates, T. (eds.) Proceedings 11th International Conference on Grammatical Inference (ICGI 2012). JMLR Workshop and Conference Proceedings, September 5-8, vol. 21, pp. 4–18. University of Maryland, College Park (2012)
5. Aarts, F., Schmaltz, J., Vaandrager, F.W.: Inference and Abstraction of the Biometric Passport. In: Margaria, T., Steffen, B. (eds.) ISoLA 2010, Part I. LNCS, vol. 6415, pp. 673–686. Springer, Heidelberg (2010)
6. Angluin, D.: Learning regular sets from queries and counterexamples. Inf. Comput. 75(2), 87–106 (1987)
7. Helmink, L., Sellink, M.P.A., Vaandrager, F.W.: Proof-Checking a Data Link Protocol. In: Barendregt, H., Nipkow, T. (eds.) TYPES 1993. LNCS, vol. 806, pp. 127–165. Springer, Heidelberg (1994)
8. Howar, F., Steffen, B., Jonsson, B., Cassel, S.: Inferring Canonical Register Automata. In: Kuncak, V., Rybalchenko, A. (eds.) VMCAI 2012. LNCS, vol. 7148, pp. 251–266. Springer, Heidelberg (2012)
9. Merten, M., Howar, F., Steffen, B., Cassel, S., Jonsson, B.: Demonstrating Learning of Register Automata. In: Flanagan, C., König, B. (eds.) TACAS 2012. LNCS, vol. 7214, pp. 466–471. Springer, Heidelberg (2012)
10. Merten, M., Steffen, B., Howar, F., Margaria, T.: Next Generation LearnLib. In: Abdulla, P.A., Leino, K.R.M. (eds.) TACAS 2011. LNCS, vol. 6605, pp. 220–223. Springer, Heidelberg (2011)
11. Raffelt, H., Steffen, B., Berg, T., Margaria, T.: LearnLib: a framework for extrapolating behavioral models. STTT 11(5), 393–407 (2009)

Efficient and Trustworthy Tool Qualification
for Model-Based Testing Tools

Jörg Brauer[1], Jan Peleska[1,2,*], and Uwe Schulze[2,**]

[1] Verified Systems International GmbH, Bremen, Germany
[2] Department of Mathematics and Computer Science, University of Bremen,
Germany

Abstract. The application of test automation tools in a safety-critical
context requires so-called tool qualification according to the applicable
standards. The objective of this qualification is to justify that verification
steps automated by the tool will not lead to faulty systems under test
to be accepted as fit for purpose. In this paper we review the tool qualification requirements of the standards ISO 26262 (automotive domain)
and the new RTCA DO-178C (avionic domain) and propose a general
approach on how to qualify model-based testing tools according to these
standards in an efficient and at the same time reliable way. Our approach
relies on a lightweight error detection mechanism based on the idea of
replaying test executions against the model. We further show how the
error detection capabilities can be integrated into a convincing argument
for tool qualification, going through the necessary verification activities
step-by-step. We highlight the key steps for the RT-Tester Model-Based
Test Generator, which is used in test campaigns in the automotive, railway and avionic domains. The approach avoids having to qualify several
complex components present in model-based testing tools, such as code
generators for test procedures and constraint solving algorithms for test
data elaboration.

1 Introduction

In model-based testing, a test model is used to define the expected behavior
of the system-under-test (SUT). From this formal specification of the desired
system behavior, test cases are generated, which are then executed against the
SUT[1]. The generation of test cases is frequently based on techniques such as abstract interpretation [3] and SMT solving [8], which exercise the semantic structure of the model to automatically calculate these test cases; such techniques

---

* The author's contribution has been developed during the course of the project "Ver-
ifikation von Systemen synchroner Softwarekomponenten" (VerSyKo) funded by the
German ministry for education and research (BMBF).
** The author's research is funded by the EU FP7 COMPASS project under grant
agreement no.287829.
[1] It is important to note that correctness of model-based test generators relies on the
consistency and completeness of test models, since test cases are derived directly
from the models. It is thus assumed that the test models have undergone review.

B. Nielsen and C. Weise (Eds.): ICTSS 2012, LNCS 7641, pp. 8–23, 2012.

are also implemented in our tool-suite RT-Tester Model-Based Test Generator (RTT-MBT) [12]. The resulting test cases are then specified as sequences of input data — including timing constraints — that stimulate computations of the SUT conforming to the test case specifications. In addition to the input stimulations, RTT-MBT automatically generates test oracles that run concurrently with the SUT, checking the responses of the SUT against the test model on-the-fly. In combination, the stimulation component and the test oracles form a test procedure which is compiled and executed in a test execution environment (TE). The test execution environment then generates a so-called *execution log*, which contains the data observed and recorded during test case execution.

1.1 Model-Based Testing in Industry and Tool Qualification

The success of model-based testing in industry has been stimulated by the success of model-driven software development in general. Indeed, compared to conventional approaches, model-based testing has proven to increase both, quality and efficiency of test campaigns [10], which may explain the industrial interest in model-based methods, especially from domains such as automotive, avionics, and railway industry. However, all tools that automate process steps in the development and verification of safety-critical systems (e. g. code generators, compilers, model checkers, test automation tools) need to be qualified since they automate a life cycle activity so that a manual inspection of its outcome (e. g., generated source code, object code, verification or test results) is rendered superfluous. In this situation it has to be ensured that the tool performing this automation cannot inject errors into the artifacts produced; otherwise, this would induce the risk of a faulty system component to be accepted as fit for purpose.

The ISO 26262 [6] standard currently implemented in the automotive domain presents guidelines for the development of safety-related systems in road vehicles. This standard is an exemplar of a standard prescribing required properties for development and verification automation tools. The standard [6, Sect. 11.4] itself expresses the aim of tool qualification as follows:

> *"The objective of the qualification of software tools is to provide evidence of software tool suitability for use when developing a safety-related item or element, such that confidence can be achieved in the correct execution of activities and tasks required by ISO 26262."*

The key steps of providing the required evidence are defined in the standard. First of all, qualifying a tool for a development process necessitates to determine the tool impact and its error detection capabilities. These two factors are combined to form an overall *tool confidence level*. Of course, the more severe the developed system component, the stricter the requirements imposed onto the tool. Yet, an interesting aspect of ISO 26262 [6, Sect. 11.4.4.1] is that tools with maximal *tool error detection capabilities* do not require qualification measures at all, as long as error detection is perfectly reliable. Hence, if a tool is capable of detecting its own malfunctioning, the entire tool qualification process for ISO 26262 can be simplified in a significant way.

1.2 Tool Qualification for ISO 26262

Malfunction of a test-case and test procedure generator such as RTT-MBT introduces two hazards which may result in a situation where a requirement allocated
to a safety-related item[2] is violated, due to malfunction of this item:

- **Hazard 1: undetected SUT failures.** A deviation of the observed SUT
  behavior from its expected behavior specified in the test model may potentially remain undetected if the generator creates erroneous test oracles failing
  to detect this deviation during test executions.
- **Hazard 2: undetected coverage failures.** The test execution fails to meet
  the pre-conditions which are necessary in order to cover a given test case,
  but the test oracles indicate TEST PASSED because the observed execution
  is consistent with the model. If this situation remains undetected, it may be
  assumed that the SUT performs correctly with respect to the specified test
  case, while in fact the test procedure tested "something else".

The qualification goal required by ISO 26262 states that any possible hazard
introduced by the tool will eventually be detected [6, Sect. 11.4.3.2]. The identification of components of model-based test generators relevant for qualification,
as well as trustworthy, yet lightweight methods for satisfying this objective are
topic of this paper. Of course, formal verification of RTT-MBT as a whole to
prove the absence of defects is an unrealistic mission, as the state-of-the-art represents verifying functional correctness of systems that involve approximately
10,000 lines of C code [7], and RTT-MBT consists of approx. 250,000 lines of
C/C++ code. To qualify RTT-MBT for use in the development of software of
high quality assurance levels (according to ISO 26262 and other standards such
as RTCA DO-178C), it is thus necessary to combine formal verification with testing and effective tool error detection. In the following, we discuss the verification
strategies we applied to RTT-MBT and the tool error detection mechanism.

The key idea of our approach to tool qualification is simple: Rather than attempting *a priori* verification for the test generator by proving conformance of
generated test procedures with the model, we focus on the *a posteriori* error detection capabilities of RTT-MBT, regarding the consistency of the test execution
log with the model. This is performed by *replaying* the execution log on the test
model. The key functionality for replay of test execution is defined as follows:

- A simulation of the test model is generated that uses exactly the input data
  to the SUT that was used during test procedure execution.
- The respective simulation contains the *expected* SUT outputs as calculated
  from the test model. These outputs are compared to the outputs *observed*
  during test procedure execution and documented in the test execution log.
  Any deviations are recorded in the replay verification results.
- The actual model and test coverage achieved by the simulation is recorded
  in the replay verification results, too.

---

[2] That is, a software or embedded HW/SW control system tested by means of procedures generated by the tool.

Using this strategy, the impact of errors in the test generator are localized. In essence, it suffices to show that replay detects any deviation of the concrete test execution from the test model. Establishing this correctness argument is strictly easier than proving correctness of the entire test generation functionality. In principle, replay could be performed on-the-fly, concurrently to the test execution. Yet, we describe it as an *a posteriori* activity, to be performed offline after the execution has been completed, since hard real-time test engines running HW/SW or system integration tests often do not have sufficient spare computing power to cope with additional model executions for replay purposes.

1.3   Contributions and Outline

In summary, this paper presents the following contributions:

- We present an analysis that relates properties of model-based test generators to requirements for tool qualification posed by ISO 26262.
- We identify classes of hazards introduced by test generators and provide an analysis of parts of a test generator that are relevant to qualification.
- We introduce a lightweight framework for replaying concrete test executions with the aim of identifying erroneous test case executions.
- We show how the different verification activities, consisting of design analyses, formal verification, structural testing and tool error detection are combined to form a convincing case in point for customers and certification authorities.

The exposition of this paper is laid out as follows: First, Sect. 2 presents an impact analysis that connects the test generator to the demands posed by the ISO 26262. Then, Sect. 3 identifies those parts of a test generator that are relevant for tool qualification and discusses the details of the verification strategies applied. Following, Sect. 4 studies properties of the replay and constructs a correctness argument from the architecture, before Sect. 5 discusses differences between ISO 26262 and RTCA DO-178C w.r.t. test-case generators. Finally, the paper concludes with a survey of related work in Sect. 6 and a discussion in Sect. 7.

2   Tool Classification According to ISO 26262

To assess the qualification requirements for a model-based test-case generator, it is necessary to analyze hazards potentially inflicted by the tool, as well as the impact of these hazards. The second important aspect are the tool error detection capabilities of a tool with respect to its own malfunction. Based on this analysis, particular requirements are imposed onto the tool, which are discussed in the remainder of this section.

2.1   Impact Analysis

ISO 26262 defines two different *tool impact (TI) levels* for software tools of any kind: **TI0** is applicable iff malfunctioning of the tool can under no circumstances introduce a hazard; otherwise, **TI1** shall be chosen [6, Sect. 11.4.3.2].

Assuming correctness and completeness of the test models[3] potential malfunction of a model-based test-case generator introduces the hazards 1 (undetected SUT failures) and 2 (undetected coverage failures) introduced in Sect. 1. These hazards clearly imply tool impact level **TI1** for model-based test-case generators.

2.2   Tool Error Detection Capabilities

The probability of preventing or detecting an erroneous tool output is expressed by *tool error detection classes TD* [6, Sect. 11.4.3.2]. If there is high confidence in the ability of a tool to detect its own malfunctioning, then **TD1** is the appropriate classification. Lower classes such as **TD3** or **TD4** are applicable if there is low confidence in the tool's error detection facilities, or if no such mechanism exists. To achieve **TD1**, we specify one tool-external measure — that is, a guideline to be respected by the test engineers applying the tool — and three tool-internal measures, that is, measures implemented in software.

External Measure. Every test execution of test procedures generated by RTT-MBT shall be replayed.

Independently of the specific functionality of RTT-MBT, this external measure is mandatory to enforce anyway, since every testing activity for safety-critical systems requires a verification of the test results. The replay function as introduced in Sect. 1 can be considered as a tool-supported review of this kind, because it verifies whether the test execution observed complies with the model and whether the intended test cases have really been executed. To enable the external measure above, or, equivalently, to achieve **TD1**, we implement three tool-internal measures with the following objectives:

Internal Measure #1. Every change of input data to the SUT is correctly captured by logging commands in the test stimulator of the test procedure.

Internal Measure #2. Every change of SUT output data is correctly captured by logging commands in the test oracles of the generated test procedure.

Internal Measure #3. The replay mechanism detects (1) every deviation of the SUT behavior observed during test execution from the SUT behavior expected according to the test model, and (2) every deviation of the test cases actually covered during the test execution from the test cases planned to be covered according to the test generator.

---

[3] Since models represent abstractions of a real system, correctness and completeness is usually defined according to some conformance relation between model and SUT. In our case – since the SUT never blocks inputs – conformance means that for any given timed trace of inputs (1) the SUT produces the same observable outputs as the model, modulo tolerances regarding timing and floating point values, and (2) that the ordering of inputs and outputs, when restricted to a sequential sub-component of the model, is the same for model and SUT (partial ordering of observable I/Os).

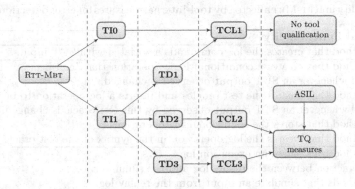

Fig. 1. Relation between tool impact (**TI**), error detection (**TD**) and automotive safety integrity level (**ASIL**)

The effectiveness of internal measures 1 — 3 clear implies the desired **TD1** capability, as long as test engineers comply with the external measure above.

For the tool-internal measures to be effective, two prerequisites of the overall test system need to be satisfied: (1) All logging commands in the test procedures are correctly executed and recorded in the execution log, and (2) the test model is complete and correct. Clearly, the first prerequisite is delegated to the test execution environment, a component which is independent of the functionality discussed in this paper and has to be qualified on its own. Satisfying the second prerequisite is the duty of test engineers that use a model-based test generator.

2.3   Tool Confidence Level

Pairing the tool impact **TI** with the appropriate tool error detection capability **TD** yields the associated *tool confidence level TCL* [6, Sect. 11.4.3.2]. It is remarkable that for a tool with impact level **TI1** and error detection class **TD1** (such as RTT-MBT), no qualification whatsoever is required according to [6, Sect. 11.4.4.1]. Otherwise, tool qualification measures have to be adopted according to the automotive safety integrity level (**ASIL**) of the system under test. This situation is depicted in Fig. 1. High confidence in the error detection capabilities of a tool thus eases the tool qualification significantly, which motivates the desire for trustworthy, lightweight error detection integrated into the tool.

3   Verification for Qualification

The overall architecture of RTT-MBT is depicted in Fig. 2. A parser component translates an input model written in UML or SysML, which is given as an XML export of some modeling tool, into an intermediate model representation (IMR, the abstract syntax tree of the model) that is used by both the test-case generation and the replay facilities. The test-case generator uses techniques such as SMT solving, abstract interpretation and code generation in order to generate test inputs and the corresponding test procedures. In contrast to this, the

Table 1. Functionality in RTT-MBT affected by tool-internal measures for error detection

Measure	Affected Functionality
#1	The method that creates the log commands associated with SUT inputs.
#2	The method that creates a conditional logic operation that shall be executed whenever an SUT output observed is changed. The method that creates the test oracles and inserts a log operation to be executed whenever an SUT output observed by this test oracle is changed. The method that stores the conditional log operations. The method that creates the log operation in the syntax of the test oracle.
#3	The method that parses an execution log. The interaction between the replay log and the simulator. The methods that simulate an input from the replay log. The method comparing the observed SUT outputs with the expected SUT outputs calculated by the simulator The methods that manage the internal memory during simulation. The methods that determine whether the test cases covered during replay are identical to those observed during a concrete execution.

sole purpose of the replay mechanism is to simulate an execution of a concrete execution log on the test model. Test-case generation and replay are thus independent components that have also been developed with independence. The test generator, however, is responsible for the generation of log commands in test procedures, and the replay mechanism depends on their correct generation (recall the tool-internal measures discussed in Sect. 2.2). Therefore this part of the generator (it is a sub-component of the test procedure generator) receives increased attention during verification.

3.1   Identification of Relevant Components

The parser is responsible for translating an input model into an IMR. It has thus to be qualified as errors in this component may mask failures of the test generator and the replay. To identify classes and methods reachable from the parser, we use data-flow analysis and code inspection. Apart from the parser itself, the relevant classes most notably include the IMR used within RTT-MBT.

As argued in Sect. 2.2, a replay that implements the tool-internal measures eliminates the need to qualify test generation. This strategy entails that the replay needs to be qualified, as tool error detection is delegated to the replay component. It is noteworthy that test generation is much more complex than replay. Complementing test generators by replay mechanisms thus reduces the workload for qualification significantly: the existence of tool error detection turns test generation — with the exception of the log command generator — into a component whose outputs need not be verified. As before, we apply data-flow analysis to identify classes and methods that are involved during replay. The result of this analysis includes, most notably, the IMR, the memory model storing states during model simulation, the simulator, and the parser for the test execution log.

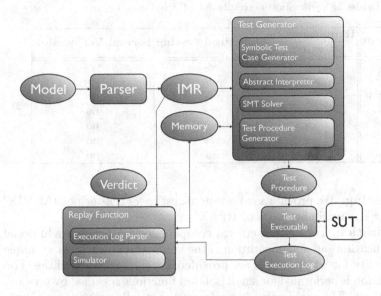

Fig. 2. High-level architecture of RTT-MBT

3.2   Identification of Tool-Internal Measures

Additionally, we performed a design review to identify those parts of RTT-MBT implementing the tool-internal measures 1—3 for error detection. The results of this analysis are given in Tab. 1. These parts must under any circumstances be implemented correctly. Special attention should thus be paid during the verification of the methods highlighted in Tab. 1.

3.3   Verification Activities

To verify the correctness of each involved component, we apply different verification activities. The main verification activity is (software integration) testing, though this process is augmented with formal verification for the most critical software parts. The combination of methods applied conforms to the requirements of RTCA DO-178B for developing software of the highest criticality (Level A): (1) The development process for the replay component has been controlled according to [15, Tab. A-1,A-2]. (2) High-level and low-level requirements specified for the replay mechanism have been verified with independence according to the approach defined in [15, Tab. A-3,A-4]. (3) The source code has been inspected, formally verified and tested according to [15, Tab. A-5, A-6, A-7]. (4) The configuration management and software quality assurance processes have been set up for the whole RTT-MBT product in a way conforming to [15, Tab. A-8,A-9], respectively.

Requirements-based testing. For each high-level and low-level requirement of the test generator, we provide normal behavior tests as well as robustness tests that investigate the stability of RTT-MBT.

Table 2. Verification activities for affected components

Component	Requirements testing	Structural testing	Formal Verification
Measure #1	yes	yes	yes
Measure #2	yes	yes	yes
Measure #3	yes	yes	no
Parser	yes	yes	no
IMR	yes	yes	no
Replay	yes	yes	no
Generation	no	no	no

Structural testing. We provide a collection of test cases that achieve MC/DC coverage for the reachable parts of RTT-MBT.

Formal Verification. For certain critical components, we perform additional formal verification and documentation of the verification results. An example of functionality for which proofs are provided are the logging facilities. Formal verification is performed for small isolated functions specified by pre- and post-conditions. The verification is performed manually using Hoare Logic. The small size of the verified functions indicated that manual proofs were acceptable and could be checked independently by a verification specialist.

A summary of the verification activities for each component is given in Tab. 2. We define the following general criteria for the testing process of the involved components, before discussing the details for the strategy applied to the parser.

Pass/fail criteria. The test passes if the expected results are produced without deviation; otherwise, it fails.

Test end criteria. The test ends when all test cases have passed and the test suite resulted in a 100% MC/DC coverage for the involved methods.

General test strategy. Each method shall be tested as follows:
  - The test cases for verifying the methods are elaborated.
  - A test model is selected which is suitable for the test cases under consideration. Test cases shall cover both normal behavior and robustness.
  - A replay file is selected which is based on a test execution whose test procedure was generated with the selected model and which is suitable for the test cases under consideration.
  - The replay function is activated with the model and replay file as inputs.
  - The replay results consist of the pass/fail results achieved during the replay, and the list of test cases covered during the replay.
  - The replay results are verified with respect to the expected results. It is checked that the replay result is pass if and only if the replay file corresponds to a correct model computation. Evaluating the replay file against the model, it is checked against the model that the list of covered test cases produced during replay is correct and complete.
  - The MC/DC coverage achieved during the execution of the test suite is checked whether it results in 100% for the methods identified above.

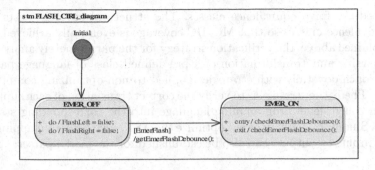

Fig. 3. A simple state machine

- If some code portions could not be covered by the test suite designed according to the guidelines listed here, it is admissible to perform unit tests on the methods not completely covered so far. The unit tests shall check the expected results by means of post conditions. The associated unit test cases specify the data needed to cover the missing code portions as test condition, and the post condition as expected result.

Test Strategy for the Parser Component. The IMR of a model is the basis for all further functionality of RTT-MBT. Errors in the IMR can therefore mask failures in the test data generation as well as in the replay. Thus the parser component setting up the IMR has to be qualified. The IMR is a representation of the abstract syntax tree (AST) of the model restricted to those UML/SysML elements which are supported by RTT-MBT. An example of a simple state machine, which is part of a test model, is shown in Fig. 3. The corresponding IMR is shown in Fig. 4. In addition to the IMR, a model of the internal memory representation is generated, which is used during simulations to store the values of variables and control states. Both the AST and the memory model are used as inputs to the replay and must thus be qualified.

For requirements-based tests of the parser, models serve as input that have been designed to specifically test one or more syntactic UML/SysML feature supported by the parser. Their respective XML representations are the test inputs to the parser, which generates both, the IMR and the memory model, from the test model. The IMR is then verified to be a valid representation of the model. For each test model, we handcraft an AST corresponding to the expected IMR. The result generated by the parser is then checked against this expected AST.

The memory model is an algorithmically simple component. Qualification amounts to verifying that for each control state and each variable, an appropriate entry in the internal memory is initialized. Whenever a value is stored in the memory, its internal state shall correctly reflect the update. It also needs to be ensured that support for data types is exhaustive. These properties are checked using a combination of requirements-based integration tests and unit tests which, e.g., systematically probe all data types. The inputs for the requirements-based test procedures form equivalence classes. The structural coverage tests refine these equivalence classes so that MC/DC coverage is eventually achieved.

As explained above, the verification strategy for the parser merely analyzes the correct parsing and transformation of a pre-defined class of language patterns. This approach dovetails with strategies applied to non-optimizing compilers [4, Sect. 2.1]. There, the strategy is to verify the correct translation of each supported symbol in a high-level programming language into the corresponding assembly fragment. Since RTT-MBT does not optimize the AST, such a direct mapping from expected inputs to outputs can also be established for the model parser.

4   Error Detection Using Replay

Objectives. In this section we elaborate a formal argument to show that replay — if correctly implemented — enforces the tool error detection class **TD1** as required. Let us briefly recall the scenarios that may occur once a generated test case is executed: (1) If test execution fails, manual investigation is required to justify the deviations, identify an erroneous test case, fix the SUT, or refine the test model. (2) If test execution passes, this may be due to one of the following reasons: (a) The test cases were generated correctly from the test model and the SUT conforms these test cases, or (b) some test cases were incorrectly generated[4] from the test model, but the SUT behavior still conforms to these faulty cases. Tool error detection thus needs to classify only test case executions that pass. In the following, we build towards a correctness argument for the replay.

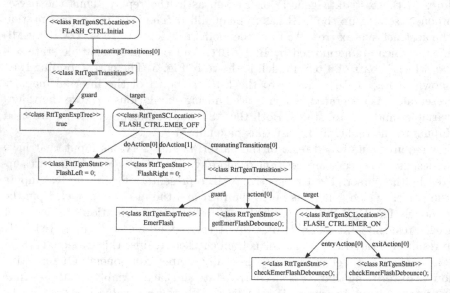

Fig. 4. IMR of the state machine in Fig. 3

---

[4] This means that either the test data is inappropriate for the test objective, or the check of expected results is faulty.

Prerequisites. The SUT **S** communicates with the test environment through finite sets of input signals $\mathcal{I} = \{i_1, \ldots, i_m\}$ and output signals $\mathcal{O} = \{o_1, \ldots, o_n\}$ such that $\mathcal{I} \cap \mathcal{O} = \varnothing$. We denote the set of overall signals by $\mathcal{S} = \mathcal{I} \cup \mathcal{O}$. Further, each signal $s \in \mathcal{S}$ is assigned a type drawn from a finite class $\mathbb{T} = \{\mathbb{N}, \mathbb{B}, \mathbb{Q}, \ldots\}$ of types using a map $\sigma : \mathcal{S} \to \mathbb{T}$. An input to the SUT is then given as a triple $\langle t, i, v \rangle$ where $t \in \mathbb{R}$ is a time-stamp, $i \in \mathcal{I}$ is an input signal and $v \in \sigma(i)$ is an assignment to i. Likewise, an output from the SUT to the test environment is a triple $\langle t, o, v \rangle$ with $t \in \mathbb{R}$, $o \in \mathcal{O}$, and $v \in \sigma(o)$.

Model Semantics. The desired behavior of the SUT is specified by means of a (deterministic) test model **M**. The model **M** is syntactically reproduced by a parser that has been qualified. Syntactic correctness of **M** can thus be assumed. Semantically, **M** can be interpreted as the (possibly infinite) set of (infinite) computation paths it defines, which we denote by $[\![\mathbf{M}]\!]$. Since **M** is deterministic, a path $\pi \in [\![\mathbf{M}]\!]$ is uniquely determined through its observable input-output behavior, i.e., partial (timed) assignments of the above form to the signals in $\mathcal{S}$.

Test Generation. Formally, a test generator is a function that computes a finite set of finite traces from **M**, which we denote $[\![\mathbf{M}]\!]_{\mathsf{TC}}$. If correct, each $\pi_{\mathsf{TC}} \in [\![\mathbf{M}]\!]_{\mathsf{TC}}$ is the finite prefix of a computation path π through the test model (the prefix relation is denoted by $\pi_{\mathsf{TC}} \prec \pi$). Since the test generator is not qualified, and is thus an untrusted component, we have to assume that such a corresponding path does not necessarily exist. We define:

Definition 1. *Let $\pi_{\mathsf{TC}} \in [\![\mathbf{M}]\!]_{\mathsf{TC}}$. The predicate* correct *on π_{TC} is defined as:*

$$\mathsf{correct}(\pi_{\mathsf{TC}}) \Leftrightarrow \exists \pi \in [\![\mathbf{M}]\!] : (\pi_{\mathsf{TC}} \prec \pi)$$

Test Execution. Given $\pi_{\mathsf{TC}} \in [\![\mathbf{M}]\!]_{\mathsf{TC}}$, the test procedure that executes π_{TC} generates an execution log that can be interpreted as a finite trace π_{exec}. As before, we interpret the semantics $[\![\mathbf{S}]\!]$ of an SUT **S** as the set of its feasible execution traces; clearly, $\pi_{\mathsf{exec}} \in [\![\mathbf{S}]\!]$. Observe that π_{exec} is not required to be identical to π_{TC}: timings and floating point values may deviate within specified limits, and only a partial ordering of I/Os has to be observed as explained in Sect. 2.1. However, if π_{exec} conforms to π_{TC} the test passes, which we denote by $\mathsf{pass}_{\pi_{\mathsf{TC}}}(\pi_{\mathsf{exec}})$. Since the execution log is compared to a trace from an untrusted generator, we cannot infer correctness of the test execution with respect to **M**.

Proposition 1. *Let $\pi_{\mathsf{TC}} \in [\![\mathbf{M}]\!]_{\mathsf{TC}}$ and $\pi_{\mathsf{exec}} \in [\![\mathbf{S}]\!]$. Then*

$$(\mathsf{correct}(\pi_{\mathsf{TC}}) \wedge \mathsf{pass}_{\pi_{\mathsf{TC}}}(\pi_{\mathsf{exec}})) \Rightarrow (\exists \pi \in [\![M]\!] : \mathsf{pass}_{\pi}(\pi_{\mathsf{exec}}))$$

Replay. Formally, the replay mechanism can be interpreted as a predicate replay:

Definition 2. *Let $\pi_{\mathsf{exec}} \in [\![\mathbf{S}]\!]$ denote an execution of $\pi_{\mathsf{TC}} \in [\![\mathbf{M}]\!]_{\mathsf{TC}}$ such that $\mathsf{pass}_{\pi_{\mathsf{TC}}}(\pi_{\mathsf{exec}})$. The predicate* replay $: [\![\mathbf{S}]\!] \to \mathbb{B}$ *is defined as:*

$$\mathsf{replay}(\pi_{\mathsf{exec}}) \Leftrightarrow \exists \pi \in [\![\mathbf{M}]\!] : (\pi_{\mathsf{TC}} \prec \pi) \wedge \mathsf{pass}_{\pi_{\mathsf{TC}}}(\pi_{\mathsf{exec}})$$

Since correctness of the implementation of the replay mechanism is ensured, we safely assume that $\mathsf{replay}(\pi_{\mathsf{exec}}) = \mathsf{true}$ iff π_{exec} is the prefix of a path $\pi \in [\![\mathbf{M}]\!]$ such that $\mathsf{pass}_\pi(\pi_{\mathsf{exec}})$. We thus obtain the correctness argument:

Proposition 2. *Let* $\pi_{\mathsf{exec}} \in [\![\mathbf{S}]\!]$ *denote an execution of* $\pi_{\mathsf{TC}} \in [\![\mathbf{M}]\!]_{\mathsf{TC}}$ *such that* $\mathsf{pass}_{\pi_{\mathsf{TC}}}(\pi_{\mathsf{exec}})$. *Then,* $\mathsf{correct}(\pi_{\mathsf{TC}}) \Leftrightarrow \mathsf{replay}(\pi_{\mathsf{exec}})$.

In consequence, given a generated test $\pi_{\mathsf{TC}} \in [\![\mathbf{M}]\!]_{\mathsf{TC}}$ and an execution $\pi_{\mathsf{exec}} \in [\![\mathbf{S}]\!]$ that passes, π_{TC} is the finite prefix of a path $\pi \in [\![\mathbf{M}]\!]$ iff $\mathsf{replay}(\pi_{\mathsf{exec}})$ as desired, which ultimately provides a proof of correctness of the mechanism.

5   Compatibility with RTCA DO-178C

The avionic software development standard RTCA DO-178B [15] was one of the first standards to explicitly address tool qualification. The requirements are less strict than the ones imposed by ISO 26262 discussed so far in this paper. The updated standard RTCA DO-178C [16], however, devotes a whole companion standard [17] to tool qualification. When planning to use test and verification tools in both the automotive and the avionic domain it is thus useful to elaborate a consolidated qualification strategy that is consistent with both standards.

Project-specific tool qualification. The avionic standards emphasize that tool qualification cannot be unconditionally granted for any development or verification tool, but has to be performed with respect to a specific project [17, p. 5]. Practically speaking, certain tool components may only be universally qualified if it can be justified that these components' behavior does not depend on a specific project or target system to be developed. All other components have to be re-qualified for each development and verification campaign. For test automation tools this implies that the interfaces between test tool and SUT have to be specifically qualified, because correctly calculated test data may be passed along the wrong interfaces to the SUT. Conversely, erroneous SUT outputs may be passed along a wrong interface where the data appears to be correct. Moreover, it has to be verified that the interface-specific refinements and abstractions performed by the test automation tool (e. g., transforming abstract values used on model level to concrete communication telegrams and vice versa) are correct.

Tool criticality assessment. Both ISO26262 and RTCA DO-178C / DO-330 require that the qualification effort to be invested shall depend on the impact that tool malfunctions could have on the target system under consideration. The automotive and the avionic standards, however, differ in one crucial aspect. ISO26262 classifies the criticality of a tool alone on the basis whether erroneous tool behavior may result in erroneous target system behavior, and whether tool malfunction can be detected with high or low confidence [6, Sect. 11.4.3.2]. RTCA DO-178C distinguishes between development tools whose outputs become part of the airborne software and verification tools (including test automation tools) whose malfunction could only lead to an error in the target system remaining undetected (criteria 1 and 2 in [16, Sect. 12.2.2]).

As a consequence, DO-178C assigns only *tool qualification level* **TQL4** to tools that automate verification and test of software of the highest criticality (i.e., Level A) [16, Tab. 12-1]. This requires the elaboration of operational and functional requirements and their verification, the verification of protection mechanisms, and requirements-based testing [16, Tab. T-0 – T-7]. Yet, neither tests against the detailed design, nor code coverage of any measure are required.

By way of contrast, ISO26262 assigns **TCL1** to tools classified by **TI1** and **TD1**, as the one considered in this paper [6, Sect. 11.4.3.2]. Since no qualification whatsoever is required for **TCL1**, no requirements-based testing is is needed. It remains to prove, however, that the tool indeed fulfills **TD1** (*"there is a high degree of confidence that a malfunction or an erroneous output from the software tool will be prevented or detected"*, [6, Sect. 11.4.3.2, b)]). It is remarkable, though that the standard does not elaborate on how error detection should be verified. From the general qualification requirements [6, Sect. 11.], however, we conclude that this should be done with the highest possible effort associated with the target system's criticality. For the highest criticality level (denoted ASIL D) the standard requires alternatively the evaluation of the development process in combination with a comprehensive validation or — this is the procedure applied for RTT-MBT in this paper — development in compliance with a safety standard, such as RTCA DO-178B [6, p. 23, Tab. 2, Ex. 3]. This implies, e.g., that detailed tests to achieve MC/DC code coverage have to be performed for the replay.

We conclude that the tool qualification requirements of ISO26262 and RTCA DO-178C / DO-330 are complementary in the sense that the former put emphasis on an in-depth verification of the error detection mechanism with highest confidence, while the latter requires comprehensive requirements-based testing.

6 Related Work

The idea of replaying a test execution in a simulator is, of course, not new. The overall approach is frequently referred to as the *capture and replay* paradigm, and has long been studied in different contexts such as testing of concurrent programs [2]. However, the classical approach of capture/replay testing is to capture user-interaction and then replay the recorded inputs within test cases, as opposed to automatic test-case generation. This paradigm differs from the one implemented in RTT-MBT, although we integrate a replay function into our work to detect deviations of a generated test case from the test model. To our best knowledge, our approach is the first to combine replay with model-based methods for error detection within a test-case generator. Our contribution is not a theoretical one, but comes from an industrial perspective. Tool qualification is compulsory for software that is applied in development processes of safety-critical systems. For ISO 26262, the tool qualification requirements in a general context were recently studied by Hillebrand et al. [5]. Most relevant to our work, the authors study verification measures for error detection, which are classified as *prevention, review,* and *test* [5, Sect. 4.6]. According to this classification, our approach falls into the categories *review* and *test*, as the results of the test-case generator undergo review and are automatically tested against the test model.

Recently, there has been impressive progress on verified compilers [9,11] that, in theory, do not require further qualification measures. França et al. [4] report on their experiences of introducing the verified COMPCERT compiler into development processes for airborne software. Yet, it is important to note that even a verified compiler contains non-verified components, which may introduce bugs. Indeed, Regehr [14] discovered defects in the COMPCERT front-end responsible for type-checking, thereby showing that proofs of functional correctness of core components do not provide sufficient evidence to construct an overall correctness argument. Our approach can be seen as a practical response to this situation since we evaluate the correctness of the outputs on a *per test* basis.

A notable difference between ISO 26262 and RTCA DO-178C is that the latter standard distinguishes between tools that mutate the software (such as code generators) and those that only analyze it (such as stack analyzers). The qualification measures imposed onto analyzers or test-case generators are less strict in RTCA DO-178C. Further details on this issue in the context of RTCA DO-178C (that are likewise applicable to DO-178B), and also additional information about the qualification process for formal verification tools, are given by Souyris et al. [18]. This recent paper can be seen as a wrap-up of a paper by the same authors that studied the same problem more than a decade ago [13], and also contains details about how different formal methods tools are used within Airbus. Qualification for RTCA DO-178B was mentioned earlier by Blackburn and Busser [1]. There, the authors describe the tool T-VEC, which is used in the qualification process to test itself. However, rather than using automatic replay, they manually define expected outputs and compare them to derived test procedures [1, Sect. 5]. By way of contrast, our approach delegates the manual specification of expected outputs to the design of the test model — a step that is necessary in model-based testing anyway — and the execution of test procedures.

7   Concluding Discussion

This paper advocates the use of replay for tool error detection in model-based test generators as a key mechanism for qualifying such a tool according to ISO 26262, since it provides trustworthy, yet simple and cost effective, error detection. By providing full tool error detection capabilities, the approach thus smoothly integrates with the requirements of ISO 26262 for the highest tool confidence level. It is noteworthy, however, that the mechanism does not ensure the absence of errors in the entire tool, but only in the functionality that is indeed used.

We have to point out, however, that the qualification achieved for ISO 26262 cannot be directly used to gain qualification credit according to RTCA DO-178C: the latter standard requires comprehensive requirements-based testing of *all* tool capabilities, while being less strict with respect to the verification of error detection mechanisms, which are considered simply as tool capabilities to be verified by means of robustness tests. The verification techniques to achieve this are the same as the ones used for qualification according to ISO 26262.

References

1. Blackburn, M.R., Busser, R.D.: T-VEC: A Tool for Developing Critical Systems. In: Compass, pp. 237–249. IEEE Computer Society Press (1996)
2. Carver, R.H., Tai, K.C.: Replay and Testing for Concurrent Programs. IEEE Software 8(2), 66–74 (1991)
3. Cousot, P., Cousot, R.: Abstract Interpretation: A Unified Lattice model for Static Analysis of Programs by Construction or Approximation of Fixpoints. In: POPL, pp. 238–252. ACM Press (1977)
4. França, R.B., Favre-Felix, D., Leroy, X., Pantel, M., Souyris, J.: Towards Formally Verified Optimizing Compilation in Flight Control Software. In: PPES. OASICS, vol. 18, pp. 5–9–68. Schloss Dagstuhl (2011)
5. Hillebrand, J., Reichenpfader, P., Mandic, I., Siegl, H., Peer, C.: Establishing Confidence in the Usage of Software Tools in Context of ISO 26262. In: Flammini, F., Bologna, S., Vittorini, V. (eds.) SAFECOMP 2011. LNCS, vol. 6894, pp. 257–269. Springer, Heidelberg (2011)
6. International Organization for Standardization. ISO 26262 - Road Vehicles - Functional Safety - Part 8: Supporting Processes. ICS 43.040.10 (2009)
7. Klein, G., Andronick, J., Elphinstone, K., Heiser, G., Cock, D., Derrin, P., Elkaduwe, D., Engelhardt, K., Kolanski, R., Norrish, M., Sewell, T., Tuch, H., Winwood, S.: seL4: Formal Verification of an Operating-System Kernel. Commun. ACM 53(6), 107–115 (2010)
8. Kroening, D., Strichman, O.: Decision Procedures. Springer (2008)
9. Leroy, X.: Formal Verification of a Realistic Compiler. Commun. ACM 52(7), 107–115 (2009)
10. Löding, H., Peleska, J.: Timed Moore Automata: Test Data Generation and Model Checking. In: ICST, pp. 449–458. IEEE Computer Society (2010)
11. Myreen, M.O.: Verified Just-in-Time Compiler on x86. In: POPL, pp. 107–118. ACM (2010)
12. Peleska, J., Vorobev, E., Lapschies, F.: Automated Test Case Generation with SMT-Solving and Abstract Interpretation. In: Bobaru, M., Havelund, K., Holzmann, G.J., Joshi, R. (eds.) NFM 2011. LNCS, vol. 6617, pp. 298–312. Springer, Heidelberg (2011)
13. Randimbivololona, F., Souyris, J., Baudin, P., Pacalet, A., Raguideau, J., Schoen, D.: Applying Formal Proof Techniques to Avionics Software: A Pragmatic Approach. In: Wing, J.M., Woodcock, J., Davies, J. (eds.) FM 1999. LNCS, vol. 1709, pp. 1798–1815. Springer, Heidelberg (1999)
14. Regehr, J.: The Future of Compiler Correctness (2010), http://blog.regehr.org/archives/249
15. RTCA SC-167/EUROCAE WG-12. Software Considerations in Airborne Systems and Equipment Certification. Number RTCA/DO-178B. RTCA, Inc., 1140 Connecticut Avenue, N.W., Suite 1020, Washington, D.C. 20036 (December 1992)
16. RTCA SC-205/EUROCAE WG-71. Software Considerations in Airborne Systems and Equipment Certification. Number RTCA/DO-178C. RTCA, Inc., 1140 Connecticut Avenue, N.W., Suite 1020, Washington, D.C. 20036 (December 2011)
17. RTCA SC-205/EUROCAE WG-71. Software Tool Qualification Considerations. Number RTCA/DO-330. RTCA, Inc. (December 2011)
18. Souyris, J., Wiels, V., Delmas, D., Delseny, H.: Formal Verification of Avionics Software Products. In: Cavalcanti, A., Dams, D.R. (eds.) FM 2009. LNCS, vol. 5850, pp. 532–546. Springer, Heidelberg (2009)

Managing Execution Environment Variability during Software Testing: An Industrial Experience

Aymeric Hervieu[1,2], Benoit Baudry[2], and Arnaud Gotlieb[3]

[1] KEREVAL, Thorigné Fouillard, France
[2] INRIA Rennes Bretagne Atlantique, Rennes, France
{Aymeric.Hervieu,Benoit.Baudry}@inria.fr
[3] Certus Software V&V Center, SIMULA RESEARCH LAB., Lysaker, Norway
arnaud@simula.no

Abstract. Nowadays, telecom software applications are expected to run on a tremendous variety of execution environments. For example, network connection software must deliver the same functionalities on distinct physical platforms, which themselves run several distinct operating systems, with various applications and physical devices. Testing those applications is challenging as it is simply impossible to consider every possible environment configuration. This paper reports on an industrial case study called BIEW (Business and Internet EveryWhere) where the combinatorial explosion of environment configurations has been tackled with a dedicated and original methodology devised by KEREVAL, a french SME focusing on software testing services. The proposed solution samples a subset of configurations to be tested, based on environment modelling, requirement analysis and systematic traceability. From the experience on this case study, we outline the challenges to develop means to select relevant environment configurations from variability modelling and requirement analysis in the testing processes of telecom software.

1 Introduction

Business and Internet EveryWhere TM (BIEW) is an Internet connection software developed by Orange, a worldwide Telecom Company. BIEW has been designed to fulfil professional needs in mobility. It aims to provide user the ability to connect to the internet through different means, from everywhere. BIEW is able provide an internet connection using 3G, Wifi or Ethernet protocols. Today the application is used by more than 1.5 millions users from all around the world. For the end user the application overrides the connection manager of the operating system, and gathers in the same application different ways to connect to Internet. Fig. 1 presents a screenshot of the application where the grey panel represents state of the connection: mean, time, connexion quality, and amount of data transferred. At the bottom, a set of icons permits users to access to the various functionalities of the application. As it has to provide users the ability to connect to Internet through different protocols, the application has to

B. Nielsen and C. Weise (Eds.): ICTSS 2012, LNCS 7641, pp. 24–38, 2012.

handle a large number of physical devices. The application has been specified to behave correctly on more than 2,000,000 different environments, composed of operating systems, 3G, Wifi dongles, browsers and mail clients. A the end of the project, specifications of the application contained 1493 requirements. As Internet connection is business critical for a company like Orange, the acceptance testing phase of the BIEW software is a major step in the life cycle of the software. A major dysfunction of the application would have serious financial and reputation consequences for the company. In the previous testing rounds of the application most of the testing activities were based on the craft and experience of software testers. There was no formalized acceptance test process and test teams had no vision of the general efficiency of their test activities.

As the project grew, the number of requirements increased and tests activities only based on manual craft and experience appeared to be insufficient. The testers did not have the necessary expertise in requirements management and systematic environment modelling to handle the growing number of different conditions under which the test cases had to be executed. As this process was highly challenging, KEREVAL, a french SME focusing on software testing services, has been solicited to develop a dedicated testing methodology based on

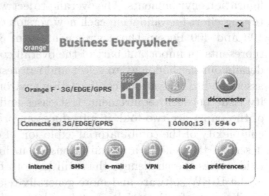

Fig. 1. Screenshot of the application

variability modelling, requirement analysis and systematic traceability between requirements and test cases. To validate this application, we faced to 3 challenges.

1. The first challenge is the explosion of environment configurations, due to the heterogeneity of devices available to the end-user. We were asked to find a systematic selection strategy to reduce the number of configurations under which the system has to be tested ;
2. The second challenge is the reduction of the effort to deploy a configuration to run a set of test cases. To deploy an environment configuration, the testers have to install an Operating System (OS), to set up drivers and plug in devices, and finally to configure the application. These tasks are time-consuming and we were asked to find ways to reuse environment configurations as much as possible ;
3. The last challenge is to keep track of the relations between requirements, environment configurations and test cases. Any change in the requirements or the environment configurations may affect the testing strategy and then needs to facilitated by means of a better traceability.

Unfortunately, the literature contains few industrial reports explaining how these challenges can be efficiently handled. Olsen et al. recently presented in [1] an approach for testing professional printers, that has been deployed by a Big Company. The authors considered a controller having a large number of input parameters and chose to model the environment of the controller (i.e., logical relations between parameters) with propositional logic formula. Based on these formula, they generated test cases covering the pairwise combinatorial testing criterion, and executed them on the system. In the BIEW project, a model of the environment is insufficient to generate test cases and test cases need to be generated from test requirements. More over, the owner of BIEW (i.e., Orange) considered worth reaching the coverage of test requirements rather than any other testing criterion.

This paper reports on the methodology we designed and deployed at KEREVAL, to validate the 1493 BIEW test requirements over the different configuration environments. The overall project was intended to last for 5 years. The testing effort for validating each new version of BIEW was estimated in between 100 and 400 Person-Days, with a mean of 300 Person-Days, meaning that it represents an important part of the overall cost of the development. This paper details our methodology to select and run tests cases, to manage the variability associated to the various configuration environments, to deal with the traceability issue between requirement, test cases and environments. The contributions of the paper are two-fold: it introduces an original methodology to manage the complexity of the combinatorial explosion of configuration environments and it describes the benefits and limitations of our implementation of this methodogy ; it identifies the challenges that still have to be handled to improve the testing of the BIEW software and more generally telecom software applications.

The rest of this article contains three sections. Sec.2 describes the testing methodology through its main components, i.e., inputs processing, environment variability modelling, test requirements management, test case generation and traceability management. Sec.3 reports on the implementation of this methodology, its industrial adoption and discusses of its benefits and limitations. This section also introduces new research perspectives by identifying several key scientific challenges. Finally, Sec.4 concludes the paper.

2   A Methodology to Manage Test Requirements and Test Cases on a Large Number of Configuration Environments

The French SME KEREVAL, specialized in testing services, designed a methodology to manage test requirements and test cases on a large number of configuration environments. The complete methodology is depicted in Fig.2. It takes both environment specifications and requirements as inputs, and produces concrete test cases and several variability matrix that capture test case execution verdicts. These variability matrix specify the test cases that are executed in selected configuration environments. The process includes 5 steps showed with diamonds shapes in Fig.2, namely *environment analysis*, *requirement analysis*, *test case selection*, *variability matrix design* and *test case execution*:

1. In the *environment analysis* step, the validation engineer converts the specification document into a set of environmental features (e.g., OS, browser, etc.) ;
2. In the *requirement analysis* step, the validation engineer splits the set of customer-oriented test requirements into environment-dependent requirements and environment-independent requirements. The former ones are tagged with the set of environmental features on which they depend ;
3. In the *test cases selection* step, the validation engineer extracts test cases from the requirement analysis phase ;
4. The *variability matrix design* step produces the variability matrix that associate the set of environmental configurations to each test case. The matrix also store the test verdict for each test case with its associated set of configurations, when it becomes available ;
5. Finally, the *test case execution* is a process where the validation engineer distributes individual tasks to the engineer in charge of the settings of a test environment and the execution of the tests cases ;

The rest of the section is devoted to the detailed presentation of these steps, which composes the methodology introduced in this paper.

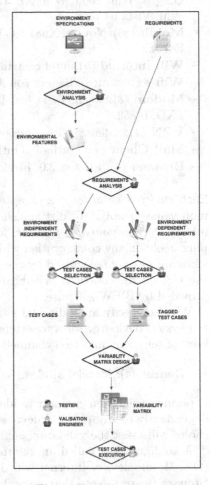

Fig. 2. Test design process

2.1 Environment Analysis

Provided by Orange, a document specification describes an unstructured list of environment items (e.g., OS, browsers, ...). A very first step of our process is to analyse this document and to extract a structured view of the environment under the form of possible configurations. By gathering items corresponding to physical devices or software artefacts, called *environmental features* our process leads to identify possible distinct configurations under the form of *environment configurations*. For the BIEW software, we identified 8 distinct *environmental features*:

- **OS** (5): Win. 2000, Win. XP 32 bits, Win. XP 64 bits, Win. Vista 32 bits, Win. Vista 64 bits
- **Mobile** (25): Novatel Xu870, GT Max GX0301, Lucent Merlin U530, Huawei E870...
- **Wifi internal** (5): intel centrino 2100, 2200, 2915, 3945,
- **Wifi external**(8): Sagem 706 A, Sagem 703...
- **Modem** (8):Sagem F@st 800 USB, Thomson ST330, Siemens A100, ZTE ZXDSL 852...
- **VPN** (4): Safenet, Cisco, Avasy
- **Mail Client** (4): Outlook, Outlook Express, Windows Live Mail, empty
- **Browser** (4): Firefox 2.0, Firefox 1.5, Internet Explorer 5.5, empty

Each *environmental feature*, except **OS**, is optional, that's why each has a common value : empty. We distinguished Wifi Internal and Wifi External features into to 2 *environmental features*, for 2 reasons. Wifi External devices can be plug freely on any configuration while internal devices cannot. Wifi Internal devices are already recognized by the Operating System, drivers are embedded in the OS, on the contrary, Wifi External may sometime require external driver provided by BIEW software.

We also specify an additional *environmental feature*, which is not associated to physical devices or software artefacts. This *environmental feature* contains the kind of telecommunication channel:

- **Bearer** (4): Mobile, Modem, Wifi, Undef

It permits validation engineer to identify certain telecommunication channel independently of any physical devices. Section 2.2 illustrates how this modelling choice will assist the validation engineer .

A configuration, called an *environment configuration*, is a tuple of 9 values: (OS, Mobile device, Internal wifi device, Wifi USB device, Mail client, VPN, Browser,Bearer). Note that *environment configurations* do not necessarily represent actual configuration as, for example, nothing forbids 2 web browsers to be installed within the same machine. Note also that some configurations are not necessarily a *valid environment configurations* because some combinations are forbidden. For example, Firefox 1.5 cannot be installed on Windows Vista 64 bits. According to our definitions, the number of possible *environment configurations* (valid and invalid) is exactly 2560000 [1].

The *environmental feature* **Bearer** will be set up at Undef (undefined) value if a tester selects an *environment configuration* containing more than 1 mean of connection. i.e. in the case of an environment configuration containing a **mobile device** Novatel Xu870 and **Wifi External** device Sagem 706. The main weakness of this step of the process is that invalid configurations are not exclude. Informal knowledge of the tester is not captured.

---

[1] $\sharp OS * \sharp Mobile * \sharp WiFiInternal * \sharp WiFiExternal * \sharp Modem * \sharp VPN * \sharp Mail * \sharp Browser$.

2.2   Requirements Analysis

Requirements have been produced by Orange, and used by developers to write the specification of the BIEW application. The requirements are gathered by *functional domains*, which correspond to the major functionalities of BIEW : e.g. `Power Management` , `POP Locator`, `Startup Preferences` ... In this project, 43 functional domains corresponding to 1493 requirements, are identified. Fig.3 shows a requirement extracted from the functional domain `Wifi Management`. Requirements are composed of a header, including a unique ID, a version number a small summary of the requirement goal, and a detailed explanation of the expected application behaviour on a given situation. Based on the identified *environmental features*, validation engineers decide whether a functional domain is dependent on the environment or not. Classification of a functional domain as dependent or independent of the environment is made after discussions with project managers, software engineers and software testers. For the BIEW application, 33 functional domains (including 841 requirements) are classified as environment-dependent while 10 of them (including the remaining 652 requirements) are environment-independent. Environment-independent functional domains contain requirements that are not dependent of the environment. Each requirement of an environment-dependent functional domain can be tagged with up to 2 tags. *Tags* values correspond to *environmental features*. When a tag is assigned to a requirement, it means that the requirement should be tested in every possible values of the tag. For example, if a requirement r is tagged with OS, then r should be tested over Windows XP 32 bits, Windows XP 64 bits, ... The requirement shown in Fig.3 belongs to an environment-dependent functional domain. As this requirement describes a situation where BIEW depends on the devices wired to the machine, it includes a tag `[WIFI]`. Thus, for this requirement, BIEW should be tested with all the possible Wifi settings. A requirement tagged `[BEARER]` means that the requirement does not directly depend of physical device, but depends on the nature of the telecommunication channel.

The identification of environment dependency is a complex task as it requires a deep understanding of the application domain, thus requiring extensive discussions among the project members: software developers and testers. We estimated that the time spent to identify requirements dependencies was about 15 Person-days.

```
[RQ 02000 _V8.0.1_ Select Wifi device in Settings][WIFI]
The user can also select the Wifi device in the settings. He can choose
in a listof all devices authorized by the customisation and detected by the
Client Software Suite on the PC.
```

Fig. 3. Environment-dependent requirement

2.3   Test Cases Selection

During this step, test cases are selected for each requirement. An example of such a test case is given in Fig.4. Each test case is composed of:

- A unique identification number, which links the test case with the requirement it originates, for traceability;
- A *tag* (optional), which allows validation engineers to identify the environment dependency;
- Pre-requisites that describe the necessary conditions for the test case to be executable;
- A test objective, that is the goal of the test case;
- A test procedure, that gives the detailed plan for executing the test case.

Test case is written in Quality Center (QC), and associated to its requirement. QC permits to maintain the traceability between requirements and test cases. When a requirement evolves, is modified, added, or suppress,the impacted test cases are distinguished. During a test campaign, validation engineer executes the test case, and reports verdict in Quality Center. For BIEW, 3102 test cases are selected from the requirements, among which 1231 are associated to environment-dependent functional domain.

[353-RQ01980][WIFI]
Objective: Check the prompt display for one descriptor and one security key WPA2.
Pre Requise:
Business EveryWhere Kit installed.
Acces Point AP1 selected
Wireless lan seted up with WPA 2 security
Test Procedure:
- Launch the BIEW application
- Click on the button connect, on the main screen
- Select the access Point AP1

Fig. 4. An example of a Test case

2.4   Variability Matrix Design

The tag is used to reduce the number of test execution to perform for a given test case. This is basically the approach we adopted to reduce the combinatorial explosion:

- if a test case has no tag, then only a single environment configuration is selected for test case execution ;
- if a test case has a single dependency, all the environment configurations related to the environmental feature are used for test case execution. For example, if the feature is WIFI, then all the WIFI-environment configurations are selected;
- if the test case has two tags, then all the combinations of environment configurations will be selected for test case execution.

A *Variability matrix* is designed for each of 43 functional domain. When the domain is environment-independent, then the test cases have to be executed on a single environment configuration. On the contrary, test cases originating from environment-dependent functional domain have to be executed on several environment configurations. A variability matrix (as the one shown in Fig.4), captures the dependency in this latter case. In this matrix, each row corresponds to a test case, while columns represent environment configuration and environment configurations combination. As the environment dependency has been limited to 2 *environmental features*, only two levels of combination are possible. In the matrix of Fig.5, the first columns include informations such as the test case name, its priority, its environmental features and its status. Of course, status are only available once test execution has been started. A status can be either `Passed`, `Failed` or `Not completed`, corresponding to the state of the test execution process. A color is associated to each element of the matrix: grey means that the test case, within the considered configuration, is not required to be executed, white means that the test case has to be executed, green means `Passed`, red means `Failed`, while N/A means `Not applicable`. This latter case holds for test case that cannot be executed on a given *environment configuration*. When a test cases has been run on all the *environment configurations* then its statuts is turned `Passed` or `Failed`, depending on the results over all the environment configurations. If the test case fail for at least one *environment configuration* then, its status is turned `Failed`. Variability matrix are then associated to their *functional domain* in QC. Thanks to these rules, only 10603 test case executions were run instead of 33685 + 1871, while the overall environment diversity of the test cases was preserved. The quality of the test suite was evaluated by 2 distinct entities. Developers of the application where executed test cases during development steps put in excerpt a several defects. This test step permits developers to fix quickly the application. The second is an independent entity the Orange development team.This entity is a branch of Orange group which valid the release of a major version. The second entity identified few defects. Now, a part the validation process of the branch, for BIEW 9, relies on our test platform. We were not able to extract relevant metrics to illustrate the quality of the test suite. We obtained those information thought discussions other the different stakeholder.

Projet ouvert : BESS_V8_0				Vista Business												
			120 test(s) >	Centrino 2100	Centrino 2200	Centrino 2915	Centrino 3945	Dongle Inventel InexQ	Inventel Cohiba	Sagem 703	Sagem 760A	Sagem 760N	Caméo	Broadcom Devices	Centrino 2100	Centrino 2200
Plan: Name	Plan: Dependancies	Plan: Priority	Status	20	44	20	20	20	80	20	20	20	20	20	15	15
353 - RQ 01500	Aucun	P1 - Important	Passed						OK							
353 - RQ 02900 - 002	OS + Wifi	P0 - Indispensable	No Run									NA	NA	NA		
353 - RQ 03000	OS + Wifi	P0 - Indispensable	Failed									[illegible]	[illegible]	[illegible]		
353 - RQ 03050	OS + Wifi	P0 - Indispensable	Failed									OK	OK	[illegible]		
353 - RQ 03200	Aucun	P0 - Indispensable	Passed						OK							

Fig. 5. Variability matrix

2.5   Test Case Management and Execution

In the BIEW project, we gathered 1493 requirements and classified them in terms of functional domains. For each functional domain, identified as environment dependent, we associated a specific variability matrix. As a result, test cases were formally associated to the requirements for faciliting traceability.

In order to monitor test activities, we associated a status to each requirement in our methodology. The status of a requirement depends on the state of execution of its associated test cases. There are five possible values for the status of a req:

- NOT COVERED: if there is no test case associated to the req. ;
- FAILED: if at least one of the test cases failed ;
- PASSED: if all the test cases successfully passed, in all the environments specified by the variability matrix ;
- NOT COMPLETED: at least one of the test cases associated to the req. has not yet been executed ;
- NOT RUNNED: none of the test cases associated to the req. has been executed ;

Of course, the main relevant metric used during the acceptance testing phase is the number of covered requirements (and their status). Using this metric, the validation engineer can follow quite easily the evolution of the project and can provide informations related to the state and quality of the deliverables to the development team. Fig. 6 shows a screenshot of the Quality Center (QC) tool that has been used in the BIEW project. QC centralizes and reports on all the test activities of the project. On the left, all the requirements classified by functional domain are shown. For each functional domain, the validation engineer follows test activities through the diagrams shown on the right.

During test execution, the validation engineer assigns to each tester a subset of existing variability matrix. The testers are then responsible of the execution of test cases, as they are specified in the distinct matrix. A test case assembles 3 elements: an *environment configuration*, a test input and a test verdict. Note however, that a matrix does not specify the order on which the test cases have to be executed. Testers have to select a *environment configuration* according to the availability of material (e.g., USB sticks, SIM card) and to prioritize theexecution of test cases based on their knowledge of the fault-proness of the configuration. When *environment configurations* contain items tagged as [Bearer], it means that the test case execution does not require a particular physical device to be set up. Then, the tester can select an environment configuration with any item to perform test case execution.

3   Benefits, Limitations and Possible Innovations

KEREVAL has developed a cost-effective systematic methodology that relies on two key-components: the formalization of execution environment as a set of

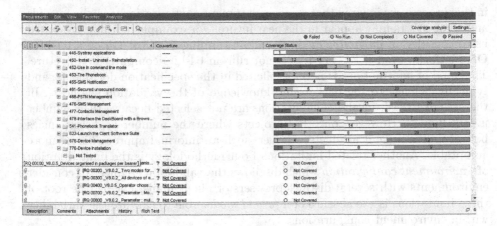

Fig. 6. Screenshot of the test project in Quality Center

environmental features and the analysis of customer-oriented requirements to clarify their dependency on *functional domains*. Since the methodology keeps track of the link between requirements and test cases, much testing effort is saved by limiting the number of test cases executed on each environment. The testing effort is also reduced during test cases design, as their dependency to environment has been explicited. Still, the methodology is perfectible. Let us review the limitations we considered, the identification of which could serve as a basis to improve the methodology.

- In the methodology, *environmental features* are totally independent from each other, while in fact, there are many dependencies among them ;
- Several configuration environments, having distinct sets of *environmental features*, are in fact redundant, meaning that test efforts could be saved if we could capture redundant environments ;
- In the methodology, we considered that a maximum of 2 tags could be associated to each requirement for facilitating the representation of dependencies of requirement to the environmentconfigurations ;
- Requirements and environments often change from one version to another of the BIEW software. In our methodology, we did not consider the benefice that could be brought by an impact analysis of these changes ;

In this section, we review each of these limitations by identifying their roots, and, by studying existing research results, we propose and discuss potential improvements of the methodology.

3.1 Explicit Representation of the Variability within Environment Configurations

For BIEW, Orange provided us an informal description of the environment configurations, from which, we extracted a list of environmental features. However, in this process, we ignored that some environment configurations may be invalids and some others may appear in the near future. For example, nothing prevented us to consider an *environment configuration* running **Firefox 1.5** on a **64-bits OS** platform, even if Firefox 1.5 cannot run on 64-bits computer architecture. This kind of informations is never explicited in the specification documents, and typically belongs to the background knowledge of the validation engineers. In the case of BIEW, invalid configurations are not selected because their number is still limited. However, on other projects where the number of discrepancies between environment artefacts is larger, such an informal approach is no more acceptable. Another related limitation of our methodology is the limited notion of *environment configuration* which disallows the validation engineer to consider environments with several distinct browsers or client mails. For us, the root of these limitations is the absence of a *formal model* able to capture the variability within environment configurations.

In the literature, feature modelling, introduced by Kang in [2], enables complex and inter-dependant environment variability representation. Feature modelling introduces a tree-based graphical representation of the variability within a set of components of a system, or a set of options within a product line, or a set of features of an environment representation . Looking at the so-called *Feature Model*, which basically captures a set of propositional logic formula representing distinct environments, we modelled the dependencies within environment configurations of BIEW. Fig. 7 is an excerpt of this Feature Model, where the discrepancy between Firefox 1.5 and 64-bits architecture can be explicited using a special operator, called **Mutex** (i.e., exclusive disjunction). In this model, an operator OR can be used to represent configurations with several browsers, enabling the selection of environments with multiple features. The overall Feature Model we built for BIEW is composed of 66 features and implicitly represents 8, 243, 200 distinct configurations. Using a Feature Model, a number of manual activities for the testing of BIEW could be automated. Benavides et al. [3] surveyed the automated analysis of Feature Models and identified key analyses, such as the so-called *valid product* and *valid partial product* operations that could be useful in our case:

- *Valid product* verifies that a given environment configuration respects all the constraints of a Feature Model. For example, a configuration with both Firefox 1.5 and any 64-bits architecture will be automatically rejected. Implementations of this operation relies on the usage of SAT-solving or Constraint Programming techniques.
- *Valid partial product* is a similar operation over only a subset of features, and enables in addition the automatic completion of a partial environment configuration.

To sum up, we think that capturing the distinct environment configurations with a formal model of the variability will be useful to improve the test management and execution of the BIEW software.

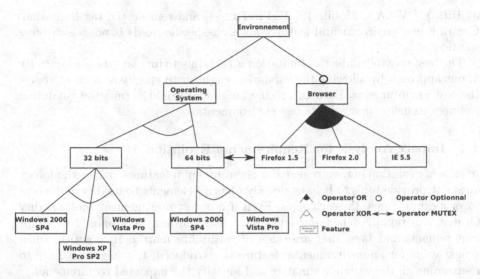

Fig. 7. Excerpt of the feature model representing the execution environment of the BIEW application

3.2   Elimination of Redundant Configuration Environments

In our methodology, the validation engineer identifies the dependency among *environmental features*, through a careful analysis of the specification documents and the customer-oriented test requirements. These dependencies are captured within *variability matrix*. However, a detailed analysis of the *variability matrix* shows that several test environments are redundants. In fact, requirements from distinct functional domains can be tagged with the same features, leading to the creation of distinct matrix, although they represent similar *environment configurations*. We identified 149 such duplicated environment configurations over the 390 configurations used during the overall test project.

3.3   Improving the Internal Representation

Our methodology involves the tagging of requirements with *environmental features*, to identify their environmental dependencies. Each requirement is tagged with 1 or 2 environmental features because we used a simple two-dimensional representation (i.e., *variability matrix*) for specifying the link between the environment configurations and the requirements.Then tagged requirements are tested under all the combinations of the items of the values.

The current modelling does not permit the validation engineer to define precisely test environments. For example, validation engineer cannot specify that a requirement has to be tested over 1 operating system 32 bits, and 1 operating system 64 bits, under a WLAN and a mobile connexion, with Internet Explorer, and Firefox. To design a test environment according to the depicted process validation engineer needs to 3 new environmental features ({ 1 OS 32 Bits, 1 OS

64 Bits }, { WLAN, Mobile }, { IE,FireFox }), and remove the tag limitation. Creating new environmental features for each specific needs is not a satisfying solution.

The best way to handle this limitation is certainly to increase the declarativity of our approach by allowing the validation engineer to specify at a finest coarse the test environments. Domain specific languages would permit the validation engineer to define precisely its test environments.

3.4   Impact Analysis for Requirements Evolution

In case of evolution of requirements or environmental features, our methodology does not provide tools to help us quickly identify elements to modify and adapt to properly manage these changes. Even if our test management tool, Quality Center, can rapidly detect impacted test cases, nothing is proposed to adapt requirements and tags, that are store in variability matrix. In practice, when a new value for an environmental feature is introduced, test engineers have to re-examine all the variability matrix and identify the impacted requirements.

The literature contains many propositions to handle efficiently these evolutions. For example, Hartman et al. in [4] proposes to use Feature modelling with dependencies to manage context evolutions. Metzeger et al. [5] introduced *xlink* to link two distinct variability models, while Than Tun et al [6] used xlinks to formally establish the relation between a set of requirements to a set of features. Then, using these xlinks, their approach permits the validation engineers to select configurations that cover a selected subset of requirements. We think that this approach is valuable and could be implemented in our specific case for handling the evolution of requirements or environmental features.

3.5   Test Criteria over the Environment Dependency

As exhaustive testing of every requirement on every possible environment configuration is impossible, test criteria have to be introduced in any methodology aiming at testing telecom software applications. In the case of BIEW, we implicitly considered every pair of values for environmental features, meaning that we tested the dependency to the environment with pairwise testing, a Combinatorial Interaction Testing (CIT) criterion [7].

A limitation of original approaches of CIT is however that it did not consider constraints among the variables [7,8]. In the case of BIEW there are constraints among the environment features that capture the restrictions in configuration environments (see Sec.3.1). Recently, several authors proposed means to generate test configurations from feature models with constraints [9,10,11,12]. The authors of this article also contributed to this domain with a similar approach based on Constraint Programming [13]. Generating pairwise-covering configurations has also been studied for other representations of variability and constraints, e.g., [14]. Another intersting extension of CIT approaches is their ability to handle other testing criteria than pairwise. For example, it is possible to consider 3-wise or even N-wise combinations between the variables. We think that qualifying our test methodology with respect to these criteria will be helpful to improve our understanding of the achieved level of quality. This would be helpful in the discussions with our customer to adjust precisely the methodology with the expected level of quality.

4   Conclusion and Perspectives

This paper presents a methodology we designed at KEREVAL to validate a telecom software application on a large number of distinct environment configurations. The main challenge we dealt with consisted to handle the potential combinatorial explosion of the number of possible configurations. In the proposed methodology, we adopted an approach that links the requirements to the environment through the usage of *environmental features*, and dedicated *variability matrix*. We performed a systematic identification of the dependencies between requirements and environmental features and thus were able to construct. We also kept the traceability between test cases, environments and requirements by using these elements. Thanks to this testing methodology, we showed that 70% of the test definition/execution effort could be saved over an exhaustive testing approach. However, we also identified several limitations in our methodology and the paper shows that is a large room for improvements. Among them, the absence of a formal representation of the variability (e.g., Feature Model) is the main limitation to address the problem of the combinatorial explosion of the number of environments to consider. We can also mention the need for impact analysis of requirements and environment change.

Our future plan includes a better formalization of the methodology, through the usage of variability models. Recent works on feature modelling enable automated analysis and then could be highly beneficial in the context of BIEW [6,5,4,3]. We also plan to reason over variability models in order to generate test configurations that respect Combinatorial Interaction Testing criteria [13]. Following an approach inspired by xlink introduced by Hartmann and Than Tun [6,4], we will also exploit these variability models to facilitate impact analysis of change in requirements and environmental features. On another side, we would like to evaluate the potential of our methodology on other projects. In some sense, BIEW was a first industrial application that allowed us to identify the limitations of the approach. KEREVAL is involved in several distinct telecom application testing projects (e.g., the testing of mobile phone applications on 15 distinct platforms) and BIEW was the only project on which such a variability management approach was deployed. We are convinced that a fine-tuned methodology for managing distinct environment configurations is essential to save effort and cost in these kind of projects.

Acknowledgements. We thank Ludovic Rocher and Mokrane Kessaci for their precise answers to our multiple questions related to the BIEW project. We also thank Orange company which allowed us to use the result of the BIEW testing project in this paper.

References

1. Olsen, P., Foederer, J., Tretmans, J.: Model-Based Testing of Industrial Transformational Systems. In: Wolff, B., Zaïdi, F. (eds.) ICTSS 2011. LNCS, vol. 7019, pp. 131–145. Springer, Heidelberg (2011)
2. Kang, K., Cohen, S., Hess, J., Novak, W., Peterson, S.: Feature-Oriented Domain Analysis (FODA) Feasibility Study, Software Engineering Institute, Tech. Rep. CMU/SEI-90-TR-21 (November 1990)
3. Benavides, D., Segura, S., Ruiz-Cortés, A.: Automated analysis of feature models: A detailed literature review. Information Systems (35), 615–636 (2010)
4. Hartmann, H., Trew, T.: Using feature diagrams with context variability to model multiple product lines for software supply chains. In: Proceedings of the 2008 12th International Software Product Line Conference (2008)
5. Disambiguating the Documentation of Variability in Software Product Lines: A Separation of Concerns, Formalization and Automated Analysis (2007)
6. Than Tun, T., Boucher, Q., Classen, A., Hubaux, A., Heymans, P.: Relating requirements and feature configurations: a systematic approach. In: Proceedings of the 13th International Software Product Line ConferenceTha (2009)
7. Cohen, D.M., Dalal, S.R., Fredman, M.L., Patton, G.C.: The aetg system: An approach to testing based on combinatorial design. IEEE Transactions on Software Engineering 23(7), 437–444 (1997)
8. Lei, Y., Tai, K.-C.: In-parameter-order: A test generation strategy for pairwise testing. In: HASE 1998, pp. 254–261 (1998)
9. Oster, S., Markert, F., Ritter, P.: Automated Incremental Pairwise Testing of Software Product Lines. In: Bosch, J., Lee, J. (eds.) SPLC 2010. LNCS, vol. 6287, pp. 196–210. Springer, Heidelberg (2010)
10. Perrouin, G., Sen, S., Klein, J., Baudry, B., Le Traon, Y.: Automated and scalable t-wise test case generation strategies for software product lines. In: ICST 2010, Paris, France (2010)
11. Lamancha, B.P., Usaola, M.P.: Testing Product Generation in Software Product Lines Using Pairwise for Features Coverage. In: Petrenko, A., Simão, A., Maldonado, J.C. (eds.) ICTSS 2010. LNCS, vol. 6435, pp. 111–125. Springer, Heidelberg (2010)
12. Johansen, M.F., Haugen, Ø., Fleurey, F.: Properties of Realistic Feature Models Make Combinatorial Testing of Product Lines Feasible. In: Whittle, J., Clark, T., Kühne, T. (eds.) MODELS 2011. LNCS, vol. 6981, pp. 638–652. Springer, Heidelberg (2011)
13. Hervieu, A., Baudry, B., Gotlieb, A.: Pacogen: Automatic generation of pairwise test configurations from feature models. In: Proc. of the 22nd IEEE Int. Symp. on Softw. Reliability Engineering (ISSRE 2011), Hiroshima, Japan (November 2011)
14. Garvin, B.J., Cohen, M.B., Dwyer, M.B.: An improved meta-heuristic search for constrained interaction testing. In: Proceedings of the 2009 1st International Symposium on Search Based Software Engineering, SSBSE 2009, pp. 13–22. IEEE Computer Society, Washington, DC (2009), http://dx.doi.org/10.1109/SSBSE.2009.25

A Technique for Agile and Automatic Interaction Testing for Product Lines

Martin Fagereng Johansen[1,2], Øystein Haugen[1], Franck Fleurey[1],
Erik Carlson[3], Jan Endresen[3], and Tormod Wien[3]

[1] SINTEF ICT, Pb. 124 Blindern, 0314 Oslo, Norway
{Martin.Fagereng.Johansen,Oystein.Haugen,Franck.Fleurey}@sintef.no
[2] Institute for Informatics, University of Oslo, Pb. 1080 Blindern, 0316 Oslo, Norway
[3] ABB, Bergerveien 12, 1375 Billingstad, Norway
{erik.carlson,jan.endresen,tormod.wien}@no.abb.com

Abstract. Product line developers must ensure that existing and new features work in all products. Adding to or changing a product line might break some of its features. In this paper, we present a technique for automatic and agile interaction testing for product lines. The technique enables developers to know if features work together with other features in a product line, and it blends well into a process of continuous integration. The technique is evaluated with two industrial applications, testing a product line of safety devices and the Eclipse IDEs. The first case shows how existing test suites are applied to the products of a 2-wise covering array to identify two interaction faults. The second case shows how over 400,000 test executions are performed on the products of a 2-wise covering array using over 40,000 existing automatic tests to identify potential interactions faults.

Keywords: Product Lines, Testing, Agile, Continuous Integration, Automatic, Combinatorial Interaction Testing.

1 Introduction

A product line is a collection of products with a considerable amount of hardware or code in common. The commonality and differences between the products are usually modeled as a feature model. A product of a product line is given by a configuration of the feature model, constructed by specifying whether features are including or not. Testing product lines is a challenge since the number of possible products grows exponentially with the number of choices in the feature model. Yet, it is desirable to ensure that the valid products function correctly.

One approach for testing product lines is combinatorial interaction testing [1]. Combinatorial interaction testing is to first construct a small set of products, called a covering array, in which interaction faults are most likely to show up and then to test these products normally. We have previously advanced this approach by showing that generating covering arrays from realistic features models is tractable [2] and by providing an algorithm that allows generating covering arrays for product lines of the size and complexity found in industry [3].

B. Nielsen and C. Weise (Eds.): ICTSS 2012, LNCS 7641, pp. 39–54, 2012.

In its current form, the application of combinatorial interaction testing to testing product lines is neither fully automatic nor agile; a technique for automatic and agile testing of product lines based on combinatorial interaction testing is the contribution of this paper, presented in Section 3. The technique is evaluated by applying it to test two industrial product lines, a product line of safety devices and the Eclipse IDEs; this is presented in Section 4.

In Section 4.1 it is shown how the technique can be implemented using the Common Variability Language (CVL) [4] tool suite. (CVL is the language of the ongoing standardization effort of variability languages by OMG.) Five test suites were executed on 11 strategically selected products, the pair-wise covering array, of a product line of safety devices to uncover two unknown and previously undetected bugs.

In Section 4.3 it is shown how the technique can be implemented using the Eclipse Platform plug-in system. More than 40,000 existing automatic tests were executed on 13 strategically selected products, the pair-wise covering array, of the Eclipse IDE product line, producing more than 400,000 test results that reveal a multitude of potential interaction faults.

2   Background and Related Work

2.1   Product Lines

A product line [5] is a collection of products with a considerable amount of hardware or code in common. The primary motivation for structuring one's products as a product line is to allow customers to have a system tailored for their purpose and needs, while still avoiding redundancy of code. It is common for customers to have conflicting requirements. In that case, it is not even possible to ship one product for all customers.

The Eclipse IDE products [6] can be seen as a software product line. Today, Eclipse lists 12 products (which configurations are shown in Table 1a[1]) on their download page[2].

One way to model the commonalities and differences in a product line is using a feature model [7]. A feature model sets up the commonalities and differences of a product line in a tree such that configuring the product line proceeds from the root of the tree. Figure 1 shows the part of the feature model for the Eclipse IDEs that is sufficient to configure all official versions of the Eclipse IDE. The figure uses the common notation for feature models; for a detailed explanation of feature models, see Czarnecki and Eisenecker 2000 [8].

2.2   Product Line Testing

Testing a product line poses a number of new challenges compared to testing single systems. It has to be ensured that each possible configuration of the product

---

[1] http://www.eclipse.org/downloads/compare.php, retrieved 2012-04-12.
[2] http://eclipse.org/downloads/, retrieved 2012-04-12.

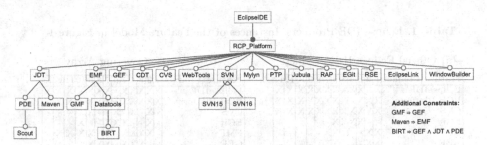

Fig. 1. Feature Model for the Eclipse IDE Product Line

line functions correctly. One way to validate a product line is through testing, but testing is done on a running system. The software product line is simply a collection of many products. One cannot test each possible product, since the number of products in general grows exponentially with the number of features in the product line. For the feature model in Figure 1, there are 356, 352 possible configurations.

Reusable Component Testing. In a survey of empirics of what is done in industry for testing software product lines [9], we found that the technique with considerable empirics showing benefits is *reusable component testing*. Given a product line where each product is built by bundling a number of features implemented in components, reusable component testing is to test each component in isolation. The empirics have later been strengthened; Ganesan et al. 2012 [10] is a report on the test practices at NASA for testing their Core Flight Software System (CFS) product line. They report that the chief testing done on this system is reusable component testing [10].

Interaction Testing. There is no single recommended approach available today for testing interactions between features in product lines efficiently [11], but there are many suggestions. Some of the more promising suggestions are combinatorial interaction testing [1], discussed below; a technique called ScenTED, where the idea is to express the commonalities and differences on the UML model of the product line and then derive concrete test cases by analyzing it [12]; and incremental testing, where the idea is to automatically adapt a test case from one product to the next using the specification of similarities and differences between the products [13]. Kim et al. 2011 [14] presented a technique where they can identify irrelevant features for a test case using static analysis.

Combinatorial Interaction Testing: Combinatorial interaction testing [1] is one of the most promising approaches. The benefits of this approach is that it deals directly with the feature model to derive a small set of products (a covering array) which products can then be tested using single system testing techniques, of which there are many good ones [15].

Table 1. Eclipse IDE Products, Instances of the Feature Model in Figure 1

(a) Official Eclipse IDE products

Feature\Product	1	2	3	4	5	6	7	8	9	10	11	12
EclipseIDE	X	X	X	X	X	X	X	X	X	X	X	X
RCP_Platform	X	X	X	X	X	X	X	X	X	X	X	X
CVS	X	X	X	X	X	X	X	X	X	X	X	X
EGit	-	-	X	X	X	X	-	-	-	-	-	-
EMF	X	X	-	-	X	X	-	-	-	-	-	-
GEF	X	X	-	-	X	X	-	-	-	-	-	-
JDT	X	X	-	-	X	X	X	-	X	-	-	X
Mylyn	X	X	X	X	X	X	X	X	X	X	X	-
WebTools	-	X	-	-	-	X	-	-	-	X	-	-
RSE	-	X	X	X	-	-	X	X	-	-	-	-
EclipseLink	-	X	-	-	-	X	-	-	X	-	-	-
PDE	-	X	-	-	X	X	X	-	X	-	-	X
Datatools	-	X	-	-	-	-	X	-	-	-	-	-
CDT	-	-	X	X	-	-	-	X	-	-	-	-
BIRT	-	-	-	-	-	X	-	-	-	-	-	-
GMF	-	-	-	-	X	-	-	-	-	-	-	-
PTP	-	-	-	-	-	-	X	-	-	-	-	-
Scout	-	-	-	-	-	-	-	X	-	-	-	-
Jubula	-	-	-	-	-	-	-	-	X	-	-	-
RAP	-	-	-	X	-	-	-	-	-	-	-	-
WindowBuilder	X	-	-	-	-	-	-	-	-	-	-	-
Maven	X	-	-	-	-	-	-	-	-	-	-	-
SVN	-	-	-	-	-	-	-	-	-	-	-	-
SVN15	-	-	-	-	-	-	-	-	-	-	-	-
SVN16	-	-	-	-	-	-	-	-	-	-	-	-

(b) Pair-wise Covering Array

Feature\Product	1	2	3	4	5	6	7	8	9	10	11	12	13
EclipseIDE	X	X	X	X	X	X	X	X	X	X	X	X	X
RCP_Platform	X	X	X	X	X	X	X	X	X	X	X	X	X
CVS	-	X	-	X	-	X	-	-	X	-	-	-	-
EGit	-	X	-	-	X	X	X	-	-	X	-	-	-
EMF	-	X	X	X	X	-	-	X	X	X	X	X	-
GEF	-	-	X	X	X	-	X	X	X	-	-	X	-
JDT	-	X	X	X	X	-	X	-	X	X	-	X	-
Mylyn	-	X	-	X	-	-	X	X	-	-	-	-	-
WebTools	-	-	X	X	X	-	X	-	-	X	X	-	-
RSE	-	X	X	-	X	X	-	-	-	-	-	-	-
EclipseLink	-	X	X	-	-	X	-	X	X	-	-	-	-
PDE	-	X	-	X	X	-	X	-	X	-	-	X	-
Datatools	-	X	X	X	X	-	-	-	X	-	X	X	-
CDT	-	-	X	X	-	X	-	X	X	-	-	-	-
BIRT	-	-	-	X	X	-	-	-	X	-	-	X	-
GMF	-	-	X	X	X	-	-	X	X	-	-	-	-
PTP	-	-	X	-	X	X	-	X	X	-	-	-	-
Scout	-	X	-	X	-	-	X	-	X	-	-	-	-
Jubula	-	-	X	X	-	X	-	X	-	X	-	-	-
RAP	-	X	X	-	-	X	X	-	X	-	-	-	-
WindowBuilder	-	X	-	X	-	X	-	X	-	-	-	-	-
Maven	-	X	X	-	-	-	-	X	X	-	-	-	-
SVN	-	X	-	-	X	X	X	X	X	-	X	-	X
SVN15	-	X	-	X	-	X	-	X	-	-	-	-	X
SVN16	-	-	-	-	X	X	-	X	-	X	-	-	-

There are three main stages in the application of combinatorial interaction testing to a product line. First, the feature model of the system must be made. Second, the t-wise covering array must be generated. We have developed an algorithm that can generate such arrays from large features models [3][3]. These products must then be generated or physically built. Last, a single system testing technique must be selected and applied to each product in this covering array.

Table 1b shows the 13 products that must be tested to ensure that every pair-wise interaction between the features in the running example functions correctly. Each row represents one feature and every column one product. 'X' means that the feature is included for the product, '-' means that the feature is not included. Some features are included for every product because they are core features, and some pairs are not covered since they are invalid according to the feature model.

Testing the products in a pair-wise covering array is called 2-wise testing, or pair-wise testing. This is a special case of t-wise testing where $t = 2$. t-wise testing is to test the products in a covering array of strength t. 1-wise coverage means that every feature is at least included and excluded in one product, 2-wise coverage means that every combination of two feature assignments are in the covering array, etc. For our running example, 3, 13 and 40 products is sufficient to achieve 1-wise, 2-wise and 3-wise coverage, respectively.

---

[3] See [3] for a definition of covering arrays and for an algorithm for generating them.

Empirical Motivation. An important motivation for combinatorial interaction testing is a paper by Kuhn et al. 2004 [16]. They indicated empirically that most bugs are found for 6-wise coverage, and that for 1-wise one is likely to find on average around 50%, for 2-wise on average around 70%, and for 3-wise around 95%, etc.

Garvin and Cohen 2011 [17] did an exploratory study on two open source product lines. They extracted 28 faults that could be analyzed and which was configuration dependent. They found that three of these were true interaction faults which require at least two specific features to be present in a product for the fault to occur. Even though this number is low, they did experience that interaction testing also improves feature-level testing, that testing for interaction faults exercised the features better. These observations strengthen the case for combinatorial interaction testing.

Steffens et al. 2012 [18] did an experiment at Danfoss Power Electronics. They tested the Danfoss Automation Drive which has a total of 432 possible configurations. They generated a 2-wise covering array of 57 products and compared the testing of it to the testing all 432 products. This is possible because of the relatively small size of the product line. They mutated each feature with a number a mutations and ran test suites for all products and the 2-wise covering array. They found that 97.48% of the mutated faults are found with 2-wise coverage.

3 Proposed Technique

We address two problems with combinatorial interaction testing of software product lines in our proposed technique. A generic algorithm for automatically performing the technique is presented in Section 3.2, an evaluation of it is presented in Section 4 and a discussion of benefits and limitations presented in Section 5.

- **The functioning of created test artifacts is sensitive to changes in the feature model:** The configurations in a covering array can be drastically different with the smallest change to the feature model. Thus, each product must be built anew and the single system test suites changed manually. Thus, plain combinatorial interaction testing of software product lines is not agile. This limits it from effectively being used during development.
- **Which tests should be executed on the generated products:** In ordinary combinatorial interaction testing, a new test suite must be made for a unique product. It does not specify how to generate a complete test suite for a product.

3.1 Idea

Say we have a product line in which two features, A and B, are both optional and mutually optional. This means that there are four situations possible: Both A and B are in the product, only A or only B is in the product and neither is in the product. These four possibilities are shown in Table 2a.

Table 2. Feature Assignment Combinations

(a) Pairs

Feature\Situation	1	2	3	4
A	X	X	-	-
B	X	-	X	-

(b) Triples

Feature\Situation	1	2	3	4	5	6	7	8
A	X	X	X	X	-	-	-	-
B	X	X	-	-	X	X	-	-
C	X	-	X	-	X	-	X	-

If we have a test suite that tests feature A, *TestA*, and another test suite that tests feature B, *TestB*, the following is what we expect: (1) When both feature A and B are present, we expect *TestA* and *TestB* to succeed. (2) When just feature A is present, we expect *TestA* to succeed. (3) Similarly, when just feature B is present, we expect *TestB* to succeed. (4) Finally, when neither feature is present, we expect the product to continue to function correctly. In all four cases we expect the product to build and start successfully.

Similar reasoning can be made for 3-wise and higher testing, which cases are shown in Table 2b. For example, for situation 1, we expect *TestA*, *TestB* and *TestC* to pass, in situation 2, we expect *TestA* and *TestB* to pass, which means that A and B work in each other's presence and that both work without C. This kind of reasoning applies to the rest of the situations in Table 2b and to higher orders of combinations.

3.2 Algorithm for Implementation

The theory from Section 3.1 combined with existing knowledge about combinatorial interaction testing can be utilized to construct a testing technique. Algorithm 1 shows the pseudo-code for the technique.

The general idea is, for each product in a t-wise covering array, to execute the test suites related to the included features. If a test suite fails for one configuration, but succeeds for another, we can know that there must be some kind of interaction disturbing the functionality of the feature.

In Algorithm 1, line 1, the covering array of strength t of the feature model FM is generated and the set of configurations are placed in CA_t. At line 2, the algorithm iterates through each configuration. At line 3, a product is constructed from the configuration c. PG is an object that knows how to construct a product from a configuration; making this object is a one-time effort. The product is placed in p. If the construction of the product failed, the result is placed in the result table, *ResultTable*. The *put* operation on *ResultTable* takes three parameters, the result, the column and the row. The row parameter can be an asterisk, '*', indicating that the result applies to all rows.

If the build succeeded, the algorithm continues at line 7 where the algorithm iterates through each test suite, *test*, of the product line, provided in a set *Tests*. At line 8, the algorithm takes out the feature, f, that is tested by the test suite *test*. The algorithm finds that in the object containing the Test-Feature-Mapping, TFM. At line 9, if this feature f is found to be included in the current

---

Algorithm 1. Pseudo Code of the Automatic and Agile Testing Algorithm

---

```
1:  CAₜ ← GenerateCoveringArray(FM, t)
2:  for each configuration c in CAₜ do
3:      p ← PG.GenerateProduct(c)
4:      if p's build failed then
5:          ResultTable.put("buildfailed", c, *)
6:      else
7:          for each test test in Tests do
8:              f ← TFM.getFeatures(test)
9:              if c has features f then
10:                 result ← p.runTest(test)
11:                 ResultTable.put(result, c, f)
12:             end if
13:         end for
14:     end if
15: end for
```

---

configuration, c, then, at line 10, the test suite is run. The results from running the test is placed in the result table[4], line 11.

3.3   Result Analysis

Results stored in a result table constructed by Algorithm 1 allow us to do various kinds of analysis to identify the possible causes of the problems.

Attributing the Cause of a Fault. These examples show how analysis of the result can proceed:

- If we have a covering array of strength 1, CA_1, of a feature model FM: If a build fails whenever f_1 is not included, we know that f_1 is a core feature.
- If we have a covering array of strength 2, CA_2, of a feature model FM in which feature f_1 and f_2 are independent on each other: If, $\forall c \in CA_2$ where both f_1 and f_2 are included, the test suite for f_1 fails, while where f_1 is included and f_2 is not, then the test suite of f_1 succeeds, we know that the cause of the problem is a disruption of f_1 caused by the inclusion f_2.
- If we have a covering array of strength 2, CA_2, of a feature model FM in which feature f_1 and f_2 are not dependent on each other: If, $\forall c \in CA_2$ where both f_1 and f_2 are included, the test suites for both f_1 and f_2 succeed, while where f_1 is included and f_2 is not, then the test suite of f_1 fails, we know that the cause of the problem is a hidden dependency from f_1 to f_2.

These kinds of analysis are possible for all the combinations of successes and failures of the features for the various kinds of interaction-coverages.

---

[4] Two examples of result tables are shown later, Tables 4b and 5b.

Of course, if there are many problems with the product line, then several problems might overshadow each other. In that case, the tester must look carefully at the error given by the test case to find out what the problem is. For example, if every build with f_1 included fails that will overshadow a second problem that f_2 is dependent on f_1.

Guarantees. It is uncommon for a testing technique to have guarantees, but there are certain errors in the feature model that will be detected.

- Feature f is not specified to be a core feature in the feature model but is in the implementation. This is guaranteed to be identified using a 1-wise covering array: There will be a product in the covering array with f not included that will not successfully build, start or run.
- Feature f_1 is not dependent on feature f_2 in the feature model, but there is a dependency in the code. This is guaranteed to be identified using a 2-wise covering array. There will be a product in the 2-wise covering array with f_1 included and f_2 not included that will not pass the test suite for feature f_1.

4   Evaluation with Two Applications and Results

4.1   Application to ABB's "Safety Module"

About the ABB Safety Module. The ABB Safety Module is a physical component that is used in, among other things, cranes and assembly lines, to ensure safe reaction to events that should not occur, such as the motor running too fast, or that a requested stop is not handled as required. It includes various software configurations to adapt it to its particular use and safety requirements.

A simulated version of the ABB Safety Module was built—independently of the work in this paper—for experimenting with testing techniques. It is this version of the ABB Safety Module which testing is reported in this paper.

Basic Testing of Sample Products. Figure 2a shows the feature model of the Safety Module. There are in total 640 possible configurations. Three of these are set up in the lab for testing purposes during development. These are shown in Figure 2b and are, of course, valid configurations of the feature model of the ABB Safety Module, Figure 2a.

The products are tested thoroughly before they are delivered to a customer. Five test suites are named in the left part of Table 3a; the right side names the feature that the test suite tests.

We ran the relevant tests from Table 3a. The results from running the relevant test suite of each relevant product are shown in Table 3b. The table shows a test suite in each row and a product in each column. When the test suite tests a feature not present in the product, the entry is blank. When the test suite tests a feature in the product, the error count is shown. All test runs gave zero errors, meaning that they were successful for the three sample products. This is also what we expected since these three test products have been used during development of the simulation model to see that it functions correctly.

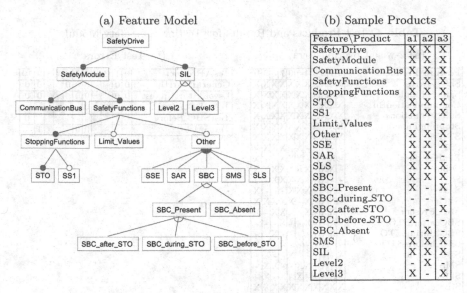

(a) Feature Model

(b) Sample Products

Feature\Product	a1	a2	a3
SafetyDrive	X	X	X
SafetyModule	X	X	X
CommunicationBus	X	X	X
SafetyFunctions	X	X	X
StoppingFunctions	X	X	X
STO	X	X	X
SS1	X	X	X
Limit_Values	-	-	-
Other	X	X	X
SSE	X	X	X
SAR	X	X	-
SLS	X	X	X
SBC	X	X	X
SBC_Present	X	-	X
SBC_during_STO	-	-	-
SBC_after_STO	-	-	X
SBC_before_STO	X	-	-
SBC_Absent	-	X	-
SMS	X	X	X
SIL	X	X	X
Level2	-	X	-
Level3	X	-	X

Fig. 2. ABB Safety Module Product Line

Table 3

(a) Feature-Test Mapping

Unit-Test Suite	Feature
GeneralStartUp	SafetyDrive
Level3StartUpTest	Level3
TestSBC_After	SBC_after_STO
TestSBC_Before	SBC_before_STO
TestSMS	SMS

(b) Test errors

Test\Product	a1	a2	a3
GeneralStartUp	0	0	0
Level3StartUpTest	0		0
TestSBC_After			0
TestSBC_Before	0		
TestSMS	0	0	0

Testing Interactions Systematically. The three sample products are three out of 640 possible products. Table 4a shows the 11 products that need to be tested to ensure that every pair of features is tested for interaction faults; that is, the 2-wise covering array of Figure 2a.

We built these products automatically and ran the relevant automatic test suite on them. Table 4b shows the result from running each relevant test suite on each product of Table 4a. If the features interact correctly, we expect that there would be no error.

As we can see, products 2, 3, 7 and 8 did not compile correctly. This proved to be because for certain configurations, the CVL variability model was built incorrectly, producing a faulty code that does not compile.

For product 9, the test suite for the SMS ("Safe Maximum Speed") feature failed. This is interesting, because it succeeded for product 4 and 5. We investigated the problem, and found that the SMS feature does not work if the break is removed from the ABB Safety Module. This is another example of an interaction

Table 4. Test Products and Results for Testing the Safety Module

(a) 2-wise Covering Array

Feature\Product	0	1	2	3	4	5	6	7	8	9	10
SafetyDrive	X	X	X	X	X	X	X	X	X	X	X
SafetyModule	X	X	X	X	X	X	X	X	X	X	X
CommunicationBus	X	X	X	X	X	X	X	X	X	X	X
SafetyFunctions	X	X	X	X	X	X	X	X	X	X	X
StoppingFunctions	X	X	X	X	X	X	X	X	X	X	X
STO	X	X	X	X	X	X	X	X	X	X	X
SS1	-	-	X	X	-	X	-	X	X	X	-
Limit_Values	-	X	-	X	-	X	X	X	-	-	X
Other	-	X	X	-	X	X	X	X	X	X	X
SSE	-	-	X	-	-	X	X	X	X	-	-
SAR	-	X	-	-	X	X	X	-	-	-	X
SBC	-	X	X	-	X	-	X	X	X	X	X
SBC_Present	-	X	X	-	X	-	-	X	X	-	X
SBC_after_STO	-	-	-	-	X	-	-	X	-	-	-
SBC_during_STO	-	X	-	-	-	-	-	X	-	-	-
SBC_before_STO	-	-	X	-	-	-	-	-	-	-	X
SBC_Absent	-	-	-	-	-	-	X	-	-	X	-
SMS	-	-	X	-	X	X	-	-	X	X	-
SLS	-	X	X	-	-	X	-	X	-	X	-
SIL	X	X	X	X	X	X	X	X	X	X	X
Level2	-	-	X	X	-	-	X	X	X	-	-
Level3	X	X	-	-	X	X	-	-	-	X	X

(b) Test Errors

Test\Product	0	1	2	3	4	5	6	7	8	9	10
GeneralStartUp	0	0	-	-	0	0	0	-	-	0	0
Level3StartUpTest	0	0			0	0				0	0
TestSBC_After					0			-			
TestSBC_Before			-								0
TestSMS			-		0	0				-	1

fault. It occurs when SMS is present, and the break is absent. The inclusion of *SBC_Absent* means that there is no break within in the implementation.

4.2 Implementation with CVL

The pseudo-algorithm for implementing the technique with the CVL [4] tool suite is shown as Algorithm 2. It is this implementation that was used to test the ABB Safety Module[5]. The algorithm assumes that the following is given to it: a CVL variability model object, VM; a coverage strength, t; a list of tests, $tests$; and that a mapping between the tests and the features, TFM.[6]

The algorithm proceeds by first generating a t-wise covering array and setting them up as resolution models in the CVL model, VM. The CVL model contains bindings to the executable model artifacts for the ABB Safety Module. Everything that is needed is reachable from the CVL model. It can thus be used to generate the executable product simulation models; the set of product models is placed in P. The algorithm then loops through each product p. For each product, it sees if the build succeeded. If it did not, that is noted in *resultTable*. If the build succeeded, the algorithm runs through each test from the test set provided. If the feature the test tests is present in the product, run the test and record the result in the proper entry in *resultTable*. The result table we got in the experiment with the ABB Safety Module is shown in Table 4b.

---

[5] The source code for this implementation including its dependencies is found on the paper's resource website: http://heim.ifi.uio.no/martifag/ictss2012/

[6] All these are available on the paper's resource website.

Algorithm 2. Pseudo Code of CVL-based version of Algorithm 1

1: $VM.GenerateCoveringArray(t)$
2: $P \leftarrow VM.GenerateProducts()$
3: **for** each product p in P **do**
4:    **if** p build failed **then**
5:       $resultTable.put("buildfailed", p, *)$
6:    **else**
7:       **for** each test $test$ in $tests$ **do**
8:          $f \leftarrow TFM.getFeatures(test)$
9:          **if** p has features f **then**
10:            $result \leftarrow p.runTest(test)$
11:            $resultTable.put(result, p, f)$
12:          **end if**
13:       **end for**
14:    **end if**
15: **end for**

4.3   Application to the Eclipse IDEs

The Eclipse IDE product line was introduced earlier in this paper: The feature model is shown in Figure 1, and a 2-wise covering array was shown in Table 1b.

The different features of the Eclipse IDE are developed by different teams, and each team has test suites for their feature. Thus, the mapping between the features and the test suites are easily available.

The Eclipse Platform comes with built-in facilities for installing new features. We can start from a new copy of the bare Eclipse Platform, which is an Eclipse IDE with just the basic features. When all features of a product have been installed, we can run the test suite associated with each feature.

We implemented Algorithm 1 for the Eclipse Platform plug-in system and created a feature mapping for 36 test suites. The result of this execution is shown in Table 5b. This experiment[7] took in total 10.8 GiB of disk space; it consisted of 40,744 tests and resulted in 417,293 test results that took over 23 hours to produce on our test machine.

In Table 5b, the first column contains the results from running the 36 test suites on the released version of the Eclipse IDE for Java EE developers. As expected, all tests pass, as would be expected since the Eclipse project did test this version with these tests before releasing it.

The next 13 columns show the result from running the tests of the products of the complete 2-wise covering array of the Eclipse IDE product line. The blank cells are cells where the feature was not included in the product. The cells with a '-' show that the feature was included, but there were no tests in the test setup for this feature. The cells with numbers show the number of errors produced by running the tests available for that feature.

---

[7] The experiment was performed on Eclipse Indigo 3.7.0. The computer on which we did the measurements had an Intel Q9300 CPU @2.53GHz, 8 GiB, 400MHz RAM and the disk ran at 7200 RPM.

Table 5. Tests and Results for Testing the Eclipse IDE Product Line, Figure 1, Using the 2-wise Covering Array of Table 1b

(a) Tests

Test Suite	Tests	Time(s)
EclipseIDE	0	0
RCP_Platform	6,132	1,466
CVS	19	747
EGit	0	0
EMF	0	0
GEF	0	0
JDT	33,135	6,568
Mylyn	0	0
WebTools	0	0
RSE	0	0
EclipseLink	0	0
PDE	1,458	5,948
Datatools	0	0
CDT	0	0
BIRT	0	0
GMF	0	0
PTP	0	0
Scout	0	0
Jubula	0	0
RAP	0	0
WindowBuilder	0	0
Maven	0	0
SVN	0	0
SVN15	0	0
SVN16	0	0
Total	40,744	14,729

(b) Results, Number of Errors

Feature\Prod.	JavaEE	1	2	3	4	5	6	7	8	9	10	11	12	13
EclipseIDE	-	-	-	-	-	-	-	-	-	-	-	-	-	-
RCP_Platform	0	17	90	94	0	0	90	0	91	87	7	0	0	10
CVS	0		0		0		0			0				
EGit		-			-		-	-					-	
EMF	-		-	-	-				-	-	-	-	-	
GEF	-			-	-			-	-	-				-
JDT	0		11	8	0	0		0	0		5	3		0
Mylyn	-		-					-		-				
WebTools	-			-	-				-			-	-	
RSE	-		-	-		-	-							
EclipseLink	-		-	-					-	-				
PDE	0		0		0	0		0		0			0	
Datatools	-		-		-	-				-		-	-	
CDT				-	-			-		-	-			
BIRT				-	-					-		-		
GMF	-			-	-				-	-				
PTP				-		-	-			-	-			
Scout		-		-			-			-				
Jubula			-	-			-			-		-		
RAP		-		-	-			-	-		-			
WindowBuilder														
Maven		-								-	-			
SVN		-			-		-	-	-	-			-	-
SVN15		-			-			-			-			-
SVN16								-	-		-		-	

Products 4–5, 7 and 11–12 pass all relevant tests. For both features CVS and PDE, all products pass all tests. For product 2–3 and 9–10, the JDT test suites produce 11, 8, 5 and 3 error respectively. For the RCP-platform test suites, there are various number of errors for products 1–3, 6, 8–10 and 13.

We executed the test several times to ensure that the results were not coincidental, and we did look at the execution log to make sure that the problems were not caused by the experimental set up such as file permissions, lacking disk space or lacking memory. We did not try to identify the concrete bugs behind the failing test cases, as this would require extensive domain knowledge that was not available to us during our research.[8]

4.4 Implementation with Eclipse Platform's Plug-in System

Algorithm 3 shows the algorithm of our testing technique for the Eclipse Platform plug-in system[9].

---

[8] We will report the failing test cases and the relevant configuration to the Eclipse project, along with the technique used to identify them.

[9] The source code for this implementation including its dependencies is available through the paper's resource website, along with the details of the test execution and detailed instructions and scripts to reproduce the experiment.

Algorithm 3. Pseudo Code of Eclipse-based version of Algorithm 1

```
 1:  CA ← FM.GenerateCoveringArray(t)
 2:  for each configuration c in CA do
 3:     p ← GetBasicEclipsePlatform()
 4:     for each feature f in c do
 5:        p.installFeature(f)
 6:     end for
 7:     for each feature f in c do
 8:        tests ← f.getAssociatedTests()
 9:        for each test test in tests do
10:           p.installTest(test)
11:           result ← p.runTest(test)
12:           table.put(result, c, f)
13:        end for
14:     end for
15:  end for
```

The algorithm assumes that the following is given: a feature model, FM, and a coverage strength, t.

In the experiment in the previous section we provided the feature model in Figure 1. The algorithm loops through each configuration in the covering array. In the experiment, it was the one given in Table 1b. For each configuration, a version of Eclipse is constructed: The basic Eclipse platform is distributed as a package. This package can be extracted into a new folder and is then ready to use. It contains the capabilities to allow each feature and test suite can be installed automatically using the following command: `<eclipse executable> -application org.eclipse.equinox.p2.director -repository <repository1,...> -installIU <feature name>` Similar commands allow tests to be executed.

A mapping file provides the links between the features and the test suites. This allows Algorithm 3 to select the relevant tests for each product and run them against the build of the Eclipse IDE. The results are put into its entry in the result table. The results from the algorithm are in a table like the one given in the experiment, shown in Table 5b.

5   Benefits and Limitations

Benefits

- **Usable:** The technique is a fully usable software product line testing technique: It scales, and free, open source algorithms and software exists for doing all the automatic parts of the technique.[10]
- **Agile:** The technique is agile in that once set up, a change in a part of the product line or to the feature model will not cause any additional manual

---

[10] Software and links available on the paper's resource website: http://heim.ifi.uio.no/martifag/ictss2012/

work. The product line tests can be rerun with one click throughout development. (Of course, if a new feature is added, a test suite for that feature should be developed.)

- **Continuous Integration**: The technique fits well into a continuous integration framework. At any point in time, the product line can be checked out from the source code repository, built and the testing technique run. For example, the Eclipse project uses Hudson [19] to check out, build and test the Eclipse IDE and its dependencies at regular intervals. Our technique can be set up to run on Hudson, and every night produce a result table with possible interaction faults in a few hours on suitable hardware.
- **Tests the feature model**: The technique tests the feature model in that errors might be found after a change of it. For example, that a mandatory relationship is missing causing a feature to fail.
- **Automatic**: The technique is fully automatic except making the test suites for each feature, a linear effort with respect to the number of features, and making the build-scripts of a custom product, a one-time effort.
- **Implemented**: The technique has been implemented and used for CVL-based product lines and for Eclipse-based product lines, as described in Section 4.
- **Run even if incomplete**: The technique can be run even if the product line test suites are not fully developed yet. It supports running a partial test suite, e.g. when only half of the test suites for the features are present, one still gets some level of verification. For example, if a new feature is added to the product line, a new test suite is not needed to be able to analyze the interactions between the other features and it using the other feature's test suites.
- **Parallel**: The technique is intrinsically parallel. Each product in the covering array can be tested by itself on a separate node. For example, executing the technique for the Eclipse IDE could have taken approximately 1/13th of the time if executed on 13 nodes, taking approximately in 2 hours instead of 23.

Limitations

- **Emergent features**: Emergent features are features that emerge from the combination of two or more features. Our technique does not test that an emergent feature works in relation to other features.
- **Manual Hardware Product Lines**: Product line engineering is also used for hardware systems. Combinatorial interaction testing is also a useful technique to use for these products lines [20]; however, the technique described in this paper is not fully automatic when the products must be set up manually.
- **Quality of the automated tests**: The quality of the results of the technique is dependent on the quality of the automated tests that are run for the features of the products.
- **Feature Interactions**: A problem within the field of feature interaction testing is how to best create tests as to identify interaction faults occur between two or more concrete features, *the feature interaction problem* [21].

Although an important problem, it is not what our technique is for. Our technique covers all simple interactions and gives insight into how they work together.

6 Conclusion

In this paper we presented a new technique for agile and automatic interaction testing for product lines. The technique allows developers of product lines to set up automatic testing as a part of their continuous integration framework to gain insight into potential interaction faults in their product line.

The technique was evaluated by presenting the results from two applications of it: one to a simulation model of the ABB safety module product line using the CVL tool suite, and one to the Eclipse IDE product lines using the Eclipse Platform plug-in system. The cases show how the technique can identify interaction faults in product lines of the size and complexity found in industry.

Acknowledgments. The work presented here has been developed within the VERDE project ITEA 2 - ip8020. VERDE is a project within the ITEA 2 - Eureka framework.

The authors would like to thank the anonymous reviewers for their helpful feedback.

References

1. Cohen, M.B., Dwyer, M.B., Shi, J.: Constructing interaction test suites for highly-configurable systems in the presence of constraints: A greedy approach. IEEE Transactions on Software Engineering 34, 633–650 (2008)
2. Johansen, M.F., Haugen, Ø., Fleurey, F.: Properties of Realistic Feature Models Make Combinatorial Testing of Product Lines Feasible. In: Whittle, J., Clark, T., Kühne, T. (eds.) MODELS 2011. LNCS, vol. 6981, pp. 638–652. Springer, Heidelberg (2011)
3. Johansen, M.F., Haugen, Ø., Fleurey, F.: An Algorithm for Generating t-wise Covering Arrays from Large Feature Models. In: Alves, V., Santos, A. (eds.) Proceedings of the 16th International Software Product Line Conference (SPLC 2012). ACM (2012)
4. Haugen, Ø., Møller-Pedersen, B., Oldevik, J., Olsen, G.K., Svendsen, A.: Adding standardized variability to domain specific languages. In: SPLC 2008: Proceedings of the 2008 12th International Software Product Line Conference, pp. 139–148. IEEE Computer Society, Washington, DC (2008)
5. Pohl, K., Böckle, G., van der Linden, F.J.: Software Product Line Engineering: Foundations, Principles and Techniques. Springer-Verlag New York, Inc., Secaucus (2005)
6. Rivieres, J., Beaton, W.: Eclipse Platform Technical Overview (2006)
7. Kang, K.C., Cohen, S.G., Hess, J.A., Novak, W.E., Peterson, A.S.: Feature-oriented domain analysis (foda) feasibility study. Technical report, Carnegie-Mellon University Software Engineering Institute (November 1990)

8. Czarnecki, K., Eisenecker, U.: Generative programming: methods, tools, and applications. ACM Press/Addison-Wesley Publishing Co., New York (2000)
9. Johansen, M.F., Haugen, Ø., Fleurey, F.: A Survey of Empirics of Strategies for Software Product Line Testing. In: O'Conner, L. (ed.) Proceedings of the 2011 IEEE Fourth International Conference on Software Testing, Verification and Validation Workshops, ICSTW 2011, pp. 266–269. IEEE Computer Society, Washington, DC (2011)
10. Ganesan, D., Lindvall, M., McComas, D., Bartholomew, M., Slegel, S., Medina, B., Krikhaar, R., Verhoef, C.: An analysis of unit tests of a flight software product line. Science of Computer Programming (2012)
11. Engström, E., Runeson, P.: Software product line testing - a systematic mapping study. Information and Software Technology 53(1), 2–13 (2011)
12. Reuys, A., Reis, S., Kamsties, E., Pohl, K.: The scented method for testing software product lines. In: Käkölä, T., Dueñas, J.C. (eds.) Software Product Lines, pp. 479–520. Springer, Heidelberg (2006)
13. Uzuncaova, E., Khurshid, S., Batory, D.: Incremental test generation for software product lines. IEEE Transactions on Software Engineering 36(3), 309–322 (2010)
14. Kim, C.H.P., Batory, D.S., Khurshid, S.: Reducing combinatorics in testing product lines. In: Proceedings of the Tenth International Conference on Aspect-oriented Software Development, AOSD 2011, pp. 57–68. ACM, New York (2011)
15. Binder, R.V.: Testing object-oriented systems: models, patterns, and tools. Addison-Wesley Longman Publishing Co., Inc., Boston (1999)
16. Kuhn, D.R., Wallace, D.R., Gallo, A.M.: Software fault interactions and implications for software testing. IEEE Transactions on Software Engineering 30(6), 418–421 (2004)
17. Garvin, B.J., Cohen, M.B.: Feature interaction faults revisited: An exploratory study. In: Proceedings of the 22nd International Symposium on Software Reliability Engineering (ISSRE 2011) (November 2011)
18. Steffens, M., Oster, S., Lochau, M., Fogdal, T.: Industrial evaluation of pairwise spl testing with moso-polite. In: Proceedings of the Sixth International Workshop on Variability Modelling of Software-intensive Systems, VaMoS 2012 (January 2012)
19. Moser, M., O'Brien, T.: The Hudson Book. Oracle Inc. (2011)
20. Johansen, M.F., Haugen, Ø., Fleurey, F., Eldegard, A.G., Syversen, T.: Generating Better Partial Covering Arrays by Modeling Weights on Sub-Product Lines. In: France, R.B., Kazmeier, J., Breu, R., Atkinson, C. (eds.) MODELS 2012. LNCS, vol. 7590, pp. 269–284. Springer, Heidelberg (2012)
21. Bowen, T., Dworack, F., Chow, C., Griffeth, N., Herman, G., Lin, Y.: The feature interaction problem in telecommunications systems. In: Seventh International Conference on Software Engineering for Telecommunication Switching Systems, SETSS 1989, pp. 59–62. IET (1989)

CaPTIF: Comprehensive Performance TestIng Framework

Daniel A. Mayer[1], Orie Steele[1], Susanne Wetzel[1], and Ulrike Meyer[2]

[1] Stevens Institute of Technology, Department of Computer Science, Hoboken, USA
[2] RWTH Aachen University, UMIC Research Center, Aachen, Germany

Abstract. In this paper we present the design and implementation of a framework for comprehensive performance evaluation of algorithms, modules, and libraries. Our framework allows for the definition of well-defined test inputs and the subsequent scheduling and execution of structured tests. In addition, the framework provides a web-based interface for user interaction and allows for the convenient browsing, plotting, and statistical analysis of test results. We furthermore report on our experience in using the new framework in the development of cryptographic protocols and algorithms—specifically in the context of secure multi-party computation.

1 Motivation

When designing practical algorithms, modules, and libraries, experimental performance evaluations are an essential part in determining their suitability for real-world applications. In particular, such performance tests can provide insights which cannot be determined through theoretical analysis alone.

The performance of algorithms in general depends on a variety of choices in the test setup. First of all, more complex algorithms or modules commonly use simpler algorithms as building blocks. When conducting performance tests, assessing the impact of choosing different building blocks providing the same functionality is naturally of great interest. In addition, an algorithm's performance behavior depends on the chosen input as well as many other parameters. When performed manually, varying the input and a larger number of other parameters is time consuming, error prone, and typically generates a large amount of data which needs to be managed and stored. In particular, storing the data such that it may be retrieved together with all the parameters used in a particular test often poses a major challenge in practice. Finally, comprehensive performance tests require an evaluation in a variety of testbeds including different computing platforms and suitable network topologies.

To address these challenges we have developed a test framework which enables structured performance tests of algorithms and modules called *CaPTIF* (*Comprehensive Performance TestIng Framework*). *CaPTIF* is a web-based system which enables its users to define, execute, and review performance tests of algorithms, modules, and libraries. The system keeps track of all parameters used, it schedules the test runs to automatically execute on available test systems,

B. Nielsen and C. Weise (Eds.): ICTSS 2012, LNCS 7641, pp. 55–70, 2012.

and it provides extensive storage and retrieval functionality for the test results. We have implemented *CaPTIF* and successfully applied it in the development of cryptographic algorithms—specifically in the context of secure multi-party computation [1,2]. In this paper, we motivate the design of *CaPTIF*, describe its implementation, and share our experience in using the framework.

Outline: We first review related techniques in Section 2. Section 3 discusses the required functionality of a suitable test framework. Section 4 describes our design decisions and Section 5 details the concrete tools we used to implement *CaPTIF*. Finally, Section 6 summarizes the lessons learned when developing and using *CaPTIF*.

2   Related Techniques

In the software development process, performance testing is commonly conducted to determine an application's performance as experienced by the user. In this context, the focus is generally not on a single application session but on the application in its entirety, i.e., one does not test a single, isolated request of a single user but rather the performance when many users interact with the application simultaneously. Software testers commonly use techniques such as load testing, stress testing, etc., to perform these kinds of tests [3]. There is a variety of commercial products and free open-source tools available for the task. For example, IBM's *Rational Performance Tester* [4] and HPs *LoadRunner* [5] both do scalability testing by generating a real work load on the application. Open-source tools such as Apache's *JMeter* [6] and *Grinder* [7] provide a similar functionality.

Motivated by the large cost for commercial performance testing tools, Chen et al. created *Yet Another Performance Testing Framework* [8]. It enables users to create custom test programs which define the business operations to be performed during the test. Chen's framework then executes these tasks concurrently. In [9], Zhang et al. present a cloud-based approach to performance testing of web services. Their system provides a frontend in which users can specify test cases which are then dispatched to Amazon EC2 [10] cloud instances for execution. Similar to all the previous tools, their system is testing the performance under concurrent user access to the system.

The tools described above are geared towards testing of production-stage applications or web-services. In contrast, in this paper the focus is on performance evaluations typically conducted at an earlier stage in the development process. Specifically, we focus on tests which are performed when individual algorithms or protocols are initially designed and implemented. This process typically involves the selection and performance assessment of appropriate building block for the newly designed algorithms or protocols. In addition, these tests are used to not only establish the feasibility of the new design but also to guide the fine-tuning of the implementation. Unlike production-ready testing, the testing in this stage is characterized by assessing and understanding the behavior of an isolated execution of a single protocol or algorithm. This test scenario gives rise to a set of

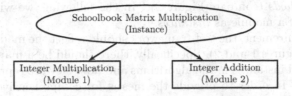

Fig. 1. *Matrix Multiplication* utilizes the modules *Integer Multiplication* and *Integer Addition.*

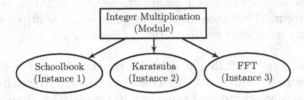

Fig. 2. Different Instances for the module *Integer Multiplication*

requirements which are not directly supported by the kind of tools mentioned above. In Section 3 we provide a detailed discussion of the requirements for a suitable test framework. To the best of our knowledge, to date there is no publicly available test framework which is focused on such comprehensive and fine-grained performance evaluation of individual protocols and algorithms. It is important to note, that we focus our discussion solely on performance evaluations and leave any kind of correctness tests such as unit tests as an independent problem.

3   Requirements for a Comprehensive Test Framework

In the following, we introduce the requirements for the design of a test framework for comprehensive performance evaluations of algorithms, modules, and libraries.

Below, we motivate that a suitable framework should reflect the modular design of the tested functionality and allow for the precise definition of test inputs. Since comprehensive testing necessitates a separation of the two, they need to be specified independently. In order to conduct a particular test, both can then seamlessly be combined. Furthermore, the framework should provide means for efficient retrieval and analysis of any test results. In the following, we will describe these requirements in greater detail.

Reflecting Modular Algorithm Design: Algorithms often have modular designs. For example, Figure 1 illustrates *Schoolbook Matrix Multiplication* which typically relies on the two *modules Integer Multiplication* and *Integer Addition.* In practice, each of these modules can be instantiated by different concrete algorithms which provide the same functionality, e.g., the module *Integer Multiplication* may be instantiated by the *Schoolbook Method, Karatsuba's Algorithm,* or

FFT-based methods (compare Figure 2).[1] In the following, we will refer to the instantiations of a module as *instances*.

As a first requirement, the test framework should reflect the modular structure (indicated in Figures 1 and 2). Specifically, there should be a mapping between the modules and instances in the algorithms and how they are represented in the test framework. In order to provide the means for comprehensively explaining the practical behavior of an instance, the test framework should then allow for flexible testing strategies based on this representation. In particular, a suitable framework should account for the relationships between modules and instances and allow for the testing of different compositions of an instance, i.e., testing for different assignments of instances to modules (e.g., which multiplication method is used to implement integer multiplication in Figure 2).

Test Input: The framework should allow for the definition of well-defined test inputs which are used when conducting a test. In particular, this definition should contain which parameters are used and which parameter(s) is (are) varied within which range. For example, for matrix multiplication, the input consists of two matrices and the parameters are the dimension of the matrices and the size of the individual matrix entries. Test inputs should be defined independently from the tested instance to allow for standardized tests in which test inputs can be re-used in different tests.

Test Execution: A test framework should allow for the execution of tests using a particular combination of an instance and a specific test input. In addition, the framework should record details on the execution environment and on the implementation of the tested instance together with the test. Moreover, in order to enable statistical analysis of the test results, the framework should support the repeated execution of any test.

Flexible Test Environment: The test framework should be flexible in how a particular test is conducted and it should allow for the assignment of a variable number of test systems to a test. For example, the test of a matrix multiplication algorithm can be carried out on a single test system while protocols[2] may need to be executed in a distributed fashion across multiple networked systems. In addition, since mobile devices increasingly gain importance as personal computing platforms, the framework should support different execution platforms such as servers, desktop machines, and mobile devices. For any test utilizing more than one single test system, the network setting has a great influence on for the overall performance and it should be tracked together with the test. For any test environment, a suitable framework should ensure exact performance

---

[1] Note that this is a simplified example which was chosen to illustrate the underlying concept. In practice, the modular structure of matrix multiplication is not as trivial as described.

[2] A protocol is an algorithm which involves multiple parties. The involved parties perform certain computations locally and exchange messages through some kind of communication channel such as a network.

measurements. In particular, this is challenging in cases where the time for a single execution of an instance is so small that a reliable measurement is not possible due to limitations of the operating system or the hardware.

Implementation Details: Since the performance of an instance may vary greatly depending on the programming language used for its implementation, a test framework should record the implementation details together with a test.

In addition, as the implementation of an instance changes over time and undergoes revisions, a suitable test framework should support efficient re-evaluation of the instance's performance during this process. In order to facilitate a correlation of the changes in the code base with the corresponding performance results, the test framework should allow for the tracking of the respective code revision (e.g., the commits in a version control system) of the instance under evaluation.

Analysis: Comprehensive performance evaluations tend to quickly result in large amounts of test results which need to be organized properly in order to be of any use. The test framework should therefore allow for a structured storing of all test results in combination with the test that produced the specific result. It should be possible to store all test results without prior post-processing in order to allow the user to perform any desired analysis on the raw test results at a later time.

After a test is completed, the test result should be available for review by the user. In particular, the framework should allow the user to efficiently select test results and to display, retrieve, or plot them. In addition, it should be possible to easily compare test results originating from different tests. To assist the user in the analysis of the test results, the framework should provide standard statistical functionality (e.g., computation of averages and error bars based on the standard deviation).

4   Design of the *CaPTIF* Framework

In this section, we introduce the design of *CaPTIF*, our implementation of a test framework which meets the requirements outlined in Section 3. For this, we will refine the description presented in Section 3 and introduce clear terms to define all of *CaPTIF*'s components. Figure 3 shows the main components of *CaPTIF* and illustrates their interdependencies. At its base, *CaPTIF* consists of four components: *Test Configuration, Test Case, Code Base and Revision,* and *Text Execution Environment.* It is important to note that all four of these components can be specified independently of each other. All four components are combined in the definition of a *Test Run.* Finally, the execution of a test run produces a *Test Result.*

To date, we have applied *CaPTIF* in the area of *secure multi-party computation* (SMPC) [1,2]. In SMPC, two or more parties wish to compute some function on their private inputs. At the conclusion of an SMPC protocol all parties have only learned the result they are entitled to and, in particular, they have learned

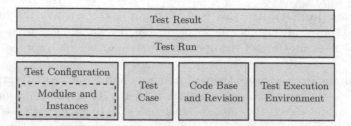

Fig. 3. Main components of *CaPTIF*

nothing about the other parties' inputs or intermediate results. It is important to note that SMPC operates without the involvement of a trusted third party (see [11] for an introduction to SMPC). Despite this original focus, the final design of *CaPTIF* is far more general and is thus applicable to much more general settings allowing for the effective performance testing of arbitrary algorithms, modules, and libraries. For the sake of clarity of presentation, in this paper we will describe the design of *CaPTIF* on the concrete example of cryptographic protocols in the context of SMPC.

4.1   Mapping Modules and Instances

In Section 3, we have motivated that instances commonly have modular structure. As a first step in our framework design, this section describes how this modular structure is reflected in *CaPTIF*.

Input Types. Since different modules require different types of input, *CaPTIF* allows for the definition of arbitrary *input types* such as integer or set of integers. For each input type it is possible to specify a set P of parameters $p_i \in P$ ($1 \leq i \leq |P|$) which fully define an input type. For example, a set of integers may be specified by the parameters *set cardinality* and *size of the individual integers in the set*.

Representing the Modular Structure. As discussed in Section 3, any *instance* may rely on different *modules* to implement its functionality and each module can be instantiated by any of the instances corresponding to that module (see Figures 1 and 2). It is important to note that any instance of a particular module may itself rely on other modules in performing its function.

To implement this requirement, *CaPTIF* allows for the specifying of any modules which are used. In this process it is required to indicate which input type (e.g., integer, set of integers) is required to test this module. For each module it is then possible to specify an arbitrary number of instances. In turn, for each instance one can assign all the modules which it relies on as well as any parameters (e.g., *cryptographic key size*) which are required for testing the instance. Overall this yields a complex tree structure which captures the relationships between all modules and instances as illustrated in Figure 4 on the example of a fictitious

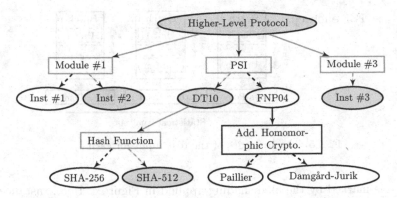

Fig. 4. Illustration of a higher-level protocol and the modules (rectangles) it utilizes. The instances (ovals) shaded in blue represent one possible configuration of the higher-level protocol.

cryptographic protocol. Here, a higher-level protocol instance is composed of three modules one of which is *Private Set Intersection* (PSI)[3] [12] (all others are left unspecified). The PSI module can be instantiated using any of the various PSI protocols proposed in the literature, e.g., *DT10* [13] or *FNP04* [12]. In turn, *DT10* uses a cryptographic hash functions and *FNP04* uses an additively homomorphic cryptosystem[4] ([15,16]) as module. Again, different instances for each of these modules exist.

Given this tree, it is possible to perform tests of any subtree rooted at an instance. For example, in Figure 4 one may test the entire high-level protocol, the implementation of DT10, the Paillier cryptosystem [15], or any other instance.

4.2 Test Configurations

Given a modular instance such as the one illustrated in Figure 4, one needs to clearly define its composition, i.e., the assignment of one instance to each module, that is to be evaluated (see Section 3). In the following we refer to this as *test configuration*.

In order to define a test configuration, *CaPTIF* first allows the choosing of the instance which is tested. Next, it is possible to assign one instance to each module within the subtree rooted at the tested instance. For this, *CaPTIF* enables the recursive selecting of one instance for each defined module until leaf nodes are reached. As an example, one possible test configuration for the Higher-Level

---

[3] PSI is a prominent SMPC protocol which has applications in a variety of contexts. In PSI, two parties each hold a private input set and at the conclusion of the protocol one party learns which set elements both have in common and the other party learns nothing.

[4] Informally, an additively homomorphic cryptosystem allows for the computation of the sum of two values solely by performing an operation on their respective ciphertexts (without knowledge of the secret key). See, e.g., [14] for an introduction.

For each c_j:

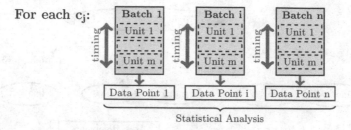

Fig. 5. The structure of the test input for each c_j

Protocol is marked by the blue shading applied in Figure 4. Here, Instance #2 is selected for Module #1, the DT10 PSI using the SHA-512 hash function for PSI, and Instance #3 for Module #3. To reiterate (see Section 4.1), *CaPTIF* does not require to start the test configuration with the root, i.e., Higher-Level Protocol in Figure 4. Instead one can test any subtree, e.g., in order to test DT10 PSI, one would start at the corresponding node and one would only specify the hash function used.

4.3 Test Cases

As established in Section 3, it is crucial to precisely define the used test input. *CaPTIF* implements this by means of a so-called *test case*[5] which is a concise descriptions of how to generate a specific test input.

To specify a test case, *CaPTIF* first requires the selection of the input type (e.g., integer, set of integers). Note that a test case can later only be used in conjunction with a test configuration which requires a test case of the same input type (see Sections 4.1 and 4.2). As motivated in Section 4.1, the input type defines the set P of all parameters $p_i \in P$ which need to be specified in order to fully define a test case of the given input type. For all parameters p_i it is possible to either specify the range (and step size) in which they are varied or set a constant value which is used for the entire test case. As an example, consider an input of type set of integers with p_1 being the size of the individual set elements and p_2 being the set cardinality. One can then choose to vary p_1 from 32 bits to 64 bits in steps of 32 bits and vary p_2 from 10 to 30 in steps of 10.

A second component of the test case is to specify so called *test units* and *test batches*—which are illustrated in Figure 5. A test unit represents a part of the test input which is used for a single execution of the tested instance. In cases where a single execution cannot be measured reliably (because the execution time is below the resolution of the timing function of the operating system), m test units are grouped together into a test batch. The execution for the tested instance is then measured and stored for the entire batch, i.e., for all m executions

---

[5] This is not to be confused with the notion of a test case used in software correctness testing [17].

in total, and thus the test result contains one data point for each batch.[6] When defining a test case, *CaPTIF* allows for the specification of the number m of test units within each batch. In addition, to allow for the computation of statistics, one can specify the desired number of batches n (see Figure 5).

Once a test case is defined in the test framework, the user can choose to automatically generate and store the corresponding test input by means of test generation scripts which are implemented as part of *CaPTIF* (see Section 5.2). The test input encompasses all the input data that is generated from a given test case.[7] For this, *CaPTIF* first converts the specified parameter ranges into sets V_{p_i} which contain all values in the given range for parameter $p_i \in P$. Subsequently, the Cartesian product $C = \prod_{p_i \in P} V_{p_i}$ of all values is computed. As a result, each tuple $c_j \in C$ $(1 \le j \le |C|)$ is a unique combination of parameter values. For example, let $P = \{p_1, p_2\}$ where p_1 and p_2 are varied as above. Then $V_{p_1} = \{32, 64\}$, $V_{p_2} = \{10, 20, 30\}$, and $C = V_{p_1} \times V_{p_2} = \{(32,10), (64,10), (32,20), (64,20), (32,30), (64,30)\}$ with $c_3 = (32,20)$. For each c_j, n batches containing m units of test input each are generated. Consequently, the overall test input consists of $|C| \cdot m \cdot n$ test units and the corresponding test result will contain a total of $n \cdot |C|$ data points. In the example above, n batches with m test units each would be generated for each pair $c_j \in \{(32,10), (64,10), (32,20), (64,20), (32,30), (64,30)\}$. Once the test input is generated, it is stored and used in all test runs involving this test case.[8]

4.4 Code Bases and Test Environments

Code Bases: CaPTIF allows for the definition of different code bases which capture different implementations or programming languages, e.g., *C++* or *Java*. For each test run it is possible to specify which code base and which code revision is used.

Test Environments: CaPTIF maintains information on the available test systems and their locations. To date, *CaPTIF*'s design refrains from defining the concrete network topology or latency between each pair of locations since this information grows quadratically in the number of locations and is difficult to maintain. Instead, keeping only the information on the location itself allows for a very good estimate of the respective topology. Moreover, one could obtain exact latency information by performing external tests on the connection between these two location. While this approach only provides for a rough estimate on the topology and latencies, we believe it is sufficient for modeling most practical scenarios.

---

[6] It is important to note that the total timing for all m execution is stored as part of the test result. In particular, we do not average over the m units i.e., we do not divide the measured timing by m.

[7] It is important to note that the test input for a multi-party protocol includes individual, yet correlated inputs for each party.

[8] It is important to note that any test input that is not automatically generated by *CaPTIF* has to be generated in a similar manner elsewhere.

4.5 Test Runs

To compose a test run, it is necessary to select the desired test configuration and the test case. In addition, an appropriate number of test systems is assigned to the test run and the underlying code base and revision must be specified.

Instead of only allowing for the collection of one time measurement per test batch, *CaPTIF* provides for flexibility by allowing for the collection of multiple *split times*. For example, when testing a cryptosystem, one may time encryption and decryption individually for each test batch.

5 Implementation

CaPTIF stores the details on all modules and instances, test configurations, test cases, test inputs, and test results for all test runs in a relational database back-end (see Section 5.1). In order to interact with the database, *CaPTIF* provides a web-based front-end. In this section, we present our choices for appropriate software frameworks, libraries, tools and the concrete implementation details. One crucial step was the selection of the development framework for the implementation of *CaPTIF*. Since *CaPTIF*'s data is not only accessed by the user but also by programs and scripts, e.g., during the generation of test inputs (see Section 5.2), the web interface should be separated logically from the data and application logic. Thus, the *Model-Viewer-Controller* (MVC) pattern [18] which supports all of these requirements was chosen as a basis for implementing *CaPTIF*. The decision for this design pattern was further supported by the fact that MVC frameworks became state-of-the-art in web application development in recent years.

Pyramid [19] is a Python MVC web framework which achieves modularity through extensive usage of the *Web Server Gateway Interface* (WSGI). This modularity and the resulting support for a wide range of different components, e.g., database abstraction and templating make this framework very flexible, light-weight, and thus well-suited for implementing *CaPTIF*. The current version of *CaPTIF* is built using pyramid in conjunction with *SQLAlchemy* [20] as *Object-Relational-Mapper* and *Mako* [21] as template engine for the web interface.

5.1 Backend Database

As stated above, *CaPTIF*'s entire data is stored in a relational database. We use the performance-oriented *MySQL* database using the *innoDB* storage engine which enforces foreign key relationships and ensures data integrity, which is crucial for maintaining all the complex relationships between *CaPTIF*'s components [22]. The entity relationship diagram for the database was carefully designed to support the efficient storage and retrieval of all required data together with its relationships and dependencies.

5.2   Test Input Generation

When defining a test case in *CaPTIF*, one can choose to automatically generate the test input based on the description given in the test case. To facilitate test input generation, an automated Python script regularly checks whether there is any test case for which no test input was generated yet. If this is the case, the script retrieves all information concerning this test case from the database. Based on the input type specified for the test case, the actual test input generation is handed off to an appropriate generator script. *CaPTIF*'s functionality can be extended by adding new generator scripts as required for any new input types that may be defined in the future. Since *CaPTIF* handles the entire interaction with the database, the input generators only need to implement the actual generation of the input.[9] The resulting test input is then stored in the backend database. For efficiency reasons, the entire test input per batch (see Figure 5) is stored as a database blob. This eliminates a great number of database joins which otherwise would cause a significant overhead when the test input is accessed. Furthermore, it makes the database schema independent of the underlying format of the test input. In particular, we store the test input in *JavaScript Object Notation* (JSON) [23] and apply a hexadecimal encoding to any integer value. In addition, since the *CaPTIF* API described in Section 5.3 utilizes JSON to encode requests and responses, storing test inputs in JSON format eliminates costly data conversion during input retrieval. Once the generation is completed, the input is marked as being available and a test run using this test input may start executing.

5.3   Test Execution

In order to facilitate the execution of test runs on different test systems, *CaPTIF* provides an *Application Programming Interface* (API). The use of this API is two-fold. First, it allows the retrieval of a test run from the database. Second, once the test run is completed, the raw test result can be pushed back into the framework where it is associated with the corresponding test run. This separation enables the execution of test runs on devices which can not communicate directly with *CaPTIF* . The latter is of particular importance when testing on mobile devices. Figure 6 outlines the workflow for the execution of a test run. *CaPTIF*'s API is implemented using HTTPS requests in JSON [23] and currently three API calls are supported:

getTestRun: Check whether a test run was scheduled to run on a particular test system.

getTestInput: Retrieve the test input associated with a specific test run and test system.

submitTestResult: Submit the test result from an individual test system to *CaPTIF*.

---

[9] Test generators may internally use a source of randomness to generate randomized input for the tests. Currently, the seed for any random number generator is not stored with the test input.

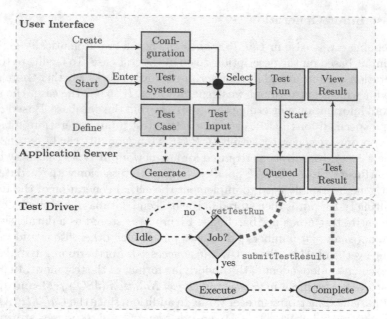

Fig. 6. Workflow when creating and executing a test run using *CaPTIF*. The figure shows the steps taken in the web interface (top), by the application server (middle), and by the test driver executing on the test systems (bottom). Dotted lines indicate automated events while solid lines are user actions.

Each data point in the test result includes all split times obtained for a test batch. Currently, each split time consists of the *user time, system time, real time,* and *maximum memory used.* However, additional metrics such as, e.g., throughput could easily be added. Below we show *CaPTIF*'s flexibility in designing the execution setting on the example of a test execution on a Linux host and on a mobile device.

Execution on a Linux Host: To execute a test, each test system periodically executes a Python test driver which calls `getTestRun` to check whether a new test run has been scheduled. If a new test run is found, it downloads the associated test input by calling `getTestInput` and executes an appropriate test program. Note that it is not possible to use a generic test program for all types of modules. This is due to the fact that the test requirements vary based on the module that is being tested. Therefore, the test driver calls a different test program[10] which can be specified in the web interface when creating the test run.

After calling the test program, the driver passes the test input via `STDIN` and waits for the test program to terminate. After completion of the test run, the driver collects the test result from `STDOUT` and submits them to *CaPTIF*

---

[10] The test program is not part of *CaPTIF* but it is created and compiled by the user ahead of time to facilitate the testing of a specific algorithm or protocol.

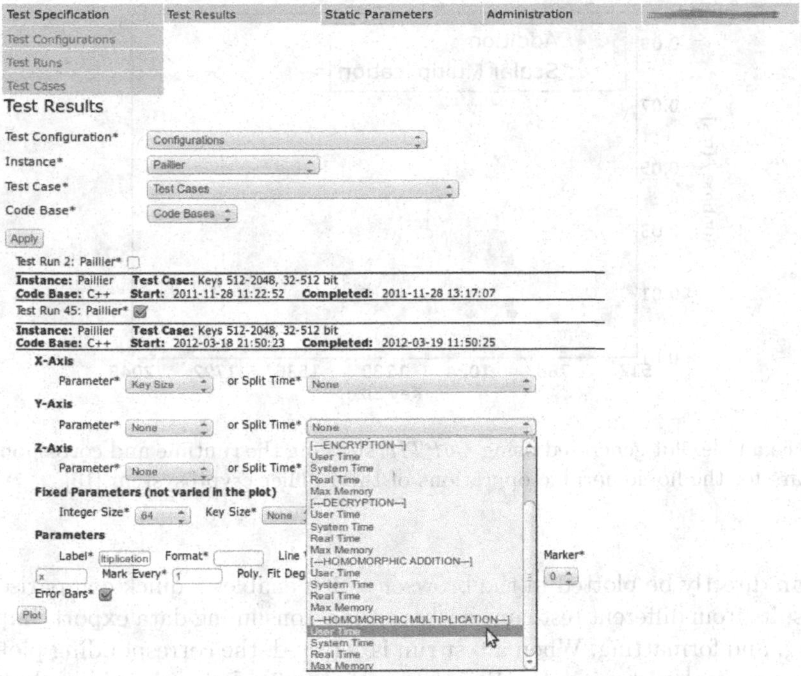

Fig. 7. Screenshot of our web interface illustrating how the plot in Figure 8 was created. The result from testing the Paillier cryptosystem [15] were selected for plotting. The plot assigns the *key size* to the x-axis, the *user time* for the homomorphic scalar multiplication to the y-axis, and fixes the integer size to 64 bits.

via `submitTestResults`. This submission also marks the test run as completed within the test database and triggers an email to the user who created the test run notifying her of the completed test.

Execution on a Mobile Device: If the test environment allows it, a mobile device may use a procedure similar to the one used for Linux hosts. However, in settings where this is not possible, a test driver can be executed on a desktop computer to retrieve the test input and test configuration for the device and store them in a temporary file. This file can then be transferred to the mobile device where the user manually executes the test program using the test input copied over from the desktop computer. Similarly, the test result is written to a file on the device, copied back to the desktop computer, and submitted to *CaPTIF*.

5.4   Result Browser

The web interface provides a result browser which can be used to review the test results. The browser displays a list of test runs which can be filtered by test configuration, test instance, test case, etc. *CaPTIF* allows that any result

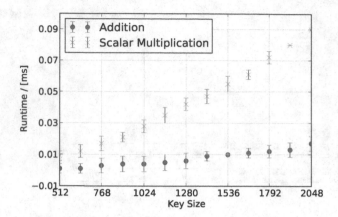

Fig. 8. Example plot generated using *CaPTIF* showing the runtime and corresponding error bars for the homomorphic operations of the Paillier cryptosystem [15]

data can directly be plotted in the browser which enables a quick comparison of test results from different test runs without time-consuming data export/import, plotting, and formatting. When a test run is selected, the corresponding plotting options are displayed using JavaScript (see Figure 7). For each axis of the plot, the user is presented with various choices for values to be plotted. One can either choose one of the parameters defined in the test case or any of the collected metrics (such as *user time*) for any of the recorded split times. If more than one parameter was varied, the remaining free parameters have to be fixed in order for the plot to be meaningful. For example, if an encryption function was tested by varying both the key size and the size of the plaintext, plotting the *user time* as a function of the plaintext size requires the specification of a fixed key size. Furthermore, if the test involved more than one party or host, the user can choose the party for which the test result is to be plotted.

In addition, one can specify a label to be displayed in the legend, the format of the plot (color, width, markers, etc.), and whether error bars should be plotted. One can also choose to fit the test result by a polynomial function. Once all details are specified, the plot is added to the list of current plots. Our implementation in *CaPTIF* leverages the Python *matplotlib* [24] to generate publication quality plots. Multiple test results can be selected for plotting and viewing in the browser. The user has the option to download the resulting figure as *Portable Network Graphics* PNG image or as *Portable Document Format* PDF. All plots created by *CaPTIF* show an average taken over all batches and units. In addition, one may download the raw timings in CSV format which enables more complex analysis using any software of choice. In addition, the web interface provides various options to customize the plot, such as the range of the axes, axes labels, figure dimensions, and a scaling factor which is useful for unit conversions (e.g., milliseconds to seconds). Figure 8 shows an example of a plot generated using *CaPTIF*.

6   Lessons Learned and Future Work

We have successfully used *CaPTIF* to conduct extensive performance evaluations of various cryptographic algorithms (e.g., cryptosystems and other cryptographic primitives), and complex multi-party protocols. These tests involved dedicated servers connected via Ethernet as well as mobile devices connected via Bluetooth and Wi-Fi. While our experience is by and large qualitative in nature and is mostly related to cryptographic settings, we believe that the lessons learned are directly transferable to the testing of general algorithms and protocols.

Before using *CaPTIF*, organizing all the parameters and details of a test run and combining them with the corresponding test results proved challenging. Our experience with *CaPTIF* shows that storing all information in a structured fashion ensures that no information is lost and that it is easily accessible and searchable at any given time. In addition, having all test results stored homogeneously in one location enables fast comparison and plotting. This centralized data storage is particularly useful to us since we are working in a team with members working from different locations.

In addition, the ability of conveniently re-using a test case to evaluate another instance or the same instance using different parameters significantly simplified testing. In particular, the obtained results can directly be compared in a meaningful manner. As part of future work we plan to extend *CaPTIF* to store additional details on test runs such as the versions of any libraries used as well as details on compiler flags, etc.

Finally, test runs can efficiently be scheduled within *CaPTIF* and they are then executed without requiring user interaction. As a result, it is no longer necessary to manually log into each test system in order to start a test run. Moreover, once a test run is completed, the next one is automatically executed which increases the utilization of the test systems and reduces turn-around time. It would be helpful if *CaPTIF* would allow for the storing of more details on the underlying network topology—one requirement discussed in Section 3 but not yet implemented in *CaPTIF*. In addition, it might be desirable to further automate the scheduling process such that test systems are assigned automatically to queued test runs. This would not only reduce the effort required to create a new test run, but it would also ensure that a test run does not wait for a specific test system while others are available. Moreover, this would allow for the execution of a single test run to be split across multiple identical test systems. Furthermore, the test driver could be extended to support the automated fetching of the required code from a repository and the building of the tested binary.

Acknowledgements. The authors would like to thank Georg Neugebauer for useful discussions during the design phase of *CaPTIF*. In part, this work was supported by NSF Award CCF 1018616, the DFG, and by the UMIC Research Center, RWTH Aachen University.

References

1. Yao, A.: Protocols for Secure Computations. In: Foundations of Computer Science, vol. 23, pp. 160–164. IEEE (1982)
2. Goldreich, O.: Foundations of Cryptography. Basic Applications, vol. 2. Cambridge University Press (2009)
3. Molyneaux, I.: The Art of Application Performance Testing, vol. 1. O'Reilly Media (2009)
4. IBM: Rational Performance Tester, http://www-01.ibm.com/software/awdtools/tester/performance/
5. Hewlett Packard: HP LoadRunner, http://www8.hp.com/us/en/software/software-product.html?compURI=tcm:245%-935779
6. Apache Software Foundation: Apache JMeter, http://jmeter.apache.org/
7. Aston, P.: The Grinder, a Java Load Testing Framework, http://grinder.sourceforge.net/
8. Chen, S., Moreland, D., Nepal, S., Zic, J.: Yet Another Performance Testing Framework. In: Australian Conference on Software Engineering (ASWEC), pp. 170–179 (2008)
9. Zhang, L., Chen, Y., Tang, F., Ao, X.: Design and Implementation of Cloud-based Performance Testing System for Web Services. In: Conference on Communications and Networking in China (CHINACOM), pp. 875–880 (2011)
10. Amazon Web Services LLC: Amazon Elastic Compute Cloud (Amazon EC2) (2012), http://aws.amazon.com/ec2/
11. Cramer, R., Damgård, I., Nielsen, J.: Multiparty Computation, an Introduction (2009)
12. Freedman, M., Nissim, K., Pinkas, B.: Efficient Private Matching and Set Intersection. In: Cachin, C., Camenisch, J.L. (eds.) EUROCRYPT 2004. LNCS, vol. 3027, pp. 1–19. Springer, Heidelberg (2004)
13. De Cristofaro, E., Tsudik, G.: Practical Private Set Intersection Protocols with Linear Complexity. In: Sion, R. (ed.) FC 2010. LNCS, vol. 6052, pp. 143–159. Springer, Heidelberg (2010)
14. Micciancio, D.: A First Glimpse of Cryptography's Holy Grail. Commun. ACM 53(3), 96–96 (2010)
15. Paillier, P.: Public-Key Cryptosystems Based on Composite Degree Residuosity Classes. In: Stern, J. (ed.) EUROCRYPT 1999. LNCS, vol. 1592, pp. 223–238. Springer, Heidelberg (1999)
16. Damgard, I., Jurik, M.: A Generalisation, a Simplification and Some Applications of Paillier's Probabilistic Public-Key System. In: Kim, K.-C. (ed.) PKC 2001. LNCS, vol. 1992, pp. 119–136. Springer, Heidelberg (2001)
17. IEEE: Standard for System and Software Verification and Validation (2012)
18. Reenskaug, T.: Model-Viewer-Controller. Technical report, XEROX PARC (1978)
19. The Pylons Project: Pyramid (2012), http://www.pylonsproject.org/
20. SQLAlchemy Authors and Contributors: SQLAlchemy, http://www.sqlalchemy.org/
21. Mako Authors and Contributors: Mako Templates for Python, http://www.makotemplates.org/
22. MySQL AB: MySQL - The World's Most Popular Open Source Database (2011), http://www.mysql.com/
23. Crockford, D.: The application/json Media Type for JavaScript Object Notation (JSON). RFC 4627 (Informational) (July 2006)
24. Hunter, J.: Matplotlib (2011), http://matplotlib.sourceforge.net/

Towards a TTCN-3 Test System for Runtime Testing of Adaptable and Distributed Systems

Mariam Lahami, Fairouz Fakhfakh, Moez Krichen, and Mohamed Jmaiel

Research Unit of Development and Control of Distributed Applications
National School of Engineering of Sfax, University of Sfax
Sokra Road km 4, PB 1173 Sfax, Tunisia
{mariam.lahami,fairouz.fakhfakh,moez.krichen}@redcad.org,
mohamed.jmaiel@enis.rnu.tn
http://www.redcad.org

Abstract. Today, adaptable and distributed component based systems need to be checked and validated in order to ensure their correctness and trustworthiness when dynamic changes occur. Traditional testing techniques can not be used since they are applied during the development phase. Therefore, runtime testing is emerging as a novel solution for the validation of highly dynamic systems at runtime. In this paper, we illustrate how a platform independent test system based on the TTCN-3 standard can be used to execute runtime tests. The proposed test system is called TT4RT: TTCN-3 test system for Runtime Testing. A case study in the telemedicine field is used as an illustration to show the relevance of the proposed test system.

1 Introduction

Nowadays, a relevant issue in the software engineering research area consists in delivering software systems able to change their configuration dynamically in order to achieve new requirements and avoid failures without service interrupting. Therefore, they evolve continuously by integrating new components, deleting faulty or unneeded ones and substituting old components by new versions at runtime. Dealing with such reconfiguration actions, the possibility of unexpected errors (components failure, connections going down, etc.) during the reconfiguration process is unavoidable.

Accordingly, a validation technique, such as testing, has to be applied in order to detect as soon as possible such inconsistencies and to check functional and non-functional requirements after each dynamic reconfiguration. Nevertheless, traditional testing techniques cannot be done for these highly evolvable systems since they are applied during the development phase.

For this reason, a recent branch of work has demonstrated the interest of using the *Runtime Testing* as a new solution for the validation of the above systems [1–8]. They have focused on building specific test infrastructures, for instance based on the JUnit Framework. None of them have used a generic test standard like TTCN-3 for the specification or the execution of runtime tests.

B. Nielsen and C. Weise (Eds.): ICTSS 2012, LNCS 7641, pp. 71–86, 2012.

Furthermore, they are using at most one technique to isolate runtime tests in the aim of reducing the interference between business and test data. To the best of our knowledge, only one approach presented in [9] uses TTCN-3 standard for online validation and testing of internet services. However, this work did not deal with test isolation issues when testing is applied in the production phase.

This paper makes a contribution in these directions by proposing a TTCN-3 test system for Runtime Testing (TT4RT). The key idea is to extend the reference architecture of the standardized TTCN-3 test system by a new module supporting different test isolation techniques. The latter is a fundamental issue that has to be tackled while executing runtime tests either components under test are testable or not testable. As illustrative example, we describe a case study in telemedicine area called Teleservices and Remote Medical Care System (TRMCS).

The remaining of this paper is structured as follows. Section 2 introduces the runtime testing approach and its challenges that we are facing.The TTCN-3 standard and its key elements are introduced in Section 3. The proposed approach is illustrated in section 4. Section 5 introduces the case study. Some scenarios are illustrated in Section 6. A brief description of related work is addressed in section 7. Finally, section 8 concludes the paper and draws some future work.

2 Runtime Testing of Dynamic and Distributed Component Based Systems

Runtime testing is a novel solution for validating highly dynamic systems. It is defined in [10] as any testing method that has to be carried out in the final execution environment of a system while it is performing its normal work. It can be performed first at deployment-time and second at service-time. The deployment-time testing serves to validate and verify the assembled system in its runtime environment while it is deployed for the first time. For systems whose architecture remains constant after initial installation, there is obviously no need to retest the system when it has been placed in-service. On the contrary, if the execution environment or the system behavior and architecture have changed, service-time testing will be a necessity to verify and validate the new system in the new situation [10].

As previously mentioned in the definition of runtime testing, any test method can be applied at runtime such unit testing, integration testing, conformance testing, etc. In our work, we support unit testing as well as integration testing. On the first hand, unit testing is used to validate that the component behavior still conforms to its specification while it is running in isolation in the execution environment. On the other hand, integration testing is used at runtime to validate that the affected component compositions by the reconfiguration action still behave as intended. In order to minimize the number of testers to be deployed and the number of test cases to be re-executed, we apply unit and integration tests only on the affected parts of the system under test by a reconfiguration action. Consequently, the testing effort, cost and time will be reduced [11].

However, other challenges still persist such as test processes interference with the business processes of the running system due to their parallel execution. The best way to resolve such problem is the application of test isolation mechanisms widely discussed in [2, 4] (such as cloning components, adding a test interface, tagging test data, blocking components during test, etc). This challenging issue is resolved in our approach by supporting the well known test isolation mechanisms in the literature. It will be discussed in depth in following sections.

3 TTCN-3 Overview

TTCN-3 (Testing and Test Control Notation Language Version 3) is a test specification language used to define test procedures for reactive black-box testing of distributed systems [12]. This test standard has been widely used in the protocol testing field and is newly addressing other kinds of applications such as service-oriented or CORBA-based systems. It is also suitable for various types of tests such as conformance, robustness, regression and functional testing.

TTCN-3 allows the specification of dynamic and concurrent test systems. In fact, it offers a test configuration system made of two kinds of test components: Main Test Component (MTC) and Parallel Test Component (PTC). For each test case, an MTC is created. PTCs can be created dynamically at any time during the execution of test case. Thus, test system can use any number of test components to realize test procedures in parallel. Communications between the test system and the SUT are established through ports.

The structure of TTCN-3 test system is depicted in Figure 1. It is made up of a set of interacting entities where each one corresponds to a specific functionality involved in the test system implementation. These entities interact together through two major interfaces: the TTCN-3 Control Interface (TCI) [13] and the TTCN-3 Runtime Interface (TRI) [14]. They are briefly described [15] as follows:

- The Test Management (TM) Entity manages the test execution.
- The Test Logging (TL) Entity is responsible for maintaining the test logs.
- The TTCN-3 Executable (TE) Entity executes the compiled TTCN-3 code.
- The Coding/Decoding (CD) Entity encodes and decodes test data types and values.
- The Component Handling (CH) Entity handles the communication between test components.
- The SUT Adapter (SA) Entity implements communication between SUT and test system.
- The Platform Adapter (PA) Entity implements timers and external functions.

TTCN-3 is used in our context to define abstract test suites following the TTCN-3 notation. In this case, test suites are specified at an abstract layer, Abstract Test Suites (ATS). This feature helps to separate test design from test implementation and makes the ATS language platform independent. Furthermore, it increases the reusability of the elaborated test cases. By doing this, we can address complexity of testing evolvable systems which are also heterogeneous in

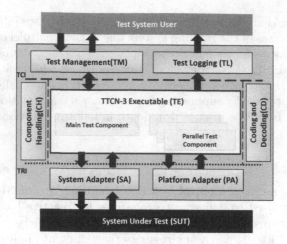

Fig. 1. TTCN-3 reference architecture

structure and technologies. Hence, different network and platforms technologies can communicate easily with the TTCN-3 test system through the adaptation layer [16]. The latter comprises three parts of the reference architecture that are Coding-Decoding entity, Test Adapter entity and Platform Adapter entity. These entities provide means to adapt the communication and the time handling between the SUT and test system in a loose coupling manner.

Due to all these features: a standardized, abstract and platform independent test-language and offering a flexible adaptation layer with the aim of facilitating interaction with the SUT, TTCN-3 was adopted in our work and also enhanced to support runtime testing.

4   The Proposed Approach: TT4RT

Our main objective is to design and build a test system that handles complexity of testing evolvable and heterogenous (both in structure and technologies) systems. Therefore, we have enhanced the TTCN-3 test system by adding two layers as depicted in Figure 2: a *Test Management Layer* and a *Test Isolation Layer*. The main purposes of these layers are described in the following:

Test Management Layer. It intends to control the execution of runtime tests. It includes a GUI component called *TTmanGUI*. The latter is responsible mainly for starting and stopping test cases. The TTmanGUI interacts with the TM entity offered by the classical TTCN-3 test system in order to achieve the test execution management and also with test isolation layer in order to prepare the test environment.

We have to mention that this layer has as input an XML file which contains the components under test, the test components to deploy and their deployment hosts as well as the test cases to execute. This file is called *Resource Aware Test*

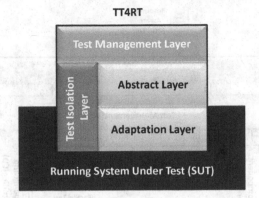

Fig. 2. Supported layers of TT4RT

Plan since the assignment of the test components to execution nodes must fit some resource constraints[1]. The structure of this file will be introduced later.

Test Isolation Layer. It aims to reduce the interference risk between test data and business data when testing is performed at runtime. It includes a component which is able to choose the most adequate test isolation technique for each component under test. This choice is suggested by using a policy called *Test Isolation Policy*. For each test request, the proposed policy is executed in order to generate the test isolation technique to apply. Our test system supports four test isolation techniques: duplication, blocking, tagging and built-in tests.

For reasons of space, these techniques are briefly introduced through some examples. For instance, if a component is not testable and it is under some timing constraints then it will be automatically duplicated. In this case, the test processes are executed in the duplicate with the aim of not disturbing the execution of the original component. Unless the component is under some timing constraints, it can be blocked until the test processes are achieved. Also, some components can be provided with some capabilities such as testability through a test interface or test awareness through a flag which lets the component under test differentiate between the test data and business data. The proposed policy treats all these conditions and produces the best solution when a test request is triggered.

Abstract Layer. As we have explained above, this layer is offered by the classical TTCN-3 test system in order to build abstract test suites. This feature makes runtime tests independent of the test execution environment and enhances their reusability and extensibility. All the specified test cases are compiled and stored in a repository in order to make them executable.

Adaptation Layer. It includes the implemented Coding/Decoding and System Adapter entities which facilitate the communication between TT4RT and the SUT in production phase.

---

[1] This assignment problem is not considered in this current work.

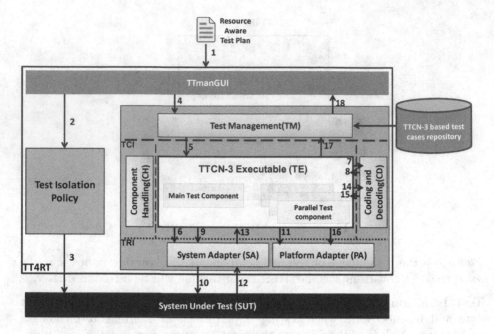

Fig. 3. The proposed workflow of the TT4RT system

In order to detail the internal interactions in TT4RT system, a workflow illustrated by the Figure 3 is given:

- When a reconfiguration action is triggered, the test plan that describes the affected parts of the SUT by this dynamic change and the test configuration used to validate it, is generated. This plan is considered as an input to the TT4RT system (Step **1**).
- Test isolation policy is called for each component under test in order to choose the best test isolation technique (Step **2**).
- The appropriate test isolation technique is then used to prepare the test environment (Step **3**).
- After preparing the test environment, the test system user initiates the test execution through the TTmanGUI and by calling the adequate method in the TM entity *TciStartTestCase* (Steps **4-5**).
- Once the test process is started, the TE entity creates the involved test components and informs the SA entity that the test case has been started with the aim of allowing the SA entity to prepare its communication facilities. This is done through the call of *triExecuteTestcase* method (Step **6**).
- Next, TE invokes the CD entity in order to encode the test data from a structured TTCN-3 value into a form that will be accepted by the SUT. This is done through the call of *encode* method (Step **7**).
- The encoded test data is passed back to the TE entity as a binary string and forwarded to the SUT via the SA entity with the *triSend* method (Steps **8-9-10**).

- After the test data is sent, a timer can be started. To achieve this, the TE invokes the *triStartTimer* method on the PA entity (Step **11**).
- The SUT returns its response to the SA entity. The given response is an encoded value that has to be decoded in order to be understandable by the TTCN-3 test system (Step **12**).
- For doing this, the SA entity forwards the encoded test data to the TE entity through the method *triEnqueueMsg* (Step **13**).
- The TE entity transmits the encoded response to the CD entity with the intention of decoding it into a structured TTCN-3 value (this is done through the call of *decode* method) (Step **14**).
- The decoded response is passed back to the TE that stops the running timer by invoking the *triStopTimer* method on the PA and finally computes the global verdict (Steps **15-16-17**).
- At last, the test system user is notified by the generated verdict (pass, fail or inconclusive) by the TTmanGUI (Step **18**).

The gains of this design are the conformance to the TTCN-3 standard, generality and platform-independency (applicable to every component based or service oriented systems), reusability and extensibility (compiled code TTCN-3 is stored as jar files in a repository and can be loaded at any time and also updated dynamically without restarting TT4RT system). Furthermore, TT4RT can be used either at deployment time or at service time to validate the SUT. Instead the classical TTCN-3 test systems which consider the SUT as a black-box, TT4RT system treats the SUT as a grey-box (the SUT is composed of a collection of interacting components and compositions under test (CUTs)). This fact can help to localize easily the faulty component or composition and to proceed enhancement of the quality and reliability of the SUT.

5   Case Study

To illustrate our approach, we choose a case study in the telemedicine field. In fact, telemedicine has become an important research issue. It merges telecommunication and information technologies in order to provide remotely clinical health care. It facilitates communications between patients who suffer from chronic health problems and medical staff. In addition, it improves the access to medical services as well as the transmission of patient data (e.g monitored vital signs, laboratory tests, etc.) especially when critical events or emergency situations occur.

As widely described in the literature [17–19], telemedicine applications have to evolve dynamically in order to fulfill new requirements such as adding new health care services, updating the existing one in order to support improvements in wireless and mobile technologies, etc. This adaptability is essential to ensure that these applications remain within the functional requirements defined by application designers, as well as maintain their performance, security and safety properties. Furthermore, the execution environment of such applications is distinguished by its hardware heterogeneity (for instance PDA, PC and sensors) and the use of large range of wireless networking solutions like wireless LANs, ad-hoc wireless networks and cellular/GSM/3G infrastructure-oriented networks.

Due to these dynamic variabilities, medical errors and degradation of QoS parameters can occur. Therefore, runtime testing is required to validate dynamic system changes. Thus, this validation technique can improve health care quality and lead to the early detection and repair of medical devices malfunctions. In the following subsections, we present the architecture of the studied telemedicine application and also its implementation.

5.1   Architecture of TRMCS Case Study

The adopted telemedicine application is called Teleservices and Remote Medical Care System (TRMCS). The main behaviors and structure of such system are inspired from [20]. As depicted in Figure 4, TRMCS system provides monitoring and assistance to patients suffering from chronic health problems. The interacting actors in the system are :

- Medical staff which is composed of physicians, nurses, etc. These health care providers can be located in their own office, hospitals or even an ambulance car.
- One or more patients who are located at their home and are equipped with wearable devices that can sense one or more vital signs such as blood pressure, respiration rate, pulse rate, oxygen saturation and body core temperature.

The wearable medical sensors measure and transmit biomedical data to local as well as remote medical data centers. They should operate autonomously and have to send alert signals when emergency problems arise.

The main functionalities that the TRMCS system supports are:

- The acquisition of biomedical data from patients equipped with wearable medical sensors.
- The processing of monitored data by generating reports.
- The transmission of the monitored data, medical images, laboratory tests to a local as well as remote medical data centers for storage.
- The analysis of monitored data by sending emergency signals when critical events are triggered or threshold conditions are reached[2].

The latter functionality is highlighted and used as proof-of-concept. Within the following studied scenario, the ability of TT4RT system to detect reconfiguration faults is demonstrated.

Studied Scenario. The initial architecture of the studied scenario is outlined in the Figure 5. Each patient sends different kind of help requests to different help centers such as doctor's office, nursery, hospital and ambulatory. This help request can be issued by the patient through a user GUI or raised automatically by the monitoring system. In this current implementation, we support three kinds of help requests: generating call, SMS or alarm signal.

---

[2] For instance, when the heart rate exceeds a certain level of tolerance.

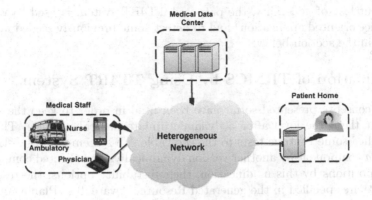

Fig. 4. Global view of Teleservices and Remote Medical Care System

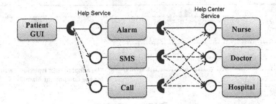

Fig. 5. The initial configuration of the studied scenario

Reconfiguration Scenario. It comes a moment when this system is changed to fulfill new requirements. For instance, the *Alarm* component is changed by a new version with the aim of increasing SUT performance and responsiveness. The new version sends the help request to the help center in a duration that does not exceed 15 time units instead of 30 time units for the old version. Once this reconfiguration is achieved, the new component and all the affected parts of the system by this modification have to be tested.

5.2 Implementation of TRMCS Case Study

In the literature, we have found some research works that use the Open Service Gateway initiative (OSGi) platform[3] to implement such case study [17, 21]. We follow the same technology choice due its dynamism (a powerful Framework to create highly dynamic applications). Thus, we implement the studied scenario using the OSGi Framework, especially OSGi iPOJO model[4]. Under OSGi architecture, software components are encapsulated into bundles which is a java archive file that contains packages and service prerequisites. These bundles are loaded and run automatically by the Apache Felix[5] 1.8 implementation.

---

[3] OSGi Alliance, http://www.osgi.org/markets/index.asp

[4] http://felix.apache.org/site/apache-felix-ipojo.html

[5] http://felix.apache.org/site/index.html

Without loss of generality, the proposed TT4RT system is used to validate this service oriented application[6] and to detect some previously seeded faults as outlined in the section below.

6   Validation of TRMCS by Using TT4RT System

The key concepts presented so far have been used in order to keep the system quality at the same level after a dynamic update has taken place. Thus, we have applied some runtime tests to the evolvable sub-system while substituting the *Alarm* component by another version dynamically. The affected components and compositions by this modification, their testability options, the test cases to execute are specified in the generated Resource Aware Test Plan as outlined in the Figure 6.

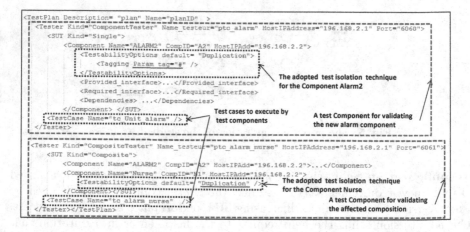

Fig. 6. The main features included in the Resource Aware Test Plan XML file

Furthermore, We have to mention that some faults have been seeded in the new configuration in order to assess the capabilities of TT4RT system to find these reconfiguration faults. It is worth noting that some inconsistencies are automatically detected by the OSGi Framework, for instance a required service crashing. Nevertheless, TT4RT is still required to detect other kinds of faults such erroneous results provided by the new service, incompatibilities between compositions, degradation of quality of service, etc.

6.1   Specifying the Abstract Test Cases

Different test cases specified following the TTCN-3 notation are available to detect reconfiguration faults. In fact, TTCN-3 standard is used to define not only

---

[6] It is worthy to note that our TT4RT system can be used to validate either object or component based applications.

the behavior of each test component but also the dynamic and concurrent test configuration of each test request. First of all, the Listing 1 bellow outlines the adopted test configuration and highlights the different test components involved in this testing process.

```
1  testcase tc_substitute_alarm() runs on mtcType system systemType {
2    var ptcType ptc_alarm,ptc_alarm_nurse,ptc_alarm_hospital,ptc_alarm_doctor;
3      ptc_alarm := ptcType.create("ptc_alarm");
4      map(ptc_alarm:ptcPort, system:systemPort);
5      ptc_alarm.start(ptcBehaviour_alarm());
6      ptc_alarm.done;
7
8      ptc_alarm_nurse := ptcType.create("ptc_alarm_nurse");
9      map(ptc_alarm_nurse:ptcPort, system:systemPort1);
10     ptc_alarm_nurse.start(ptcBehaviour_alarm_nurse());
11     ptc_alarm_nurse.done;
12
13     ptc_alarm_doctor := ptcType.create("ptc_alarm_doctor");
14     map(ptc_alarm_doctor:ptcPort, system:systemPort2);
15     ptc_alarm_doctor.start(ptcBehaviour_alarm_doctor());
16     ptc_alarm_doctor.done;
17
18     ptc_alarm_hospital := ptcType.create("ptc_alarm_hospital");
19     map(ptc_alarm_hospital:ptcPort, system:systemPort3);
20     ptc_alarm_hospital.start(ptcBehaviour_alarm_hospital());
21     ptc_alarm_hospital.done;
22 }
```

Listing 1. The test configuration

The global test process is managed by the MTC component as defined in line 1. This MTC component is responsible for dynamically creating a PTC checking the new *Alarm* component (see line 3) and also three others PTCs for validation the communication between the affected compositions (alarm-nurse, alarm-hospital, alarm-doctor) as indicated respectively in line 8, 13 and 18. To start the execution of these test components, the *map*[7] and *start* methods are used and the adequate function is called (see for example line 4 and 5).

```
1  function ptcBehaviour_alarm() runs on ptcType {
2    timer localtimer := 15.0;
3    ptcPort.send(msg_to_alarm);
4    localtimer.start;
5    alt {
6        [] ptcPort.receive("Service invoked Successfully")
7        {setverdict (pass, "Test service alarm successfully");}
8        [] ptcPort.receive
9        {setverdict (fail, "Something else received");}
10       [] localtimer.timeout
11       { setverdict (fail, "Timeout");}
12        localtimer.stop;
13    }}
```

Listing 2. An example of a PTC behavior

We have to mention that the instantiation of test components and communication links are done dynamically and the execution of their behaviors is done in a parallel manner. For instance, the next listing shows the behavior of one

---

[7] This method aims for connecting a port of a PTC to a port of SUT.

PTC validating the new *Alarm* component (*ptcBehaviour_alarm()*). As depicted in the Listing 2, a timer is defined in line 2 and started in line 4 when testing data are sent (see line 3). It is used to validate the timing behavior of the new *Alarm* component that transmits the help request in a period of time smaller than 15 time units. If this deadline is not respected by the new version (see line 10) a fail verdict is generated as indicated in line 11. Otherwise, the functional behavior is validated and accordingly a partial verdict is computed (see line 7 and 9).

For editing and compiling the specified tests, we have used respectively the CL Editor (TTCN-3 Core Language Editor) and the TThree Compiler that are included in the TTworkbench basic tool [8]. The generated Jars are stored in the repository for further use and can be dynamically loaded during the execution when runtime testing is required to validate dynamic changes.

6.2 Preparing the Test Execution Environment

Before executing the compiled tests, the test isolation policy is called in order to choose for each component under test the suitable test isolation technique. The testability options of each component involved in the testing process are specified in the resource aware test plan as depicted in Figure 6. In the current scenario, the *Alarm* component is test aware. It differentiates between test data and business data by using a test tag as illustrated in the test plan. The *Nurse* component is not testable. Thus, we use the default test isolation technique mentioned in the test plan file which is the duplication technique. In this case, a new component is created which handles the test request. Such solution aims not to disturb the original *Nurse* component. The same work is done for *Doctor* and *Hospital* components.

6.3 Executing Runtime Tests

Once the Resource Aware Test Plan is loaded and the test process is started through the TTmanGUI, the test environment is built and the test components are created dynamically. The Figure 7 highlights the main interaction between some components under test and the corresponding test components. For instance, it shows that the test component *PTC_alarm* is created in order to validate the *Alarm2* component. The latter is instructed to use both the testing data and business data. Thus, *PTC_alarm* sends inputs data which is generated with the test tag and receive outputs in order to verify that the specified timing constraint is respected by the new component. Furthermore, affected compositions are also checked by test components like *PTC_alarm_nurse*. Due to the non testability of the *Nurse* component, it has been duplicated and the duplicate component is used while testing the composition under test behavior.

We follow the same principles for the rest of the components under test as specified in the resource aware test plan. Once the PTCs components terminate

---

[8] http://www.testingtech.com/products/ttworkbench.php

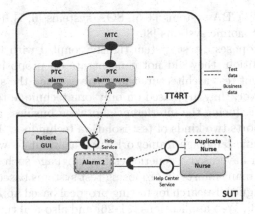

Fig. 7. Test components interaction with the affected components under test

their specified behaviors, they are removed from the test configuration. The MTC component computes the global verdict which is finally displayed to the test system user through the TTmanGUI. The latter has been implemented using the Java language and the swing package. It has been packaged as an OSGi bundle. The Figure 8 shows the proposed graphical user interface also the final verdict of the executed runtime tests.

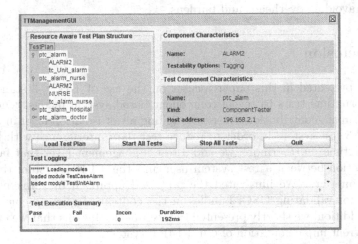

Fig. 8. Screenshot of the Prototype TTmanGUI of the TT4RT system

7   Related Work

Recent research activities have been proposed to deal with runtime testing in dynamic environments. They aim to ensure the correctness of the running system after reconfiguration. In fact, we distinguish approaches dealing with ubiquitous software systems [1], CBA systems [3–5], SOA systems [6, 7], publish/subscribe systems [2] and autonomic systems [8].

Each of them proposes a test system tightly coupled with the system under test (SUT). In addition, they did not concentrate on proposing a generic and platform independent test architecture that evolves when the system under test evolves too. Moreover, they are based on only one technique to isolate runtime tests in the aim of reducing the interference between business and test data except [8] which supports two kinds of test isolation techniques. These approaches mostly used a specific language framework such as Junit to write and execute tests. None of them have used a generic testing language such as TTCN-3.

There have been many efforts on proposing test systems based on the TTCN-3 standard. We distinguish research for testing protocol based applications [15, 22], Web services [16, 23], Web applications [24–26] and also real time and embedded systems [27, 28]. To the best of our knowledge, [9] is the only previous paper presenting ideas on using TTCN-3 standard for online validation and testing of internet services. However, this work did not deal with test isolation issues when testing is applied in the production phase.

Unlike these approaches, our work aims at proposing a generic and platform independent test system based on the TTCN-3 standard to execute runtime tests. The proposed test system supports different test isolation mechanisms in order to support testing different kinds of components: test sensitive, test aware or even non testable components. Such test system has an important impact on reducing the risk of interference between test behaviors and business behaviors as well as avoiding overheads and burdens.

8   Conclusion

The work presented in this paper focuses on the use of TTCN-3 standard for executing runtime tests to reveal component based system inconsistencies and faults. Our main contribution consists in adding a test isolation layer in the classic TTCN-3 test system in order to reduce test data interference with business data at runtime. Furthermore, we add a test management layer that facilitates the interaction between a test system user and the TT4RT system through a graphical interface. We illustrated the proposed approach by implementing a prototype for validating OSGi bundles in the context of telemedicine applications. In addition, we shortly presented the technical solutions that we employed for the current implementation of our TT4RT system.

Nevertheless, distributing test configurations in different nodes remains unsolved. Hence, we are exploring solutions in this area to distribute efficiently test components with fitting some resource and connectivity constraints. Besides, this work does not deal with test cases generation. All the executed tests are specified manually. Therefore, we aim to investigate effort in automating TTCN-3 test cases generation, especially when behavior adaptation occurs. Another area to explore is the optimization of test cases selection by re-testing only the affected parts of the system due to a reconfiguration action.

References

1. Merdes, M., Malaka, R., Suliman, D., Paech, B., Brenner, D., Atkinson, C.: Ubiquitous RATs: how resource-aware run-time tests can improve ubiquitous software systems. In: SEM 2006: Proceedings of the 6th International Workshop on Software Engineering and Middleware, pp. 55–62. ACM, New York (2006)
2. Piel, É., González-Sanchez, A., Groß, H.G.: Automating integration testing of large-scale publish/subscribe systems. In: Hinze, A., Buchmann, A.P. (eds.) Principles and Applications of Distributed Event-Based Systems, pp. 140–163. IGI Global (2010)
3. Piel, É., González-Sanchez, A.: Data-flow integration testing adapted to runtime evolution in component-based systems. In: Proceedings of the 2009 ESEC/FSE Workshop on Software Integration and Evolution @ Runtime, pp. 3–10. Association for Computing Machinery, New York (2009)
4. Gonzalez, A., Piel, E., Gross, H.G.: Architecture support for runtime integration and verification of component-based systems of systems. In: Caporuscio, M., Marco, A.D. (eds.) 23rd IEEE/ACM International Conference on Automated Software Engineering - Workshops. ASE Workshops 2008, pp. 41–48. IEEE Computer Society (September 2008)
5. Niebuhr, D., Rausch, A.: Guaranteeing correctness of component bindings in dynamic adaptive systems based on runtime testing. In: SIPE 2009: Proceedings of the 4th International Workshop on Services Integration in Pervasive Environments, pp. 7–12. ACM, New York (2009)
6. Bai, X., Xu, D., Dai, G., Tsai, W.T., Chen, Y.: Dynamic reconfigurable testing of service-oriented architecture, vol. 1, pp. 368–378 (July 2007)
7. Greiler, M., Gross, H.G., van Deursen, A.: Evaluation of Online Testing for Services – A Case Study. In: 2nd International Workshop on Principles of Engineering Service-Oriented System, pp. 36–42. ACM (2010)
8. King, T.M., Allen, A.A., Cruz, R., Clarke, P.J.: Safe Runtime Validation of Behavioral Adaptations in Autonomic Software. In: Calero, J.M.A., Yang, L.T., Mármol, F.G., García-Villalba, L.J., Li, X.A., Wang, Y. (eds.) ATC 2011. LNCS, vol. 6906, pp. 31–46. Springer, Heidelberg (2011)
9. Deussen, P.H., Din, G., Schieferdecker, I.: A TTCN-3 Based Online Test and Validation Platform for Internet Services. In: Proceedings of the The Sixth International Symposium on Autonomous Decentralized Systems (ISADS 2003). IEEE Computer Society, Washington, DC (2003)
10. Brenner, D., Atkinson, C., Malaka, R., Merdes, M., Paech, B., Suliman, D.: Reducing verification effort in component-based software engineering through built-in testing. Information Systems Frontiers 9(2-3), 151–162 (2007)
11. Lahami, M., Krichen, M., Jmaiel, M.: A distributed test architecture for adaptable and distributed real-time systems. The Journal of New technologies of Information (RNTI), CAL 2011 (2012)
12. ETSI: Methods for Testing and Specification (MTS); The Testing and Test Control Notation version 3; Part 1: TTCN-3 Core Language
13. ETSI: Methods for Testing and Specification (MTS); The Testing and Test Control Notation version 3; Part 6: TTCN-3 Control Interface (TCI)
14. ETSI: Methods for Testing and Specification (MTS); The Testing and Test Control Notation version 3; Part 5: TTCN-3 Runtime Interface (TRI)
15. Schulz, S., Vassiliou-Gioles, T.: Implementation of TTCN-3 Test Systems using the TRI. In: Proceedings of the IFIP 14th International Conference on Testing Communicating Systems XIV, pp. 425–442. Kluwer, B.V, Deventer (2002)

16. Rentea, C., Schieferdecker, I., Cristea, V.: Ensuring quality of web applications by client-side testing using ttcn-3. In: TestCom/Fates (2009)
17. Chen, I.Y., Tsai, C.H.: Pervasive Digital Monitoring and Transmission of Pre-Care Patient Biostatics with an OSGi, MOM and SOA Based Remote Health Care System. In: Sixth Annual IEEE International Conference on Pervasive Computing and Communications (PerCom), pp. 704–709 (2008)
18. Varshney, U.: Pervasive healthcare and wireless health monitoring. Mob. Netw. Appl. 12(2-3), 113–127 (2007)
19. André, F., Segarra, M.T., Zouari, M.: Distributed Dynamic Self-adaptation of Data Management in Telemedicine Applications. In: Mokhtari, M., Khalil, I., Bauchet, J., Zhang, D., Nugent, C. (eds.) ICOST 2009. LNCS, vol. 5597, pp. 303–306. Springer, Heidelberg (2009)
20. Inverardi, P., Muccini, H.: Software Architectures and Coordination Models. J. Supercomput. 24(2), 141–149 (2003)
21. Chen, I.Y., Huang, C.C.: A Service Oriented Agent Architecture To Support Tele-cardiology Services On Demand. Journal of Medical and Biological Engineering (2005)
22. Schieferdecker, I., Vassiliou-Gioles, T.: Realizing Distributed TTCN-3 Test Systems with TCI. In: Hogrefe, D., Wiles, A. (eds.) TestCom 2003. LNCS, vol. 2644, pp. 95–109. Springer, Heidelberg (2003)
23. Schieferdecker, I., Din, G., Apostolidis, D.: Distributed functional and load tests for web services. STTT 7, 351–360 (2005)
24. Stepien, B., Peyton, L., Xiong, P.: Framework Testing of Web applications using TTCN-3. Int. J. Softw. Tools Technol. Transf. 10(4), 371–381 (2008)
25. Ying Li, Q.L.: Research on Web application software load test using Technology of TTCN-3. American Journal of Engineering and Technologu Research 11, 3686–3690 (2011)
26. Din, G., Tolea, S., Schieferdecker, I.: Distributed Load Tests with TTCN-3. In: Uyar, M.Ü., Duale, A.Y., Fecko, M.A. (eds.) TestCom 2006. LNCS, vol. 3964, pp. 177–196. Springer, Heidelberg (2006)
27. Okika, J.C., Ravn, A.P., Liu, Z., Siddalingaiah, L.: Developing a ttcn-3 test harness for legacy software. In: Proceedings of the 2006 International Workshop on Automation of Software Test, pp. 104–110. ACM, New York (2006)
28. Serbanescu, D.A., Molovata, V., Din, G., Schieferdecker, I., Radusch, I.: Real-Time Testing with TTCN-3. In: Suzuki, K., Higashino, T., Ulrich, A., Hasegawa, T. (eds.) TestCom/FATES 2008. LNCS, vol. 5047, pp. 283–301. Springer, Heidelberg (2008)

Passive Interoperability Testing
for Request-Response Protocols: Method, Tool
and Application on CoAP Protocol

Nanxing Chen and César Viho

IRISA/University of Rennes 1
Campus de Beaulieu, Avenue du Général Leclerc, 35042 Rennes Cedex, France
nanxing.chen@irisa.fr, cesar.viho@irisa.fr

Abstract. Passive testing is a technique that aims at testing a running system by only observing its behavior without introducing any test
input. The non-intrusive nature of passive testing makes it an appropriate technique for interoperability testing, which is an important activity
to ensure the correct collaboration of different network components in
operational environment. In this paper we propose a passive interoperability testing approach, especially for request-response protocols in the
context of client-server communications. According to the interaction
pattern of request-response protocols, the observed interactions (trace)
between the network components under test can be considered as a set
of conversations between client and server. Then, a procedure to map
each test case into these conversations is carried out, which intends to
verify the occurrence of the generated test cases as well as to determine
whether interoperability is achieved. The trace verification procedure has
been automated in a passive testing tool, which analyzes the collected
traces and deduces appropriate verdicts. The proposed method and the
testing tool were put into operation in the first interoperability testing
event of Constrained Application Protocol (CoAP) held in Paris, March
2012 in the scope of the Internet of Things. By using this approach, an
amount of CoAP applications from different vendors were successfully
and efficiently tested, revealing their interoperability degree.

Keywords: Interoperability Testing, Passive Testing, Request-Response
Protocol, CoAP.

1 Introduction

With the development and increasing use of distributed systems, computer communication mode has changed. There is increasing use of clusters of workstations
connected by a high-speed local area network to one or more network servers.
In this environment, resource access leads to communications that are strongly
request-response oriented. This tendency resulted in a large amount of protocols such as Hypertext Transfer Protocol (HTTP)[1], Session Initiation Protocol

---

[1] http://tools.ietf.org/html/rfc2616

B. Nielsen and C. Weise (Eds.): ICTSS 2012, LNCS 7641, pp. 87–102, 2012.

(SIP)[2], and very recently the Constrained Application Protocol (CoAP) [1], etc.
Due to the heterogeneous nature of distributed systems, the interoperability of
these protocol applications is becoming a crucial issue. In this context, interoperability testing is required before the commercialization to ensure correct
collaboration and guarantee the quality of services.

This paper proposes a methodology for the interoperability testing of request-
response protocols. Specifically, we apply the technique of *passive testing*, which
aims at testing a running system by only observing its external behavior without disturbing its normal operation. The methodology consists of the following
main steps: *(i)* Interoperability test purposes extraction from the protocol specifications. Each test purpose specifies an important property to be verified. *(ii)*
For each test purpose, an interoperability test case is generated, in which the
detailed events that need to be observed are specified. *(iii)* Behavior analysis.
In order to verify whether the test purposes are reached, as well as to detect
non-interoperable behavior, traces produced by protocol implementations are
processed by keeping only the client-server *conversations* with respect to the interaction model of request-response protocols. These conversations will further
be analyzed by a trace verification algorithm to identify the occurrence of the
generated test cases and to emit an appropriate verdict for each of them.

The proposed passive interoperability testing method has been implemented
in a test tool, which was successfully put into operation during ETSI CoAP
Plugtest - the first formal CoAP interoperability testing event held in Paris,
March 2012 in the context of the Internet of Things.

This paper is organized as follows: Section 2 introduces the background and
motivation. Section 3 proposes the methodology for passive interoperability testing of request-response protocols. Section 4 describes the application of this
method on CoAP Plugtest as well as the experimental results. Finally, we conclude the paper and suggest further research directions in Section 5.

2   Background and Motivation

The request-response oriented communication is generally used in conjection
with the client-server paradigm to move the data and to distribute the computations in the system by requesting services from remote servers. The typical
sequence of events in requesting a service from a remote server is: a client entity sends a request to a server entity on a remote host, then a computation is
performed by the server entity. And, finally a response is sent back to the client.

Request-response communications are now common in the fields of networks.
Request-response exchange is typical for database or directory queries and
operations, as well as for many signaling protocols, remote procedure calls or middleware infrastructures. A typical example is REST (Representational State
Transfer) [10], an architecture for creating Web service. In REST, clients initi-
ate request to servers to manipulate resources identified by standardized Uniform
Resource Identifier (URI). E.g., the HTTP methods GET, POST, PUT and

---

[2] http://www.ietf.org/rfc/rfc3261.txt

DELETE are used to read, create, update and delete the resources. On the other hand, servers process requests and return appropriate responses. REST is nowadays popular, which is applied in almost all of the major Web services on the Internet, and considered to be used in the *Internet of Things*, aiming at extending the Web to even the most constrained nodes and networks. This goes along the lines of recent developments, such as Constrained RESTful Environments (CoRE)[3] and CoAP, where smart things are increasingly becoming part of the Internet and the Web, confirming the importance of request-response communication.

Promoted by the rapid development of computer technology, protocols using the request-response transaction communications are increasing. Normally, protocol specifications are defined in a way that the clients and servers interoperate correctly to provide services. To ensure that they collaborate properly and consequently satisfy customer expectations, protocol testing is an important step to validate protocol implementations before their commercialization. Among them, *conformance testing* [7] verifies whether a protocol application conforms to its specifications. It allows developers to focus on the fundamental problems of their protocol implementations. However, it is a well-known fact that, even following the same standard, clients and servers might not interoperate successfully due to several reasons: poorly specified protocol options, incompleteness of conformance testing, inconsistency of implementation, etc. These aspects may cause the interoperable issues in realizing different services. However, the heterogeneous nature of computer systems requires interoperability issues to be solved before the deployment of the product. Therefore, *interoperability testing* [11] is required to ensure that different protocol applications communicate correctly while providing the expected services.

To perform interoperability testing (*iop* for short in the sequel), the conventional method is the *active testing* approach (e.g. [8,4]). It requires to deploy a *test system* (TS) that stimulates the *implementations under test* (IUT) and verify their reactions. Although widely used, active testing has limitations: test can be difficult or even impossible to perform if the tester is not provided with a direct interface to stimulate the IUTs, or in operational environment where the normal operation of IUTs cannot be shutdown or interrupted for a long period of time. On the contrary, *passive testing* represents an alternative, which aims at testing a system by passively observing its inputs/outputs without interrupting its normal behavior.

Until now, passive testing has been studied and applied to computing systems to supervise distributed computations, communications networks for fault management [6], protocol testing [3,5], runtime verification [12], etc. In this paper, we will provide a passive interoperability testing methodology for request-response protocols. We have chosen to use passive testing technique for the following arguments: First, passive testing does not insert arbitrary test messages, thus is suitable for interoperability testing in operational environment as is often concerned by request-response services. Also, passive testing does not introduce extra overhead into the networks, hence is appropriate for testing in the context of Internet of Things, where devices are resource limited.

---

[3] http://datatracker.ietf.org/wg/core/charter/

The work presented in this paper is original. It involves using the non-intrusive passive testing technique to verify interoperability, where there exist only few works in the literature. Moreover, the method does not only verify whether the test purposes are reached, but also detects non-interoperable behavior. Last but not least, the procedure of trace verification is automated by implementing a tool, which was successfully put into practice for the test of an important machine-to-machine communication protocol CoAP. To our knowledge, it was the first time that passive automated interoperability testing method was applied in an interoperability testing event, which increased drastically the efficiency, while keeping the capacity of non-interoperability detection.

3 Interoperability Testing for Request-Response Protocols

3.1 Formal Model

Specification languages for reactive systems can often be given a semantics in terms of labeled transition systems. In this paper, we use the IOLTS (Input-Output Labeled Transition System) model [9], which allows differentiating input, output and internal events while precisely indicating the interfaces specified for each event.

Definition 1. An IOLTS is a tuple $M = (Q^M, \Sigma^M, \Delta^M, q_0^M)$ where Q^M is the set of states of the system M with q_0^M its initial state. Σ^M is the set of observable events at the interfaces of M. In IOLTS model, input and output actions are differentiated: We note $p?a$ (resp. $p!a$) for an input (resp. output) a at interface p. $\Gamma(q) =_{def} \{\alpha \in \Sigma^M | \exists q', (q, \alpha, q') \in \Delta^M\}$ is the set of all possible events at the state q. $\Delta^M \subseteq Q^M \times (\Sigma^M \cup \tau) \times Q^M$ is the transition relation, where $\tau \notin \Sigma^M$ stands for an internal action. A transition in M is noted by $(q, \alpha, q') \in \Delta^M$.

3.2 Testing Method Overview

The passive interoperability testing architecture (c.f. Fig.1) for request-response protocols involves a *test system* and a *system under test*, composed of two *implementations under test*, namely a *client* and a *server*. In passive iop testing, the test system has two main roles: *(i)* Observe and collect the information exchanged (trace) between the client and the server. *(ii)*Analyze the collected trace to check interoperability. Generally, trace verification can be done *online* to monitor the system and report abnormalities at any time. Elsewise it can be done *offline*, i.e, the traces during the test execution are stored in a file and will be analyzed in a posteriori manner. As passive testing does not apply any stimulus, testing activity is only based on an accurate level of observation, relying on the set up of sniffer at *point(s) of observation* (PO) to observe the messages exchanged between the client and the server. In this paper we consider *black-box* testing: the test system is not aware of the internal structure of IUTs. Only their external behavior can be verified during their interactions.

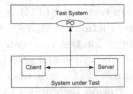

Fig. 1. Passive interoperability testing architecture

The testing procedure is illustrated in Fig.2. It consists of the following main steps:

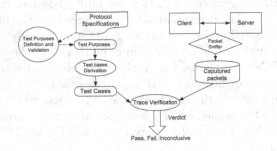

Fig. 2. Passive interoperability testing procedure

1. Interoperability test purposes (ITP) selection from protocol specifications. An ITP is in general informal, in the form of an incomplete sequence of actions representing a critical property to be verified. Generally it can be designed by experts or provided by standards guidelines for test selection. Test purpose is a commonly used method in the field of testing to focus on the most important properties of a protocol, as it is generally impossible to validate all possible behavior described in specifications. Nonetheless, an ITP itself must be correct w.r.t the specification to assure its validity. Formally, an ITP can be represented by a deterministic and complete IOLTS equipped with trap states used to select targeted behavior.
   $ITP = (Q^{ITP}, \Sigma^{ITP}, \triangle^{ITP}, q_0^{ITP})$ where:
   - $\Sigma^{ITP} \subseteq \Sigma^{S_{client}} \cup \Sigma^{S_{server}}$. where S_{client} and S_{server} are the specifications on which the IUTs are based.
   - Q^{ITP} is the set of states. An ITP has a set of trap states $Accept^{ITP}$, indicating the targeted behavior. States in $Accept^{ITP}$ imply that the test purpose has been reached and are only directly reachable by the observation of outputs produced by the IUTs.
   - ITP is complete, which means that each state allows all actions. This is done by inserting "*" label at each state q of the ITP, where "* " is an abbreviation for the complement set of all other events leaving q. By using "*" label, ITP is able to describe a property without taking into account the complete sequence of detailed specifications interaction.

2. Once the ITPs chosen, an iop test case (ITC) is generated for each ITP. An ITC is the detailed set of instructions that need to be taken in order to perform the test. The generation of iop test case can be either manual, as usually done in most of the interoperability events, also for "young" protocols whose specifications are not yet stable. ITCs can also be generated automatically by using various formal description techniques existing in the literature such as [11,4]. Formally, an iop test case ITC is represented by an IOLTS: ITC = $(Q^{ITC}, \Sigma^{ITC}, \Delta^{ITC}, q_0^{ITC})$, where q_0^{ITC} is the initial state. {*Pass, Fail, Inconclusive*} $\in Q^{ITC}$ are the trap states representing interoperability verdicts. Respectively, verdict *Pass* means the ITP is satisfied ($Accept^{ITP}$ is reached) without any fault detected. *Fail* means at least one fault is detected, while *Inconclusive* means the behavior of IUTs is not faulty, however can not reach the ITP. Σ^{ITC} denotes the observation of the messages from the interfaces. Δ^{ITC} is the transition function. In active testing, ITCs are usually controllable. i.e, ITC contains stimuli that allow controlling the IUTs. On the contrary, in passive testing, ITCs are only used to analyze the observed trace produced by the IUTs. The correct behavior of IUTs implies that the trace produced by the IUTs should exhibit the events that lead to *Pass* verdicts described in the test cases. In the sequel, an ITC is supposed to be deterministic. The set of test cases is called a *test suite*. An example of ITP and ITC can be seen on Fig.6 in Section 4.2.

3. Analyze the observed behavior of the IUTs against each test case and issue a verdict *Pass, Fail* or *Inconclusive*. In this paper we choose *offline* testing, where the test cases are pre-computed before they are executed on the trace.

3.3   Request-Response Protocol Passive Interoperability Testing

In offline passive interoperability testing for request-response protocols, the packets exchanged between the client and server are captured by a packet sniffer. The collected traces are stored in a file. They are key to conclude whether the protocol implementations interoperate (c.f. Fig.2).

In passive testing, one issue is that the test system has no knowledge of the global state where the system under test SUT can be in w.r.t a test case at the beginning of the trace. In order to realize the trace analysis, a straight way is *trace mapping* [6]. This approach compares each event in the trace produced by the SUT strictly with that in the specification. SUT specification is modeled as a Finite State Machine (FSM). Recorded trace is mapped into the FSM by backtracking. Initially, all states in the specification are the possible states that the SUT can be in. Then, the events in the trace are studied one after the other: the states which can be led to other states in the FSM by the currently checked event are replaced by their destination states of the corresponding transitions. Other states are redundant states and removed. After a number of iterations, if the set of possible states becomes empty, SUT is determined faulty. i.e., it contains a behavior which contradicts its specification as trace mapping procedure fails. This approach however, has some limitations. First, to model a complex network by a single FSM maybe complex. Moreover, this approach does not suit interoperability testing: as the SUT concerned in interoperability testing involves several IUTs, therefore to calculate their global behavior encounters state explosion.

In [5], another method called *invariant approach* was introduced. Each invariant represents an important property of the SUT extracted from the specification. It is composed of a preamble and a test part, which are cause-effect events respectively w.r.t the property. The invariant is then used to process the trace: The correct behavior of the SUT requires that the trace exhibit the whole invariant.

In this paper, we propose another solution to perform passive trace verification. The idea is to make use of the special interaction model of request-response protocols. As the interoperability testing of this kind of protocol essentially involves verifying the correct transactions between the client and the server, therefore each test case consists of the dialogues (requests and responses) made between them, and generally starts with a request from the client. A strategy is as follows: *(i)* the recorded trace is filtered to keep only the messages that belong to the tested request-response protocol. In this way, the trace only contains the conversations made between the client and the server. *(ii)* Each event in the filtered trace will be checked one after another according to the following rules, which correspond to the algorithm of trace verification (c.f. Algorithm 1). This algorithm aims at mapping the test case into the trace. i.e., to match a test case with the corresponding conversation(s) in the trace. Recall that in our work, each test case specify the events that lead to verdicts *Pass, Fail* or *Inconclusive* assigned on its trap states. Therefore, if a test case is identified on the trace, we can check whether it is respected by comparing each message of the test case with that in its corresponding conversation(s), and emitting a verdict once an associated verdict is reached.

1. If the currently checked message is a request sent by the client, we verify whether it corresponds to the first message of (at least one of) the test cases (noted TC_i) in the test suite TS. If it is the case, we keep track of these test cases TC_i, as the matching of messages implies that TC_i might be exhibited on the trace. We call these TC_i *candidate test cases*. The set of candidate test cases is noted TC. Specifically, the currently checked state in each candidate test case is kept in memory (noted $Current_i$).

2. If the currently checked message is a response sent by the server, we check if this response corresponds to an event of each candidate test cases TC_i at its currently checked state (memorized by $Current_i$). If it is the case, we further check if this response leads to a verdict *Pass, Fail* or *Inconclusive*. If it is the case, the corresponding verdict is emitted to the related test case. Otherwise we move to the next state of the currently checked state of TC_i, which can be reached by the transition label - the currently checked message. On the contrary, if the response does not correspond to any event at the currently checked state in a candidate test case TC_i, we remove this TC_i from the set of the candidate test cases TC.

3. Besides, we need a counter for each test case. This is because in passive testing, a test case can be met several times during the interactions between the client and the server due to the non-controllable nature of passive testing.

The counter $Counter_i$ for each test case TC_i is initially set to zero. Each time a verdict is emitted for TC_i, the counter increments by 1. Also, a verdict emitted for a candidate test case TC_i each time when it is met is recorded, noted $verdict.TC_i.Counter_i$. For example, $verdict.TC_1.1 = Pass$ represents a sub-verdict attributed to test case TC_1 when it is encountered the first time in the trace. All the obtained sub-verdicts are recorded in a set $verdict.TC_i$. It helps further assign a global verdict for this test case.

4. The global verdict for each test case is emitted by taking into account all its sub-verdicts recorded in $verdict.TC_i$. Finally, a global verdict for TC_i is *Pass* if all its sub-verdicts are *Pass*. *Inconclusive* if at least one sub-verdict is *Inconclusive*, but no sub-verdict is *Fail*. *Fail*, if at least one sub-verdict is *Fail*.

Algorithm 1. Trace verification for request-response protocols

---

Input: filtered trace σ, test suite TS
Output: $verdict.TC_i$
Initialization: $TC = \emptyset$, $Counter_i = 0$, $Current_i = q_0^{TC_i}$, $verdict.TC_i = \emptyset$;
while $\sigma \neq \emptyset$ **do**

    $\sigma = \alpha.\sigma'$;
    if α *is a request* **then**
        for $TC_i \in TS$ **do**
            if $\alpha \in \Gamma(Current_i)$ **then**
                $TC = TC \cup TC_i$ /*Candidate test cases are added into the candidate test case set*/;
                $Current_i = Next_i$ where $(Current_i, \alpha, Next_i) \in \Delta^{TC_i}$
            end
        end
    end
    else
        for $TC_i \in TC$ **do**
            if $\alpha \in \Gamma(Current_i)$ **then**
                $Current_i = Next_i$ where $(Current_i, \alpha, Next_i) \in \Delta^{TC_i}$;
                if $Next_i \in \{Pass, Fail, Inconclusive\}$ **then**
                    $Counter_i = Counter_i + 1$;
                    $verdict.TC_i.Counter_i = Next_i$ /* Emit the corresponding verdict to the test case*/;
                    $verdict.TC_i = verdict.TC_i \cup verdict.TC_i.Counter_i$
                end
            end
            else
                $TC = TC \setminus TC_i$
            end
        end
    end
end
return $verdict.TC_i$

The complexity of the algorithm is $O(M \times N)$, where M is the size of the trace, N the number of candidate test cases. The trace verification procedure in fact, aims at looking for the possible test cases that might be exhibited in the trace by checking each event taken in order from the trace. Regarding the transaction mode of request-response protocols, each filtered traces are in fact composed of a set of *conversations*. The objective of the algorithm is intended to match the test cases with the conversations, so that the occurrence of the test cases in the trace is identified. By comparing each message of the test case with that of its corresponding conversation(s), we can determine whether IUTs interactions are as expected as they are described by the test cases. Moreover, the possibility that a test case can appear several times in the trace is also taken into account. Therefore the global verdict for a given test case is based on the set of subverdicts, increasing the reliability of interoperability testing. Not only we can verify whether the test purposes are reached, but also non-interoperable behavior can be detected due to the difference between obtained subverdicts.

3.4   Passive Testing Tool

To realize trace verification, we have developed a passive testing tool [2], which aims to automate the process of trace verification. A description of this tool is given in Fig.3.

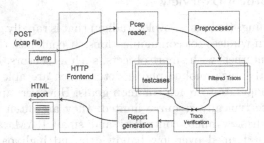

Fig. 3. Passive interoperability testing tool

The tool is implemented in language Python3[4] mainly for its advantages: easy to understand, rapid prototyping and extensive library. The tool is influenced by TTCN-3[5]. It implements basic TTCN-3 snapshots, behavior trees, ports, timers, messages types, templates, etc. However it provides several improvements, for example object-oriented message types definitions, automatic computation of message values, interfaces for supporting multiple input and presentation format, implementing generic codecs to support a wide range of protocols, etc. These features makes the tool flexible, allowing to realize passive testing.

As illustrated in Fig.3, a web interface (HTTP frontend) was developed. Traces produced by client and server implementations of a request-response protocol, captured by the packet sniffer are submitted via the interface. Specifically in our work, the traces should be submitted in pcap format[6]. Each time a trace is submitted, it is then dealt by a preprossesor to filter only the messages relevant to the tested request-response protocol, i.e., to keep only the conversations made between the client and server.

The next step is trace verification, which takes into two files as input: the set of test cases and the filtered trace. The trace is analyzed according to Algorithm 1, where test cases are verified on the trace to check their occurrence and validity.

---

[4] http://www.python.org/getit/releases/3.0/
[5] http://www.ttcn-3.org/
[6] http://www.tcpdump.org/

Finally, unrelated test cases are filtered out, while other test cases are associated with a verdict *Pass*, *Fail* or *Inconclusive*. The results are then reported from the HTTP frontend: Not only the verdict is reported, also the reasons in case of *Fail* or *Inconclusive* verdicts are explicitly given, so that users can understand the blocking issues of interoperability (c.f. a use case in Section 4.3).

4   Experimentation

The proposed passive interoperability testing method for request-response protocols has been put into operation in the CoAP Plugtest - the first formal CoAP interoperability testing event in the context of the Internet of Things.

4.1   CoAP Protocol Overview

The Internet of Things (IoT) is a novel paradigm that is rapidly gaining ground in the field of modern wireless telecommunications. It combines the general meaning of the term 'Internet' with smart objects, such as sensors, Radio-Frequency IDentication (RFID) tags, mobile phones, etc. which are able to interact with each other and cooperate to reach common goals. However, applications in the context of IoT are typically resource limited: they are often battery powered and equipped with slow micro-controllers and small RAMs and ROMs. The data transfer is performed over low bandwidth and high packet error rates, and the communication is often machine-to-machine. To deal with the various challenging issues of constrained environment, the Constrained Application Protocol (CoAP) has been designed by Constrained RESTful Environments (CoRE) working group[7] to make it possible to provide resource constrained devices with Web service functionalities.

   CoAP protocol is a request-response style protocol. A CoAP request is sent by a client to request an action on a resource identified by a URI on a server. The server then sends a response, which may include a resource representation. CoAP is consist of two-layers (c.f. Fig.4): *(i)* CoAP transaction layer deals with UDP and the asynchronous interactions. Four types of message are defined at this layer: Confirmable (CON, messages require acknowledgment), Non-Confirmable (NON, messages do not require acknowledgment), Acknowledgment (ACK, an acknowledgment to a CON message), and Reset (RST, messages indicate that a Confirmable message was received, but some context is missing to properly process it. eg. the node has rebooted). *(ii)* CoAP Request/Response layer is responsible for the transmission of requests and responses for resource manipulation and interoperation. CoAP supports four request methods: *GET* retrieves the resource identified by the request URI. *POST* requests the server to update/create a new resource under the requested URI. *PUT* requests that the resource identified by the request URI to be updated with the enclosed message body. *DELETE* requests that the resource identified by the request URI to be deleted.

---

[7] http://datatracker.ietf.org/wg/core/charter/

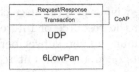

Fig. 4. Protocol stack of CoAP

4.2   Test Purposes and Test Cases

As one of the most important protocol for the future Internet of Things, the application of CoAP is potentially wide, especially concerning energy, building automation and other M2M applications that deal with manipulation of various resources on constrained networks. For that CoAP applications be widely adopted by the industry, hardware and software implementations from different vendors need to interoperate and perform well together. Regarding the specifications of CoAP [1], a set of 27 interoperability test purposes are selected. To ensure that the ITPs are correct w.r.t the specifications, the ITPs were chosen and cross-validated by experts from ETSI[8], IRISA[9] and BUPT[10], and reviewed by IPSO alliance. The test purposes concern the following properties:

- Basic CoAP methods GET, PUT, POST and DELETE. This group of tests involves in verifying that both CoAP client and server interoperate correctly w.r.t different methods as specified in [1], even in lossy context as often encountered by M2M communication. (c.f. an example in Fig.5-(a)).
- Resource discovery[11]. As CoAP applications are considered to be M2M, they must be able to discover each other and their resources. Thus, CoAP standardizes a resource discovery format defining a path prefix for resource as */.well-known/core*. The interoperability testing of resource discovery requires verifying that: when the client requests */.well-known/core* resource, the server sends a response containing the payload indicating all the available links.
- Block-wise transfer[12] : CoAP is based on datagram transports such as UDP, which limits the maximum size of resource representations (64 KB) that can be transferred. In order to handle large payloads, CoAP defines an option *Block*, in order that large sized resource representation can be divided in several blocks and transferred in multiple request-response pairs. The interoperability testing of this property therefore involves in verifying that: when the client requests or creates large payload on the server, the server should react correctly to the requests (c.f. an example in Fig.5-(b)).
- Resource observation[13] is an important property of CoAP applications, which provides a built-in push model where a subscription interface is provided for

---

[8] http://www.etsi.org/WebSite/homepage.aspx
[9] http://www.irisa.fr/
[10] http://www.bupt.edu.cn/
[11] http://tools.ietf.org/id/draft-shelby-core-link-format-00.txt
[12] http://tools.ietf.org/html/draft-ietf-core-block-08
[13] http://tools.ietf.org/html/draft-ietf-core-observe-04

client to request a response whenever a resource changes. This push is accomplished by the device with the resource of interest by sending the response message with the latest change to the subscriber. The interoperability testing of this property consists of: upon different requests sent by the client to register or cancel its interest for a specific resource, the server should react correctly. i.e., it adds the client to the list of observers for the resource in the former case, while remove it from the list in the latter case (c.f. an example in Fig.5-(c)).

The following figure demonstrates some typical examples of CoAP transactions. Fig.5-(a) illustrates a confirmable request sent by the client, asking for the resource of humidity. Upon the reception of the request, the server acknowledges the message, transferring the payload while echoing the Message ID generated by the client. Fig.5-(b) illustrate a block-wise transfer of a large payload (humidity) requested by the client. Upon the reception of the request, the server divides the resource into 4 blocks and transfers them separately to the client. Each response indicates the block number and size, as well as whether there are further blocks (indicated by value m). Fig 5-(c) illustrates an example of resource observation, including registration and cancellation. At first, the client registers its interest in humidity resource by indicating Observe option. After a while, it cancels its intention by sending another GET request on the resource without Observe option.

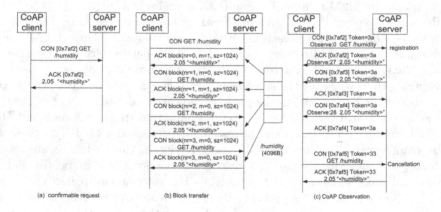

Fig. 5. CoAP transaction examples

Once the set of test purposes are defined, a test case is derived for each test purpose. The following figure shows an example. The test purpose focuses on the GET method in confirmable transaction mode. i.e., when the client sends a GET request (It implies parameters: a Message ID, Type=0 for confirmable transaction mode, Code=1 for GET method. The parameters are omitted in the figure due to the limitation of space), the server's response contains an acknowledgment, echoing the same Message ID, as well as the resource presentation (Code=69(2.05 Content)). The corresponding test case is illustrated in Fig.6-(b). The bold part of the test case represents the expected behavior that leads to *Pass* verdict. Behavior that is not forbidden by the specifications leads to *Inconclusive* verdict (for example, response contains a code other than 69. These events are noted by *m* in the figure for the sake of simplicity). However other unexpected behavior leads to *Fail* verdict (labeled by *Otherwise*). The test cases are derived, validated by the experts of IRISA, BUPT, ETSI and IPSO Alliance w.r.t the specifications of CoAP. They are implemented in the testing tool, taking into account all the verdicts. For simplicity, during the test event, only expected behavior to be observed is provided to the users as test specification document (Fig.6-(c)). Nevertheless, in case of *Inconclusive* or *Fail* verdicts, an explication will be provided to the users.

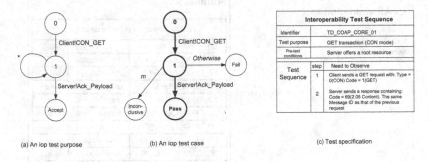

(a) An iop test purpose   (b) An iop test case   (c) Test specification

Fig. 6. Example of test purpose and test case

4.3 CoAP Plugtest

CoAP Plugtest[14] is the first formal interoperability event, held in Paris, March 2012 during two days for CoAP protocol in the scope of Internet of Things. It was co-organized by the Probe-IT[15] (the European project in the context of Internet of things), the IPSO Alliance and ETSI[16] (the European Telecommunication Standard Institute). The objective of the CoAP plugtest is to enable CoAP implementation vendors to test end to end interoperability with each other. Also, it is an opportunity for standards development organization to review the ambiguities in the protocol specifications. 15 main developers and vendors of CoAP implementations, such as Sensinode[17], Watteco[18], Actility[19], etc. participated in the event. Test sessions are scheduled by ETSI so that each participant can test their products with all the other partners.

---

[14] http://www.etsi.org/plugtests/coap/coap.htm
[15] http://www.probe-it.eu/
[16] http://www.etsi.org/
[17] http://www.sensinode.com/
[18] http://www.watteco.com/
[19] http://www.actility.com/

The testing method is based on the technique of passive testing as described in Section 3. During the test, the participants start launching their equipments. Packets exchanged between CoAP implementations (CoAP client and CoAP server) were captured by using *Wireshark*[20]. Captured traces were analyzed against the test cases by using the passive testing tool presented in Section 3.4. For CoAP Plugtest, the tool was developed to support the message formats of the CoAP drafts. It checks the basic message type code as well as parameters such as token or message ID. CoAP test suite is implemented. During the plugtest, 410 traces produced by the CoAP devices were captured and then submitted and processed by the passive validation tool. Received traces are filtered, parsed and analyzed against the test cases. And an appropriate verdict *Pass, Fail,* or *Inconclusive* is issued for each test purpose. A use case of the tool is as follows:

CoAP validation tool	Summary		
Version: 20120325_43	ip6-localhost (::1) vs ip6-localhost (::1)		
	TD_COAP_CORE_01	7 occurence(s)	inconc
Submit your traces (pcap format)	TD_COAP_CORE_02	2 occurence(s)	fail
Choisissez un fichier Aucun f... choisi	TD_COAP_CORE_03	2 occurence(s)	fail
	TD_COAP_CORE_04	0 occurence(s)	none
☐ I agree to leave a copy of this file on the server (for debugging purpose)	TD_COAP_CORE_05	0 occurence(s)	none
	TD_COAP_CORE_06	0 occurence(s)	none
Valider	TD_COAP_CORE_07	0 occurence(s)	none
	TD_COAP_CORE_08	0 occurence(s)	none
⑤ IRISA	TD_COAP_CORE_09	7 occurence(s)	inconc

```
Testcase TD_COAP_CORE_01

Conversation 1 -> inconc

<Frame    1: [::1                     -> ::1        ] CoAP [CON 0xaeca] GET />
   [ pass | match: CoAP (type=0, code=1)
<Frame    2: [::1                     -> ::1        ] CoAP [ACK 0xaeca] 2.16 Success >
   [ inconc | mismatch: Coap (code=69, mid=0xaeca)
          CoAP.code: ValueMismatch
               got:      89
               expected: 69
```

Fig. 7. Trace verification tool use case

The top left image is the user interface of the tool. Users can submit their traces in pcap format. Then, the tool will execute the trace verification algorithm and return back the results as shown at the top right corner in the summary table. In this table, the number of occurrence of each test case in the trace is counted, as well as a verdict *Pass, Fail* or *Inconc(lusive)* is given (For a test case which does not appear in the trace, it is marked as *"none"* and will not be verified on the trace). Moreover, users can view the details about the verdict for each test case. In this example, test case TD_COAP_CORE_1 (GET method in CON mode) is met 7 times in the trace. The verdict is *Inconclusive,* as explained by the tool: *CoAP.code ValueMismatch* (cf. the bottom of Fig.7).

---

[20] http://www.wireshark.org/

In fact, according to the test case, after that the client sends a request (with Type value 0 and Code value 1 for a confirmable GET message), the server should send a response containing Code value 69(2.05 Content). However in the obtained trace, the server's response contains Code value 80, indicating that the request is successfully received without further information. This response is not forbidden in the specification, however does not allow to satisfy the test case. In fact, the same situation exists in all the other conversations that correspond to this test case. Therefore, the global verdict for this test purpose is *Inconclusive*.

4.4 Results

The CoAP plugtest was a success with regards to the number of executed tests (3081) and the test results (shown in the sequel). The feedback from participants on the testing method and passive validation tool is positive mainly due to the following aspects:

- To our knowledge, it is the first time that an interoperability event is conducted by using automatic passive testing approach. In fact, conventional interoperability methods that rely on *active testing* are often complicated and error-prone. According to our previous experience [8], active testing requires usually experts for installation, configuration, and cannot be run reliably by the vendors. Also, test cases are not flexible, as they involve the ordering of tests, needs to re-run a test, etc. Moreover, inappropriate test configuration cause often false verdicts. By using passive testing, complicated test configuration is avoided. Bug fixes in the tool do not require re-running the test. Moreover, it provides the ability to test products in operational environment.
- Also, the passive testing tool shows its various advantages: By using passive testing tool, the participants only need to submit their traces via a web interface. The human readable test reports provided by the validation tool makes the reason of non-interoperable behavior be clear at a glance. Besides, another advantage of the validation tool is that it can be used outside of an interoperability event. In fact, the participants started trying the tool one week before the event by submitting more than 200 traces via internet. This allows the participants to prepare in advance the test event. Also, passive automated trace analysis allows to considerably increase the efficiency. During the CoAP plugtest, 3081 tests were executed within two days, which are considerable. Compared with past conventional plugtest event, e.g. IMS InterOp Plugtest[21], 900 tests in 3 days, the number of test execution and validation benefited a drastic increase.
- Moreover, the passive testing tool not only validates test purposes, but also shows its capability of non-interoperability detection: Among all the traces, 5.9% reveal non-interoperability w.r.t basic RESTful methods; 7.8% for Link Format, 13.4% for Blockwise transfer and 4.3% for resource observation. The results help the vendors discover the blocking issues and to achieve higher quality implementations.

---

[21] http://www.etsi.org/plugtests/ims2/About_IMS2.htm

5 Conclusion and Future Work

In this paper, we have proposed a passive interoperability testing methodology for request-response protocols. According to their interaction mode, the traces collected during the test were analyzed to verify the occurrence of the test cases. Also, interoperability is determined by comparing each event in the test case with that of its related conversation(s) in the trace. The trace verification procedure has been automated by implementing a testing tool, which was successfully put into operation in the first interoperability testing event of CoAP protocol, where an amount of protocol applications were tested, and non-interoperable behavior was detected. Future work intends to improve the passive validation tool. E.g online trace verification and solutions to solve message overlapping will be considered. Also, the tool is considered to be extended to a wider range of protocols and more complex test configurations.

References

1. Shelby, Z., Hartke, K., Frank, B.: Constrained application protocol (CoAP), draft-ietf-core-coap-08 (2011)
2. Baire, A., Viho, C., Chen, N.: Long-term challenges in TTCN-3 a prototype to explore new features and concepts. In: ETSI TTCN-3 User Conference and Model Based Testing Workshop Conference (2012)
3. Arnedo, J.A., Cavalli, A., Núñez, M.: Fast Testing of Critical Properties through Passive Testing. In: Hogrefe, D., Wiles, A. (eds.) TestCom 2003. LNCS, vol. 2644, pp. 295–310. Springer, Heidelberg (2003)
4. Seol, S., Kim, M., Kang, S., Chanson, S.T.: Interoperability test generation and minimization for communication protocols based on the multiple stimuli principle. IEEE Journal on selected areas in Communications 22(10), 2062–2074 (2004)
5. Zaidi, F., Cavalli, A., Bayse, E.: Network Protocol Interoperability Testing based on Contextual Signatures. In: The 24th Annual ACM Symposium on Applied Computing, SAC 2009 (2009)
6. Lee, D., Netravali, A.N., Sabnani, K.K., Sugla, B., John, A.: Passive testing and applications to network management. In: Int. Conference on Network Protocols, ICNP 1997, pp. 113–122 (1997)
7. ISO. Information Technology - Open System Interconnection Conformance Testing, Methodology and Framework, Parts 1-7. International Standard ISO/IEC 9646/1-7 (1994)
8. Sabiguero, A., Baire, A., Boutet, A., Viho, C.: Virtualized Interoperability Testing: Application to IPv6 Network Mobility. In: 18th IFIP/IEEE Int. Workshop on Distributed Syst.: Operations and Management (2007)
9. Verhaard, L., Tretmans, J., Kars, P.: Brinksma, Ed.: On asynchronous testing. In: Protocol Test Systems. IFIP Transactions, vol. C-11, pp. 55–66 (1992)
10. Fielding, R.T.: Architectural Styles and the Design of Network-based Software Architectures, Doctoral dissertation, University of California (2000)
11. Desmoulin, A., Viho, C.: Automatic Interoperability Test Case Generation Based on Formal Definitions. In: Leue, S., Merino, P. (eds.) FMICS 2007. LNCS, vol. 4916, pp. 234–250. Springer, Heidelberg (2008)
12. Falcone, Y., Fernandez, J.C., Mounier, L.: Runtime Verification of Safety-Progress Properties. In: Bensalem, S., Peled, D.A. (eds.) RV 2009. LNCS, vol. 5779, pp. 40–59. Springer, Heidelberg (2009)

Using Knapsack Problem Model to Design a Resource Aware Test Architecture for Adaptable and Distributed Systems

Mariam Lahami, Moez Krichen, Mariam Bouchakwa, and Mohamed Jmaiel

Research Unit of Development and Control of Distributed Applications
National School of Engineering of Sfax, University of Sfax
Sokra Road km 4, PB 1173 Sfax, Tunisia
{mariam.lahami,moez.krichen,mariam.bouchakwa}@redcad.org,
mohamed.jmaiel@enis.rnu.tn
http://www.redcad.org

Abstract. This work focuses on testing the consistency of distributed and adaptable systems. In this context, *Runtime Testing* which is carried out on the final execution environment is emerging as a new solution for quality assurance and validation of these systems. This activity can be costly and resource consuming especially when execution environment is shared between the software system and the test system. To overcome this challenging problem, we propose a new approach to design a resource aware test architecture. We consider the best usage of available resources (such as CPU load, memory, battery level, etc.) in the execution nodes while assigning the test components to them. Hence, this work describes basically a method for test component placement in the execution environment based on an existing model called *Multiple Multidimensional Knapsack Problem*. A tool based on the constraint programming Choco library has been also implemented.

1 Introduction

Adaptable and distributed systems are characterized by the possibility of dynamically changing their behaviors or structures at runtime in order to preserve their usefulness and achieve new requirements. They evolve continuously by integrating new components, deleting faulty or unneeded ones and substituting old components by new versions without service interruption.

In order to preserve the system safety and consistency and to check functional as well as non-functional requirements during and after dynamic adaptation, a validation technique, such as *Runtime Testing*, has to be applied. It is defined in [1] as any testing method that has to be carried out in the final execution environment of a system while it is performing its normal work.

In a previous work [2], we have proposed a flexible and evolvable distributed test architecture made of two kinds of test components. These test components execute unit tests (respectively integration tests) on the affected components (respectively component compositions) with the aim of detecting reconfiguration faults. To do

B. Nielsen and C. Weise (Eds.): ICTSS 2012, LNCS 7641, pp. 103–118, 2012.
© IFIP International Federation for Information Processing 2012

this, they send stimuli to the System Under Test (SUT) in order to verify that it responds as expected. The main challenging problem here is that the test execution is done while the SUT is running. Also, test components are usually deployed and executed in the same execution environment with the SUT. Consequently, SUT performance can be highly influenced especially when execution nodes have scarce resources or testing processes are very resource consuming.

Therefore, placing efficiently test components can be a useful solution to reduce runtime testing cost. This activity has to be resource aware by respecting all resource constraints in order not to disturb the SUT performance and not burden the execution nodes.

Various research efforts have addressed the resource aware testing activity such as [3,4]. They focus mainly on optimizing the generation of test cases with the best usage of available resources. To our best knowledge, there is only two visible research works [5,6] being carried out the issue of test component placement with respecting only some resource constraints and some user preferences. Connectivity constraints which are stated with the aim of reducing communications cost over the network between components under test and testers are ignored in these approaches.

In this paper, we propose a resource aware test architecture design phase before executing runtime tests while the system evolves dynamically. Essentially, we have studied the issue of test component placement in a shared execution environment with the SUT. Two main kinds of constraints are considered : resource and connectivity constraints. Hence, the most important question to be tackled in this paper is: How to place test components in the adequate nodes in order to fit these constraints? To solve this problem, we have modeled it using an existing model in the combinatorial optimization area, called *Multiple Multidimensional Knapsack Problem*. In addition, an implementation of a tool based on the Choco solver has been presented. Also, some experiments have been done to evaluate the proposed approach.

The remainder of this paper is organized as follows. We begin by a motivating example in Section 2. A brief description of related work is addressed in section 3. Section 4 overviews the resource aware test architecture design phase and outlines particularly the test component placement over the execution nodes fitting resource and connectivity constraints. In Section 5, we present our test component placement method based on the Knapsack Problem (KP) model. First, we introduce concisely the background of the standard KP and its diverse forms. Next, we illustrate the mathematical modeling of the placement problem using a new KP variant called *Multiple Multidimensional Knapsack Problem*. The realization of this approach is provided in Section 6. Some experiments for execution time measuring of the placement method are conducted in section 7. Finally, Section 8 concludes the paper and draws some future work.

2   Motivating Example

Consider an execution environment made of four nodes ($N1, N2, N3$ and $N4$) which are offering some free resources as illustrated in table 1. Some software components ($C1,C2,C3,C4$ and $C5$) are running and distributed among these nodes. We assume that a dynamic reconfiguration occurs and all these components are affected by this modification. Thus, they have to be tested in order to ensure that they still behave as intended.

Table 1. Execution node characteristics

Nodes	Free RAM	CPU Load	Components
$N1$	50 %	20 %	$C1, C2$
$N2$	40 %	30 %	$C3$
$N3$	35 %	50%	$C4$
$N4$	60 %	60 %	$C5$

Table 2. Test component characteristics

Testers	Required RAM	CPU usage	CUTs
$T1$	10 %	10 %	$C1$
$T2$	10 %	5 %	$C2$
$T3$	15 %	10 %	$C4$
$T4$	20 %	15 %	$C5$

For this reason, some test components have to be deployed in this shared execution environment. These test components require some computational resources as depicted in table 2. With the aim of not disturbing the running SUT and reducing test burdens, they have to be assigned to the execution nodes efficiently while fitting some resource constraints. In this example, we consider just two kinds of computational resources: RAM and CPU. It is worthy to note that others resources like battery level and hard disk space can be included. Furthermore, we assume for simplicity that memories and processors in execution nodes have approximately the same capacities.

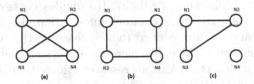

Fig. 1. Execution environment modeling using graphs

Besides resource constraints, connectivity issue in the execution environment has to be also tackled. If all nodes are connected together as a strongly connex graph or even a connex graph (see Figure 1 (a), (b)), test components can be assigned to any node in the environment in order to perform runtime tests. Nevertheless, we are faced sometimes with some connectivity problems[1] that can be arisen due to Firewalls, non-routing networks [7], node mobility, etc. In this case, connectivity constraints have to be considered while assigning test components to nodes. For example, while non routing is performed between the node $N4$ and the rest of the execution environment as depicted in Figure 1 (c) the test component $T4$, which is responsible of testing the component under test (CUT) $C5$, can be hosted only in the node $N4$. It is not allowed to place $T4$ in $N1$, $N2$ or even $N3$ because no route is available to communicate

---

[1] For instance, wireless communication networks are characterized by frequent and unpredictable changes in connectivity.

with the component under test $C5$. In the same way, the other test components can be assigned to any node except $N4$. This illustrative example is detailed progressively in the following sections of the paper. Placement solutions are also given in section 5.

3   Related Work

Since runtime testing is performed while the system is operational, the business process execution may be affected by testing activities and the system performance may be negatively influenced. Therefore, test isolation techniques (such as SUT duplication, tagging, SUT blocking, etc.) are required to separate testing processes from business processes [8,9,10]. In addition, testing activities have to be resource aware with the aim of minimizing execution nodes burdens while runtime tests are executed. The first issue is out of the scope of this paper. We mainly concentrate on studying the resource aware testing activity [3,4].

Fitting resource and connectivity constraints while testing distributed and adaptable systems at runtime is included in a larger class called *context aware testing* [11,12]. The latter has recently emerged to validate especially new class of software systems which are context aware and adaptive, also known as *Ubiquitous* or *Pervasive* systems [4]. This kind of systems can sense their surrounding environment and adapt their behavior accordingly. In [13], the author generally defines the context as any information that can be used to characterize the situation of an entity (which can be a person, a machine or any object including a service, a software component, or data). He divides context into two main categories: external context (which contains information about the users, their location, time, etc.) and resource context (which describes the available resources on nodes and communication links like memory, CPU load, battery level, bandwidth between two nodes, etc.). Various research efforts have addressed testing activity with considering resource context such as [3,4]. They focus mainly on optimizing the generation of test cases with the best usage of available resources but without studying the placement and the deployment cost of test components.

To our best knowledge, there is only two visible research works related to test component placement under resource constraints and user preferences. In the first work [5], the authors propose a function for distributing a set of test components, which are belonging to a test configuration implemented in TTCN-3 standard[2][14], on different test nodes (computers that are dedicated for test execution). The proposed mathematical function is applied at deployment time separately for each test component in order to assign it to a node where it will be deployed and also executed. It considers two types of parameters when distributing test components in the adequate test nodes: external parameters such as CPU load, memory consumption and internal parameters like the number of components that can be hosted in a specific test node. The second work presented in [6] mainly focuses on the dynamic deployment of test components also

---

[2] Testing and Test Control Notation version 3 (TTCN-3) standard offers a standardized test notation and an execution platform facilitating the deployment and the execution of test components, http://www.ttcn-3.org/

implemented in TTCN-3 standard. It proposes an approach for designing load tests and distributing test components efficiently with considering the available workstation resources. The major problem here is that these approaches do not define explicitly the proposed distributed function used for test components assignment to test nodes. Moreover, they focus mainly on computational resources and they ignore connectivity constraints.

Unlike these approaches, our work aims at defining a novel method for assigning test components to execution nodes in a way fitting both resource and connectivity constraints. This challenging issue has been widely addressed in other research areas. First, an interesting work is presented in [15] that aims to optimize resource allocation and the placement of Java components by using a graph mapping approach. The latter consists in modeling the application by a software graph and the execution environment by a hardware graph. The main purpose here is to map as best as possible the software graph on the hardware graph. Other approaches have studied the placement issue based on constraint programming, which aims to model and solve combinatory problems, such as [16,17]. By extending the *Multiple Knapsack Problem* model, [16] proposes a method for assigning sensors in virtual environments. Hermenier [17] presents a flexible architecture that adapts the placement of virtual machines in grids with response to requirements analysis, resources states and some placement constraints defined by the user. The problem here is similar to *Two-Dimensional Bin Packing* problem. The classical problem consists in packing objects with different volumes into a finite number of bins having a predefined capacity in a way that minimizes the number of bins used. Following the same principle, Hermenier's work aims to minimize the number of nodes in the grid involved in the placement of virtual machines while satisfying resource constraints such as CPU load and memory consumption. Both introduced approaches use the Choco solver [18] in order to solve the placement problem. In the rest of this paper, our proposal that is inspired from the constraint programming based approaches will be highlighted.

4   Resource Aware Test Architecture Design

After a dynamic evolution of the system, runtime testing process is started to validate these changes. Only the affected parts of the system are considered in the testing activity. In Figure 2, two fundamental steps are outlined: *Test Architecture Design* and *Test Component Placement*. They will be detailed in the following subsections.

4.1   Test Architecture Design

This activity consists in defining for each affected component or composition the kind of test component to deploy and the test cases to execute. As illustrated in Figure 3, the elements involved in a distributed test architecture (DTA), their kind and their number depend on the affected parts of the system by a reconfiguration action. In our previous work [2], we defined a *Single Component Tester* (SCT) which is in charge of executing unit tests once a single component

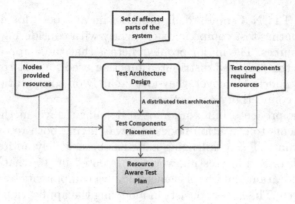

Fig. 2. Resource Aware Test Architecture Design

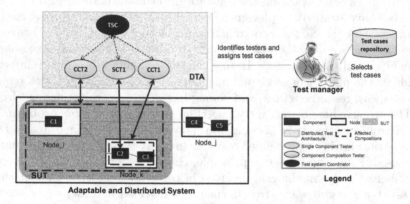

Fig. 3. Overview of a detailed Distributed Test Architecture

has been changed or newly added at runtime. Moreover, *Component Composition Tester* (CCT) is introduced to validate the affected component compositions. These two kinds of testers communicate with a *Test System Coordinator* (TSC) which is charged with generating a global verdict depending on local verdicts of SCTs and CCTs.

In this work, we suppose that for each adaptation process a test manager which is responsible for controlling and managing all the runtime testing processes is introduced. It defines the adequate test architecture and assigns test cases. We also assume that during deployment phase, test cases are available and stored in a repository for further use. They can be also updated or new ones can be added if behavioral adaptations occur.

4.2   Test Component Placement

Once the distributed test architecture is elaborated, we have to assign its constituents to the execution nodes. It is worth noting that in this work we focus on assigning mainly single components testers to the execution nodes. The placement issue of component composition testers is out the scope of this paper.

Test component placement is more challenging when tests are executed at runtime. In fact, test components may share the same execution environment with the running SUT. This may burden some execution nodes of the SUT and may have a bad impact on the SUT performance. Also, it may sometimes cause malfunctions. To resolve this problem, we concentrate in this work on proposing a new method for adapting the test components deployment at runtime to the resource situation of the execution nodes and also to connectivity constraints.

– Consideration of Resource Allocation Issue

We first introduce the considered resources for nodes as well as for test components. For each node in the execution environment, three resources are monitored during SUT execution: the available memory, the provided CPU and the battery level. The value of each resource can be directly captured on each node through the use of internal monitors. These values are measured after the runtime reconfiguration and before starting the testing activity.

For each test component, we introduce the memory size (the memory occupation needed by a test component in execution), CPU load and battery consumption properties. We suppose that these properties values are provided by the test manager. It is also worth noting that some techniques are available in the literature for obtaining the required resources by testers. For example in [5], the authors propose a preliminary test to learn about some required resources such as the amount of memory allocated by a test component, the time needed to execute the test behavior, etc.

– Consideration of Connectivity Issue

Regarding the connectivity constraints, we consider that each test component has to find at least one route to communicate with the component under test. As mentioned before, this constraint can be ignored when all nodes are communicating together. In this case, the execution environment is modeled as a connected graph. Recall that in the graph theory, a graph is connected if for every pair of vertices, there is a path in the graph between those vertices. Hence, each test component can be assigned to any node and it can communicate with the node under test either locally or remotely.

In the worst case, whereas some connectivity problems occur [7], the execution environment is considered not connected. In this situation, the graph is obviously decomposed in several *connected components* as we have seen in the illustrative example (see Figure 1 (c)). Therefore, for each test component we have to pinpoint a set of forbidden nodes to avoid when the placement procedure is done. For instance, the set of forbidden nodes for the test component $T1$ contains $N4$. From a technical perspective, either depth-first[3] or breadth-first[4] algorithm can

---

[3] http://en.wikipedia.org/wiki/Depth-first_search
[4] http://en.wikipedia.org/wiki/Breadth-first_search

be used to firstly identify the connected components and secondly to compute the forbidden nodes for each test component involved in the test architecture.

We can also associate for each node a profit. While the tester is placed in the same node with the component under test, the profit is maximal because the communications cost over the network will be reduced. It decreases once the tester is placed far from the component under test.

In the rest of this paper, we suppose that the execution environment has been modeled as a connex graph. Even when the obtained graph is disconnected, we have to compute the connected components and apply the same adopted method for placement to these sub-graphs. In the next section, we formalize the placement problem using a variant of the Knapsack Problem under assumptions like: provided resources for each node are accessible and required resources for each test component are available too.

5   Mathematical Modeling of the Test Component Placement

5.1   Background

The *Knapsack Problem* (KP) is a well-studied, $\mathcal{NP}$-hard combinatorial optimization problem. It has been used to model different applications for instance in computer science and financial management. It considers a set of n objects $O = o_1, \ldots, o_n$ and a knapsack of capacity W. Each object o_j has an associated profit p_j and weight w_j. The objective is to find a subset $S \subseteq O$ in such a way that the weight sum over the objects in S does not exceed the knapsack capacity and yields a maximum profit [19,20,21].

The most basic form of *Knapsack Problem* (KP) is formulated as follows:

$$KP = \begin{cases} maximize \quad z = \sum_{j=1}^{n} p_j x_j \\ subject \quad to \quad \sum_{j=1}^{n} w_j x_j \leq W \\ x_j \in \{0,1\} \quad \forall j \in \{1, \cdots, n\} \end{cases}$$

In the literature, we found many variants of this problem. Due to space limitations, we describe in details only the two models used in our context:

The Multidimensional Knapsack Problem (MDKP). is also called Multiply constrained Knapsack Problem or m-dimensional knapsack problem. It can be viewed as a resource allocation model and can be modeled as follows:

$$MDKP = \begin{cases} maximize \quad z = \sum_{j=1}^{n} p_j x_j \\ subject \quad to \quad \sum_{j=1}^{n} w_{ij} x_j \leq c_i \quad \forall i \in \{1, \cdots, m\} \\ x_j \in \{0,1\} \quad \forall j \in \{1, \cdots, n\} \end{cases}$$

Where a set of n items with profits $p_j > 0$ and m resources with capacities $c_i > 0$ are given. Each item j consumes an amount $w_{ij} \geq 0$ from each resource i. The 0-1 decision variables x_j indicate which items are selected. The main purpose is to choose a subset of items with maximum total profit. Selected items must not exceed resource capacities. This is expressed by the knapsack constraints [21]. Obviously, the KP is a special case of the multidimensional knapsack problem with $m = 1$.

The 0-1 Multiple Knapsack Problem (0-1 MKP). is the problem of assigning a subset of n items to m distinct knapsacks having different capacities [22,23]. It is also referenced as the 0-1 integer programming problem or the 0-1 linear programming problem. More formally, a MKP is stated as follows:

$$
MKP = \begin{cases}
maximize \quad z = \sum_{i=1}^{m} \sum_{j=1}^{n} p_j x_{ij} \\
subject \quad to \quad \sum_{j=1}^{n} w_j x_{ij} \leq W_i \quad \forall i \in \{1, \cdots, m\} \\
\sum_{i=1}^{m} x_{ij} \leq 1 \quad \forall j \in \{1, \cdots, n\} \\
x_{ij} \in \{0, 1\} \quad \forall j \in \{1, \cdots, n\} \quad and \quad \forall i \in \{1, \cdots, m\}
\end{cases}
$$

5.2   Our Mathematical Modeling

Mathematically, our placement problem can be modeled by merging the two introduced knapsack variants: multidimensional and multiple knapsack problems. The obtained model is called *Multiple Multidimensional Knapsack Problem* (MMKP). It is worthy to note that this new variant of the standard KP has rarely been addressed in the literature except in [24]. We assume that the execution environment consists of m nodes and we have n test components that may be assigned to them. We attempt to find an optimal solution of test component placement not violating resource and connectivity constraints and also maximizing their placement profit. We can formulate this problem using the MMKP variant as follows:

$$
MMKP = \begin{cases}
maximize \quad \mathcal{Z} = \sum_{i=1}^{n} \sum_{j=1}^{m} p_{ij} x_{ij} \quad (1) \\
subject \quad to \quad \sum_{i=1}^{n} x_{ij} dc_i \leq c_j \quad \forall j \in \{1, \cdots, m\} \quad (2) \\
\sum_{i=1}^{n} x_{ij} dr_i \leq r_j \quad \forall j \in \{1, \cdots, m\} \quad (3) \\
\sum_{i=1}^{n} x_{ij} db_i \leq b_j \quad \forall j \in \{1, \cdots, m\} \quad (4) \\
\sum_{j=1}^{m} x_{ij} = 1 \quad \forall i \in \{1, \cdots, n\} \quad (5) \\
x_{ij} \in \{0, 1\} \quad \forall i \in \{1, \cdots, n\} \quad and \quad \forall j \in \{1, \cdots, m\}
\end{cases}
$$

The provided resources by the m nodes are given through three vectors: C that contains the provided CPU, R that provides the available RAM and B that contains the battery level of each node.

$$C = \begin{pmatrix} c_1 \\ c_2 \\ \vdots \\ c_m \end{pmatrix} \quad R = \begin{pmatrix} r_1 \\ r_2 \\ \vdots \\ r_m \end{pmatrix} \quad B = \begin{pmatrix} b_1 \\ b_2 \\ \vdots \\ b_m \end{pmatrix}$$

In addition, the required resources for each test component are illustrated over three vectors: D_c that carries the required CPU, D_r that contains the required RAM and D_b that contains the required Battery by each tester.

$$D_c = \begin{pmatrix} dc_1 \\ dc_2 \\ \vdots \\ dc_n \end{pmatrix} \quad D_r = \begin{pmatrix} dr_1 \\ dr_2 \\ \vdots \\ dr_n \end{pmatrix} \quad D_b = \begin{pmatrix} db_1 \\ db_2 \\ \vdots \\ db_n \end{pmatrix}$$

Similarly, we define the two dimensional variable, x_{ij} as follows:

$$x_{ij} = \begin{cases} 1 & \text{if } \textit{tester i is assigned to node j} \\ 0 & \text{otherwise} \end{cases}$$

We may find a feasible solution of test component placement if the objective function (1) is omitted. Otherwise, an optimal solution is computed that maximizes the placement profit. For doing this, a matrix $\mathcal{P}$ has been introduced which is filled with a profit value of each test component in response to execution nodes. This matrix depends on the length path between the node under test[5] and the node hosting the test component. The profit p_{ij} can be equal to a predefined value $maxP$ if the test component i is assigned to a node j which corresponds to the node under test. It can be equal to $maxP - l$ if the test component i is assigned to a node j reachable from the node under test via a path having the length l. The constraints (2),(3) and (4) ensure that the overall required resources by the testers can not exceed the available resources in each node. They are called knapsack constraints similar to the standard knapsack problem. The equality (5) indicates that all testers have to be assigned to the execution nodes and each of them has to be placed in at most one node.

It is worthy to note that in this work we have chosen the distance between nodes as criteria for filling the matrix $\mathcal{P}$. However, other placement criteria can be used such as bandwidth utilization. Furthermore, this solution is dedicated for a connected network. Even if some connectivity problems occur, we apply the proposed model for each connected component in the network. Thus, we obtain in this case partial placement solution.

---

[5] The node hosting the component under test

5.3   Illustration

We use the previously studied example in section 2 to illustrate the feasibility of our proposal. In case of connectivity problem as shown in Figure 1 (c), the node $N4$ is forbidden to host testers $T1, T2$ and $T3$. In this case, the placement problem is divided into two sub-problems. In the first one, we consider the connected nodes ($N1, N2$ and $N3$) while searching placement solution for test components $T1, T2$ and $T3$. In the second one, we study the possibility of assigning the test component $T4$ to $N4$. In the following, we detail the first sub-problem as illustrated in Figure 4. First, we introduce for instance the RAM and CPU constraints for the node $N1$ when all nodes in the network are connected:

$$10x_{11} + 10x_{21} + 15x_{31} \leq 50. \tag{1}$$

$$10x_{11} + 5x_{21} + 10x_{31} \leq 20. \tag{2}$$

Next, the objective function is formed as follows with considering that the $maxP$ value is equal to α and $maxP - 1$ is equal to β in this example.

$$\mathcal{Z} = \alpha x_{11} + \beta x_{21} + \beta x_{31} + \alpha x_{12} + \beta x_{22} + \beta x_{32} + \beta x_{13} + \beta x_{23} + \alpha x_{33}. \tag{3}$$

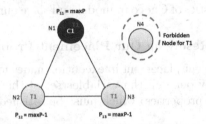

Fig. 4. Illustration Example

The formed MMKP seeks to maximize the equation (3) subject to the constraints such as defined in equations (1) and (2). In the following, we illustrate the derivation of an exact solution of such problem using a well known constraint programming solver called Choco.

6   Realization

To solve our test component placement problem which is modeled as MMKP, we propose a tool illustrated in Figure 5. As inputs, it takes three XML[6] files: nodes provided resources, testers required resources and tester profits. As output, it generates an XML based resource aware test plan which contains for each tester the adequate host to be deployed on. The core of this tool is based on the open source Choco Java library. In the following subsections, we first introduce the Choco library. Next, we demonstrate the mapping between the mathematical formalism to the Choco Java code.

---

[6] eXtensible Markup Language.

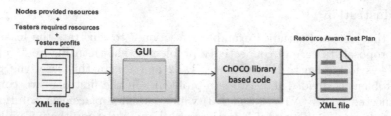

Fig. 5. Architecture of Choco based tool

6.1   Choco Library

Choco is introduced in [18] as a Java library for constraint satisfaction problems (CSP) and constraint programming (CP). It is an open source software which offers a problem modeler and a constraint programming solver. The first one is able to manipulate a large variety of variable types and supports over 70 constraints. The second one can be used in satisfaction mode by computing one solution, all solutions or iterating them. Also, it can be used in an optimization mode (maximization and minimization). We selected this solver because it seems to be one of the most popular within the research community and because it is reliable and stable open source Java solver. In the following, we show how to make use of these two fundamental characteristics of Choco to model and solve our placement problem.

6.2   Modeling and Resolving Our Placement Problem with Choco

To solve the test component placement in execution nodes formulated as MMKP, we use Choco library by defining the variables set of the problem and stating constraints (conditions, properties) which must be satisfied by the solution.

```
1  //Model declaration
2  CPModel model = new CPModel();
3  // Variables declaration
4  IntegerVariable[][] X = new IntegerVariable[n][m];
5  for (int i = 0; i < n; i++) {
6  for (int j = 0; j < m; j++) {
7          X[i][j] = Choco.makeIntVar("X" + i+j, 0, 1);}}
8  //objective variable declaration
9  IntegerVariable Z = Choco.makeIntVar("gain", 1, 1000000,Options.V_OBJECTIVE);
10 //Constraints definition
11 // ...
12 Constraint[] rows = new Constraint[n];
13 for (int i = 0; i < n; i++)
14    rows[i] = Choco.eq(Choco.sum(X[i]), 1);}
15 model.addConstraints(rows);
16 //Objective function
17 IntegerExpressionVariable []exp1=new IntegerExpressionVariable [n];
18 for (int i = 0; i < n; i++)
19    exp1[i]=Choco.scalar(g[i], X[i]);
20 model.addConstraint(Choco.eq(Choco.sum(exp1),Z));
21 //Solve the problem
22 Solver s = new CPSolver();
23 s.read(model);
24 s.maximize(s.getVar(Z), false);
```

Listing 1. Choco code example

The above Listing 1 presents a brief overview of the model translation from the mathematical representation of our problem to Choco code. In line 7, it shows the declaration of the x_{ij} variable and its domain. Moreover, we display in line 9 the declaration of the objective function that maximize the gain of test component placement. Stating the constraint (5) using the Choco syntax has been illustrated in line 14. To solve the placement problem, two cases exist : obtaining a satisfying solution or an optimal solution. The latter case is illustrated in the line 24.

7   Experimentation

In this section, we present some experiments that are conducted to evaluate the execution time (order of milliseconds) needed for the placement phase. Two cases have been studied in the following subsections. First, we measure the time needed by calculating a satisfying solution. Next, we compute the execution time while optimal solution is required.

All of the experiments were conducted on a PC with Intel Core 2 Duo CPU and 2 GB of main memory having as operating system Microsoft vista. The number of nodes is equal to the number of testers in all the experiments that we have done. Also, we have to note that each experiment is carried out five times to derive the precise average execution time of the placement phase.

7.1   Computation of a Feasible Solution

The graph of Figure 6 shows the average execution time required by the Choco solver to compute a satisfying solution. Analysis of the results indicates that the average time required for assigning test components to execution nodes increases with the increase in number of test components and nodes. The proposed solver may resolve this $\mathcal{NP}$-hard problem in a reasonable amount of time while the number of test components and nodes does not exceed some dozens. Such solution can be sufficient especially when the affected parts of the system to validate after dynamic reconfiguration are not important also when the execution environment is not large.

7.2   Computation of an Optimal Solution

Recall that in this case we search for an exact solution that maximizes the placement profits by assigning test components to the adequate execution nodes. By computing such solution, we aim to reduce the communication cost over the network between the test components and the components under test. As illustrated in Figure 7, the calculation of the optimal solution takes a significant time especially when the number of test components and nodes increases. We have to note that this computation technique can be opted when the dynamic changes are not frequently done. Thus, we have enough time to validate them. Otherwise, it can be enhanced by the use of some predefined heuristics in Choco library.

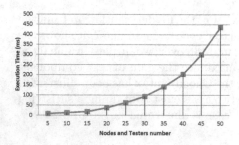
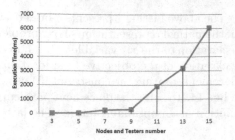

Fig. 6. Execution time needed for computing a feasible solution

Fig. 7. Execution time needed for computing an optimal solution

8　Conclusion

In this paper, we have studied the runtime testing of adaptable and distributed systems after the occurrence of dynamic changes. This resource intense testing method is often performed in a resource constrained execution environment. For this reason, defining efficiently the distributed test architecture and the assignment of its components to the execution nodes can be a useful solution for either respecting resource constraints or reducing the cost of testing activity.

To do this, we have proposed a new approach for resource aware test architecture design of adaptable and distributed systems. Our main contribution in this work consists in proposing a method for test component placement in the execution nodes while respecting resource and connectivity constraints. This $\mathcal{NP}$-hard problem has been formulated as a multiple multidimensional knapsack problem. We have also implemented a tool facilitating the resolution of our problem using the Choco Java library.

As future work, we will enhance the proposed solution by adding other resource constraints such as network bandwidth or by associating different weights with the considered resources. Moreover, it is obvious that for large scale systems or systems having hard realtime timing constraints, the proposed method is not suitable. In this case, it might take a lot of time to find the exact solution. Therefore, we investigate effort in enhancing the proposed technique using heuristics.

References

1. Brenner, D., Atkinson, C., Malaka, R., Merdes, M., Paech, B., Suliman, D.: Reducing verification effort in component-based software engineering through built-in testing. Information Systems Frontiers 9(2-3), 151–162 (2007)
2. Lahami, M., Krichen, M., Jmaiel, M.: A Distributed Test Architecture for Adaptable and Distributed Real-Time Systems. In: Journées Nationales IDM, CAL, et du GDR GPL, Lille, France (June 2011)
3. Zhang, X., Shan, H., Qian, J.: Resource-Aware Test Suite Optimization. In: Proceedings of the 2009 Ninth International Conference on Quality Software, QSIC 2009, pp. 341–346. IEEE Computer Society, Washington, DC (2009)

4. Merdes, M., Malaka, R., Suliman, D., Paech, B., Brenner, D., Atkinson, C.: Ubiquitous RATs: how resource-aware run-time tests can improve ubiquitous software systems. In: SEM 2006: Proceedings of the 6th International Workshop on Software Engineering and Middleware, pp. 55–62. ACM, New York (2006)
5. Din, G., Tolea, S., Schieferdecker, I.: Distributed Load Tests with TTCN-3. In: TestCom 2006: Proceedings of International Conference for Testing of Communicating Systems, 18th IFIP TC6/WG6.1, pp. 177–196 (May 2006)
6. Csorba, M., Eottevenyi, D., Palugyai, S.: Experimenting with Dynamic Test Component Deployment in TTCN-3. In: 3rd International Conference on Testbeds and Research Infrastructure for the Development of Networks and Communities, TridentCom 2007, pp. 1–8 (May 2007)
7. Maassen, J., Bal, H.E.: Smartsockets: solving the connectivity problems in grid computing. In: Proceedings of the 16th International Symposium on High Performance Distributed Computing, HPDC 2007, pp. 1–10. ACM, New York (2007)
8. Piel, É., González-Sanchez, A., Groß, H.G.: Automating Integration Testing of Large-Scale Publish/Subscribe Systems. In: Hinze, A., Buchmann, A.P. (eds.) Principles and Applications of Distributed Event-Based Systems, pp. 140–163. IGI Global (2010)
9. Gonzalez, A., Piel, E., Gross, H.G., Glandrup, M.: Testing Challenges of Maritime Safety and Security Systems-of-Systems. In: Proceedings of the Testing: Academic & Industrial Conference - Practice and Research Techniques, pp. 35–39. IEEE Computer Society, Washington, DC (2008)
10. King, T.M., Allen, A.A., Cruz, R., Clarke, P.J.: Safe Runtime Validation of Behavioral Adaptations in Autonomic Software. In: Calero, J.M.A., Yang, L.T., Mármol, F.G., García-Villalba, L.J., Li, X.A., Wang, Y. (eds.) ATC 2011. LNCS, vol. 6906, pp. 31–46. Springer, Heidelberg (2011)
11. Mei, L.: A context-aware orchestrating and choreographic test framework for service-oriented applications. In: ICSE Companion, pp. 371–374. IEEE (2009)
12. Flores, A., Augusto, J.C., Polo, M., Varea, M.: Towards context-aware testing for semantic interoperability on PvC environments. In: SMC (2), pp. 1136–1141. IEEE (2004)
13. Rodriguez, I.B.: Dynamic Software Architecture Management for Collaborative Communicating Systems. PhD thesis, University of Sfax & University of Toulouse (March 2011)
14. ETSI ES 201 873-1 (V3.1.1): Methods for Testing and Specification (MTS); The Testing and Test Control Notation version 3; Part 1: TTCN-3 Core Language (2005)
15. Portigliatti, V., Philippe, L.: Java Components with constraints and preferences in automatic administration of execution and placement. In: PDP, pp. 266–273. IEEE Computer Society (2003)
16. Pizzocaro, D., Chalmers, S., Preece, A.: Sensor assignment in virtual environments using constraint programming. In: Ellis, R., Allen, T., Petridis, M. (eds.) The Twenty-seventh SGAI International Conference on Innovative Techniques and Applications of Artificial Intelligence Applications and Innovations in Intelligent Systems XV: Proceedings of AI 2007. Winner of Best Poster Presentation, AI 2007, pp. 333–338. Springer (2007)
17. Hermenier, F., Lorca, X., Cambazard, H., Menaud, J.M., Jussien, N.: Reconfiguration dynamique du placement dans les grilles de calculs dirigée par des objectifs. In: 6ième Conférence Francophone sur les Systèmes d'Exploitation (CFSE 2006), Fribourg, Switzerland (2008)

18. Jussien, N., Rochart, G., Lorca, X.: Choco: an Open Source Java Constraint Programming Library. In: CPAIOR 2008 Workshop on Open-Source Software for Integer and Contraint Programming (OSSICP 2008), pp. 1–10, Paris, France (2008)
19. Cotta, C., Troya, J.: A hybrid genetic algorithm for the 0-1 multiple knapsack problem. Artificial Neural Nets and Genetic Algorithms 3, 251–255 (1998)
20. Pospíchal, P., Schwarz, J., Jaroš, J.: Parallel Genetic Algorithm Solving 0/1 Knapsack Problem Running on the GPU. In: 16th International Conference on Soft Computing, MENDEL 2010, pp. 64–70. Brno University of Technology (2010)
21. Puchinger, J., Raidl, G.R., Pferschy, U.: The Core Concept for the Multidimensional Knapsack Problem. In: Gottlieb, J., Raidl, G.R. (eds.) EvoCOP 2006. LNCS, vol. 3906, pp. 195–208. Springer, Heidelberg (2006)
22. Martello, S., Toth, P.: Solution of the zero-one multiple knapsack problem. European Journal of Operational Research 4(4), 276–283 (1980)
23. Jansen, K.: Parameterized approximation scheme for the multiple knapsack problem. In: Proceedings of the Twentieth Annual ACM-SIAM Symposium on Discrete Algorithms, SODA 2009, Philadelphia, PA, USA. Society for Industrial and Applied Mathematics, pp. 665–674 (2009)
24. Song, Y., Zhang, C., Fang, Y.: Multiple multidimensional knapsack problem and its applications in cognitive radio networks. In: Military Communications Conference, MILCOM 2008, pp. 1–7. IEEE (November 2008)

Off-Line Test Case Generation for Timed Symbolic Model-Based Conformance Testing*

Boutheina Bannour[1], Jose Pablo Escobedo[2],
Christophe Gaston[2], and Pascale Le Gall[3]

[1] Sherpa Engineering, 92250, La Garenne Colombes, France
b.bannour@sherpa-eng.com
[2] CEA LIST, Point Courrier 174, 91191, Gif-sur-Yvette, France
{jose-pablo.escobedo,christophe.gaston}@cea.fr
[3] Laboratoire MAS, Grande Voie des Vignes, 92195 Châtenay-Malabry, France
pascale.legall@ecp.fr

Abstract. Model-based conformance testing of reactive systems consists in taking benefit from the model for mechanizing both test data generation and verdicts computation. On-line test case generation allows one to apply adaptive on-the-fly analyzes to generate the next inputs to be sent and to decide if observed outputs meet intended behaviors. On the other hand, in off-line approaches, test suites are pre-computed from the model and stored under a format that can be later performed on test-beds. In this paper, we propose a two-passes off-line approach where: for the submission part, a test suite is a simple timed sequence of numerical input data and waiting delays, and then, the timed sequence of output data is post-processed on the model to deliver a verdict. As our models are Timed Output Input Symbolic Transition Systems, our off-line algorithms involve symbolic execution and constraint solving techniques.

Keywords: Model-based testing, off-line testing, real-time systems, test suite generation, verdict computation, symbolic execution, timed output-input symbolic transition systems.

1 Introduction

Using formal methods to generate test cases and to compute verdicts has been widely studied in the frame of Model Based Testing. In the domain of reactive systems, models are often given as *labeled transition systems* which describe the expected sequences of input and output data (called *traces*). Real executions of the System Under Test (SUT) can also be seen as traces. Testing an SUT comes to interact with it to build traces which are analyzed regarding to its model to provide verdicts. In black box testing, an SUT is often hardly controllable at the test execution phase, typically because, for the sake of abstraction, its reference model may include non-deterministic situations (*i.e.* after a given trace, several outputs may occur). For this reason, when dealing with automatic test case

---

* Work partially supported by the ITEA project openETCS.

B. Nielsen and C. Weise (Eds.): ICTSS 2012, LNCS 7641, pp. 119–135, 2012.

generation, approaches in which inputs to be sent to the SUT are computed on-the-fly are very popular: they permit to stimulate it in a flexible manner depending on observed SUT executions, and depending on the goal of the testing process in terms of behaviors to cover. Such approaches are often qualified as *on-line testing*.

The other alternative consists in: computing the full input sequence; submitting the sequence to the SUT; storing the output sequence of the SUT during the execution phase; computing *a posteriori* a verdict by analyzing the trace resulting from the merge of input and output sequences. Such approaches, qualified as *off-line testing* ones, have several advantages. First, computed input sequences can be stored and later translated into several formats, in particular to become compatible with various home made test benches in different industrial contexts. This allows one to avoid the intertwining (unavoidable in on-line approaches) of the test generation/test execution/verdict computation processes, which may be technically hard to achieve. Second, tests can be replayed as many times as desired which makes off-line methods particularly well-adapted for non-regression testing. Third, by construction, no constraint solving delays can interfere with the test data execution. To sum up, off-line testing eases the deployment of input sequences in the test environment and enables their reuse.

However, a particular source of concern about off-line testing is to know at which instants precisely the tester has to send the successive data of the input sequence. Those instants can be identified from the knowledge of a clock cycle or of an hypothesis of an instantaneous reaction in synchronous frameworks (e.g. testing from the clocked data-flow language Lustre in [10] or from Finite State Machines –FSM– in [11]). In asynchronous systems, the waiting delay between two successive inputs is important because the SUT takes time to compute outputs to be sent, and because sending an input before the output computation is complete, or after it is completed, leads to define different execution traces. Therefore, timed models introducing time delays between communication actions are good candidates to support input sequence generation. Moreover, in order to properly identify the trace observed at the test execution step, one needs a mechanism to know the order of occurrences between inputs and outputs: in fact, measuring delays between outputs permits to reconstruct the full trace of inputs, outputs and delays.

In this paper, we propose an off-line testing approach in a timed model-based framework. The approach is decoupled in different steps: (*a*) the coverage-based selection of an input sequence with delays; (*b*) the execution of the SUT for the input sequence which generates an output sequence with delays as a result. Input and output sequences are then merged to generate a complete execution trace; (*c*) the verdict computation based on a traversal of the model guided by the execution trace. The first and last steps are conducted off-line with Timed Input Output Symbolic Transition Systems (TIOSTS) for models. TIOSTS are extensions of Input/Output Symbolic Transition Systems (IOSTS) [8] and of Timed Automata (TA) [1], in which both data and time properties are expressed symbolically. Our framework is situated within the context of the *tioco* conformance relation [5, 9, 14].

Section 2 gives preliminaries about time and data denotation as first order structures. In Section 3, we recall the *tioco* setting. Then, we present the syntax of TIOSTS and give their semantics as timed traces in Section 4. We show in the same section how to compute these traces using symbolic execution techniques. In Section 5, we introduce our off-line testing algorithm. Section 6 reviews relevant state of the art concerning timed conformance testing.

2   Data and Time Denotation

We use classical multi-typed first order logic to symbolically denote data and time. A *signature* Ω is a triple (S, Op, P) where S is a set of *types*, Op (resp. P) is a set of *operations* (resp. *predicates*) provided with a profile in S^+ (resp. S^*). For any set V of variables typed in S, we note $T_\Omega(V)$ (resp. $P_\Omega(V)$) the set of *terms* (resp. *predicate terms*) over V and Ω inductively defined as usual. An Ω-*model* $M = \bigcup_{s \in S} M_s$ is provided with a function $\overline{f} : M_{s_1} \times \cdots \times M_{s_n} \to M_s$ (resp. a predicate $\overline{p} : M_{s_1} \times \cdots \times M_{s_n}$) for each $f : s_1 \cdots s_n \to s$ in Op (resp. for each $p : s_1 \cdots s_n$ in P). *Substitutions* (resp *interpretations*) are applications from V to $T_\Omega(V)$ (resp. M) preserving types and can be canonically extended to $T_\Omega(V)$.[1] The set $Sen_\Omega(V)$ of all *formulas* contains the predicate terms (including the truth values $\top$ and $\bot$ denoting resp. the true and false values), the equalities $t = t'$ for t, t' terms of the same type and all formulas built over the usual connectives $\neg, \vee, \wedge$ and quantifiers $\forall x, \exists x$ with x variable of V.

The satisfaction of a formula φ by an interpretation $\nu : V \to M$ is denoted $M \models_\nu \varphi$ where $M \models_\nu t = t'$ (resp. $M \models_\nu p(t_1, \ldots, t_n)$ with $t_1, \ldots, t_n$ terms of $T_\Omega(V)$) is defined by $\nu(t) = \nu(t')$ (resp. $(\nu(t_1), \ldots, \nu(t_n)) \in \overline{p}$), and connectives and quantifiers are handled as usual in more complex formulas.

We suppose that Ω contains a particular type *time* to denote durations. For readability sake, M_{time} is denoted D (for *Duration*) and is assimilated to the set of positive (or null) real numbers.[2] Op and P contain some classical operations $+ : time \times time \to time$, $- : time \times time \to time$, or predicates $<, \leq: time \times time$, provided by default with their usual meanings.[3]. Variables of type *time* are called *clocks* For a set of clocks T, we note $Sen_{time}(T)$ the set of formulas only containing conjunctions of formulas of the form $z \leq d$, $d \leq z$, $z < d$ or $d < z$, where d is a constant and z is in T.

In the sequel, $\Omega = (S, Op, P)$ and M are supposed given.

3   System Under Test

In order to reason about Systems Under Test, we denote them as Timed Input Output Labeled Transition Systems (TIOLTS) [6,9,14]. TIOLTS are automata whose transitions are labeled either by actions (inputs, outputs) or by delays. For simplicity, the unobservable action τ is not introduced (see [2]).

---

[1] The set of applications from A to B is denoted as B^A.
[2] In practice, any set of values used in a constraint solver for approaching real numbers.
[3] For simplicity, $\overline{+}, \overline{<} \ldots$ are also denoted by $+, <$.

Let C be a set of *channels*. The *set of actions over* C, denoted $Act_M(C)$, is $I_M(C) \cup O_M(C)$ where $I_M(C) = \{c?v \mid v \in M, c \in C\}$ denotes the set of *inputs* and $O_M(C) = \{c!v \mid v \in M, c \in C\}$ denotes the set of *outputs*. Thus, $c?v$ (resp. $c!v$) stands for the reception (resp. emission) of v by the SUT on the channel c.

Definition 1 (*TIOLTS*). *A TIOLTS over* C *is a triple* (Q, q_0, Tr) *where* Q *is a set of* states, $q_0 \in Q$ *is the* initial state, *and* $Tr \subseteq Q \times (Act_M(C) \cup D) \times Q$ *is a set of* transitions.

For any $tr = (q, a, q')$ of Tr, $source(tr)$, $act(tr)$, and $target(tr)$ stand respectively for q, a, and q'. The set of *paths* of a TIOLTS $\mathbb{A} = (Q, q_0, Tr)$ is the set $Path(\mathbb{A}) \subseteq Tr^*$ containing the empty sequence ε and all sequences $tr_1 \ldots tr_n$ such that $source(tr_1) = q_0$, and for all $i < n$, $target(tr_i) = source(tr_{i+1})$.[4] Let p be a path of $\mathbb{A}$, the *trace of* p, denoted as $trace(p)$, is ε if $p = \varepsilon$, $trace(p')$ if $p = p'.tr$ with $act(tr) = 0$, and $act(tr).trace(p')$ if $p = p'.tr$ with $act(tr) \neq 0$. $Traces(\mathbb{A})$ is the set of traces of all paths of $Path(\mathbb{A})$. The set $TTraces(\mathbb{A})$ of *timed traces of* $\mathbb{A}$ is the smallest set containing $Traces(\mathbb{A})$ and such that:

- for any $\sigma = \sigma'.d.\sigma''$ in $TTraces(\mathbb{A})$, $\sigma'.d_1.d_2.\sigma''$ is in $TTraces(\mathbb{A})$,
- for any $\sigma = \sigma'.d_1.d_2.\sigma''$ in $TTraces(\mathbb{A})$, $\sigma'.d.\sigma''$ is in $TTraces(\mathbb{A})$,
- for any $\sigma.r$ in $TTraces(\mathbb{A})$ with r in $Act_M(C) \cup (D \setminus \{0\})$, σ is in $TTraces(\mathbb{A})$,

where d, d_1 and d_2 are any delays of $D \setminus \{0\}$ verifying $d = d_1 + d_2$.

We introduce a normalization operation whose purpose is to compute a trace in which the occurring delays are the largest possible (by adding all consecutive delays of a trace). Let σ be a trace of $(Act_M(C) \cup (D \setminus \{0\}))^*$, $\overline{\sigma}$ is ε if $\sigma = \varepsilon$, $\overline{\sigma'}.a$ if $\sigma = \sigma'.a$ with $a \in Act_M(C)$, and $\overline{\sigma'}.(d_1 + \cdots + d_n)$ if $\sigma = \sigma'.d_1 \cdots d_n$ where for all $i \leq n$, $d_i \in D \setminus \{0\}$, and σ' is either ε or terminated by an action in $Act_M(C)$.

We naturally define the trace duration as the sum of all delays occurring in a trace. More precisely, for a trace σ, $duration(\sigma)$ is 0 if $\sigma = \varepsilon$, $duration(\sigma')$ if $\sigma = \sigma'.r$ with $r \in Act_M(C)$, and $duration(\sigma') + d$ if $\sigma = \sigma'.d$ with $d \in D \setminus \{0\}$.

Definition 2 (*SUT*). *A SUT over* C *is a TIOLTS* $\mathbb{S} = (Q, q_0, Tr)$ *over* C *satisfying the following properties:*

- **Input enableness**: $\forall\, q \in Q$, $c \in C$, $v \in M$, *there exists* $(q, c?v, q')$ *in* Tr,
- **Time elapsing**: $\forall q \in Q$ *s.t. there is no transition of the form* $(q, c!v, q')$ *in* Tr, *then there exists* (q, d, q') *in* Tr *with* d *in* $D \setminus \{0\}$.

Input enableness condition is very classical: it expresses that an SUT cannot refuse an input. **Time elapsing** condition expresses that the absence of a reaction amounts to observe no reaction during a strictly positive delay.

The conformance relation *tioco* [5,7,9,14] defines the correctness of an SUT w.r.t a TIOLTS model.

---

[4] A^* is the set of words on A with ε as the empty word and "." as the concatenation law.

Definition 3 (tioco). *Let* $\mathbb{S}$ *be an SUT and* $\mathbb{A}$ *a TIOLTS, both defined over* C. $\mathbb{S}$ *conforms to* $\mathbb{A}$, *denoted* $\mathbb{S}$ *tioco* $\mathbb{A}$, *if and only if for any* σ *in* $TTraces(\mathbb{A})$ *and* r *in* $O_M(C) \cup (D \backslash \{0\})$ *we have:*

$$\sigma.r \in TTraces(\mathbb{S}) \Longrightarrow \sigma.r \in TTraces(\mathbb{A})$$

In the Introduction, we argued that test data, in off-line testing, is made of a test input sequence to be submitted to the SUT and of a test output sequence produced by the SUT. A natural testing hypothesis expresses that when these two sequences are grouped, they form a trace of the SUT. In order to make the connection between test data and the SUT, we start by introducing some functions to handle traces: the projection function allows us to extract a subtrace, and the merge allows to combine two traces according to delays occurring in them. Formally, for any trace σ, the *input projection of* σ, denoted $\sigma_{\downarrow I}$, is: ε if $\sigma = \varepsilon$; $\sigma'_{\downarrow I}$ if $\sigma = \sigma'.o$ with $o \in O_M(C)$, and $\sigma'_{\downarrow I}.x$ if $\sigma = \sigma'.x$ with $x \in I_M(C) \cup (D \backslash \{0\})$. Similarly, the *output projection of* σ, denoted $\sigma_{\downarrow O}$, is defined by exchanging the roles of inputs and outputs. Let us define the merge operation by induction on the trace structure. For that purpose, let us consider two traces σ_i in $(I_M(C) \cup (D \backslash \{0\}))^*$ and σ_o in $(O_M(C) \cup (D \backslash \{0\}))^*$ defined over C. $Merge(\sigma_i, \sigma_o)$ is defined as follows:

- σ_o (resp. σ_i) if $\sigma_i = \varepsilon$ (resp. $\sigma_o = \varepsilon$),
- $o.Merge(\sigma_i, \sigma')$ if $\sigma_o = o.\sigma'$ with $o \in O_M(C)$,
- $i.Merge(\sigma', \sigma_o)$ if $\sigma_i = i.\sigma'$ with $i \in I_M(C)$ and $\sigma_o = d.\sigma'$ with $d \in D \backslash \{0\}$,
- with $\sigma_i = d_i.\sigma'_i$, $d_i \in D \backslash \{0\}$, and $\sigma_o = d_o.\sigma'_o$, $d_o \in D \backslash \{0\}$
  - $d_i.Merge(\sigma'_i, (d_o - d_i).\sigma'_o)$ if $d_i < d_o$
  - $d_i.Merge(\sigma'_i, \sigma'_o)$ if $d_i = d_o$
  - $d_o.Merge((d_i - d_o).\sigma'_i, \sigma'_o)$ if $d_o < d_i$.

For merging two traces beginning with an input i and then an output o, we choose to prioritize the output o: if from the point of view of the tester, i and o are perceived as occurring at the same time, it is likely that o follows from the previous inputs of the input sequence, not from i. Thus, placing o before i in the merging trace explicits that i cannot be a cause of o.

As already explained, off-line test input sequences are modeled as sequences of inputs and strictly positive delays.

Definition 4 (input sequence). *An input sequence over* C *is a sequence of* $(I_M(C) \cup (D \backslash \{0\}))^*$.

Once an input sequence is considered, the test execution phase amounts to play it on $\mathbb{S}$ so that it produces an output sequence σ_o made of outputs and strictly positive delays. Modeling $\mathbb{S}$ as a TIOLTS leads to the following facts:

- there exists a trace σ of $TTraces(\mathbb{S})$, such that the input (resp. output) projection of σ corresponds to the submitted input sequence (resp. the output sequence collected when executing the input sequence);
- the duration of the test output sequence is strictly greater than the one of the input sequence. Indeed, when collecting the output sequence, the tester will at least wait a moment after sending the last input to the SUT.

Definition 5 (execution). *Let* $\mathbb{S}$ *be an SUT over* C, *and let* σ_i *be an input sequence over* C.

An execution *of* σ_i *on* $\mathbb{S}$, *is defined as a sequence* σ_o *of* $(O_M(C) \cup (D \backslash \{0\}))^*$ *verifying:* (1) $Merge(\sigma_i, \sigma_o) \in TTraces(\mathbb{S})$ *and* (2) $duration(\sigma_o) > duration(\sigma_i)$. σ_o *is called an* output sequence *of* σ_i *for* $\mathbb{S}$ *and we note* $\sigma_i \rightsquigarrow_\mathbb{S} \sigma_o$.

The condition (2) ensures that the trace $Merge(\sigma_i, \sigma_o)$ is terminated by either an output or a delay, as verified on the example of Figure 1. Moreover, let us point out that due to non-determinism, there can exist two distinct traces σ_o and σ'_o such that $\sigma_i \rightsquigarrow_\mathbb{S} \sigma_o$ and $\sigma_i \rightsquigarrow_\mathbb{S} \sigma'_o$.

test input sequence
$4 \cdot c?a \cdot 23 \cdot e?x \cdot 39 \cdot c?w$ **SUT**   **test output sequence**
$12 \cdot c!b \cdot 31 \cdot e!y \cdot 65 \cdot c!m$

Corresponding timeline
$4 \cdot c?a \cdot 8 \cdot c!b \cdot 15 \cdot e?x \cdot 16 \cdot e!y \cdot 23 \cdot c?w \cdot 42 \cdot c!m$

Fig. 1. Example of merging two test traces

Timed Input Output Symbolic Transition Systems (TIOSTS) are models where data and time are symbolically specified. They are well-accepted concise representations of TIOLTS: symbolic data allow one to characterize internal states, to express firing conditions of transitions and to denote exchanged messages, while real-time properties are handled with constraints and resets on clock variables.

Since *tioco* defines conformance of an SUT w.r.t. a TIOLTS specification, TIOSTS model semantics (Definition 8) is given in the form of TIOLTS.

4   Timed Input Output Transition Systems

TIOSTS are defined over a signature $\Sigma = (C, A, T)$ where C is a set of channels, A is a set of variables (whose type is not *time*) called *attribute variables*, and T is a set of clocks. The set of symbolic actions $Act(\Sigma)$ is $I(\Sigma) \cup O(\Sigma)$ with $I(\Sigma) = \{c?x | x \in A, c \in C\}$ and $O(\Sigma) = \{c!t | t \in T_\Omega(A), c \in C\}$.

Definition 6 (TIOSTS). *A TIOSTS over* Σ *is a triple* (Q, q_0, Tr), *where* Q *is a set of states,* $q_0 \in Q$ *is the initial state and* Tr *is a set of transitions of the form* $(q, \phi, \psi, \mathbb{T}, act, \rho, q')$ *where* $q, q' \in Q$, $\phi \in Sen_{time}(T)$, $\psi \in Sen_\Omega(A)$, $\mathbb{T} \subseteq T$, $act \in Act(\Sigma)$, *and* $\rho : A \to T_\Omega(A)$ *is a substitution s.t.* x *does not occur in* ψ *if act is of the form* $c?x$.

When firing a transition $(q, \phi, \psi, \mathbb{T}, act, \rho, q')$, ϕ is a formula constraining the delay at which the action act occurs, ψ is a firing condition on attribute variables, ρ assigns new values to attribute variables, and clocks in $\mathbb{T}$ are reset. The restriction about the occurrence of the reception variable x in the firing condition ψ is due to the fact that both formulas ϕ and ψ are evaluated precisely at the reception instant.

Example 1 (Trajectory module of a Flight Management System).

The *Trajectory* module is embedded in a plane and orchestrates the computation of plane trajectories. Figure 2 depicts its specification: it waits to receive the current location of the aircraft (transition $q_0 \to q_1$); it sends a request to access the flight plan in less than 1 time units (transition $q_1 \to q_2$); then, either it receives the requested flight plan in less than 2 time units (transition $q_2 \to q_3$) or it does not receive it and sends an error message to its environment in less than 3 time units (transition $q_2 \to q_0$); after this step, the trajectory module sends a request for parameters (typically, fuel quantity, speed, etc.) related to the state of the plane (transition $q_3 \to q_4$), and again either receives them in less than 1 time unit or sends a warning message in less than 2 time units (two transitions $q_4 \to q_5$); then, the module sends in less than 1 time unit the location, the flight plan and the parameters to a calculator (transitions $q_5 \to q_6$), which replies by sending the new trajectory of the plane in less than 2 time units (transition $q_6 \to q_7$) unless it fails to meet the time constraint, in which case the module sends an error message in less than 3 time units; if the calculator succeeds to react on time, the computed navigation commands are transmitted to the environment (transition $q_7 \to q_0$) in a total of less than 9 time units.

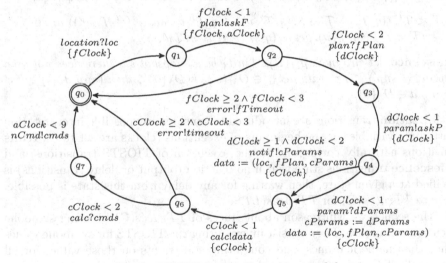

Fig. 2. TIOSTS for the Trajectory module

Executions of TIOSTS transitions are called *runs* and modeled as TIOLTS transitions whose states are called *snapshots*:

Definition 7 (runs of transitions). *Let $\mathbb{G} = (Q, q_0, Tr)$ be a TIOSTS over Σ. The set $Snp_M(\mathbb{G})$ of snapshots of $\mathbb{G}$ is the set $Q \times D \times M^{A \cup T}$. For any $tr = (q, \phi, \psi, \mathbb{T}, act, \rho, q') \in Tr$, the set of runs of tr is the set $Run(tr) \subseteq Snp_M(\mathbb{G}) \times Act_M(C) \times Snp_M(\mathbb{G})$ s.t. $((q, \mathcal{T}, \nu), act_M, (q', \mathcal{T}', \nu')) \in Run(tr)$ iff there exist $d \in D$ and $\nu^i : A \cup T \to M$ satisfying:*

- $\mathcal{T}' = \mathcal{T} + d$,
- for all $w \in T$, $\nu^i(w) = \nu(w) + d$,
- if $act = c!t$ then for all $x \in A$, $\nu^i(x) = \nu(x)$,
- if $act = c?x$ then for all $y \in A \setminus \{x\}$, $\nu^i(y) = \nu(y)$,

such that we have: $act_M = \nu^i(act)$, $\forall x \in A, \nu'(x) = \nu^i(\rho(x))$, $\forall w \in \mathbb{T}, \nu'(w) = 0$, $\forall w \in (T \setminus \mathbb{T}), \nu'(w) = \nu^i(w)$, $M \models_{\nu_i} \phi$ and $M \models_{\nu_i} \psi$.

Based on runs of transitions, we associate a TIOLTS to a TIOSTS:

Definition 8 (TIOLTS associated to a TIOSTS). The TIOLTS over C associated to $\mathbb{G}$, denoted $LTS_{\mathbb{G}} = (Snp_M(\mathbb{G}) \cup \{init, q_\delta\}, init, Tr')$, is defined as follows: $init, q_\delta$ are two distinct states not belonging to $Snp_M(\mathbb{G})$ and Tr' is the smallest subset of $(Snp_M(\mathbb{G}) \cup \{init, q_\delta\}) \times (Act_M(C) \cup D) \times (Snp_M(\mathbb{G}) \cup \{q_\delta\})$ s.t.

Initialization: for any $((q_0, 0, \nu_0), act_M, (q, \mathcal{T}, \nu)) \in Run(tr)$ with $tr \in Tr$ and $\forall w \in T, \nu_0(w) = 0$,

- if $0 < \mathcal{T}$, $(init, \mathcal{T}, (q_0, \mathcal{T}, \nu_0))$ and $((q_0, \mathcal{T}, \nu_0), act_M, (q, \mathcal{T}, \nu))$ are in Tr',
- else $(\mathcal{T} = 0)$ $((q_0, 0, \nu_0), act_M, (q, 0, \nu))$ is in Tr',

Runs: for $((q, \mathcal{T}, \nu), act_M, (q', \mathcal{T}', \nu')) \in Run(tr)$ with $tr \in Tr$ and $q \neq q_0$,

- if $\mathcal{T} < \mathcal{T}'$, $((q, \mathcal{T}, \nu), \mathcal{T}' - \mathcal{T}, (q, \mathcal{T}', \nu))$, $((q, \mathcal{T}', \nu), act_M, (q', \mathcal{T}', \nu'))$ are in Tr',
- else $(\mathcal{T} = \mathcal{T}')$ $((q, \mathcal{T}, \nu), act_M, (q', \mathcal{T}, \nu'))$ is in Tr',

Quiescence: let snp in $Snp_M(\mathbb{G}) \cup \{init\}$ be a snapshot s.t. there does not exist $(snp, act_M, snp') \in Tr'$ with $act_M \in O_M(C) \cup (D \setminus \{0\})$, then $(snp, d, q_\delta) \in Tr'$ for any $d \in D \setminus \{0\}$.

Initialization transitions are introduced to consider any possible interpretation of attribute variables at the beginning of executions (clocks are set to 0), **Runs** transitions naturally correspond to the execution of TIOSTS transitions, and **Quiescence** transitions state that if no reaction (output or delay transitions) is specified at a given state, then waiting for any delay from this state is possible. We note $TTraces(\mathbb{G})$ for $TTraces(LTS_{\mathbb{G}})$.

In the sequel, we will reason about traces of $TTraces(\mathbb{G})$ by using symbolic execution techniques. They consist in: executing the TIOSTS for symbolic values rather than numerical ones, and computing constraints on those values for all possible TIOSTS executions. In order to represent symbolic values, we suppose that a set of fresh variables $F = \bigcup_{s \in S} F_s$ is given. Symbolic states are structures used to store pieces of information concerning an execution:

Definition 9 (symbolic state). A symbolic state for $\mathbb{G}$ is a tuple $(q, \theta, \pi, \vartheta, \lambda)$ where $q \in Q$, $\theta \in Sen_{time}(F_{time})$, $\pi \in Sen_\Omega(F)$, $\vartheta \in T_\Omega(F_{time})$ and $\lambda : A \cup T \to T_\Omega(F)$ is an application preserving types.
We note S the set of all symbolic states over F.

For a symbolic state $\eta = (q, \theta, \pi, \vartheta, \lambda)$, q denotes the state reached after an execution leading to η, θ is a constraint on symbolic delay values called *time path condition*, π is a constraint on symbolic data values called *data path condition*, ϑ denotes the duration from the beginning of the execution leading to η, and λ denotes terms over symbolic variables in F that are assigned to variables of A.

In the sequel, Σ_F stands for (F, C). Moreover for any symbolic state $\eta = (q, \theta, \pi, \vartheta, \lambda)$, $q(\eta)$, $\theta(\eta)$, $\pi(\eta)$, $\vartheta(\eta)$ and $\lambda(\eta)$ stand resp. for q, θ, π, ϑ and λ. For an application $\lambda : A \cup T \to T_\Omega(F)$, we extend it in a canonical way to $T_\Omega(A \cup T)$, $Sen_\Omega(A \cup T)$ and $Act(\Sigma)$. All these extensions are also simply denoted by λ. The symbolic execution of a TIOSTS is based on symbolic executions of transitions:

Definition 10 (symbolic execution of transitions). *Let* $\mathbb{G} = (Q, q_0, Tr)$ *be a TIOSTS over* Σ *and* $tr = (q, \phi, \psi, \mathbb{T}, act, \rho, q')$ *be in* Tr. *A symbolic execution of* tr *from* η *in* S *is* $st = (\eta, act_F, \eta') \in S \times Act(\Sigma_F) \times S$ *such that* $q(\eta') = q'$, $\vartheta(\eta') = \vartheta(\eta) + z$ *where* $z \in F_{time}$ *is a new fresh variable, and there exists* $\lambda^i : A \cup T \to T_\Omega(F)$ *satisfying:*

- *if* $act \in O(\Sigma)$, *then that for all* $x \in A$, $\lambda^i(x) = \lambda(x)$,
- *if* $act \in I(\Sigma)$ *of the form* $c?y$ *then* $\lambda^i(y)$ *is a fresh variable of* F *and for all* $x \in A \setminus \{y\}$, $\lambda^i(x) = \lambda(x)$,
- *for all* $w \in T$ *we have* $\lambda^i(w) = \lambda(w) + z$,

such that $act_F = \lambda^i(act)$, *for all* $x \in A$, $\lambda(\eta')(x) = \lambda^i(\rho(x))$, *for all* $w \in (T \setminus \mathbb{T})$, $\lambda(\eta')(w) = \lambda^i(w)$, *for all* $w \in \mathbb{T}$, $\lambda(\eta')(w) = 0$, *Finally* $\pi(\eta') = \pi(\eta) \wedge \lambda^i(\psi)$ *and* $\theta(\eta') = \theta(\eta) \wedge \lambda^i(\phi)$.

The variable z is called the *delay of* st and is denoted $delay(st)$. $source(st)$, $act(st)$ and $target(st)$ stand respectively for η, act_F and η'. In the sequel, for any symbolic transition $st = (\eta, act_F, \eta')$, we note $Fresh(st) = \{delay(st)\}$ if $act \in O(\Sigma)$ and $Fresh(st) = \{delay(st), \lambda^i(y)\}$ if $act = c?y$. The symbolic execution tree associated to the TIOSTS is then defined as follows:

Definition 11 (symbolic execution of a TIOSTS). *A symbolic execution of* $\mathbb{G} = (Q, q_0, Tr)$ *is a couple* $SE(\mathbb{G}) = (Init, ST)$ *where:*

- *Init* $= (q_0, \top, \top, 0, \lambda_0)$ *is such that* $\forall x \in T, \lambda_0(x) = 0$ *and for all distinct variables* x, y *in* A, $\lambda_0(x)$ *and* $\lambda_0(y)$ *are distinct variables of* F,
- *ST is the set of all symbolic executions* st *of* tr *in* Tr *from* $\eta \in S$ *with* $q(\eta) = source(tr)$ *and* $Fresh(st) \cap \lambda_0(A) = \emptyset$. *Moreover for any two distinct* $st_1, st_2 \in ST$, $Fresh(st_1) \cap Fresh(st_2) = \emptyset$.

Example 2 (Symbolic execution). Figure 3 depicts the symbolic execution of the Trajectory module of Example 1. For the sake of clarity: only one path of the tree is shown, representing a complete cycle of the *Trajectory* module, transitions deviating from this path are cut; we show the delay of the transition together with its symbolic action; and, only the information associated with symbolic state η_1 is detailed –note that values of clocks are actually summations of delays (e.g. $fClock_1$ represents the summation $0 + z_1$).

In order to deal with quiescence, we complete symbolic executions by new transitions. Contrarily to TIOLTS, transitions of TIOSTS carry actions that are necessarily inputs or outputs (not delays). For this reason, we artificially introduce a new symbol $\delta!$ denoting the absence of reactions.

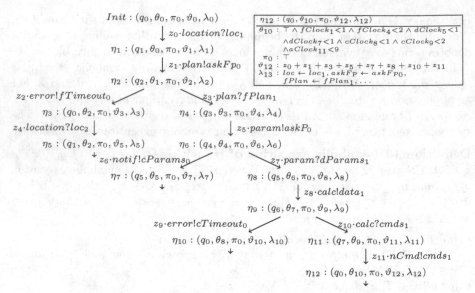

Fig. 3. Symbolic execution for the Trajectory module example

Definition 12 (quiescence enrichment). *Let $SE(\mathbb{G}) = (Init, ST)$ be a symbolic execution. For all $\eta \in S$ let us note $React(\eta)$ the set of st in ST with source$(st) = \eta$ and act$(st) \in O(\Sigma_F)$. The* quiescence enrichment *of $SE(\mathbb{G})$ is the couple $SE(\mathbb{G}_\delta) = (Init, ST \cup \Delta ST)$ where for all $\eta \in S$:*

- **Time based quiescence:** *Let $\theta_\delta(\eta)$ be $\top$ if $React(\eta) = \emptyset$ and let $\theta_\delta(\eta)$ be $\bigwedge_{st \in React(\eta)} \forall delay(st).\neg(\theta(target(st)))$ otherwise. Then, $(\eta, \delta!, \eta_\delta^t) \in \Delta ST$ with $\eta_\delta^t = (q_\delta, \theta(\eta) \wedge \theta_\delta(\eta), \pi(\eta), \vartheta(\eta) + z, \lambda(\eta))$ with z is a new variable in F_{time}.*
- **Data based quiescence:** *Let $\pi_\delta(\eta)$ be $\top$ if $React(\eta) = \emptyset$ and let $\pi_\delta(\eta)$ be $\bigwedge_{st \in React(\eta)} \neg \pi(target(st))$ otherwise. Then, $(\eta, \delta!, \eta_\delta^d) \in \Delta ST$ with $\eta_\delta^d = (q_\delta, \theta(\eta), \pi(\eta) \wedge \pi_\delta(\eta), \vartheta(\eta) + z, \lambda(\eta))$ with z is a new variable in F_{time}.*

Time based quiescence transitions can be executed only if no transition labeled by an output can be executed anymore due to unsatisfiable time constraints. By noting that $delay(st)$ is the symbolic delay associated wit the transition st, $\theta_\delta(\eta)$ precisely states that for all output transitions st of source η, whatever the delay is, the time path condition $(\theta(target(st)))$ to fire st cannot be satisfied. Similarly, **Data based quiescence** transitions can be executed only if no transition labelled by an output can be executed anymore due to unsatisfiable data constraints.

Example 3 (Quiescence enrichment).

The *Trajectory* module example takes all possible deadlock situations into account. This is normal, since in an flight management system, we do not want to have any of those situations. For illustration purposes, let us consider $Init$, since there is no output transition leaving from it, a **Data based quiescence** is detected, and as according to Definition 12, the transition $(Init, \delta!, \eta_\delta^d)$ is added to the tree, representing the fact that the module can remain silent until it receives a location from the environment. If we consider η_1, let us examine if we can detect a **Time based quiescence**. That is, let us examine the formula $\forall z_1.\neg(\theta_1)$, where $\theta_1 = fClock_1 < 1$. Since $fClock_1 = 0 + z_1$, there is no way that for all $z_1, z_1 \geq 1$ is true. Thus, no **Time based quiescence** is added to the tree.

$SE(\mathbb{G})_\delta$ characterizes in an intentional way the set of all timed traces of the TIOLTS associated to $\mathbb{G}$: we define paths of $SE(\mathbb{G})_\delta$ as finite sequences $st_1 \cdots st_n$ of transitions of ST, such that $source(st_1) = Init$ and for every $i < n$, we have $target(st_i) = source(st_{i+1})$. For any finite path $p = st_1 \cdots st_n$, $target(p)$ is $Init$ if $n = 0$ and $target(st_n)$ otherwise. We note $Path(SE(\mathbb{G})_\delta)$ the set of all such paths. For a path p, we note $Seq(p)$ the sequence defined as ε if $p = \varepsilon$, $Seq(p').delay(st)$ if p is of the form $p'.st$ with $act(st) = \delta!$ and $Seq(p').delay(st).act(st)$ if p is of the form $p'.st$ with $act(st) \neq \delta!$. The set $TTraces(p)$ is defined as $\{\sigma | \exists \nu.(M \models_\nu \theta(target(p)) \wedge \pi(target(p)) \wedge \overline{\sigma} = \nu(Seq(p)))\}$.[5] We note $TTraces(SE(\mathbb{G})_\delta)$ the set $\bigcup_{p \in Path(SE(\mathbb{G})_\delta)} TTraces(p)$.

5 Off-Line Testing Algorithms

We present our algorithms w.r.t. the input sequence selection, the test execution, and the verdict computation.

Input Sequence Selection. We propose to extract input sequences, as introduced in Definition 4, from $SE(\mathbb{G})_\delta$. Following our previous works [7,8], we propose to use paths of $SE(\mathbb{G})_\delta$ as *test purposes*, that is, we build input sequences corresponding to traces of a selected path. Given a test purpose p in $Path(SE(\mathbb{G})_\delta)$, an input sequence is built by applying the input projection on a trace chosen in $TTraces(p)$. Indeed, such input sequences are clearly good candidates to put the SUT $\mathbb{S}$ in a configuration where $\mathbb{S}$ can reach the test purpose. Therefore, we introduce the *set* $IS(p) = \{\sigma_{\downarrow I} \mid \sigma \in TTraces(p)\}$ *of input sequences of* p. We can capture the set $IS(p)$ by simply building the corresponding normalized traces and by highlighting the interpretations which satisfy the constraints defining the target state of p:

$$\{\nu(Seq(p))_{\downarrow I} \mid \nu \models \theta(target(p)) \wedge \pi(target(p))\}$$

Thus, defining a normalized input sequence for p comes to exhibit an interpretation $\nu : F \to M$ that satisfies both the time and data path conditions of the target of p by constraint solving techniques, to compute $\nu(Seq(p))$, and finally "forget" output in the result thanks to the $\downarrow_I$ operator. We suppose that an SUT $\mathbb{S}$, a test purpose p and an input sequence $\sigma_{\downarrow I}^p$ are given (σ^p is thus a timed trace of p, normalized or not).

Test Execution. As discussed in Section 3, the *test execution* is to submit $\sigma_{\downarrow I}^p$ to $\mathbb{S}$, which in turn sends an output sequence σ_o, such that $\sigma_{\downarrow I}^p \leadsto_\mathbb{S} \sigma_o$. We note

---

[5] An interpretation ν can be extended to sequences as follows: $\nu(Seq(p)) = \varepsilon$ if $p = \varepsilon$, $\nu(Seq(p)) = \nu(\omega).\nu(a)$ if $Seq(p) = \omega.a$ with $a \in Act(\Sigma_F)$ and $\nu(Seq(p)) = \nu(\omega).\nu(d)$ if $Seq(p) = \omega.d$ with $d \in T_\Omega(F)_{time}$.

$\sigma_{\mathbb{S}} = Merge(\sigma^p_{\downarrow_I}, \sigma_o)$. Recall that, due to potential non determinism of $\mathbb{G}$, even in the case $\mathbb{S}$ *tioco* $\mathbb{G}$, we may have $\sigma_{\mathbb{S}} \neq \sigma^p$.

Verdict Computation. Our algorithm takes as inputs three arguments, $SE(\mathbb{G})_\delta$, p and $\sigma_{\mathbb{S}}$, and computes verdicts concerning the correctness of $\mathbb{S}$ assessment and concerning the coverage of p by $\sigma_{\mathbb{S}}$. This algorithm can be seen as an off-line version of the one defined in [7]. We begin by introducing some intermediate definitions that are needed in the algorithm. A *context* is a mathematical structure denoting a path of $SE(\mathbb{G})_\delta = (Init, ST)$ potentially covered by a trace, together with additional identification constraints induced by the trace. Formally, a context is a tuple (η, f_t, f_d, d) where: $\eta \in S$ denotes the target state of the potentially covered path; $f_t \in Sen_{Time}(F_{time})$ expresses identification constraints between time variables of F and numerical delays occurring in the trace; $f_d \in Sen_\Omega(F)$ expresses identification constraints between data variables and values emitted and received in the trace; and finally, d is a numerical delay that identifies how much time has elapsed in the given context. Intuitively, when time elapses, if there is no modification of state, then the value d is simply increased, else, the value d is reset to 0. In the sequel, $state((\eta, f_t, f_d, d))$ names the state η. Since there may be more than one path which is covered by a trace, we manipulate sets of contexts. We introduce the function $Next(a, SC)$, which computes the set of all contexts that can be reached from a given set of contexts SC, when an action occurs or a delay elapses, i.e. $a \in Act_M(C) \cup (D \setminus \{0\})$:

Case. $a \in Act_M(C)$ of the form $c\triangle t$ with $\triangle \in \{?, !\}$: if there exists $(\eta, f_t, f_d, d) \in SC$, and a symbolic transition $st = (\eta, c\triangle u, \eta')$ in ST, then:

$$(\eta', f_t \wedge d = delay(st), f_d \wedge (t = u), 0) \in Next(a, SC)$$

provided that both $f_t \wedge d = delay(st) \wedge \theta(\eta')$ and $f_d \wedge \pi(\eta')$ are satisfiable.

Case. $a \in D \setminus \{0\}$: if there exists $(\eta, f_t, f_d, d) \in SC$, and a symbolic transition st in ST with $source(st) = \eta$, then:

$$(\eta, f_t \wedge \exists delay(st).(delay(st) \geq d + a \wedge \theta(target(st))), f_d, d + a) \in Next(a, SC)$$

provided that $f_t \wedge \exists delay(st).(delay(st) \geq d+a \wedge \theta(target(st))) \wedge \theta(\eta)$ is satisfiable.

The general idea of the algorithm is to read one by one the elements of the trace $\sigma_{\mathbb{S}}$, and to compute either the next set of contexts or to emit a verdict. Let us suppose that $\sigma_{\mathbb{S}}$ can be written as $\sigma_{pref}.a.\sigma_{suf}$ where a is an action or a delay. $SC(a)$ is a notation grouping the set of contexts SC reached after reading the beginning $\sigma_{pref}.a$ of the trace and the last analyzed element a. At the initialization step, when no element of $\sigma_{\mathbb{S}}$ has been analyzed, then we use the symbol $\_$, that is $SC(\_)$. The algorithm is then given as a set of rules of the form:

$$\frac{SC(a) \quad \sigma_{suf}}{Result} \ cond$$

σ_{suf} is the remaining trace to be analyzed with respect to the first analyses stored in $SC(a)$, to $SE(\mathbb{G})_\delta$, and to p; $cond$ is a set of conditions that has to be satisfied so that the rule can be applied; and $Result$ is either a verdict or of the form $SC'(a') \ \sigma'_{suf}$. Moreover, if $\sigma_{suf} = \varepsilon$ then $Result$ is necessarily a verdict since the initial trace $\sigma_{\mathbb{S}}$ is fully analyzed. If $Result$ is $SC'(a') \ \sigma'_{suf}$, then σ_{suf}

can be written as $a'.\sigma'_{suf}$. We will access respectively to a' and σ'_{suf} from σ_{suf} by using the usual notations $head(\sigma_{suf})$ and $tail(\sigma_{suf})$.

Rule 0 corresponds to the initialization phase: the set of contexts contains only one context stating that we begin at the symbolic state $Init$, there are no constraints identified yet, and the associated delay is 0. **Rule 1** is applied to compute a new set of contexts. This is done as long as SC is not empty and there are still elements of the trace to read. There are five verdicts: $FAIL$ is emitted when the trace denotes an incorrect behavior (**Rule 2**); $PASS$ is emitted when the trace denotes a correct behaviors, and the test purpose is the only path covered (**Rule 3**); $WEAK\_PASS$ is emitted when the trace denotes a correct behavior, the test purpose is covered but there exists at least one other path covered (**Rule 4**); $INCONC_r$ is emitted when the trace denotes a correct behavior, a path is covered but not the test purpose (**Rule 5**); $INCONC_i$ is emitted when the trace is not included in $SE(\mathbb{G})_\delta$ due to input under-specification (**Rule 6**).

Rule 0: Initialization
$$\overline{\{(Init, \top, \top, 0)\}(\_)\ \sigma_\mathbb{S}}$$

Rule 1: An action or a delay is read from the trace, SC is not empty.
$$\frac{SC(a)\ \sigma}{Next(head(\sigma), SC)(head(\sigma))\ tail(\sigma)}\ SC \neq \emptyset,\ \sigma \neq \epsilon$$

Rule 2: An unspecified output o or delay d is read from the trace.
$$\frac{SC(a)\ \sigma}{FAIL}\ SC = \emptyset;\ a \in O_M(C) \cup D \setminus \{0\}$$

Rule 3: The read action permits to cover the test purpose, and no other paths.
$$\frac{SC(a)\ \sigma}{PASS}\ \sigma = \epsilon; \forall ct \in SC, state(ct) = target(p); SC \neq \emptyset$$

Rule 4: The read action permits to cover the test purpose, and at least one other path.
$$\frac{SC(a)\ \sigma}{Weak\_PASS}\ \begin{array}{l} \sigma = \epsilon; \exists ct \in SC, state(ct) = target(p); \\ \exists ct' \in SC, state(ct') \neq target(p); SC \neq \emptyset \end{array}$$

Rule 5: Some paths are covered but not the test purpose.
$$\frac{SC(a)\ \sigma}{INCONC_r}\ \sigma = \epsilon; \forall ct \in SC, state(ct) \neq target(p); SC \neq \emptyset$$

Rule 6: An unspecified input i is read.
$$\frac{SC(a)\ \sigma}{INCONC_i}\ SC = \emptyset;\ a \in I_M(C)$$

In contrast with algorithms in [7, 8], there are two kinds of inconclusive verdicts. $INCONC_r$ corresponds to the classical one, while $INCONC_i$ is produced when $\sigma_\mathbb{S}$ is of the form $\sigma_{pref}.a.\sigma_{suf}$, where σ_{pref} is in $SE(\mathbb{G})_\delta$ while $\sigma_{pref}.a$ with $a \in I_M(C)$ is not. This situation does not occur in on-line testing algorithms, because they are in charge of stimulating the SUT so that it strictly follows the test purpose, and emits a verdict as soon as the test purpose cannot be covered anymore. On the contrary, unless $\sigma_\mathbb{S}$ can be decomposed as $\sigma_{pref}.a.\sigma_{suf}$, where σ_{pref} is a specified timed trace and $\sigma_{pref}.a$ is not (in which case either $FAIL$ or $INCONC_i$ depending on the nature of a), all actions of $\sigma_\mathbb{S}$ will be analyzed even though the emission of $PASS$ is not possible anymore. This choice is made in order to always emit $FAIL$ for a trace revealing a non conformance, even if we may be sure (several steps before) that $PASS$ can not be emitted anymore.

Example 4. Let us apply our rule-based algorithm to the *Trajectory* module example. Let us suppose that there is a mapping between messages and integers. Then, we choose the path of Figure 3 leading to η_{13}, representing a complete loop for the module, i.e., the path p:

$$z_0 \cdot location?loc_1 \cdot z_1 \cdot plan!askFp_0 \cdot z_3 \ldots z_8 \cdot calc!data_1 \cdot z_{10} \cdot calc?cmds_1 \cdot z_{12} \cdot nCmd!cmds_1.$$

Thus, the tester chooses the appropriate values and performs the *input projection* of the trace, obtaining $\sigma^p_{\downarrow I}$:   0.1 *location*?4 2.8 *plan*?5 1.8 *param*?2 1 *calc*?1. Let us assume that the SUT *responds* with $\sigma_{\downarrow O}$:   0.2 *plan*!8 2.1 *error*!6 0.1 *nCmd*!3 4.3 . By applying the merge operation on $\sigma^p_{\downarrow I}$ and $\sigma_{\downarrow O}$, we obtain the trace σ:

0.1 *location*?4 0.1 *plan*!8 2.1 *error*!6 0.1 *nCmd*!2 0.5 *plan*?5 2 *param*?2 1 *calc*?1 1 . Figure 4 illustrates the application of the rule-based algorithm to σ.

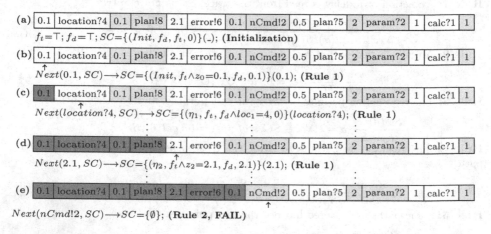

Fig. 4. Off-line Test Algorithm operating on a trace of the *Trajectory* module. At any iteration, before the execution of any rule, σ is the non-dark-gray-shadowed part of the depicted trace, $head(\sigma)$ is the element pointed by the arrow, a is the first element at its left (when it applies), and $queue(\sigma)$ is the right-side remainder. In **(a)**, SC represents the set of context after initialization. **(b)**–**(d)** represent the application of **Rule 1**, updating SC by reading the first element of the trace (and applying the $Next()$ function). In **(e)**, the observed delay causes the verdict to emit $FAIL$, since $Next()$ returns an empty set.

What is interesting to notice in Figure 4 is that, if use an on-line test purpose-guided algorithm as in [7], we emit the verdict $INCONC$ as soon as we find the delay 2.1 of output *error*!6 (**(d)** in the figure). One advantage of this off-line algorithm is that we can emit better verdicts (less $INCONC$) since we are analyzing the entire trace.

6 Related Work

Model-based conformance testing with *tioco* was addressed in [4,5,7] where models are essentially timed automata (TA) [1] (without symbolic data). Authors in [5] have defined a pure on-the-fly testing algorithm. Without any preprocessing on the model, at each moment, the algorithm computes on-the-fly a random input and its corresponding submission delay from the model and checks outputs and their timing against the model. This is reiterated until a verdict is emitted. In [4], authors model the testing activity with the help of test cases which are deterministic timed automata with inputs and outputs, whose states are labeled by verdicts. These test cases are derived from a given test purpose and result from some approximate determinisation mechanisms preserving the *tioco* conformance relation. Such a design of test cases tends to reduce choice points at runtime: however, decisions have still to be made when running test cases on SUT, for example, concerning the choice between waiting for a delay or sending a data to the SUT. So [4] may be viewed as a mixed approach, off-line for the selection, by converting a test purpose as a test case, on-line for guiding the progress in the test case during the execution. Recently, authors of [2, 3, 7, 15] have defined seemingly different reference models where both time and data are represented symbolically as extensions to TA or/and input output symbolic transition systems (IOSTS) [8,13], still based on *tioco*. In addition, approaches [2, 7] have suggested on-line testing algorithms guided by a test purpose: in [7], symbolic execution paths are selected as test purposes while the work in [2] is conducted in the spirit of [4]. To our knowledge, we are the first to propose in the context of the *tioco* conformance relation a framework where test inputs are presented statically, without any further processing to be done, while remaining executable and usable for verdict computation.

7 Conclusion

We have proposed an off-line testing approach based on the *tioco* conformance relation and on TIOSTS models which handle both data and time symbolically. The approach includes three steps: (1) first, test input sequences are extracted from a TIOSTS; for this, traces are extracted from paths of the symbolic execution tree by using solving constraints and projection techniques; (2) test executions produce output sequences that are merged with input sequences to form input output traces; (3) resulting traces are analyzed in order to provide verdicts. We highlight a verdict, specific to our off-line approach: the verdict $INCONC_i$, stating that an input can become unspecified in the context of the test execution even if it was a specified input in the context of the test selection. Our approach has been implemented using the symbolic execution tool Diversity. Diversity is an extension of the tool AGATHA [12] that integrates several sat-solvers and can analyze several languages, in particular TIOSTS or UML sequence diagrams extended with time constraints [3, 7].[6] Concerning data, our implementation handles booleans, presburger integers, and could be extended to

---

[6] *e.g.* CVC3 http://www.cs.nyu.edu/acsys/cvc3/

any decidable data theory as in [8]. Until now, we have not investigaged zone-based techniques usually undertaken with timed automata, essentially because run-time efficiency is not of primary importance in an off-line framework. We are investigating techniques to reduce the occurrence of inconclusive verdicts. As several reactions are possible after a given trace, the submission of an input sequence to SUT may result in a trace which runs outside the test purpose without questioning conformance. To control non-determinism as much as possible, we are studying under which hypotheses we can over constrain the input sequence computation in order to force a correct SUT to follow a given path.

References

1. Alur, R., Dill, D.L.: The Theory of Timed Automata. In: Huizing, C., de Bakker, J.W., Rozenberg, G., de Roever, W.-P. (eds.) REX 1991. LNCS, vol. 600, Springer, Heidelberg (1992)
2. Andrade, W.L., Machado, P.D.L., Jéron, T., Marchand, H.: Abstracting Time and Data for Conformance Testing of Real-Time Systems. In: Proc. of Int. Conf. Software Testing, Verification and Validation (ICSTW) Workshops. IEEE (2011)
3. Bannour, B., Gaston, C., Servat, D.: Eliciting unitary constraints from timed Sequence Diagram with symbolic techniques: application to testing. In: Proc. of Int. Conf. Asia-Pacific Software Engineering Conference (APSEC). IEEE (2011)
4. Bertrand, N., Jéron, T., Stainer, A., Krichen, M.: Off-Line Test Selection with Test Purposes for Non-deterministic Timed Automata. In: Abdulla, P.A., Leino, K.R.M. (eds.) TACAS 2011. LNCS, vol. 6605, pp. 96–111. Springer, Heidelberg (2011)
5. Bohnenkamp, H.C., Belinfante, A.: Timed Testing with TorX. In: Fitzgerald, J.S., Hayes, I.J., Tarlecki, A. (eds.) FM 2005. LNCS, vol. 3582, pp. 173–188. Springer, Heidelberg (2005)
6. Briones, L.B., Brinksma, E.: A Test Generation Framework for *quiescent* Real-Time Systems. In: Grabowski, J., Nielsen, B. (eds.) FATES 2004. LNCS, vol. 3395, pp. 64–78. Springer, Heidelberg (2005)
7. Escobedo, J.P., Gaston, C., Le Gall, P.: Timed Conformance Testing for Orchestrated Service Discovery. In: Proc. of Int. Conf. Formal Aspects of. Component Software (FACS). Springer (2011)
8. Gaston, C., Le Gall, P., Rapin, N., Touil, A.: Symbolic Execution Techniques for Test Purpose Definition. In: Uyar, M.Ü., Duale, A.Y., Fecko, M.A. (eds.) TestCom 2006. LNCS, vol. 3964, pp. 1–18. Springer, Heidelberg (2006)
9. Krichen, M., Tripakis, S.: Black-box time systems. In: Proc. of Int. SPIN Workshop Model Checking of Software. Springer (2004)
10. Marre, B., Arnould, A.: Test Sequences Generation from LUSTRE Descriptions: GATeL. In: Proc. of Int. Conf. Automated Software Engineering (ASE). IEEE (2000)
11. Petrenko, A., Yevtushenko, N.: Testing from Partial Deterministic FSM Specifications. IEEE Trans. Comput. (2005)

12. Rapin, N., Gaston, C., Lapitre, A., Gallois, J.-P.: Behavioural unfolding of formal specifications based on communicating automata. In: Proc. of Workshop on Automated technology for verification and analysis, ATVA (2003)
13. Rusu, V., du Bousquet, L., Jéron, T.: An Approach to Symbolic Test Generation. In: Grieskamp, W., Santen, T., Stoddart, B. (eds.) IFM 2000. LNCS, vol. 1945, pp. 338–357. Springer, Heidelberg (2000)
14. Schmaltz, J., Tretmans, J.: On Conformance Testing for Timed Systems. In: Cassez, F., Jard, C. (eds.) FORMATS 2008. LNCS, vol. 5215, pp. 250–264. Springer, Heidelberg (2008)
15. von Styp, S., Bohnenkamp, H., Schmaltz, J.: A Conformance Testing Relation for Symbolic Timed Automata. In: Chatterjee, K., Henzinger, T.A. (eds.) FORMATS 2010. LNCS, vol. 6246, pp. 243–255. Springer, Heidelberg (2010)

Querying Parametric Temporal Logic Properties on Embedded Systems

Hengyi Yang, Bardh Hoxha, and Georgios Fainekos

School of Computing, Informatics and Decision Systems Engineering,
Arizona State University
{hyang67,bhoxha,fainekos}@asu.edu

Abstract. In Model Based Development (MBD) of embedded systems, it is often desirable to not only verify/falsify certain formal system specifications, but also to automatically explore the properties that the system satisfies. Namely, given a parametric specification, we would like to automatically infer the ranges of parameters for which the property holds/does not hold on the system. In this paper, we consider parametric specifications in Metric Temporal Logic (MTL). Using robust semantics for MTL, the parameter estimation problem can be converted into an optimization problem which can be solved by utilizing stochastic optimization methods. The framework is demonstrated on some examples from the literature.

1 Introduction

Software development for embedded control systems is particularly challenging. The software may be distributed with real time constraints and must interact with the physical environment in non trivial ways. Multiple incidents and accidents of safety critical systems [1,2] reinforce the need for design, verification and validation methodologies that provide a certain level of confidence in the system correctness and robustness.

Recently, there has been a trend to develop software for safety critical embedded control systems using the Model Based Design (MBD) paradigm. Among the benefits of the MBD approach is that it provides the possibility for automatic code generation. Based on a level of confidence on the automatic code generation process, some of the system verification and validation can be performed at earlier design stages using only models of the system. Due to the importance of the problem, there has been a substantial level of research on testing and verification of models of embedded and hybrid systems (see [3] for an overview).

In [4], we investigated a new approach for testing embedded and hybrid systems against formal requirements in Metric Temporal Logic (MTL) [5]. Our work was premised on the need to express complex design requirements in a formal logic for both requirements analysis and requirements verification. Based on the concept of robustness of MTL specifications [6], we were able to pose the property falsification/testing problem as an optimization problem. In particular, robust MTL semantics provide the user with an application depended

B. Nielsen and C. Weise (Eds.): ICTSS 2012, LNCS 7641, pp. 136–151, 2012.

measure of how far a system behavior is from failing to satisfy a requirement. Therefore, the goal of an automatic test generator is to produce a sequence of tests by gradually reducing that positive measure until a system behavior with a negative robustness measure is produced. In other words, we are seeking to detect system behaviors that minimize the specification robustness measure.

Unfortunately, the resulting optimization problem is non-linear and non-convex, in general. Moreover, embedded system models frequently contain black boxes as subcomponents. Thus, only stochastic optimization techniques can be employed for solving the optimization problem and, in turn, for solving the initial falsification problem. In our previous research [7,8,4], we have explored the applicability of various stochastic optimization methods to the MTL falsification problem with great success.

In this work, we take the MTL falsification method one step further. Namely, not only would we like to detect a falsifying behavior if one exists, but also we would like to be able to explore and determine system properties. Such a property exploration framework can be of great help to the practitioner. In many cases, the system requirements are not well formalized or understood at the initial system design stages. Therefore, if the specification can be falsified, then it is natural to ask for what parameter values the system still falsifies the specification.

In more detail, given an MTL specification with an unknown or uncertain parameter [9], we automatically formulate an optimization problem whose solution provides a range of values for the parameter such that the specification does not hold on the system. In order to solve the resulting optimization problem, we utilize our MTL falsification toolbox S-TaLiRo [10], which contains a number of stochastic optimization methods [7,8,4]. Finally, we demonstrate our framework on a challenge problem from the industry [11] and we present some experimental results on a small number of benchmark problems.

2   Problem Formulation

In this work, we take a general approach in modeling real-time embedded systems that interact with physical systems that have non-trivial dynamics. In the following, we will be using the term *hybrid systems* or *Cyber-Physical Systems* (CPS) for such systems to stress the interconnection between the embedded system and the physical world.

We fix $N \subseteq \mathbb{N}$, where $\mathbb{N}$ is the set of natural numbers, to be a finite set of indexes for the finite representation of a system behavior. In the following, given two sets A and B, B^A denotes the set of all functions from A to B. That is, for any $f \in B^A$ we have $f : A \to B$.

We view a system Σ as a mapping from a compact set of *initial operating conditions* X_0 and *input signals* $\mathbf{U} \subseteq U^N$ to *output signals* Y^N and *timing* (or *sampling*) functions $\mathfrak{T} \subseteq \mathbb{R}_+^N$. Here, U is a compact set of possible input values at each point in time (input space), Y is the set of output values (output space), $\mathbb{R}$ is the set of real numbers and $\mathbb{R}_+$ the set of positive reals.

We impose three assumptions / restrictions on the systems that we consider:

1. The input signals (if any) must be parameterizable using a finite number of parameters. That is, there exists a function $\mathfrak{U}$ such that for any $u \in \mathbf{U}$, there exist two parameter vectors $\lambda = [\lambda_1 \ldots \lambda_m]^T \in \Lambda$, where Λ is a compact set, and $t = [t_1 \ldots t_m]^T \in \mathbb{R}_+^m$ such that $m \ll \max N$ and for all $i \in N$, $u(i) = \mathfrak{U}(\lambda, t)(i)$.
2. The output space Y must be equipped with a generalized metric $\mathbf{d}$ which contains a subspace Z equipped with a metric d.
3. For a specific initial condition x_0 and input signal u, there must exist a unique output signal $\mathbf{y}$ defined over the time domain R. That is, the system Σ is deterministic.

Further details on the necessity and implications of the aforementioned assumptions can be found in [12].

Under Assumption 3, a system Σ can be viewed as a function $\Delta_\Sigma : X_0 \times \mathbf{U} \to Y^N \times \mathfrak{T}$ which takes as an input an initial condition $x_0 \in X_0$ and an input signal $u \in \mathbf{U}$ and it produces as output a signal $\mathbf{y} : N \to Y$ (also referred to as *trajectory*) and a timing function $\tau : N \to \mathbb{R}_+$. The only restriction on the timing function τ is that it must be a monotonic function, i.e., $\tau(i) < \tau(j)$ for $i < j$. The pair $\mu = (\mathbf{y}, \tau)$ is usually referred to as a *timed state sequence*, which is a widely accepted model for reasoning about real time systems [13]. A timed state sequence can represent a computer simulated trajectory of a CPS or the sampling process that takes place when we digitally monitor physical systems. We remark that a timed state sequence can represent both the internal state of the software/hardware (usually through an abstraction) and the state of the physical system. The set of all timed state sequences of a system Σ will be denoted by $\mathcal{L}(\Sigma)$. That is,

$$\mathcal{L}(\Sigma) = \{(\mathbf{y}, \tau) \mid \exists x_0 \in X_0 \,.\, \exists u \in \mathbf{U} \,.\, (\mathbf{y}, \tau) = \Delta_\Sigma(x_0, u)\}.$$

Our high level goal is to explore and infer properties that the system Σ satisfies by observing its response (output signals) to particular input signals and initial conditions. We assume that the system designer has some partial understanding about the properties that the system satisfies or does not satisfy and he/she would like to be able to precisely determine these properties. In particular, we assume that the system developer can formalize the system properties in Metric Temporal Logic (MTL) [5], but some parameters are unknown. Such parameters could be unknown threshold values for the continuous state variables of the hybrid system or some unknown real time constraints.

Example 1. *As a motivating example, we will consider a slightly modified version of the Automatic Transmission model provided by Mathworks as a Simulink demo[1]. Further details on this example can be found in [14,15,12].*

The only input u to the system is the throttle schedule, while the break schedule is set simply to 0 for the duration of the simulation which is $T = 30$ sec.

---

[1] Available at: http://www.mathworks.com/products/simulink/demos.html

The physical system has two continuous-time state variables which are also its outputs: the speed of the engine ω (RPM) and the speed of the vehicle v, i.e., $Y = \mathbb{R}^2$ and $\mathbf{y}(t) = [\omega(t)\ v(t)]^T$ for all $t \in [0, 30]$. Initially, the vehicle is at rest at time 0, i.e., $X_0 = \{[0\ 0]^T\}$ and $x_0 = \mathbf{y}(0) = [0\ 0]^T$. Therefore, the output trajectories depend only on the input signal u which models the throttle, i.e., $(\mathbf{y}, \tau) = \Delta_\Sigma(u)$. The throttle at each point in time can take any value between 0 (fully closed) to 100 (fully open). Namely, $u(i) \in U = [0, 100]$ for each $i \in N$. The model also contains a Stateflow chart with two concurrently executing Finite State Machines (FSMs) with 4 and 3 states, respectively. The FSMs model the logic that controls the switching between the gears in the transmission system. We remark that the system is deterministic, i.e., under the same input u, we will always observe the same output $\mathbf{y}$.

In our previous work [12,10,7], on such models, we demonstrated how to falsify requirements like: "The vehicle speed v is always under 120km/h or the engine speed ω is always below 4500RPM." A falsifying system trajectory appears in Fig. 1. In this work, we provide answers to queries like "What is the fastest time that ω can exceed 3250 RPM" or "For how long can ω be below 4500 RPM".

Formally, in this work, we solve the following problem.

Problem 1 (Temporal Logic Parameter Estimation Problem). *Given an MTL formula $\phi[\theta]$ with a single unknown parameter $\theta \in \Theta = [\theta_m, \theta_M] \subseteq \mathbb{R}$, a hybrid system Σ, and a maximum testing time T, find an optimal range $\Theta^* = [\theta_m^*, \theta_M^*]$ such that for any $\zeta \in \Theta^*$, $\phi[\zeta]$ does not hold on Σ, i.e., $\Sigma \not\models \phi[\zeta]$.*

Ideally, by solving Problem 1, we would also like to have the property that for any $\zeta \in \Theta - \Theta^*$, $\phi[\zeta]$ holds on Σ, i.e., $\Sigma \models \phi[\zeta]$. However, even for a given ζ, the problem of algorithmically computing whether $\Sigma \models \phi[\zeta]$ is not easy to solve for the classes of hybrid systems that we consider in this work.

An overview of our proposed solution to Problem 1 appears in Fig. 2. The sampler produces a point x_0 from the set of initial conditions, a parameter vector λ that characterizes the control input signal u and a parameter θ. The vectors x_0 and λ are passed to the system simulator which returns an ex-

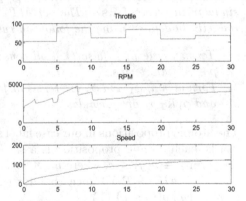

Fig. 1. Example 1: A piecewise constant input signal u parameterized with $\Lambda \in [0, 100]^6$ and $t = [0, 5, 10, 15, 20, 25]$ and the corresponding output signals that falsify the specification

ecution trace (output trajectory and timing function). The trace is then analyzed by the MTL robustness analyzer which returns a robustness value representing the best estimate for the robustness found so far. In turn, the robustness score computed is used by the stochastic sampler to decide on a next input to analyze.

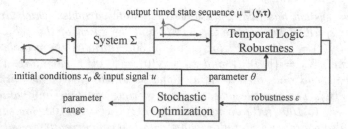

Fig. 2. Overview of the solution to the MTL parameter estimation problem on CPS

The process terminates after a maximum number of tests or when no improvement on the parameter estimate θ has been made after a number of tests.

3   Robustness of Metric Temporal Logic Formulas

Metric Temporal Logic (MTL) was introduced in [5] in order to reason about the quantitative timing properties of boolean signals. In the following, we present directly MTL in Negation Normal Form (NNF) since this is needed for the presentation of the new results in Section 5. We denote the extended real number line by $\overline{\mathbb{R}} = \mathbb{R} \cup \{\pm\infty\}$.

Definition 1 (Syntax of MTL in NNF). *Let $\overline{\mathbb{R}}$ be the set of truth degree constants, AP be the set of atomic propositions and $\mathcal{I}$ be a non-empty non-singular interval of $\overline{\mathbb{R}}_{\geq 0}$. The set MTL of all well-formed formulas (wff) is inductively defined using the following rules:*

- *Terms: True ($\top$), false ($\bot$), all constants $r \in \overline{\mathbb{R}}$ and propositions p, $\neg p$ for $p \in AP$ are terms.*
- *Formulas: if ϕ_1 and ϕ_2 are terms or formulas, then $\phi_1 \vee \phi_2$, $\phi_1 \wedge \phi_2$, $\phi_1 \mathcal{U}_{\mathcal{I}} \phi_2$ and $\phi_1 \mathcal{R}_{\mathcal{I}} \phi_2$ are formulas.*

The atomic propositions in our case label subsets of the output space Y. In other words, each atomic proposition is a shorthand for an arithmetic expression of the form $p \equiv g(y) \leq c$, where $g : Y \to \mathbb{R}$ and $c \in \mathbb{R}$. We define an observation map $\mathcal{O} : AP \to \mathcal{P}(Y)$ such that for each $p \in AP$ the corresponding set is $\mathcal{O}(p) = \{y \mid g(y) \leq c\} \subseteq Y$.

In the above definition, $\mathcal{U}_{\mathcal{I}}$ is the timed *until* operator and $\mathcal{R}_{\mathcal{I}}$ the timed *release* operator. The subscript $\mathcal{I}$ imposes timing constraints on the temporal operators. The interval $\mathcal{I}$ can be open, half-open or closed, bounded or unbounded, but it must be non-empty ($\mathcal{I} \neq \emptyset$) (and, practically speaking, non-singular ($\mathcal{I} \neq \{t\}$)). In the case where $\mathcal{I} = [0, +\infty)$, we remove the subscript $\mathcal{I}$ from the temporal operators, i.e., we just write $\mathcal{U}$, and $\mathcal{R}$. Also, we can define *eventually* ($\Diamond_{\mathcal{I}}\phi \equiv \top \mathcal{U}_{\mathcal{I}}\phi$) and *always* ($\Box_{\mathcal{I}}\phi \equiv \bot \mathcal{R}_{\mathcal{I}}\phi$).

Before proceeding to the actual definition of the robust semantics, we introduce some auxiliary notation. A metric space is a pair (X, d) such that the topology of the set X is induced by a metric d. Using a metric d, we can define the distance of a point $x \in X$ from a set $S \subseteq X$. Intuitively, this distance is the shortest distance from x to all the points in S. In a similar way, the depth of a point x in a set S is defined to be the shortest distance of x from the boundary of S. Both the notions of distance and depth will play a fundamental role in the definition of the robustness degree.

Definition 2 (Signed Distance). *Let $x \in X$ be a point, $S \subseteq X$ be a set and d be a metric on X. Then, we define the Signed Distance from x to S to be*

$$\mathbf{Dist}_d(x, S) := \begin{cases} -\mathbf{dist}_d(x, S) := -\inf\{d(x,y) \mid y \in S\} & \text{if } x \notin S \\ \mathbf{depth}_d(x, S) := \mathbf{dist}_d(x, X \backslash S) & \text{if } x \in S \end{cases}$$

We remark that we use the extended definition of the supremum and infimum, i.e., $\sup \emptyset := -\infty$ and $\inf \emptyset := +\infty$.

MTL formulas are interpreted over timed state sequences μ. In the past [6], we proposed multi-valued semantics for MTL where the valuation function on the predicates takes values over the totally ordered set $\overline{\mathbb{R}}$ according to a metric d operating on the output space Y. For this purpose, we let the valuation function be the depth (or the distance) of the current point of the signal $\mathbf{y}(i)$ in a set $\mathcal{O}(p)$ labeled by the atomic proposition p. Intuitively, this distance represents how robustly is the point $\mathbf{y}(i)$ within a set $\mathcal{O}(p)$. If this metric is zero, then even the smallest perturbation of the point can drive it inside or outside the set $\mathcal{O}(p)$, dramatically affecting membership.

For the purposes of the following discussion, we use the notation $\llbracket \phi \rrbracket$ to denote the robustness estimate with which the timed state sequence μ satisfies the specification ϕ. Formally, the valuation function for a given formula ϕ is $\llbracket \phi \rrbracket :$ $(Y^N \times \mathfrak{T}) \times N \to \overline{\mathbb{R}}$. In the definition below, we also use the following notation : for $Q \subseteq R$, the *preimage* of Q under τ is defined as : $\tau^{-1}(Q) := \{i \in N \mid \tau(i) \in Q\}$.

Definition 3 (Robustness Estimate). *Let $\mu = (\mathbf{y}, \tau) \in \mathcal{L}(\Sigma)$, $r \in \overline{\mathbb{R}}$ and $i, j, k \in N$, then the robustness estimate of any formula MTL ϕ with respect to μ is recursively defined as follows*

$$\llbracket r \rrbracket(\mu, i) := r \qquad \llbracket \top \rrbracket(\mu, i) := +\infty \qquad \llbracket \bot \rrbracket(\mu, i) := -\infty$$

$$\llbracket p \rrbracket(\mu, i) := \mathbf{Dist}_d(\mathbf{y}(i), \mathcal{O}(p)) \qquad \llbracket \neg p \rrbracket(\mu, i) := -\mathbf{Dist}_d(\mathbf{y}(i), \mathcal{O}(p))$$

$$\llbracket \phi_1 \vee \phi_2 \rrbracket(\mu, i) := \max(\llbracket \phi_1 \rrbracket(\mu, i), \llbracket \phi_2 \rrbracket(\mu, i))$$

$$\llbracket \phi_1 \wedge \phi_2 \rrbracket(\mu, i) := \min(\llbracket \phi_1 \rrbracket(\mu, i), \llbracket \phi_2 \rrbracket(\mu, i))$$

$$\llbracket \phi_1 \mathcal{U}_{\mathcal{I}} \phi_2 \rrbracket(\mu, i) := \sup_{j \in \tau^{-1}(\tau(i) + \mathcal{I})} \left(\min(\llbracket \phi_2 \rrbracket(\mu, j), \inf_{i \leq k < j} \llbracket \phi_1 \rrbracket(\mu, k)) \right)$$

$$\llbracket \phi_1 \mathcal{R}_{\mathcal{I}} \phi_2 \rrbracket(\mu, i) := \inf_{j \in \tau^{-1}(\tau(i) + \mathcal{I})} \left(\max(\llbracket \phi_2 \rrbracket(\mu, j), \sup_{i \leq k < j} \llbracket \phi_1 \rrbracket(\mu, k)) \right)$$

Recall that we use the extended definition of supremum and infimum. When $i = 0$, then we simply write $\llbracket \phi \rrbracket(\mu)$.

The robustness of an MTL formula with respect to a timed state sequence can be computed using several existing algorithms [6,15,16].

4 Parametric Metric Temporal Logic over Signals

In many cases, it is important to be able to describe an MTL specification with unknown parameters and, then, infer the parameters that make the specification true/false. In [9], Asarin et. al. introduce Parametric Signal Temporal Logic (PSTL) and present two algorithms for computing approximations for parameters over a given signal. Here, we review some of the results in [9] while adapting them in the notation and formalism that we use in this paper.

We will restrict the occurrences of unknown parameters in the specification to a single parameter that may appear either in the timing constraints of a temporal operator or in the atomic propositions.

Definition 4 (Syntax of Parametric MTL (PMTL)). *Let λ be a parameter, then the set of all well formed PMTL formulas is the set of all well formed MTL formulas where either λ appears in an arithmetic expression, i.e., $p[\lambda] \equiv g(y) \leq \lambda$, or in the timing constraint of a temporal operator, i.e., $\mathcal{I}[\lambda]$.*

We will denote a PMTL formula ϕ with parameter λ by $\phi[\lambda]$. Given some value $\theta \in \Theta$, then the formula $\phi[\theta]$ is an MTL formula.

Since the valuation function of an MTL formula is a composition of minimum and maximum operations quantified over time intervals, a formula $\phi[\lambda]$ is monotonic with respect to λ.

Example 2. *Consider the PMTL formula $\phi[\lambda] = \Box_{[0,\lambda]}p$ where $p \equiv (\omega \leq 3250)$. Given a timed state sequence $\mu = (\mathbf{y}, \tau)$ with $\tau(0) = 0$, for $\theta_1 \leq \theta_2$, we have: $[0, \theta_1] \subseteq [0, \theta_2] \implies \tau^{-1}([0, \theta_1]) \subseteq \tau^{-1}([0, \theta_2])$. Therefore, $[\![\phi[\theta_1]]\!](\mu) = \inf_{i \in \tau^{-1}([0,\theta_1])}(-\mathbf{Dist}_d(\mathbf{y}(i), \mathcal{O}(p))) \geq \inf_{i \in \tau^{-1}([0,\theta_2])}(-\mathbf{Dist}_d(\mathbf{y}(i), \mathcal{O}(p))) = [\![\phi[\theta_2]]\!](\mu)$. That is, the function $[\![\phi[\theta]]\!](\mu)$ is non-increasing with θ. See Fig. 3 for an example using an output trajectory from the system in Example 1.*

The previous example can be formalized in the following result.

Proposition 1. *Consider a PMTL formula $\phi[\lambda]$ such that it contains a subformula $\phi_1 Op_{\mathcal{I}[\lambda]} \phi_2$ where $Op \in \{\mathcal{U}, \mathcal{R}\}$. Then, given a timed state sequence $\mu = (\mathbf{y}, \tau)$, for $\theta_1, \theta_2 \in \overline{\mathbb{R}}_{\geq 0}$, such that $\theta_1 \leq \theta_2$, and for $i \in N$, we have:*

1. *if (i) $Op = \mathcal{U}$ and $\sup \mathcal{I}[\lambda] = \lambda$ or (ii) $Op = \mathcal{R}$ and $\inf \mathcal{I}[\lambda] = \lambda$, then $[\![\phi[\theta_1]]\!](\mu, i) \leq [\![\phi[\theta_2]]\!](\mu, i)$, i.e., the function $[\![\phi[\lambda]]\!](\mu, i)$ is nondecreasing with respect to λ, and*
2. *if (i) $Op = \mathcal{R}$ and $\sup \mathcal{I}[\lambda] = \lambda$ or (ii) $Op = \mathcal{U}$ and $\inf \mathcal{I}[\lambda] = \lambda$, then $[\![\phi[\theta_1]]\!](\mu, i) \geq [\![\phi[\theta_2]]\!](\mu, i)$, i.e., the function $[\![\phi[\lambda]]\!](\mu, i)$ is non-increasing with respect to λ.*

Proof (Sketch). The proof is by induction on the structure of the formula and it is similar to the proofs that appear in [6].

For completeness, we present the case $[\![\phi_1 \mathcal{U}_{\langle \alpha, \lambda \rangle} \phi_2]\!](\mu, i)$, where $\langle \in \{[, (\}$ and $\rangle \in \{],)\}$. The other cases are either similar or they are based on the monotonicity of the operators max and min. Let $\theta_1 \leq \theta_2$, then:

$$[\![\phi_1 \,\mathcal{U}_{\langle\alpha,\theta_1\rangle}\,\phi_2]\!](\mu, i) \leq \max\left([\![\phi_1 \,\mathcal{U}_{\langle\alpha,\theta_1\rangle}\,\phi_2]\!](\mu, i), [\![\phi_1 \,\mathcal{U}_{\overline{\langle}\theta_1,\theta_2\rangle}\,\phi_2]\!](\mu, i)\right)$$
$$= [\![\phi_1 \,\mathcal{U}_{\langle\alpha,\theta_2\rangle}\,\phi_2]\!](\mu, i)$$

where $\overline{\langle} \in \{[, (\}$ such that $\langle\alpha,\theta_1\rangle \cap \overline{\langle}\theta_1,\theta_2\rangle = \emptyset$ and $\langle\alpha,\theta_1\rangle \cup \overline{\langle}\theta_1,\theta_2\rangle = \langle\alpha,\theta_2\rangle$. □

We can derive similar results when the parameter appears in the numerical expression of the atomic proposition.

Proposition 2. *Consider a PMTL formula $\phi[\lambda]$ such that it contains a parametric atomic proposition $p[\lambda]$ in a subformula. Then, given a timed state sequence $\mu = (\mathbf{y}, \tau)$, for θ_1, $\theta_2 \in \overline{\mathbb{R}}_{\geq 0}$, such that $\theta_1 \leq \theta_2$, and for $i \in N$, we have:*

1. *if $p[\lambda] \equiv g(x) \leq \lambda$, then $[\![\phi[\theta_1]]\!](\mu, i) \leq [\![\phi[\theta_2]]\!](\mu, i)$, i.e., the function $[\![\phi[\lambda]]\!](\mu, i)$ is nondecreasing with respect to λ, and*
2. *if $p[\lambda] \equiv g(x) \geq \lambda$, then $[\![\phi[\theta_1]]\!](\mu, i) \geq [\![\phi[\theta_2]]\!](\mu, i)$, i.e., the function $[\![\phi[\lambda]]\!](\mu, i)$ is non-increasing with respect to λ.*

Proof (Sketch). The proof is by induction on the structure of the formula and it is similar to the proofs that appear in [6].

For completeness, we present the base case $[\![p[\lambda]]\!](\mu, i)$ where $p[\lambda] \equiv g(x) \leq \lambda$. Since $\theta_1 \leq \theta_2$, $\mathcal{O}(p[\theta_1]) \subseteq \mathcal{O}(p[\theta_2])$. We will only present the case for which $\mathbf{y}(i) \notin \mathcal{O}(p[\theta_2])$. We have:

$$\mathcal{O}(p[\theta_1]) \subseteq \mathcal{O}(p[\theta_2]) \implies \mathbf{dist}_d(\mathbf{y}(i), \mathcal{O}(p[\theta_1])) \geq \mathbf{dist}_d(\mathbf{y}(i), \mathcal{O}(p[\theta_2])) \implies$$
$$\mathbf{Dist}_d(\mathbf{y}(i), \mathcal{O}(p[\theta_1])) \leq \mathbf{Dist}_d(\mathbf{y}(i), \mathcal{O}(p[\theta_2])) \implies [\![p[\theta_1]]\!](\mu, i) \leq [\![p[\theta_2]]\!](\mu, i)\square$$

The results presented in this section can be easily extended to multiple parameters. However, in this work, we will focus on a single parameter in order to derive a more tractable optimization problem.

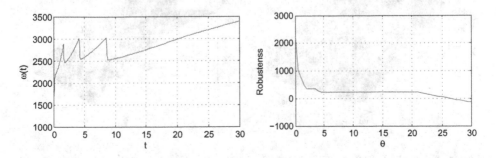

Fig. 3. Example 2. Left: Engine speed $\omega(t)$ for constant throttle $u(t) = 50$. Right: The robustness of the specification $\Box_{[0,\theta]}(\omega \leq 3250)$ with respect to θ.

5   Temporal Logic Parameter Bound Computation

The notion of robustness of temporal logics will enable us to pose the parameter estimation problem as an optimization problem. In order to solve the resulting optimization problem, falsification methods and S-TaLiRo can be utilized in order to estimate Θ^* for Problem 1.

As described in the previous section, the parametric robustness functions that we are considering are monotonic with respect to the search parameter. Therefore, if we are searching for a parameter over an interval $\Theta = [\theta_m, \theta_M]$, we know that Θ^* is going to be either of the form $[\theta_m, \theta^*]$ or $[\theta^*, \theta_M]$. In other words, depending on the structure of $\phi[\lambda]$, we are either trying to minimize or maximize θ^* such that for all $\theta \in \Theta^*$, we have $[\![\phi[\theta]]\!](\Sigma) = \min_{\mu \in \mathcal{L}_\tau(\Sigma)}[\![\phi[\theta]]\!](\mu) \leq 0$.

Example 3. *Let us consider again the automotive transmission example and the specification $\phi[\lambda] = \square_{[0,\lambda]}p$ where $p \equiv (\omega \leq 4500)$. The specification robustness $[\![\phi[\theta]]\!](\Delta_\Sigma(u))$ as a function of θ and the input u appears in Fig. 4 (left) for constant input signals. The creation of the graph required $100 \times 30 = 3,000$ tests. The contour under the surface indicates the zero level set of the robustness surface, i.e., the θ and u values for which we get $[\![\phi[\theta]]\!](\Delta_\Sigma(u)) = 0$. From the graph, we can infer that $\theta^* \approx 2.8$ and that for any $\theta \in [2.8, 30]$, we have $[\![\phi[\theta]]\!](\Sigma) \leq 0$. The approximate value of θ^* is a rough estimate based on the granularity of the grid that we used to plot the surface.*

In summary, in order to solve Problem 1, we would have to solve the following optimization problem:

$$\text{optimize} \quad \theta \tag{1}$$
$$\text{subject to} \quad \theta \in \Theta \text{ and } [\![\phi[\theta]]\!](\Sigma) = \min_{\mu \in \mathcal{L}_\tau(\Sigma)} [\![\phi[\theta]]\!](\mu) \leq 0$$

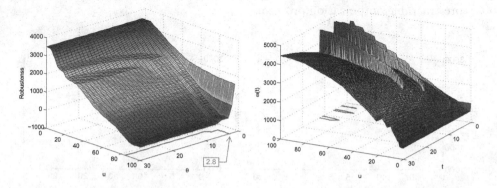

Fig. 4. Example 3: Left: Specification robustness as a function of the parameter θ and the constant input u. Right: Engine speed $\omega(t)$ as a function of the constant input u and time t. The contours indicate the u-t combinations for which $\omega(t) = 4500$.

However, $[\![\phi[\theta]]\!](\Sigma)$ neither can be computed using reachability analysis algorithms nor is known in closed form for the systems that we are considering. Therefore, we will have to compute an under-approximation of Θ^*.

Our focus will be to formulate an optimization problem that can be solved using stochastic search methods. In particular, we will reformulate optimization problem (1) into a new one where the constraints due to the specification are incorporated into the cost function:

$$\text{optimize}_{\theta \in \Theta} \left(\theta + \begin{cases} \gamma \pm [\![\phi[\theta]]\!](\Sigma) & \text{if } [\![\phi[\theta]]\!](\Sigma) \geq 0 \\ 0 & \text{otherwise} \end{cases} \right) \tag{2}$$

where the sign $(\pm)$ and the parameter γ depend on whether the problem is a maximization or a minimization problem. The parameter γ must be properly chosen so that the optimum of problem (2) is in Θ if and only if $[\![\phi[\theta]]\!](\Sigma) \leq 0$. In other words, we must avoid the case where for some θ, we have $[\![\phi[\theta]]\!](\Sigma) > 0$ and $(\theta + [\![\phi[\theta]]\!](\Sigma)) \in \Theta$. Therefore, if the problem in Eq. (1) is feasible, then the optimum of equations (1) and (2) is the same.

5.1 Non-increasing Robustness Functions

First, we consider the case of non-increasing robustness functions $[\![\phi[\theta]]\!](\Sigma)$ with respect to the search variable θ. In this case, the optimization problem is a minimization problem.

To see why this is the case, assume that $[\![\phi[\theta_M]]\!](\Sigma) \leq 0$. Since for $\theta \leq \theta_M$, we have $[\![\phi[\theta]]\!](\Sigma) \geq [\![\phi[\theta_M]]\!](\Sigma)$, we need to find the minimum θ such that we still have $[\![\phi[\theta]]\!](\Sigma) \leq 0$. That θ will be θ^* since for all $\theta' \in [\theta^*, \theta_M]$, we will have $[\![\phi[\theta']]\!](\Sigma) \leq 0$.

We will reformulate the problem of Eq. (2) so that we do not have to solve two separate optimization problems. From (2), we have:

$$\min_{\theta \in \Theta} \left(\theta + \begin{cases} \gamma + \min_{\mu \in \mathcal{L}_\tau(\Sigma)} [\![\phi[\theta]]\!](\mu) & \text{if } \min_{\mu \in \mathcal{L}_\tau(\Sigma)} [\![\phi[\theta]]\!](\mu) \geq 0 \\ 0 & \text{otherwise} \end{cases} \right) =$$

$$= \min_{\theta \in \Theta} \left(\theta + \min_{\mu \in \mathcal{L}_\tau(\Sigma)} \begin{cases} \gamma + [\![\phi[\theta]]\!](\mu) & \text{if } [\![\phi[\theta]]\!](\mu) \geq 0 \\ 0 & \text{otherwise} \end{cases} \right) =$$

$$= \min_{\theta \in \Theta} \min_{\mu \in \mathcal{L}_\tau(\Sigma)} \left(\theta + \begin{cases} \gamma + [\![\phi[\theta]]\!](\mu) & \text{if } [\![\phi[\theta]]\!](\mu) \geq 0 \\ 0 & \text{otherwise} \end{cases} \right) \tag{3}$$

where $\gamma \geq \max(\theta_M, 0)$.

The previous discussion is formalized in the following result.

Proposition 3. *Let θ^* and μ^* be the parameters returned by an optimization algorithm that is applied to the problem in Eq. (3). If $[\![\phi[\theta^*]]\!](\mu^*) \leq 0$, then for all $\theta \in \Theta^* = [\theta^*, \theta_M]$, we have $[\![\phi[\theta]]\!](\Sigma) \leq 0$.*

Proof. If $[\![\phi[\theta^*]]\!](\mu^*) \leq 0$, then $[\![\phi[\theta^*]]\!](\Sigma) \leq 0$. Since $[\![\phi[\theta]]\!](\Sigma)$ is non-increasing with respect to θ, then for all $\theta \in [\theta^*, \theta_M]$, we also have $[\![\phi[\theta]]\!](\Sigma) \leq 0$.

Since we are utilizing stochastic optimization methods [7,10,8,4] to solve problem (3), if $\llbracket \phi[\theta^*] \rrbracket (\mu^*) > 0$, then we cannot infer that the system is correct for all parameter values in Θ.

Example 4. *Using Eq. (3) as a cost function, we can now compute the optimal parameter for Example 3 using our toolbox* S-TaLiRo *[10]. In particular, using Simulated Annealing as a stochastic optimization function,* S-TaLiRo *returns* $\theta^* \approx 2.45$ *as optimal parameter for constant input* $u(t) = 99.8046$. *The corresponding temporal logic robustness for the specification* $\square_{[0,2.45]}(\omega \leq 4500)$ *is* -0.0445. *The total number of tests performed for this example was 500 and, potentially, the accuracy of estimating* θ^* *can be improved if we increase the maximum number of tests. However, we remark that based on several tests the algorithm converges to a good approximation within 200 tests.*

5.2   Non-decreasing Robustness Functions

The case of non-decreasing robustness functions is symmetric to the case of non-increasing robustness functions. In particular, the optimization problem is a maximization problem. We will reformulate the problem of Eq. (2) so that we do not have to solve two separate optimization problems. From (2), we have:

$$
\max_{\theta \in \Theta} \left(\theta + \begin{cases} \gamma - \min_{\mu \in \mathcal{L}_\tau(\Sigma)} \llbracket \phi[\theta] \rrbracket (\mu) & \text{if } \min_{\mu \in \mathcal{L}_\tau(\Sigma)} \llbracket \phi[\theta] \rrbracket (\mu) \geq 0 \\ 0 & \text{otherwise} \end{cases} \right) =
$$

$$
= \max_{\theta \in \Theta} \left(\theta + \begin{cases} \gamma + \max_{\mu \in \mathcal{L}_\tau(\Sigma)} (-\llbracket \phi[\theta] \rrbracket (\mu)) & \text{if } \max_{\mu \in \mathcal{L}_\tau(\Sigma)} (-\llbracket \phi[\theta] \rrbracket (\mu)) \leq 0 \\ 0 & \text{otherwise} \end{cases} \right) =
$$

$$
= \max_{\theta \in \Theta} \left(\theta + \max_{\mu \in \mathcal{L}_\tau(\Sigma)} \begin{cases} \gamma - \llbracket \phi[\theta] \rrbracket (\mu) & \text{if } -\llbracket \phi[\theta] \rrbracket (\mu) \leq 0 \\ 0 & \text{otherwise} \end{cases} \right) =
$$

$$
= \max_{\theta \in \Theta} \max_{\mu \in \mathcal{L}_\tau(\Sigma)} \left(\theta + \begin{cases} \gamma - \llbracket \phi[\theta] \rrbracket (\mu) & \text{if } \llbracket \phi[\theta] \rrbracket (\mu) \geq 0 \\ 0 & \text{otherwise} \end{cases} \right) \tag{4}
$$

where $\gamma \leq \min(\theta_m, 0)$.

The previous discussion is formalized in the following result.

Proposition 4. *Let* θ^* *and* μ^* *be the parameters returned by an optimization algorithm that is applied to the problem in Eq. (4). If* $\llbracket \phi[\theta^*] \rrbracket (\mu^*) \leq 0$, *then for all* $\theta \in \Theta^* = [\theta_m, \theta^*]$, *we have* $\llbracket \phi[\theta] \rrbracket (\Sigma) \leq 0$.

Proof. If $\llbracket \phi[\theta^*] \rrbracket (\mu^*) \leq 0$, then $\llbracket \phi[\theta^*] \rrbracket (\Sigma) \leq 0$. Since $\llbracket \phi[\theta] \rrbracket (\Sigma)$ is non-decreasing with respect to θ, then for all $\theta \in [\theta_m, \theta^*]$, we also have $\llbracket \phi[\theta] \rrbracket (\Sigma) \leq 0$.

Again, if $\llbracket \phi[\theta^*] \rrbracket (\mu^*) > 0$, then we cannot infer that the system is correct for all parameter values in Θ.

Example 5. *Let us consider the specification* $\phi[\lambda] = \square_{[\lambda,30]}(\omega \leq 4500)$ *on our running example. The specification robustness* $\llbracket \phi[\theta] \rrbracket (\Delta_\Sigma(u))$ *as a function of* θ *and the input* u *appears in Fig. 5 (left) for constant input signals. The creation*

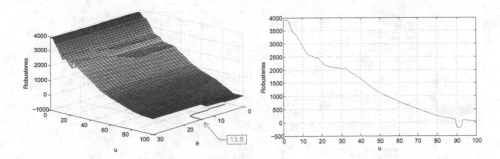

Fig. 5. Example 5. Left: Specification robustness as a function of the parameter θ and the constant input u. Right: The robustness function $[\![\Box_{[12.59,30]}(\omega \leq 4500)]\!](\Delta_\Sigma(u))$.

of the graph required $100 \times 30 = 3,000$ tests. The contour under the surface indicates the zero level set of the robustness surface, i.e., the θ and u values for which we get $[\![\phi[\theta]]\!](\Delta_\Sigma(u)) = 0$. We remark that the contour is actually an approximation of the zero level set computed by a linear interpolation using the neighboring points on the grid. From the graph, we could infer that $\theta^* \approx 13.8$ and that for any $\theta \in [0, 13.8]$, we would have $[\![\phi[\theta]]\!](\Sigma) \leq 0$. Again, the approximate value of θ^* is a rough estimate based on the granularity of the grid.

Using Eq. (4) as a cost function, we can now compute the optimal parameter for Example 3 using our toolbox S-TaLiRo [10]. S-TaLiRo returns $\theta^* \approx 12.59$ as optimal parameter for constant input $u(t) = 90.88$ within 250 tests. The temporal logic robustness for the specification $\Box_{[12.59,30]}(\omega \leq 4500)$ with respect to the input u appears in Fig. 5 (right). Some observations: (i) The $\theta^* \approx 12.59$ computed by S-TaLiRo is actually very close to the optimal value since for $\theta^* \approx 12.79$ the system does not falsify any more. (ii) The systematic testing that was used in order to generate the graph was not able to accurately compute a good approximation to the parameter unless even more tests (> 3000) are generated.

6   Experiments and a Case Study

The parametric MTL exploration of embedded systems was motivated by a challenge problem published by Ford in 2002 [11]. In particular, the report provided a simple – but still realistic – model of a powertrain system (both the physical system and the embedded control logic) and posed the question whether there are constant operating conditions that can cause a transition from gear two to gear one and then back to gear two. Such a sequence would imply that the transition was not necessary in the first place.

The system is modeled in Checkmate [17]. It has 6 continuous state variables and 2 Stateflow charts with 4 and 6 states, respectively. The Stateflow chart for the shift scheduler appears in Fig. 6. The system dynamics and switching conditions are linear. However, some switching conditions depend on the inputs to the system. The latter makes the application of standard hybrid system verification tools not a straightforward task.

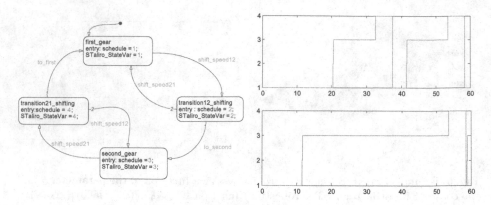

Fig. 6. Left: The shift scheduler of the powertrain challenge problem. Right: Shift schedules. The numbers on the y-axis correspond to the variables in the states of the shift scheduler. Right Top: The shift schedule falsifying requirement ϕ_{e1}. Right Bottom: The shift schedule falsifying requirement $\phi_{e3}[0.4273]$.

In [15], we demonstrated that S-TaLiRo [10] can successfully solve the challenge problem (see Fig. 6) by formalizing the requirement as an MTL specification $\phi_{e1} = \neg\Diamond(g_2 \wedge \Diamond(g_1 \wedge \Diamond g_2))$ where g_i is a proposition that is true when the system is in gear i. Stochastic search methods can be applied to solve the resulting optimization problem where the cost function is the robustness of the specification. Moreover, inspired by the success of S-TaLiRo on the challenge problem, we tried to ask a more complex question. Namely, does a transition exists from gear two to gear one and back to gear two in less than 2.5 sec? An MTL specification that can capture this requirement is $\phi_{e2} = \Box((\neg g_1 \wedge X g_1) \rightarrow \Box_{[0,2.5]}\neg g_2)$.

The natural question that arises is what would be the smallest time for which such a transition can occur? We can formulate a parametric MTL formula to query the model of the powertrain system: $\phi_{e3}[\lambda] = \Box((\neg g_1 \wedge X g_1) \rightarrow \Box_{[0,\lambda]}\neg g_2)$. We have extended S-TaLiRo to be able to handle parametric MTL specifications. The total simulation time of the model was 60 sec and the search interval was $\Theta = [0, 30]$. S-TaLiRo returned $\theta^* \approx 0.4273$ as the minimum parameter found (See Fig. 6) using about 300 tests of the system.

In Table 6, we present some experimental results. Since no other technique can solve the parameter estimation problem for MTL formulas over hybrid systems, we compare our method with the falsification methods that we have developed in the past [12,7]. A detailed description of the benchmark problems can be found in [12,7] and the benchmarks can be downloaded with the S-TaLiRo distribution[2]. In order to be able to compare the two methods, when performing parameter estimation, we regard a parameter value less than the constant in the MTL formula as falsification. Notably, for benchmark problems that are easier to falsify, the parameter estimation method incurs additional cost in the sense of reduced number of falsifications. On the other hand, on hard problem instances,

---

[2] https://sites.google.com/a/asu.edu/s-taliro/

Table 1. Experimental Comparison of Falsification (FA) vs. Parameter Estimation (PE). Each instance was run for 100 times and each run was executed for a maximum of 1000 tests. Legend: **#Fals.**: the number of runs falsified, **Parameter Estimate**: ⟨min, average, max⟩ of the parameter value computed, **dnf**: did not finish.

Benchmark Problem			#Fals.		Parameter Estimate
Specification	Instance	FA	PE		PE
$\phi_2^{AT}[\lambda] = \neg\Diamond(p_1^{AT} \wedge \Diamond_{[0,\lambda]} p_2^{AT})$	$\phi_2^{AT}[10]$	96	84		⟨7.7, 9.56, 16.84⟩
$\phi_3^{AT}[\lambda] = \neg\Diamond(p_1^{AT} \wedge \Diamond_{[0,\lambda]} p_3^{AT})$	$\phi_3^{AT}[10]$	51	0		⟨10.00, 10.22, 14.66⟩
$\phi_4^{AT}[\lambda] = \neg\Diamond(p_1^{AT} \wedge \Diamond_{[0,\lambda]} p_2^{AT})$	$\phi_4^{AT}[7.5]$	0	0		⟨7.57, 7.7, 8.56⟩
$\phi_5^{AT}[\lambda] = \neg\Diamond(p_1^{AT} \wedge \Diamond_{[0,\lambda]} p_2^{AT})$	$\phi_5^{AT}[5]$	0	0		⟨7.56, 7.74, 9.06⟩
	$\phi_{e3}[2.5]$	dnf	93		⟨1.28, 2.26, 6.82⟩

the parameter estimation method provides us with parameter ranges for which the system fails the specification. Moreover, on the powertrain challenge problem, the parameter estimation method actually helps in falsifying the system. We conjecture that the reason for this improved performance is that the timing requirements on this problem are more important than the state constraints.

7   Related Work

The topic of testing embedded software and, in particular, embedded control software is a well studied problem that involves many subtopics well beyond the scope of this paper. We refer the reader to specialized book chapters and textbooks for further information [18,19]. Similarly, a lot of research has been invested on testing methods for Model Based Development (MBD) of embedded systems [3]. However, the temporal logic testing of embedded and hybrid systems has not received much attention [20,21,4,22].

Parametric temporal logics were first defined over traces of finite state machines [23]. In parametric temporal logics, some of the timing constraints of the temporal operators are replaced by parameters. Then, the goal is to develop algorithms that will compute the values of the parameters that make the specification true under some optimality criteria. That line of work has been extended to real-time systems and in particular to timed automata [24] and continuous-time signals [9]. The authors in [25,26] define a parametric temporal logic called quantifier free LTL over real valued signals. However, they focus on the problem of determining system parameters such that the system satisfies a given property rather than on the problem of exploring the properties of a given system.

Another related research topic is the problem of Temporal Logic Queries [27,28]. In detail, given a model of the system and a temporal logic formula ϕ, a subformula in ϕ is replaced with a special symbol ?. Then, the problem is to determine a set of Boolean formulas such that if these formulas are placed into the placeholder ?, then ϕ holds on the model.

8 Conclusions

An important stage in Model Based Development (MBD) of embedded control software is the formalization of system requirements. We advocate that Metric Temporal Logic (MTL) is an excellent candidate for formalizing interesting design requirements. In this paper, we have presented a solution on how we can explore system properties using Parametric MTL (PMTL) [9]. Based on the notion of robustness of MTL [6], we have converted the parameter estimation problem into an optimization problem which we solve using S-TaLiRo [10]. Even though this paper presents a method for estimating the range for a single parameter, the results can be easily extended to multiple parameters as long as the robustness function has the same monotonicity with respect to all the parameters. Finally, we have demonstrated that the our method can provide interesting insights to the powertrain challenge problem [11].

Acknowledgments. This work was partially supported by a grant from the NSF Industry/University Cooperative Research Center (I/UCRC) on Embedded Systems at Arizona State University and NSF awards CNS-1116136 and CNS-1017074.

References

1. Lions, J.L., Lbeck, L., Fauquembergue, J.L., Kahn, G., Kubbat, W., Levedag, S., Mazzini, L., Merle, D., O'Halloran, C.: Ariane 5, flight 501 failure, report by the inquiry board. Technical report, CNES (1996)
2. Hoffman, E.J., Ebert, W.L., Femiano, M.D., Freeman, H.R., Gay, C.J., Jones, C.P., Luers, P.J., Palmer, J.G.: The near rendezvous burn anomaly of december 1998. Technical report, Applied Physics Laboratory, Johns Hopkins University (1999)
3. Tripakis, S., Dang, T.: Modeling, Verification and Testing using Timed and Hybrid Automata. In: Model-Based Design for Embedded Systems, pp. 383–436. CRC Press (2009)
4. Nghiem, T., Sankaranarayanan, S., Fainekos, G.E., Ivancic, F., Gupta, A., Pappas, G.J.: Monte-carlo techniques for falsification of temporal properties of non-linear hybrid systems. In: Proceedings of the 13th ACM International Conference on Hybrid Systems: Computation and Control, pp. 211–220. ACM Press (2010)
5. Koymans, R.: Specifying real-time properties with metric temporal logic. Real-Time Systems 2, 255–299 (1990)
6. Fainekos, G.E., Pappas, G.J.: Robustness of temporal logic specifications for continuous-time signals. Theoretical Computer Science 410, 4262–4291 (2009)
7. Sankaranarayanan, S., Fainekos, G.: Falsification of temporal properties of hybrid systems using the cross-entropy method. In: ACM International Conference on Hybrid Systems: Computation and Control (2012)
8. Annapureddy, Y.S.R., Fainekos, G.E.: Ant colonies for temporal logic falsification of hybrid systems. In: Proceedings of the 36th Annual Conference of IEEE Industrial Electronics, pp. 91–96 (2010)
9. Asarin, E., Donzé, A., Maler, O., Nickovic, D.: Parametric Identification of Temporal Properties. In: Khurshid, S., Sen, K. (eds.) RV 2011. LNCS, vol. 7186, pp. 147–160. Springer, Heidelberg (2012)

10. Annapureddy, Y.S.R., Liu, C., Fainekos, G.E., Sankaranarayanan, S.: S-TaLiRo: A Tool for Temporal Logic Falsification for Hybrid Systems. In: Abdulla, P.A., Leino, K.R.M. (eds.) TACAS 2011. LNCS, vol. 6605, pp. 254–257. Springer, Heidelberg (2011)
11. Chutinan, A., Butts, K.R.: Dynamic analysis of hybrid system models for design validation. Technical report, Ford Motor Company (2002)
12. Abbas, H., Fainekos, G.E., Sankaranarayanan, S., Ivancic, F., Gupta, A.: Probabilistic temporal logic falsification of cyber-physical systems. ACM Transactions on Embedded Computing Systems (2011) (in press)
13. Alur, R., Henzinger, T.A.: Real-Time Logics: Complexity and Expressiveness. In: Fifth Annual IEEE Symposium on Logic in Computer Science, pp. 390–401. IEEE Computer Society Press, Washington, D.C (1990)
14. Zhao, Q., Krogh, B.H., Hubbard, P.: Generating test inputs for embedded control systems. IEEE Control Systems Magazine, 49–57 (August 2003)
15. Fainekos, G., Sankaranarayanan, S., Ueda, K., Yazarel, H.: Verification of automotive control applications using s-taliro. In: Proceedings of the American Control Conference (2012)
16. Donze, A., Maler, O.: Robust Satisfaction of Temporal Logic over Real-Valued Signals. In: Chatterjee, K., Henzinger, T.A. (eds.) FORMATS 2010. LNCS, vol. 6246, pp. 92–106. Springer, Heidelberg (2010)
17. Silva, B.I., Krogh, B.H.: Formal verification of hybrid systems using CheckMate: a case study. In: Proceedings of the American Control Conference, vol. 3, pp. 1679–1683 (2000)
18. Conrad, M., Fey, I.: Testing automotive control software. In: Automotive Embedded Systems Handbook. CRC Press (2008)
19. Koopman, P.: Better Embedded System Software. Drumnadrochit Education LLC (2010)
20. Plaku, E., Kavraki, L.E., Vardi, M.Y.: Falsification of LTL Safety Properties in Hybrid Systems. In: Kowalewski, S., Philippou, Λ. (eds.) TACAS 2009. LNCS, vol. 5505, pp. 368–382. Springer, Heidelberg (2009)
21. Tan, L., Kim, J., Sokolsky, O., Lee, I.: Model-based testing and monitoring for hybrid embedded systems. In: Proceedings of the 2004 IEEE International Conference on Information Reuse and Integration, pp. 487–492 (2004)
22. Zuliani, P., Platzer, A., Clarke, E.M.: Bayesian statistical model checking with application to simulink/stateflow verification. In: Proceedings of the 13th ACM International Conference on Hybrid Systems: Computation and Control, pp. 243–252 (2010)
23. Alur, R., Etessami, K., La Torre, S., Peled, D.: Parametric temporal logic for model measuring. ACM Trans. Comput. Logic 2, 388–407 (2001)
24. Di Giampaolo, B., La Torre, S., Napoli, M.: Parametric Metric Interval Temporal Logic. In: Dediu, A.-H., Fernau, H., Martín-Vide, C. (eds.) LATA 2010. LNCS, vol. 6031, pp. 249–260. Springer, Heidelberg (2010)
25. Fages, F., Rizk, A.: On temporal logic constraint solving for analyzing numerical data time series. Theor. Comput. Sci. 408, 55–65 (2008)
26. Rizk, A., Batt, G., Fages, F., Soliman, S.: On a Continuous Degree of Satisfaction of Temporal Logic Formulae with Applications to Systems Biology. In: Heiner, M., Uhrmacher, A.M. (eds.) CMSB 2008. LNCS (LNBI), vol. 5307, pp. 251–268. Springer, Heidelberg (2008)
27. Chan, W.: Temporal-Logic Queries. In: Emerson, E.A., Sistla, A.P. (eds.) CAV 2000. LNCS, vol. 1855, pp. 450–463. Springer, Heidelberg (2000)
28. Chechik, M., Gurfinkel, A.: TLQSolver: A Temporal Logic Query Checker. In: Hunt Jr., W.A., Somenzi, F. (eds.) CAV 2003. LNCS, vol. 2725, pp. 210–214. Springer, Heidelberg (2003)

State Estimation and Property-Guided Exploration for Hybrid Systems Testing

Thao Dang and Noa Shalev*

VERIMAG/CNRS,
Centre Equation
2 Avenue de Vignate, 38610 Gières, France
{Thao.Dang,Noa.Shalev}@imag.fr

Abstract. This paper is concerned with model-based testing of hybrid systems. The first result is an algorithm for test generation which enhances the coverage of critical trajectories by using a random walk. The second result is a framework for practical testing that includes a state estimator. When the state of a system under test cannot be directly observed, it is necessary to reconstruct the trajectory of the real system in order to produce a verdict whether the system violates a property. To do so, we integrate in our tester a hybrid observer, the goal of which is to provide an estimate for the current location and the continuous state of the system under test based on the information on the input and the output of the system.

1 Introduction

We describe some recent progress in model-based testing of hybrid systems, systems combining continuous and discrete dynamics. Such systems have been widely accepted as a mathematical model for many applications in embedded systems and cyber-physical systems. In our previous work [7], we introduced a test coverage measure, based on the notion of star discrepancy of a set of points, which indicates how well the states visited by a test suite represent the whole reachable space. We then designed a test generation algorithm, called gRRT [7] which can be seen as a coverage guided version of the RRT (Rapidly-exploring Random Tree) algorithm for robotic planning [12]. Our algorithm has been successfully applied to a number of analog circuits and control applications. In this paper, we propose a new version of the test generation algorithm that is not only guided by the coverage but also by the property to verify. We focus on covering the trajectories that violate a property of interest and exploiting the discrete structure of the hybrid system. More concretely, we are interested in finding a search strategy that allows achieving a high probability of reaching some set of states. In the current version of the gRRT algorithm, we sample a

---

* This work was supported by the Agence Nationale de la Recherche (VEDECY project - ANR 2009 SEGI 015 01).

B. Nielsen and C. Weise (Eds.): ICTSS 2012, LNCS 7641, pp. 152–167, 2012.

goal hybrid state according to some distribution reflecting the current coverage information. The probability that a state is sampled to be a goal state depends on the current state coverage, which tends to a 'uniform' coverage over the global hybrid state space. In this work, we propose a new sampling method in order to bias the exploration towards some critical paths. To do so, we specify some desired stationary probability distribution over the regions (which reflect the objective of our biased exploration) and use the Metropolis-Hastings algorithms to compute a transition probability matrix of a random walk on a discrete abstraction of the hybrid system under study. An advantage of this random exploration is that one can use the bound on the expected number of transitions necessary to reach a given region as a criterion to determine the desired stationary probability distribution and guide the exploration towards critical behaviors more efficiently.

In addition, we address the partial observability problem to extend our framework to more practical testing settings. When not all discrete transitions and not all components of the continuous states are observable, to produce a verdict it is necessary to reconstruct the trajectory of the system under test. To do so, we integrate in our tester a hybrid observer, the goal of which is to provide an estimate for the current location and the continuous state of the system under test, based on the information on the input and the output of the system.

Hybrid systems testing has recently attracted the attention of researchers, which is attested by a number of publications on the topics (see for example [9,4,17,10] and references therein). However, to our knowledge, partial observability is not yet considered. Our work on testing under partial observability is inspired by a number of existing results in testing for discrete and timed systems (see for example [11,8,1]). In some of these works (such as [8]), game theoretic approaches are used. Applying this idea to hybrid systems is however difficult since this often requires complex and expensive set computations. Our approach is rather based on the idea of estimating the state of the system using the well-established results on observer design for continuous systems [14,5]. Concerning the use of random walks in test generation, this idea has recently been intensively applied for software testing, in particular, one could mention the tool MaTeLo developped by the company All4tec[1]. In this work, we make use of Metropolis-Hastings algorithms which have been successful for network protocol design (see for example [16]).

The paper is organized as follows. We first recall the testing framework and basic definitions. We then show how to combine a random walk with the coverage-guided test generation algorithm. The next section is devoted to the problem of designing an algorithm for test execution under partial observability. Finally we present some experimental results obtained for two well-known analog and mixed-signal circuit benchmarks.

---

[1] http://www.all4tec.net/

2   Model-Based Testing of Hybrid Systems

2.1   Model

We use a conformance testing framework based on the hybrid automaton model [2]. Intuitively, a hybrid automaton is an automaton where each location is associated with a distinct continuous mode and the switching between the continuous modes is described by discrete transitions. In this work we focus on discrete-time hybrid automata.

Definition 1. *A discrete-time hybrid automaton is a tuple $\mathcal{A} = (\mathcal{X}, Q, E, F, \mathcal{I}, \mathcal{G})$ where*

- *$\mathcal{X}$ is the continuous state space and is a bounded subset of $\mathbb{R}^n$;*
- *Q is a (finite) set of locations;*
- *$E \subseteq Q \times Q$ is a set of discrete transitions;*
- *$F = \{F_q \mid q \in Q\}$ such that for each $q \in Q$, $F_q = (f_q, \mathcal{U}_q)$ defines a difference equation*

$$x[k + 1] = f_q(x[k], u[k])$$

  for each location q; $x \in \mathcal{X}$ is the continuous state, $u(\cdot) \in \mathcal{U}_q$ is the input of the form $u : \mathcal{N}^+ \to U_q \subset \mathbb{R}^m$. The set $\mathcal{U}_q$ is the set of admissible inputs.
- *$\mathcal{I} = \{\mathcal{I}_q \subseteq \mathcal{X} \mid q \in Q\}$ is a set of staying conditions;*
- *$\mathcal{G} = \{\mathcal{G}_e \mid e \in E\}$ is a set of guards such that for each discrete transition $e = (q, q') \in E$, $\mathcal{G}_e \subseteq \mathcal{I}_q$;*

A *hybrid state* is a pair (q, x) where $q \in Q$ and $x \in \mathcal{X}$. The initial state of the automaton is denoted by (q_0, x_0). A state (q, x) of $\mathcal{A}$ can change in two ways as follows: by a *continuous evolution* (that is, the continuous state x evolves according to the dynamics f_q while the location q remains constant) and by a *discrete evolution* (that is, x satisfies the guard condition of an outgoing transition, the system changes the location by taking this transition).

Unlike *continuous evolutions*, *discrete evolutions* are instantaneous, which means that they do not take time. This model allows capturing *non-determinism* in both continuous and discrete dynamics. This non-determinism is useful for describing disturbances from the environment and imprecision in modelling and implementation.

2.2   Testing Problem

Specification and System Under Test. Our testing goal is to study the conformance relation between the behaviors of a system under test (SUT) and a specification. The specification is modeled by a hybrid automaton $\mathcal{A}$ and the system under test by another hybrid automaton $\mathcal{A}_s$ (we may not know the hybrid automaton $\mathcal{A}_s$). The tester applies the control inputs to the SUT and observes the outputs to produce one of the following verdicts: 'pass' (the observed behavior is allowed by the specification), 'fail' (the observed behavior is not allowed by the specification). In this work, we use the trace inclusion to define conformance relation. Intuitively, the system under test $\mathcal{A}_s$ conforms to the specification $\mathcal{A}$ if under every admissible control action sequence, the set of observation sequences of $\mathcal{A}_s$ is included in that of $\mathcal{A}$ (see [7] for more detail).

Inputs. An input of the system which is controllable by the tester is called a *control input*; otherwise, it is called a *disturbance input*. All the continuous inputs are assumed to be controllable by the tester. The discrete transitions could be controllable or uncontrollable.

We use the following assumption about the inputs: disturbance actions are of higher priority than control actions. This means that when a control action and a disturbance action are simultaneously enabled, the disturbance action takes place first.

Observations. In our previous work, the locations and the continuous states of the hybrid automata $\mathcal{A}$ and $\mathcal{A}_s$ are observable. In this work, we use a less restrictive assumption: the location and the continuous state are not directly observable, and the tester needs to deduce this information from some continuous observations. We define an observation function as follows: $h : \mathcal{X} \to \mathbb{R}^d$. In the following we consider only scalar observation functions, that is $d = 1$. Intuitively, the tester cannot directly observe the continuous state, and the outputs of its sensors can be modeled by: $y[k] = h(x[k])$.

Test Cases and Test Executions. In our framework, a *test case* is represented by a tree where each node is associated with a hybrid state and each edge of the tree is associated with a control action. A physical test execution can be described as follows: the tester applies a control input sequence to the system and measures the observations. This procedure leads to a set of observation sequences since multiple runs are possible due to non-determinism. In practical systems, due to actuator and sensor imprecision, control inputs and observations are subject to errors. The issues related to error in measurements and actuators are treated in [7] and we do not discuss them here.

Coverage-guided Test Generation. We proposed in [7] a notion of *state coverage* that describes how 'well' the visited states represent the reachable set. This measure is defined using the *star discrepancy* notion in statistics, which characterises the uniformity of the distribution of a point set within a region. Note that the reachable sets of hybrid systems are often non-convex with complex geometric form, therefore considering only corner cases does not always cover the behaviors that are important for reachabiliiy properties, especially in high dimensions. Our current method for test generation is based on a randomized exploration of the reachable state space of the system. It is an extension of the Rapidly-exploring Random Tree (RRT) algorithm, a successful motion planning technique for finding robotic trajectories in an environment with obstacles [12]. Furthermore, we combine it with a guiding tool in order to achieve a good coverage of the system's behaviors we want to test. The new results presented in this paper are twofold. First, we provide a new test generation algorithm guided by the coverage measure and additionally by the property to test via a random walk. Furthermore, we address a testing problem under partial observability where the hybrid state should be deduced from a sequence of observations.

3   Combining the Coverage-Guided Exploration and Random Walks

The main steps of the coverage-guided test generation algorithm [7] are the following: (1) a goal state is sampled, and this sampling is guided so that the goal state lies in the regions where the local coverage of the visited states is still low; (2) a neighbor state of the goal state is determined, from which an appropriate control input is applied to steer the system towards the goal state.

When using the state coverage measure to guide the test generation process, the whole reachable space is 'equally' important for the exploration and the test generation tries not to leave a large part of the reachable space unvisited. The resulting test suite is appropriate when different qualitative behaviors of the system need to be explored. However, when some regions in the state space or some traces are of particular interest, we want to bias the execution towards those regions and traces. To this end, during the test generation we combine the coverage-guided sampling with a guiding method based on a random walk.

To define a random walk, we first partition the continuous state space into a set of regions and from there we construct a directed graph G which roughly overapproximates the specification automaton $\mathcal{A}$. Then, the sampling process consists of two steps:

1. Perform a random walk on the resulting graph G to determine a goal region.
2. Within the goal region we use the coverage-guided test generation algorithm [7] to sample the goal state.

In the following we explain the first step of the sampling process. Let $G = (V_G, E_G)$ be the underlying graph obtained by partioning the continuous state space; V_G is the set of nodes and E_G is the set of directed edges between the nodes. The partition must capture the discrete transitions of $\mathcal{A}$ and separate critical regions from the rest. In this work, we use axis-aligned hyperplanes to define a partition. As future work, more general polyhedral partitions will be considered and this requires adapting the coverage definition which is currently based on a box partition of the continuous state space.

Given a node $w \in V_G$, an adjacent node of w is a node $v \in V_G$ such that there exists an edge in E_G that connects w to v. Let $A_G(w)$ be the set of all the adjacent nodes of w. A random walk[2] on G specifies a run where the node to be visited next is selected from the adjacent vertices at random with a transition probability $P(G) = (p_{wv})_{w,v \in V_G} \in [0,1]^{V_G \times V_G}$ such that for all $w \in V_G \sum_{v \in A_G(w)} p_{wv} = 1$ and for any $v \in V_G \; p_{wv} = 0$ if $v \notin A_G(w)$.

A random walk on G starting at a vertex $w \in V_G$ under the transition matrix $P(G)$ is an infinite sequence of random variables $\eta_i \in V_G$ such that $\eta_0 = w$ with the probability 1, and for all $i \geq 0$ the probability that $\eta_{i+1} = w'$, provided that the probability that $\eta_i = v$ is $p(v, w')$. The hitting time from w to v under the transition matrix $P(G)$ is defined as $H_P(w, v) = \mathcal{E}[\inf i \mid \eta_i = v]$, which is the expectation of the smallest numbers of steps needed to reach v from w.

In order to bias the exploration towards the critical regions, we define a target probability distribution

$$\pi = \{\pi_v \mid v \in V_G\}.$$

The regions we want to explore are given a higher target probability. To achieve this target probability distribution, we use the Metropolis-Hastings method since it guarantees that the stationary distribution of such a random walk on the graph G is the target distribution π [16]. Given two nodes w and v, we assign a probability to the edge from w to v:

$$\begin{cases} p_{wv} = \dfrac{1}{deg(w)} min\{\dfrac{deg(w)\pi_v}{deg(v)\pi_w}, 1\} & \text{if } v \text{ is adjacent node of } w \\ p_{wv} = 1 - \sum_{w' \neq w} p_{ww'} & \text{if } v = w \\ p_{wv} = 0 & \text{otherwise} \end{cases}$$

where $deg(w)$ is the degree of the vertex w. The additional reason we choose to use the Metropolis-Hastings method in this work is that it has good hitting times, which are of $\mathcal{O}(rN_v^2)$ where N_v is the number of vertices and $r = \max\{\dfrac{\pi_w}{\pi_v} \mid w, v \in V_G\}$. As mentioned earlier, this algorithm has been successfully applied to many applications, in particulat in network protocols.

4   Hybrid State Estimation

We now proceed with our second result. As mentioned earlier, the tester needs to deduce the current location and the current continuous state from the continuous observations.

---

[2] For a detailed introduction to random walks on a graph, the reader is referred to [15].

4.1 Continuous State Estimation

We first describe a method for estimating the state of a continuous system, which is used in the next section to handle hybrid systems. Thus, for simplicity of presentation, we drop the location index q from the equations of the dynamics, that is

$$x[k+1] = f(x[k], u[k])$$
$$y[k] \quad = h(x[k])$$

This method is based on the Newton observer method for non-linear systems [14]. During the test execution, to estimate $x[k]$ at each time point k, the tester needs a sufficient long sequence of observations. This is indeed related to observability of the system f and is explained in the following.

Let $U_{k,k+N-1}$ be a vector of N consecutive inputs that is to be applied to the system at time k:

$$U_{k,k+N-1} = \begin{pmatrix} u[k] \\ u[k+1] \\ \ldots \\ u[k+N-1] \end{pmatrix}$$

Under this continuous input sequence $U_{k,k+N-1}$ and starting from the state $x[k]$ (that we need to estimate), the system under test produces a vector of observations

$$Y_{k,k+N-1} = \begin{pmatrix} y[k] \\ y[k+1] \\ \ldots \\ y[k+N-1] \end{pmatrix}$$

We define the following vector of functions:

$$H(x, U_{0,N-1}) = \begin{pmatrix} h(x) \\ h \circ f^{u[0]}(x) \\ \ldots \\ h \circ f^{u[N-1]}(x) \circ \ldots \circ f^{u[0]}(x) \end{pmatrix}$$

where $\circ$ denotes the following composition operator: given two functions $\alpha :$ $X \to Y$ and $\beta : Y \to Z$, the function resulting from composing α with β is $\beta \circ \alpha : X \to Z$ such that for a given $y \in Y$, $\beta \circ \alpha(y) = \beta(\alpha(x))$. In the above since the inputs are fixed in the functions f, we write them as superscripts of f.

From the results on observativility of continuous systems, we know that if the system is N-observable (with $N \geq 1$) at state $\tilde{x}$ if there any sequence U of N control inputs such that $\tilde{x}$ is the unique solution of the following equation:

$$H(\tilde{x}, U) = H(\xi, U)$$

In the above, ξ is the unknown variable. Here N is the minimum number of observations required to reconstruct the state.

We assume now that the system is N-observable [14], and thus to estimate the state at time $k \geq 0$ it suffices to solve the following equation:

$$Y_{k,k+N-1} - H(\xi, U_{k,k+N-1}) = 0 \tag{1}$$

Intuitively, to estimate the state at time point k, we need to apply a sequence $U_{k,k+N-1}$ of N next input values to obtain a sequence $Y_{k,k+N-1}$ of observations. Then, we solve the above equation with $\xi \in \mathbb{R}^n$ as the unknown variables. We let $N = n$, so that the Jacobian matrix of the vector H of functions is square. Then, to determine ξ, we can use Newton's algorithm as follows[3]:

$$\xi^{i+1} = \xi^i + [\frac{\partial H}{\partial x}(\xi^i, U_{k,k+N-1})]^{-1}(Y_{k,k+N-1} - H(\xi^i, U_{k,k+N-1})$$

A detailed discussion on the standard convergence theorem for this algorithm can be found in [13]. The convergence of Newton's algorithm depends on the initial estimate and the second derivatives $||\frac{\partial^2 H}{\partial x^2}||$ which measures the nonlinearity degree of the equation (1). For linear systems, the initial estimate can be arbitrarily far from the exact solution; however, when $||\frac{\partial^2 H}{\partial x^2}||$ is large (that is, the system is very nonlinear), the initial estimate needs to be more accurate.

4.2   Testing Execution with Hybrid State Estimation

Let T be the tree generated from the specification $\mathcal{A}$, starting from the initial continuous state x_0. Now we use this tree to test the system against the specification $\mathcal{A}_s$. From the above discussion on observablity of continuous systems, to extend to the hybrid systems we need to assume that the discrete transitions can occur at times of multiples of N steps. The test execution procedure described in Algorithm 1 uses the following assumption. At any time step of the algorithm, the tester can apply many input sequences and observe the corresponding observation sequences (which may require restarting the execution of the system from the initial state to restore the current state). Initially, the system could be in any location; thus S_{init} covers all the locations.

At each iteration i (which corresponds to a time segment of length N), the tester keeps a set S_i of possible states visited before time iN. Since the discrete transitions are instantaneous, we also need to include all possible discrete successors (represented by the operator $Succ_d$).

For each of possible states (q, x) in S_i, the tester chooses from the tree a possibly feasible sequence of N inputs. It is important to note that, according to our assumption during the next N steps no discrete transition can occur. The tester then applies the chosen sequence to the system under test and observes the corresponding sequence Y of outputs. Using Newton's algorithm, we compute an estimator ξ of the state at time iN. There are two cases:

---

[3] In the case that there are more equations than states, the inverse should be replaced by a pseudo-inverse [13].

Algorithm 1. Test execution

/* Input: Test tree T */

$i = 0$
$S_{init} = \{(q, x_0) \mid q \in Q\}$
$S_n = S_{init} \cup Succ_d(S_{init})$
repeat
    $S_i = S_n \cup Succ_d(S_n)$
    $S_n = \emptyset$
    for all $(q, x) \in S_i$ **do**
        $U = InputSeq(T, (q, x))$ /* Choose an input sequence U of length N and feasible at (q, x) */
        $Y = Observation(U)$ /* Apply the input sequence U to the system and observe the corresponding outputs */
        $\xi = Newton(q, U, Y)$ /* Using Newton's algorithm to estimate the state at the current time iN */

        if $(\|\xi - x\| \leq \varepsilon)$ **then**
            $S_n = S_n \cup \{Succ_c((q, x), U)\}$ /* Adding all the continuous successors to the set S_n, they will be explored in the next iteration */
        end if
    end for
    if $(S_n = \emptyset)$ **then**
        RETURN 'fail' **verdict**
    end if
    $i++$
until $i = i_{max} \vee S_n = \emptyset$

1. If the estimator ξ is ε-close to the corresponding state x in the tree, we add it to the set S_n of new possible states which will be treated in the next iteration. The threshold ε is used to account for numerical error in Newton's algorithm and possible measurement error.
2. Otherwise, we continue with another possible current state in S_i.

After applying the above treatment to all the possible states in S_i, if the set S_n of new possible states is empty, the algorithm declares the verdict 'fail'; otherwise it continues. Note that to initialize the estimates in Newton's algorithm we use the last estimates of the previous iteration, in order to obtain a good convergence of the estimation algorithm.

Theorem 1. *If the algorithm returns the 'fail' verdict, the system under test does not conform to the specification.*

Proof. We first prove the following proposition by induction. Let us suppose that the set S_{i+1} at the beginning of the loop 'REPEAT... UNTIL' contains all the visited state during the interval $[iN, (i + 1)N]$ (this is true for $i = 0$), we prove that the set S_{i+2} contains all the visited states up to time $(i + 2)N$.

Indeed, for any state $(q, x) \in S_{i+1}$, all the states which can be reached from (q, x) by a discrete transition are already included in S_{i+1}. Hence, in order to include all the state reachable in N next step from S_{i+1}, it suffices to consider only the continuous dynamics. Since by applying Newton's algorithm to each state $(q, x) \in S_{i+1}$ as above we can estimate the continuous states, if the estimates do not match the expected states stored in the tree T, the successors of (q, x) are not the states visited so far. It then follows that in the iteration $i + 2$, the algorithm discards only the states which cannot be visited up to time $(i + 2)N$, and at the same time the algorithm includes all the states which are possibly visited up to time $(i + 2)N$. Thus, the proposition is proved.

From this proposition, it is easy to see that when the algorithm returns 'fail', that is the set of possible states is empty, the system under test is not conform to the specification.   ∎

5   Experimental Results

We implemented the above algorithms and incorporated their implementations in the tool HTG [6]. The enhancement of the test generation algorithm allowed us to increase the efficiency of the tool. In addition, the tool can now be used for test execution in practical settings with partial observability. In this section, to show the improvement in the test generation, we present the results obtained for a well-known benchmark of ring oscillator circuit. The second case study is a Delta-Sigma circuit, which is used to illustrate the state estimation feature.

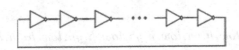

Fig. 1. Ring oscillator circuit

5.1   Ring Oscillator

The ring oscillator circuit is described in Figure 1, given in SPICE netlist formalism[4]. This circuit has one input variable, which is the source voltage of the circuit. Its values is between $1.6V$ and $2.4V$. There are 9 state variables, which are the output voltages of each inverter. We want to test whether the output voltages could reach a value lower that $-2.15V$.

In the result of the test generation without using random walk (shown in Figure 2), the maximum value of the output voltage of the last inverter is 0, and its minimum value is $-2.1458V$. The computation time for generating 10000 points is $60s$.

---

[4] The tool HTG can accept SPICE netlists as input. For more detail on the tool, see [6].

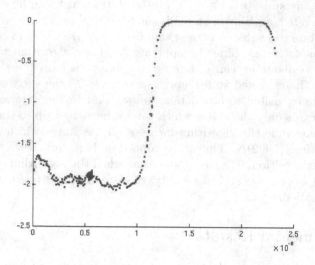

Fig. 2. The output voltage of the last inverter, obtained without using random walk

In the next experiment, we partitioned the continuous state space into two regions corresponding to two 'binary' states of the outputs of the inverters:

$$v_1 = (low, high, low, high, low, high, low, high, low)$$

$$v_2 = (high, low, high, low, high, low, high, low, high)$$

We used a random walk with the target probability distribution for these two regions: $\pi_1 = 0.8$ and $\pi_2 = 0.2$. The Metropolis-Hastings algorithm produced the following transition probability matrix:

from → to	0	1
0	0.875	0.125
1	0.5	0.5

In the result of the test generation using random walk (shown in Figure 3), the maximum value of the output voltage of the last inverter is 0, and its minimum value is $-2.1725V$. The computation time for generating 10000 points is $55s$. We can see that by favoring the region corresponding the low level of the voltage, a lower value of the voltage was discovered, and a violation of the property was detected.

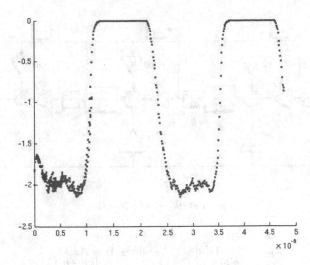

Fig. 3. The output voltage of the last inverter, obtained with a random walk

5.2   Delta-Sigma Circuit

The second case study is a third-order Delta-Sigma modulator [3], which is a mixed-signal circuit shown in Figure 4. When the input is positive and its value is less than 1, the output takes the $+1$ value more often and the quantization error is fed back with negative gain and accumulated in the integrator $\frac{1}{z-1}$. Then, when the accumulated error reaches a certain threshold, the quantizer switches the value of the output to -1 to reduce the mean of the quantization error.

The specification of a third-order Delta-Sigma modulator is modeled as a hybrid automaton, shown in Figure 4. The discrete-time dynamics of the system is as follows: $x[k+1] = Ax[k] + bu[k] - sign(y[k])a$, $y([k] = c_3x_3[k] + b_4u[k]$ where $x[k] \in \mathbb{R}^3$ is the integrator states, $u[k] \in \mathbb{R}$ is the input, $y[k] \in \mathbb{R}$ is the input of the quantizer. Thus, its output is $v[k] = sign(y[k])$, and one can see that whenever v remains constant, the system's dynamics is affine continuous.

In this study we first generated the test tree for the above hybrid automaton used as the specification automaton (see Figures 5 and 6). Our system under test is an implementation of the Delta-Sigma in SPICE netlists. The observation function $h(x) = 0.1x_1 + 0.2x_2 + 0.5x_3$. The initial state is in $[-0.01, 0.01]^3$ and the input values $u \in [-0.5, 0.5]$.

Figure 7 shows the result of the test execution using the hybrid state estimation, which state that for a bounded time the implementation is conform to the specification automaton. In this figure, the horizontal axis is time. The points drawn with $*$ sign are the estimates of x_2 obtained from the observations on the implementation. The circle points correspond to the possible states in the first location and the $+$ points correspond to the possible states in the second location.

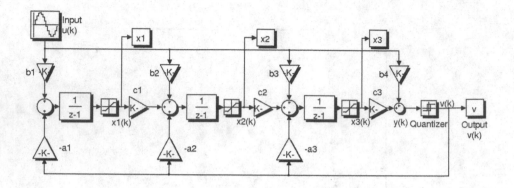

$$c_3 x_3[k] + u[k] >= 0$$

$$
\boxed{\begin{array}{l} v[k] = -1 \\ x[k+1] = Ax[k] + \\ \quad bu[k] + a \end{array}}
\qquad
\boxed{\begin{array}{l} v[k] = +1 \\ x[k+1] = Ax[k] \\ \quad +bu[k] - a \end{array}}
$$

$$c_3 x_3[k] + u[k] < 0$$

Fig. 4. Model of a third-order modulator: Saturation blocks model saturation of the integrators

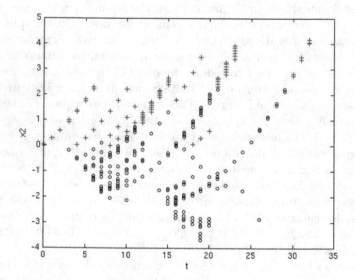

Fig. 5. Test generation result for the first location. The points drawn with the + sign correspond to the states from which a discrete transition to the second location takes place.

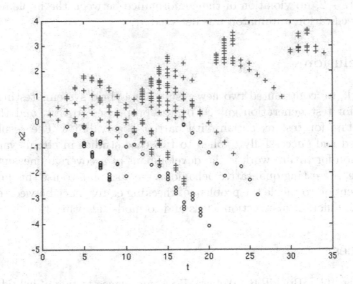

Fig. 6. Test generation result for the second location. The points drawn with the circle sign correspond to the states from which a discrete transition to the first location takes place.

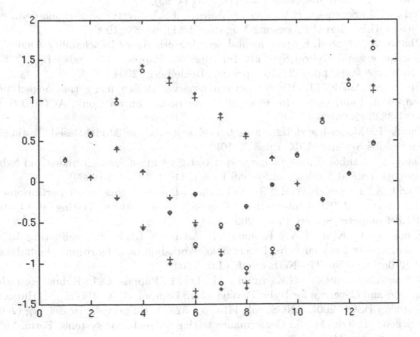

Fig. 7. Test execution result (over time) for the Delta-Sigma circuit

With $\varepsilon = 1e - 2$, no violation of the conformance between the implementation and the specification automaton was detected.

6   Conclusion

In this work, we contributed two new results for hybrid systems testing: one is a method for test generation guided by the properties to test, and the other is a procedure for test execution with partial observability. The results were implemented and successfully applied to two case studies in circuit validation. One direction for future work is the development of a coverage measure which can capture interesting qualitative behaviors. We also plan to use this procedure for test execution to tackle the problem of checking equivalence between different models with different abstraction levels and to model identification.

References

1. Aichernig, B.K., Brandl, H., Wotawa, F.: Conformance testing of hybrid systems with qualitative reasoning models. Electron. Notes Theor. Comput. Sci. 253(2), 53–69 (2009)
2. Alur, R., Courcoubetis, C., Halbwachs, N., Henzinger, T.A., Ho, P.-H., Nicollin, X., Olivero, A., Sifakis, J., Yovine, S.: The algorithmic analysis of hybrid systems. Theoretical Computer Science 138(1), 3–34 (1995)
3. Aziz, P.M., Sorensen, H.V., van der Spiegel, J.: An overview of sigma-delta converters. IEEE Signal Processing Magazine 13(1), 61–84 (1996)
4. Bhatia, A., Frazzoli, E.: Incremental Search Methods for Reachability Analysis of Continuous and Hybrid Systems. In: Alur, R., Pappas, G.J. (eds.) HSCC 2004. LNCS, vol. 2993, pp. 142–156. Springer, Heidelberg (2004)
5. Biyik, E., Arcak, M.: Hybrid newton observer design using the inexact newton method and gmres. In: Proc. 2006 American Control Conf., ACC 2006, pp. 3334–3339 (2006)
6. Dang, T.: Model-based testing of hybrid systems. In: Model-Based Testing for Embedded Systems. CRC Press (2010)
7. Dang, T., Nahhal, T.: Coverage-guided test generation for continuous and hybrid systems. Formal Methods in System Design 34(2), 183–213 (2009)
8. David, A., Larsen, K.G., Li, S., Nielsen, B.: Timed testing under partial observability. In: 2nd IEEE International Conference on Software Testing, ICST 2009. IEEE Computer Society Press (2009)
9. Esposito, J., Kim, J.W., Kumar, V.: Adaptive RRTs for validating hybrid robotic control systems. In: Proceedings Workshop on Algorithmic Foundations of Robotics, Zeist, The Netherlands (July 2004)
10. Julius, A.A., Fainekos, G.E., Anand, M., Lee, I., Pappas, G.J.: Robust Test Generation and Coverage for Hybrid Systems. In: Bemporad, A., Bicchi, A., Buttazzo, G. (eds.) HSCC 2007. LNCS, vol. 4416, pp. 329–342. Springer, Heidelberg (2007)
11. Krichen, M., Tripakis, S.: Conformance testing for real-time systems. Form. Methods Syst. Des. 34(3) (2009)
12. LaValle, S., Kuffner, J.: Rapidly-exploring random trees: Progress and prospects, 2000. In: Workshop on the Algorithmic Foundations of Robotics (2000)

13. Luenberger, D.G.: Optimization by Vector Space Methods. Wiley, New York (1969)
14. Moraal, P., Grizzle, J.W.: Observer design for nonlinear systems with discrete-time measurements. IEEE Transactions on Automatic Control 40(3) (1995)
15. Motowani, R., Raghavan, P.: Randomized Algorithms. Cambridge University Press, New York (1995)
16. Nonaka, Y., Ono, H., Sadakane, K., Yamashita, M.: The hitting and cover times of metropolis walks. Theor. Comput. Sci. 411(16-18), 1889–1894 (2010)
17. Plaku, E., Kavraki, L., Vardi, M.: Hybrid Systems: From Verification to Falsification. In: Damm, W., Hermanns, H. (eds.) CAV 2007. LNCS, vol. 4590, pp. 463–476. Springer, Heidelberg (2007)

Extending Coverage Criteria by Evaluating Their Robustness to Code Structure Changes

Angelo Gargantini, Marco Guarnieri, and Eros Magri

Dip. di Ing. dell'Informazione e Metodi Matematici, Università di Bergamo, Italy
{angelo.gargantini,marco.guarnieri,eros.magri}@unibg.it

Abstract. Code coverage is usually used as a measurement of testing quality and as adequacy criterion. Unfortunately, code coverage is very sensitive to modifications of the code structure, and, therefore, the same test suite can achieve different degrees of coverage on the same program written in two syntactically different ways. For this reason, code coverage can provide the tester with misleading information.

In order to understand how a testing criterion is affected by code structure modifications, we introduce a way to measure the sensitivity of coverage to code changes. We formalize the modifications of the code structure using semantic preserving code-to-code transformations and we propose a framework to evaluate coverage robustness to these transformations, extending actual existing coverage criteria.

This allows us to define which programs and which test suites can be considered robust with respect to a certain set of transformations. We can identify when the obtained coverage is fragile and we extend the concept of coverage criterion by introducing an index that measures the fragility of the coverage of a given test suite. We show how to compute the fragility index and we evidence that also well-written industrial code and realistic test suites can be fragile. Moreover, we suggest how to deal with this kind of testing fragility.

1 Introduction

The notion of code coverage and testing criteria dates back to the early sixties [14,19]. Although, as Dijkstra claimed in 1972 [6], "program testing can be used to show the presence of bugs, but never their absence", the initial research focused on finding *ideal* testing criteria, i.e. those capable, under certain assumptions, of demonstrating the absence of errors in programs by testing them [10]. Researchers soon realized that finding such ideal testing criteria was impractical if not impossible [23] and the community started to introduce, compare, and study testing criteria, which are not ideal but they have proved to be useful to measure the quality of testing and to find faults in programs. However, there still exists some skepticism around the actual significance of coverage criteria. It is well known that some faults may be completely missed by test suites adequate to some coverage criteria (for instance statement coverage cannot discover omission faults) and that testing criteria are very sensitive to the structure and to the syntax of the code, regardless its actual behavior. Rajan et al. [17] show that

B. Nielsen and C. Weise (Eds.): ICTSS 2012, LNCS 7641, pp. 168–183, 2012.

the MCDC, required by FAA for software on commercial airplanes, and often considered a very tough criterion to achieve, can be easily cheated by simple folding/unfolding of conditions inside guards.

Despite their weakness, coverage criteria give an immediate and easy to compute (at least for simple criteria) feedback about the quality of the testing activity. Once a test suite has been developed or built, one wants to know which parts of the code are exercised and which are not, and this information can be simply obtained by running the code with the tests. Coverage is often used as acceptance threshold: if a test suite achieves a given coverage, it is considered adequate, and the tested software accepted as *good*. For this reason, reaching a given level of coverage becomes a critical factor during the testing activity.

We can state that the coverage data are easily obtained and are widely used as acceptance measure, but have a questionable significance. In this paper we try to augment the information one can retrieve from the coverage data by considering also the structure of the code and its possible transformations.

There are two main scenarios in which it is important knowing how the coverage offered by a test suite behaves with respect to the changes in the code structure.

A. The code has been transformed *in the past* before being tested and the coverage may depend on the transformations applied. In this way, testing criteria can easily be cheated, and hence an additional measure of the coverage fragility helps in identifying well-tested classes from poorly tested ones.

B. The code structure will change *in the future* without changing the semantics of the program by applying some refactoring rules, by some automatic transformations, or by introducing particular patterns. This may influence the coverage after the application of these transformations. In this context, the tester would like to know if the level of coverage provided by the test suite will be preserved, i.e., if the coverage is robust w.r.t. future changes.

In this paper we make use of code transformations that preserve code functional behavior to model code changes. We formally define when a test suite achieves a *fragile* vs *robust* coverage. Roughly speaking, a fragile coverage depends on the structure and syntax of the code, and the test suite would not achieve the same level of coverage on the transformed code. A robust coverage and a robust test suite do not suffer from modifications of the code structure. We introduce a measure of fragility by extending the usual coverage criteria.

In Section 2 we present some related work on testing, coverage, and code transformations. Section 3 presents the theoretical framework in which our work will be integrated and contains some examples of useful code transformations. In Section 4 we show the limitations of actual coverage criteria in terms of their fragility with respect to code changes by giving several examples in which the obtained coverage is fragile. We introduce and formally define the concept of coverage robustness and several measure of coverage fragility. Section 5 reports some experiments. In Section 7 we present our conclusions.

2   Related Work

The concept of code coverage was first clearly introduced by Miller and Maloney from the US Chemical Corps in 1963 [14], although some similar concepts were already introduced by Senko from IBM [19]. Miller and Maloney observed that it is not sufficient to know that a program passes all the tests, since each test case checks a portion of the program and some portions may be not tested at all. They developed a model of programs based on flow charts and logical trees and required that every case is tested at least once. Following their approach, various notions of code coverage have been proposed as a measure for test suite quality, including statement coverage, branch coverage, method coverage, MCDC, and others [15]. These criteria consider the code structure, give a measure of the adequacy of the testing activity, and they can be used to drive the testing activity itself, for instance, requiring that certain tests must be generated. These criteria do not guarantee that the program is correct if it passes adequate testing, i.e. they are not *ideal* [10]. However, they have practical utility and they are generally required for commercial software. For instance, the Modified Condition Decision Coverage (MCDC) [5], is required for safety critical aviation software by the RCTA/DO-178B standard. The basic assumption is that a test suite is likely to be effective at revealing faults if it exercises the code where the fault is located. Therefore, increased code coverage is expected to correlate with more revealed faults, although other factors may influence the actual outcome [16]. Staats et al. [20] show that test suites generated specifically to satisfy coverage criteria achieve poor results in terms of effectiveness, whereas the use of coverage criteria as a supplement to random testing provides an improvement in the effectiveness of the generated test suites.

It is well known that coverage criteria can be very sensitive to code structure both if they are used for measuring test adequacy and if they are used for test generation. Regarding the adequacy, there are several works arguing that code coverage is not robust to code structure transformations. In [13], the authors show how very simple transformations (like adding a new empty line) can confuse code coverage tools. More severe issues are presented in [17]. In that paper, the authors prove that the MCDC metrics is highly sensitive to the structure of the implementation and can therefore be misleading as a test adequacy criterion. They present six programs in two versions each: with and without expression folding (i.e., inlining). They find that the same test suites performed very diversely on the two versions. Their suggestion is either (1) to introduce a new coverage metrics that takes the use of inlined condition into consideration, or (2) a canonical way of structuring code so that such conditions do not occur in the first place. Their approach differ from ours, since we propose a framework able to evaluate *existing* coverage criteria with respect to their robustness to code structure and syntax changes and to *extend* them by computing some information about their robustness/fragility. No change of the existing code is required in our approach either.

So far, the main solution in the literature to overcome coverage criteria weaknesses has been trying to introduce more powerful and tough testing criteria. For instance, testing criteria that consider also the information flow can be introduced. In [18], the authors define a family of program test data selection criteria derived from data flow analysis techniques similar to those used in compiler optimization. We believe that introducing complex coverage criteria may be avoided if code transformations are taken into account as proposed in our approach.

Testing criteria are very sensitive to code structure also when used for test generation. Often the structure of the code makes hard the generation of tests, i.e. it reduces its *testability*, especially when test generation is performed automatically. The automated generation of adequate test data can be impeded by properties of the code itself (for example, flags, side effects, and unstructured control flow). For this reason *testability transformations* are introduced [11]. A testability transformation is a code-to-code transformation that aims to improve the ability of a given test generation method to generate test data for the original program. A first difference between our approach and the work of Harman et al. is that we do not tackle the problem of test suite generation but we only want to measure the robustness of a given test suite in order to obtain a measurement of how much the coverage is affected by modifications in the code structure. Another difference is that *testability transformations* are not semantic preserving while the transformations defined in our work do not modify the semantics of the program. We will also show that the use of *testability transformations* should be carefully considered because the test suite generated from a transformed program P' that achieves a certain coverage C' may not achieve the same level of coverage C on the original program P.

Transformations and code coverage is studied by Weissleder [22]. In this case the transformation is used to obtain information of the coverage over the original code from the information about the coverage over the transformed code. The goal is to find a transformation such that if a test suite achieves the coverage C_1 over the transformed code, than the same test suite achieves the coverage C_2 over the original code. In this case C_1 *simulates* the coverage C_2.

The fact that transformations can disrupt coverage is also tackled by Kirner. In [12], he addresses the challenge of ensuring that the structural code coverage achieved for a program P is preserved when P is transformed. If the code transformation fulfills some formal properties, than it preserves also the coverage. The considered code transformations allow to obtain machine level code from higher level programs. He also identifies three classes of transformations: 1. the ones that change the reachability of program elements, 2. the ones that add new paths to the program and 3. the ones that preserve the coverage. His work is more focused on preserving structural code coverage into compilers and code generators, whereas our work is more focused on measuring the impact of transformations of the code structure on the coverage.

3   Theoretical Background

Testing criteria, often called *coverage criteria*, have the main goal of measuring the test quality. They are used as a metrics to quantify the coverage of the control flow of a program achieved by a test suite. Usually they are also used as a stopping rule to decide when the testing process can stop and the software can be accepted. Studying coverage criteria, defining new ones, and providing empirical evidence of their fault detection capability have been a major research focus for the last three decades. First of all, we introduce a framework defining them formally, mainly taken from [24], where the reader can find an exhaustive treatment of the subject. For the purpose of our paper we do not consider directly the use of testing criteria for test suite generation, and we focus on *program based structural testing*, that does not consider the specification and defines testing requirements only in terms of program elements (statements, conditions, and so on). Given the set of programs P and the set of all the test suites TS, we define a testing criterion in the following way.

Definition 1. *Testing Criteria. A testing criterion is a function C, $C : P \times TS \to [0,1]$. $C(p, ts) = r$ means that the adequacy of testing the program p by the test set ts is of degree r according to the criterion C. The greater the real number r, the more adequate the test suite ts is.*

Given a fixed value r', such that $0 \le r' \le 1$, which represents the lower expected coverage for the criterion C applied to the program $p \in P$, we can consider the test suite $ts \in TS$ as adequate for testing program p iff $C(p, ts) \ge r'$.

In program based structural testing, coverage requirements are expressed in terms of the coverage achieved over a particular set of elements in the structure of the program under test (e.g. the set of all the statements for *statement coverage* or the set of all the conditions for *condition coverage*). We will focus on classical coverage criteria [3,15], including the statement and branch coverage and the Modified Condition Decision Coverage (MCDC) [5].

3.1   Code Transformations

There exist several, theoretically infinite, programs which have the same behaviour but have different code structure and thus can achieve different results in terms of coverage for a particular criterion. So how, given a program $p \in P$, can we obtain new programs with the same behaviour of p? We can do this by means of *code-to-code transformations*, which are functions that take as input a program p and return another program p'. Formally, a transformation t is a function $P \longrightarrow P$, where P is the set of all the programs.

However not all the transformations produce a transformed program with the same behaviour of the original program. This kind of transformations are called Semantic Preserving Transformations (SPT). A SPT [2] is a code-to-code transformation that modifies the syntax of the program to which it is applied, without changing its semantics. Thus given a SPT $t \in T$, where T is the set of all the SPTs, and a program $p \in P$, p and $t(p)$ must have the same behaviour. In the following of the paper we will consider only SPTs and, thus, we will call them just transformations.

In the following we present five SPTs which we will use in the paper as a case study. Each transformation is identified by using a transformation schema, composed by two snippets of code. The first one, called input pattern, defines on which snippets of code the transformation can be applied. The second one, called output pattern, defines how the transformed piece of code will look like.

Several new transformations can be obtained by combining already defined transformations. Given a sequence of transformations T, we define the transformation t_{seqT} as the application of the transformations in T in sequence, i.e. $t_{seqT} = t_1 \circ \ldots \circ t_n$ where $t_{seqT}, t_1, \ldots, t_n \in T$. Given a transformation t, we define the transformation $\tilde{t}$ as the iterative application of t until the program is no longer modified by t. Given a certain transformation t, we can define the inverse transformation t^{-1} by exchanging the input pattern and the output pattern.

In this paper, we consider the following transformations.

Externalized Complex Flag. This transformation was already identified by Rajan et al. [17], which showed its effects on MCDC criterion, and by Harman et al. [11], which showed how it can be used in order to enhance the test generation phase. It has the following schema:

```
boolean x;                                boolean x;
...                                       ...
x = complexBoolExpr; //A     t_ecf        x = complexBoolExpr;
...                          ⇒            ...
if (...x...) { //B                        if (... complexBoolExpr ...) {
...                                       ...
}                                         }
```

In the schema, complexBoolExpr is a Boolean expression that contains at least one Boolean operator, and the statements between the point A and B do not change the value of x, and of the variables referenced in complexBoolExpr. We briefly call this transformation t_{ecf}. By applying $\tilde{t}_{ecf}$ to a program p we obtain a new program $\tilde{t}_{ecf}(p)$ in which all the flags in *if statements* are expanded to their definition. Several refactoring patterns [8] can be partially mapped on this transformation or its inverse, i.e. *Inline Temp Variable* (in case the variable is boolean and it is inlined in an *if statement*), *Remove Control Flag, Introduce Explaining Variable*.

Boundary Extraction. This transformation t_b acts on an *if statement* and splits it into several *if statements* if it contains a condition in the form of $a \lesseqgtr x \lesseqgtr b$, where a, b, and x are numerical constants or variables. It has the following schema:

```
                                    ... t0 ...
                                    if (x==a) {
                                        ... t1 ...
... t0 ...                          } else if (x==b) {
if (a<=x && x<=b) {                     ... t1 ...
    ... t1 ...         t_b          } else if (x>a && x<b) {
} else {              ⇒                 ... t1 ...
    ... t2 ...                      } else {
}                                       ... t2 ...
                                    }
```

Reverse Conditional. The transformation t_{rc} is associated with the *Reverse Conditional* refactoring pattern [1]. It simply inverts the condition of the *if statement* and exchange the *then block* and the *else block* between them, and *cond* is a boolean expression. It has the following schema:

```
if( cond ){              if(! cond) {
   ...t1...        t_rc      ...t2...
} else {            ⇒     } else{
   ...t2...                  ...t1...
}                        }
```

Flattening Conditional Expression. The transformation t_{fbc} splits all the expressions used as guards in *conditional statements* until every *if statement* has only an atomic Boolean expression as a guard. It can be defined using two schema. The first schema represents how the transformation splits a conjunctive condition:

```
                                if(cond1){
                                   if(cond2){
if(cond1 && cond2){                   ...t1...
   ...t1...             t_fbc       } else {
} else {                ⇒             ...t2...
   ...t2...                        }
}                               } else {
                                   ...t2...
                                }
```

The second schema represents how the transformation splits a disjunctive condition:

```
                                if(cond1){
                                   ...t1...
if(cond1 || cond2){             } else if(cond2){
   ...t1...             t_fbc       ...t1...
} else {                ⇒        } else {
   ...t2...                         ...t2...
}                               }
```

In both schema *cond1* and *cond2* are boolean expressions. It is a generalization of the *Consolidate Conditional Expression* refactoring pattern [8]. Note that a similar transformation may be performed during compilation (e.g. in the byte code) and therefore, a test suite that achieves the decision coverage of the original program, may not achieve the same coverage of the compiled program. This problem is also studied in [12] and it is a common transformation done when the source code is transformed into assembly code (for conjunctive expressions).

Remove Consolidate Conditional Fragment. The transformation t_{cdcf} is the inverse transformation of the one associated with the *Consolidate Conditional Fragment* refactoring pattern [8]. It simply moves into the *then block* and the *else block* the first statement after the *if statement*. It has the following schema:

```
if(cond){                if(cond) {
   ...t1...                  ...t1...
} else {         t_cdcf      statement;
   ...t2...        ⇒      } else{
}                            ...t2...
statement;                   statement;
                         }
```

Meaning of Transformations. The meaning of code transformations regarding the testing activity depends on which of two scenarios explained in the introduction we assume. If we suspect that the code was transformed in the past, code transformations bring the code to its original structure, while, if we assume that the code will be changed in the future, code transformations model the changes the code will be subject to. For instance, $t_{ecf}^{\sim}$ would undo the insertion of flags for conditions in *if statements* done in the past.

4   Coverage Robustness

4.1   Code Transformations and Coverage

Code coverage is very sensitive to the code structure and it can therefore be misleading as test adequacy criterion. This fact is well explained in [17] for MCDC in case of inlining and outlining of Boolean variables (addressed by our t_{ecf} and $t_{ecf}{}^{-1}$ transformations). Even though examples in literature are focused only on the extrapolation of a complex flag, the sensitivity of coverage criteria to code structure can be generalized for any code transformation and any code coverage criterion. Indeed we show several code fragments with the same semantics that achieve different coverage degrees with the same coverage criteria and the same test sets.

Example 1. For instance consider the following code fragment, in which in_1 and in_2 are two inputs and the guard of the conditional statement has been *outlined*, i.e. the guard is simply a Boolean variable defined in terms of other Boolean variables or expressions.

```
boolean expr_1 = in_1 || in_2;        if (in_1 || in_2){
if (expr_1){                  ⇒ₜₑcf      ...
   ...                                  }
}
```

A test suite containing only two tests (in_1=**true**, in_2=**false**) and (in_1=**false**, in_2=**false**) covers the MCDC for the *if statement*, which has a simple variable as guard, so two tests are enough. However, if we apply t_{ecf}, the transformed code were written with the condition *inlined* and thus the same test suite would not achieve the MCDC of the same code.

These simple patterns recur quite often in software and in models [17]. However, it would be not acceptable to force the developer to choose only the inlined version, in order to avoid that a full MCDC coverage is achieved with less test cases. The outlined version is more readable and maintainable since a complex expression is re-factored in an auxiliary variable. This situation can be also the result of an explicit *extract local variable* refactoring operation [8]. It could also perform better, since the Boolean flag is computed only once.

Example 2. Consider the following code, where x is an integer variable and a simplified form of boundary extraction is applied:

```
  ...                            ...
if (x>=2)  x=x+1;     ⇒ₜ_b     if (x==2)     x=x+1;
else       x=x+2;             else if (x>2)  x=x+1;
                              else           x=x+2;
```

A test suite containing only two tests (x=**0**) and (x=**5**) achieves 100% of branch coverage. However the same test suite achieves only 75% of branch coverage on the transformed code.

Example 3. Consider the following code fragment, in which a and b are Boolean variables. To achieve a full decision coverage a test suite containing only two tests ($a = $ **true**, b = **true**) and ($a = $ **false**, b = **true**), is enough.

```
                              if(a) {
if(a && b){          t_fbc      if (b){
    .... // body      ⇒          .... // body
}                             }
                          }
```

The transformation does not change the behaviour of the program, but the original test suite would cover only the first decision on the transformed program.

Example 4. Consider the following code fragment in which a is a Boolean variable and i an Integer variable:

```
                              if(a) {
if(a)                            i = i+1;
    i = i+1;                     System.out.println(i);
else             t_cdcf       } else {
    i = i+2;         ⇒          i = i+2;
System.out.println(i);         System.out.println(i);
                          }
```

The test suite containing only one test (a = **true**) achieves 60% of statement coverage. However on the code transformed by using the t_{cdcf} transformation, the same test suite achieves only 50% of coverage.

All the examples show that several programs with the same behaviour can achieve the same value of coverage with different effort from a testing point of view, i.e. the number of test cases in the test suite, only because they have a different structure. This is valid for all the structural coverage criteria.

4.2   Coverage Fragility and Robustness

First of all, we want to formalize the sensitivity of the coverage obtained by testing a program P with a test suite, with respect to a set of possible transformations of P.

Definition 2. *Fragility. Given a program $p \in P$, a coverage criterion C and a set of transformations T, we say that a test suite ts fragilely covers p, if there exists a transformation $t \in T$ such that $C(p, ts) > C(t(p), ts)$.*

Fragilely covered programs can be modified by some transformation $t \in T$ in a way that, also if the behaviour of the program remains the same, the coverage provided by ts on the transformed program $t(p)$ diminishes with respect to the coverage on the original program p.

If a test suite fragilely covers the program under test, the confidence in the measurement of the coverage is reduced because the possible high level of coverage may be due to the structure of the code. It may happen that the developer has used *in the past* a particular pattern that has increased the coverage but if the code were written in another way then the test suite would be not as good in terms of achieved coverage. Fragile coverage is not robust to transformations of the code that may be performed *in the future* either, such as refactoring techniques or compiler optimizations. This is a problem because, usually, after a SPT is applied, the test suite is not updated by the developer because he/she does not feel the need of new tests, and thus the old test suite can achieve lower coverage on the resulting code. For this reason, fragilely covered programs may need more testing, regardless the level of coverage achieved so far.

In order to reduce the fragility of a test suite, new tests must be added. Generally, the new tests are built looking at the transformed program and then added to the original test suite. However, using the transformed program to derive a completely new test suite to be applied also to the original program can cause an unexpected loss of coverage, as proved by the following theorem.

Theorem 1. *Let C be a coverage criterion, ts and ts' be two test suites, generated respectively for p and for $t(p)$, such that $ts \nsubseteq ts'$, $ts' \nsubseteq ts$, and $t \in T$ be a transformation, $C(t(p), ts') > C(t(p), ts)$ does not imply $C(p, ts') > C(p, ts)$.*

Proof. We prove the theorem by showing a case in which the converse – $C(t(p), ts') > C(t(p), ts)$ implies $C(p, ts') > C(p, ts)$ – is false. Consider the transformation t_{ecf} and the following program p and its transformed version $t_{\text{ecf}}(p)$:

```
x = a && b && c;              x = a && b && c;
if(x) {          ⟹_tecf    if(a && b && c) {
  ...                           ...
}                             }
```

Given the test suite ts, which has two test cases ($a = $ **true**, $b = $ **true**, $c = $ **false**) and ($a = $ **true**, $b = $ **true**, $c = $ **true**), and considering the condition coverage criterion, the coverage is $C(p, ts) = 1.0$ while $C(t_{\text{ecf}}(p), ts) = 4/6 = 0.66$. If we consider then a test suite ts' that has two test cases ($a = $ **false**, $b = $ **true**, $c = $ **true**) and ($a = $ **true**, $b = $ **false**, $c = $ **true**), the coverage that ts' achieves on $t_{\text{ecf}}(p)$ is $5/6 = 0.83$ and thus it improves the coverage of ts over $t_{\text{ecf}}(p)$, i.e. $C(t_{\text{ecf}}(p), ts') > C(t_{\text{ecf}}(p), ts)$. Moreover, $ts \nsubseteq ts'$, $ts' \nsubseteq ts$ is true. However, the coverage of ts' over p dimishes, since $C(p, ts') = 0.5$ whereas $C(p, ts) = 1.0$.

Theorem 1 states that, given a program p fragilely covered by a test suite ts and a transformation t, if we want to achieve a better coverage than the one obtained using the test suite ts on the program p we cannot simply generate a new test suite ts' on the program $t(p)$, because ts', also if increases the coverage on $t(p)$ with respect to ts, maybe does not increase the coverage achieved on p.

Note that transformations allowing testers to obtain programs from which tests can be generated more easily are also called *testability transformations* [11]. Theorem 1 states that the use of testability transformations should be carefully considered since they may not increase the coverage obtained on the original program, even though the coverage is increased on the transformed program.

Sometimes we want to refer to the *coverage* as either fragile or robust. In accordance with Def. 2, we can introduce the following definition.

Definition 3. *Fragile [Robust] Coverage. Given a coverage criterion C, a program p, a test suite ts for p, and T a set of code transformations, we say that the coverage of p provided by ts with respect to the coverage criterion C and the code transformations T is fragile [robust], if and only if the program p is [is not] fragilely covered by ts with respect to C and T.*

The fact that a coverage is fragile or robust strongly depends on the set of transformations T one considers. With a small set T any coverage is likely to be robust, but with a large T only the best test suites will provide the robust required coverage. For this reason, the client who requires certain levels of coverage and robustness has to provide the tester with adequate transformations in order to ensure the desired confidence in the code coverage. The given set of transformations T should depend on the expected set of SPTs that will be applied on the program or on the set of transformations applied in the past on the program. It is important to define such programs whose coverage is not affected by the application of transformations, we call them *robust* programs.

Definition 4. *Robust program Given a coverage criterion C and a set of code transformations T, we say that a program p has* robust *structure if any test suite that provides the coverage C for p, C is robust.*

Code with robust structure is of great interest for testers, since its coverage during testing cannot be diminished by code transformations, i.e. the coverage achieved by any test suite on a robust program will not diminish regardless the sequence of SPTs $t_1, \ldots, t_n \in T$ applied to it. Given a program p and a test suite ts, which achieves a certain level of coverage $C(p, ts)$ for a coverage criterion C, there are two ways to increase the achieved coverage. If the program p is robust, we can generate a new test suite ts' also transforming the program, because generating a test suite ts' that achieves a coverage higher than $C(p, ts)$ assure also that $C(p, ts') \geq C(p, ts)$. If the program is not robust the only way to increase the coverage is extending the test suite ts, because the Theorem 1 proves that generating a new test suite ts' that achieve higher coverage on a transformed version of p does not assure to obtain a better coverage on p.

4.3   Fragility and Robustness Measures

We define a measure to express how much the coverage achieved by the test suite ts on the program p with respect to the criterion C is robust to the changes in the code structure introduced by a set of SPTs T. Our metrics works with any existing coverage criterion C, without the need to introduce new and possible more complex testing criteria. This allows the tester to re-use existing criteria (and associated tools) which he/she is already familiar with.

The metrics is called *extended coverage* (because extends the usual coverage measurement with an information on how much the coverage offered by the test suite is sensitive to transformations), and it consists of a couple of values (a, b) where $a = C(p, ts)$ represent the usual coverage obtained by applying ts to the program p, whereas b is a fragility index such that $b \in [0, 1]$, and it measures the sensitivity of the coverage to modifications in the code structure. For a coverage measure in the form (a, b), $b = 0$ means that a is the robust coverage, while as $b \to 1$ the coverage a is increasingly sensitive to the transformations of the code structure. If $b = 1$ the coverage a is completely fragile.

Let p be a program, ts a test suite, and C a coverage, we define $\Delta(t) = C(p, ts) - C(t(p), ts)$ where t is a transformation. Let $pos(x)$ be a function defined as $max(0, x)$. We define three fragility indexes. The first one is simply the *averaged fragility*:

$$b_{af} = pos\left(\frac{\sum_{t \in T} \Delta(t)}{|T|}\right)$$

The second one is called *weighted fragility* and it is defined as

$$b_{wf} = \sum_{t \in T} \rho(t) * pos(\Delta(t))$$

where $\rho(t)$ is a function that defines the weight of each transformation $t \in T$, such that $\sum_{t \in T} \rho(t) = 1$. The *weighted fragility* is a useful metrics in case we want to assign a different weight to some transformations for a particular reason, e.g. the weight can represent the likelihood that a certain transformation will be applied to the code. The third fragility index is called *worst case loss of coverage*. It is an indicator of what is the maximum loss of coverage between the original program and any transformed one, and it is expressed as

$$b_{wc} = pos(max_{t \in T}(\Delta(t)))$$

In this case if the index $b_{wc} = 0$ it means that a is the robust coverage, otherwise b_{wc} indicates the maximum loss of coverage and thus the real coverage in the worst case is $C(p, ts) - b_{wc}$.

The *extended coverage* is a very useful metrics, especially if it is measured during the development phase. For instance with respect to unit testing, once the developer has measured the extended coverage, if it is not a robust coverage he/she can act in two ways to increase the robustness of the coverage: (a) he/she could extend the test suite with new test cases, maybe generated from a transformed version of the program, (b) he/she could change the structure of the code in order to remove all the points that introduces fragility issues. However, removing fragility points may be not straightforward nor possible every time (this fact highly depends on the transformations in T). Moreover transforming the code would increase the robustness at the expenses of the coverage, which would diminish. To maintain the same level of coverage, the tester should add new tests in any case.

5   Experiments

In order to evaluate how much the transformation of a program influences the robustness of the coverage offered by a test suite we have analyzed several Java programs. The selected programs vary from toy examples to complex Java libraries. The programs are the following:

LEAP: It contains one method checking whether the passed year is leap or not.
TRI: It contains a triangle classification method, which takes as input the length of the three sides and computes the type of the triangle [3].
WBS: The Wheel Brake System (WBS) is a Java implementation of the WBS case example found in ARP 4761 [4,17]. The WBS determines what pressure to apply to braking based on the environment.
TCAS: It is the Java implementation of a Traffic Collision Avoidance System (TCAS) II, required on all commercial aircraft flying in US airspace.
ASW: The Altitude Switch (ASW) is a synchronous reactive component from the avionics domain that controls the power of some devices according to the airplane altitude.

Table 1. Results in percentage of the robustness analysis for LEAP, TRI, and TCAS and their test suites, where $a = C(p, ts)$. Random1 test suite contains 100 tests, and Random2 contains 1000 tests for all projects. Evosuite has 4 tests for LEAP, 13 for TRI, and 16 for JTCAS. Handmade has 1 test for all the projects.

Program p	LEAP						TRI						TCAS					
LOC	10						35						155					
Coverage	Stmt		Branch		MCDC		Stmt		Branch		MCDC		Stmt		Branch		MCDC	
Test suite ts	a	b_{wc}	a	b_{wc}	a	b_{wc}	a	b_{wc}	a	b_{wc}	a	b_{wc}	a	b_{wc}	a	b_{wc}	a	b_{wc}
Random1	100	0	100	0	100	50	93	0	94	0	95	5	65	15	23	13	18	8
Random2	100	0	100	0	100	50	93	0	94	0	95	5	-	-	-	-	-	-
Evosuite	100	0	100	0	100	13	100	0	100	0	100	0	94	22	87	43	74	30
Handmade	100	0	100	0	100	63	100	0	100	0	100	20	26	7	3	2	3	1

JTOPAS: It is a simple, easy-to-use Java library for the common problem of parsing arbitrary text data.

ANT: Apache Ant is a Java library and command-line tool widely used to compile and build Java applications.

NXML: NanoXML is a small XML parser for Java.

Code for TACAS, JTOPAS, ANT, NXML and their unit tests can be found in the SIR repository [7]. The Java implementation of ASW is included in the Java Path Finder distribution [21].

In our study we have considered statement, branch and MCDC coverage criteria. We have studied all the transformations presented in Section 3.1, and thus $T = \{t_{\tilde{ecf}}, t_{\tilde{rc}}, t_{\tilde{b}}, t_{\tilde{fbc}}, t_{\tilde{cdcf}}\}$. For each example we have considered an handmade test suite (for TACAS, JTOPAS, ANT and NXML the considered test suite is the one presented in the SIR repository). For the smallest case studies (LEAP, TRI, WBS, and TCAS), we have also considered a test suite automatically generated by means of Evosuite [9] and random test suites with a fixed dimension of 100 and 1000 test cases. Experiments with random test suites are repeated 10 times, with different seeds, and only the averaged results are presented in this paper. For each test suite ts, for each coverage criterion C and for each program under test p, we have computed the coverage[1] achieved by ts for the criterion C on the program p and for any transformed program $t(p)$, for each $t \in T$.

Table 1 presents the results of the robustness analysis for smallest case studies (LEAP, TRI, and TCAS). For each program and test suite, the table shows the results in terms of coverage a and the *worst case loss of coverage* b_{wc} fragility index.

Table 2 shows the results of our study on the biggest case studies (ASW, TOPAS, NXML, and ANT). For each program, the table shows the results in terms of coverage achieved by the provided test suite and the two fragility indexes, the *worst case loss of coverage* b_{wc} and *averaged fragility* b_{af}.

Table 3 shows the detailed results of the robustness analysis for the WBS program. For each test case and coverage criterion, the table shows the results

---

[1] We use the CodeCover tool http://codecover.org/

Table 2. Results in percentage of the robustness analysis for ASW, TOPAS, NXML, and ANT

	ASW			TOPAS			NXML			ANT		
LOC/Classes	1497/47			10115/91			3696/34			104304/1266		
Test suite size (LOC)	965			4725			4231			24384		
Coverage	a	b_{wc}	b_{af}	a	b_{wc}	b_{af}	a	b_{wc}	b_{af}	a	b_{wc}	b_{af}
Statement	32.5	0.6	0.1	78.5	30.4	10.2	10.6	3.2	0.7	10.9	8.4	1.8
Branch	27.8	1.0	0.2	69.8	28.3	7.5	4.1	2.1	0.5	7.6	5.7	1.2
MCDC	31.1	1.1	0.2	69.4	30.6	7.6	4.8	2.6	0.5	7.6	5.9	1.3

Table 3. Results in percentage of the robustness analysis for WBS (194 lines of code)

Test suite	size	Statement Coverage C	Δ			Branch Coverage C	Δ			MCDC C	Δ		
			t_{cdcf}	t_{ecf}	t_{fbc}		t_{cdcf}	t_{ecf}	t_{fbc}		t_{cdcf}	t_{ecf}	t_{fbc}
Random1	100	58.1	34.9	0	17.7	51.4	33.7	0	19.1	50.0	31.8	4.5	17.7
Random2	1000	74.2	56.1	0	22.5	74.3	59.7	0	28.3	71.2	56.4	10.3	25.2
Evosuite	6	74.2	56.1	0	22.5	74.3	59.7	0	28.3	71.2	56.4	10.3	25.2
Handmade	1	58.1	42.4	0	17.7	50.0	39.5	0	20.2	46.3	35.8	8.1	16.5

in terms of coverage achieved by the test suite and the losses in terms of coverage on the transformed versions of the program. The table shows only the results for the t_{fbc}, t_{ecf} and t_{cdcf} transformations, because the WBS program is not influenced by the t_{rc} and t_b transformations.

All the programs and test suites considered in our study suffer from fragility problems: semantically equivalent programs achieve different results in terms of coverage, and thus SPTs can influence greatly the coverage achieved by test suites. Our results highlight the fact that some transformations influence only certain coverage criteria, e.g. t_{ecf} influences only MCDC in our study, whereas other transformations, such as t_{rc}, seems to not influence the coverage at all. For this reason, the choice of the transformations considered in the robustness analysis can significantly influence the results of the analysis itself.

No apparent correlation can be identified between the size of the test suite and their fragility: indeed, significant losses in terms of coverage exist also for big test suites, e.g. Table 3 shows that also the random test suite with 1000 test cases has high losses. Note that even if the losses in terms of coverage may be small in some cases, this is usually due to the low coverage achieved by the test suites. For instance, in the ANT case the maximum loss is 8.4%, but the coverage achieved on the original program is only 10.9%.

Test suite with high coverage, can be fragile as well: from the results, it seems that test suites generated by hand explicitly to achieve good coverage, are those with higher losses in terms of coverage. This is due both to the fact that these test suites have small sizes and also to the fact that they are created ad-hoc to obtain full coverage of the program with a particular structure and thus the coverage is more fragile than the one of a not ad-hoc test suite.

6   Threats to Validity

There are three main aspects that can pose a threat to the validity of our work.
Transformations: Although the set of selected transformations is small, in our opinion it can demonstrate the effectiveness of our approach. By extending the given set of transformations, test suites become likely less robust. The selected transformations are meaningful examples. Indeed t_{ecf} is already used in several works [11,17], whereas t_{cdcf}, t_{rc}, t_{ecf} and t_{fbc} are extracted from common refactoring techniques [8,1].

Coverage Criteria: We have considered three common structural coverage criteria, i.e. statement coverage, branch coverage and MCDC. Rajan et al. [17] show that MCDC is highly sensitive to the structure of the implementation and our experiments confirm that. Test suites adequate to other non structural coverage criteria may be less fragile.

Experiments: Our work has focused only on a limited set of Java programs. However we think that chosen programs are representative of several classes of systems, i.e. toy examples (LEAP, TRI), critical systems (WBS, ASW, TCAS), and complex Java libraries (JTOPAS, NXML, ANT). Our experiments involved 1442 classes and more than 120kLOC, and therefore the selected programs are, in our opinion, a representative sample of real Java programs. We have also used different test suites which range from manually built test suites, to test suites generated by using well-known tools.

7   Conclusions and Future Work

In this paper we have proposed a framework to evaluate the robustness of a test suite with respect to semantic preserving transformations applied to the program under test. We have introduced the concept of fragile and robust coverage and we have identified the conditions for a code to have a robust structure with respect to a certain set of transformations. Moreover, we have defined a new extended coverage metrics that takes into account the fragility of the coverage. The extended coverage does not require either a modification of the code or the introduction of new original testing criteria. It uses a fragility index to quantitatively measure the quality of test suite in terms of its robustness. In presence of fragile code, we suggest either to (1) find and remove fragility points by modifying the code or (2) increase the test suite until its robustness reaches a desired level. We have evaluated the fragility of several Java programs (from toy examples to Java library code) together with their test suites and we have found that the fragility problem occurs in all the considered programs.

In the future we plan to study the correlation between the fragility of the test suite and its fault detection capability. We also plan to define a language for the formalization and definition of semantic preserving transformations. In this way, we can easily model other transformations and also extend the theoretical framework.

Acknowledgments. The authors would like to thank Matt Staats for sharing some code examples.

References

1. Refactoring catalog - website, http://www.refactoring.com/catalog/
2. Aho, A.V., Sethi, R., Ullman, J.D.: Compilers: principles, techniques, and tools. Addison-Wesley Longman Publishing Co., Inc., Boston (1986)
3. Ammann, P., Offutt, J.: Introduction to Software Testing, 1st edn. Cambridge University Press, New York (2008)
4. ARP 4761, Guidelines and Methods for Conducting the Safety Assessment Process on Civil Airborne Systems and Equipment. Aerospace Recommended Practice, Society of Automotive Engineers, Detroit, USA (1996)
5. Chilenski, J.J., Miller, S.P.: Applicability of modified condition/decision coverage to software testing. Software Engineering Journal 9(5), 193–200 (1994)
6. Dijkstra, E.W.: Notes on structured programming. In: Dahl, O.J., Dijkstra, E.W., Hoare, C.A.R. (eds.) Structured Programming. Academic Press (1972)
7. Do, H., Elbaum, S.G., Rothermel, G.: Supporting controlled experimentation with testing techniques: An infrastructure and its potential impact. Empirical Software Engineering 10(4), 405–435 (2005)
8. Fowler, M.: Refactoring: Improving the Design of Existing Code. Addison-Wesley (August 1999)
9. Fraser, G., Arcuri, A.: Evosuite: Automatic test suite generation for object-oriented software. In: Proc. of ACM SIGSOFT ESEC/FSE, pp. 416–419 (2011)
10. Goodenough, J.B., Gerhart, S.L.: Toward a theory of test data selection. IEEE Trans. Softw. Eng. 1(2), 156–173 (1975)
11. Harman, M., Hu, L., Hierons, R., Wegener, J., Sthamer, H., Baresel, A., Roper, M.: Testability transformation. IEEE Trans. Softw. Eng. 30, 3–16 (2004)
12. Kirner, R.: Towards preserving model coverage and structural code coverage. EURASIP J. Emb. Sys., 1–16 (2009)
13. Marick, B., Smith, J., Jones, M.: How to misuse code coverage. In: Proc. of ICTCS 1999 (June 1999)
14. Miller, J.C., Maloney, C.J.: Systematic mistake analysis of digital computer programs. Commun. ACM 6, 58–63 (1963)
15. Myers, G.J.: The art of software testing, 2nd edn. Wiley (2004)
16. Namin, A.S., Andrews, J.H.: The influence of size and coverage on test suite effectiveness. In: Proc. of ISSTA 2009, pp. 57–68. ACM (2009)
17. Rajan, A., Whalen, M.W., Heimdahl, M.P.: The effect of program and model structure on mc/dc test adequacy coverage. In: Proc. of ICSE, pp. 161–170 (2008)
18. Rapps, S., Weyuker, E.: Selecting software test data using data flow information. IEEE Trans. Soft. Eng. SE-11(4), 367–375 (1985)
19. Senko, M.E.: A control system for logical block diagnosis with data loading. Commun. ACM 3, 236–240 (1960)
20. Staats, M., Gay, G., Whalen, M., Heimdahl, M.: On the Danger of Coverage Directed Test Case Generation. In: de Lara, J., Zisman, A. (eds.) FASE 2012. LNCS, vol. 7212, pp. 409–424. Springer, Heidelberg (2012)
21. Staats, M., Păsăreanu, C.: Parallel symbolic execution for structural test generation. In: Proc. of ISSTA, pp. 183–194. ACM, New York (2010)
22. Weißleder, S.: Simulated satisfaction of coverage criteria on uml state machines. In: Proc. of ICST 2010, pp. 117–126. IEEE Computer Society (2010)
23. Weyuker, E.J.: Translatability and decidability questions for restricted classes of program schemas. SIAM J. Comput. 8(4), 587–598 (1979)
24. Zhu, H., Hall, P., May, J.: Software unit test coverage and adequacy. ACM Computing Surveys 29(4), 366–427 (1997)

Using Behaviour Inference
to Optimise Regression Test Sets

Ramsay Taylor, Mathew Hall, Kirill Bogdanov, and John Derrick

Department of Computer Science, The University of Sheffield

Abstract. Where a software component is updated or replaced regression testing is required. Regression test sets can contain considerable redundancy. This is especially true in the case where no formal regression test set exists and the new component must instead be compared against patterns of behaviour derived from in-use log data from the previous version. Previous work has applied search-based techniques such as Genetic Algorithms to minimise test sets, but these relied on code coverage metrics to select test cases. Recent work has demonstrated the advantage of behaviour inference as a test adequacy metric. This paper presents a multi-objective search-based technique that uses behaviour inference as the fitness metric. The resulting test sets are evaluated using mutation testing and it is demonstrated that a considerably reduced test set can be found that retains all of the fault finding capability of the complete set.

1 Introduction

Where a software component is updated or replaced regression testing is required. It is often the case that there is no documented specification for the behaviour of the component. In the absence of a specification for the component, regression tests can be used to attempt to determine that a de-facto specification — the behaviour of the previous version — is adhered to.

In the absence of regression test sets, the only available regression test is the replay of trace data from in-service logs of the previous version. This trace data contains sequences of inputs and outputs, or sequences of function calls that are applied to the component. The traces can identify both sequences of behaviour that must be accepted, and sequences that should not occur. When sufficient log data is available this provides an accurate picture of the behaviour that the rest of the system expects from the component, so replay of traces forms a meaningful regression test.

Running regression tests is often expensive, usually due to the large number of tests that comprise a test suite. Often, multiple regression tests will exercise the same behaviour, resulting in time being spent on tests that add no value. This is especially true of test sets derived from in-service data.

An improved test suite can be developed by selecting a subset of the traces with enough traces to exercise each part of the behaviour for the lowest overall cost. Figure 1 illustrates the minimisation process. In the example, a subset of the eight regression tests is selected $(1, 4, 5)$, and must then be evaluated for its

B. Nielsen and C. Weise (Eds.): ICTSS 2012, LNCS 7641, pp. 184–199, 2012.

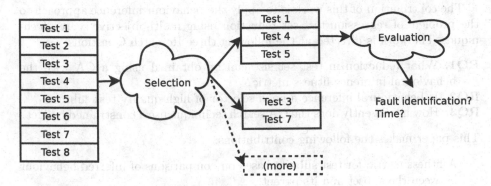

Fig. 1. Problems facing test set selection

suitability. The naive, exact solution is to repeat this process for all subsets of the test suite, but this is impractical for most test suites, and impossible for test suites generated from log data that can contain billions of lines [18]. It has been shown in [12] that finding a suitable regression test subset is NP complete and so heuristic approaches are required. A detailed survey of regression test selection literature can be found in [3].

The problem has two distinct elements. Firstly, given that considering all candidate sets is infeasible, the selection step must be performed more intelligently. Secondly, once a candidate is selected, difficulty remains in assessing its suitability as a reduced test set.

Genetic Algorithms (GAs) are one solution to the selection problem. They are a class of heuristic approaches that have been used successfully in many software engineering problems [9] and provide efficient selection of possible solutions from large search spaces. In a GA, a pool of good solutions is recombined to locate better solutions. This relies on measurement of the "fitness" of these solutions. Despite its efficiency, a GA will still consider a large number of solutions before it locates a suitable result, making its execution time highly dependent on both the accuracy and the speed of the evaluation mechanism.

Previous work has used code coverage to address the evaluation problem. Genetic Algorithm approaches to the selection of subsets were presented in [13] and [19], and sought to identify the minimum set of traces that achieves complete code coverage. Test sets selected for code coverage have been shown to provide a low "behavioural adequacy" [6] — that is, their fault finding ability is lower than test sets selected for behavioural coverage. An alternative measure of a test set is provided by behaviour inference. Using behaviour inference as a measure of test adequacy was first suggested in 1983 [17], and has been shown to provide a better foundation for selecting test sets [6]. While behavioural inference requires some computation time this grows with the number of test cases, regardless of their content. However, the time taken to execute a test set is unbounded as each test may depend on external factors such as communication, which may take an arbitrarily long time.

The contribution of this work is to apply the behaviour inference approach to the problem of regression test set reduction using multi-objective search techniques. The work is directed at the following three Research Questions:

RQ1. What reduction in test set size can be obtained using a GA with the behavioural inference fitness metric?
RQ2. Is behavioural inference a good selector of high quality test subsets?
RQ3. How intelligently does the GA search technique use a constrained budget?

This paper makes the following contributions:

– A fitness metric for test subsets based on comparisons of inferred behaviour between the subset and its parent.
– A multi-objective search approach based on the NSGA-II algorithm that applies this metric to identify a Pareto front of fast, accurate test sets.
– An evaluation of the solutions found by this approach that demonstrates the search efficiency and validates the results by comparing mutation testing outcomes between the subsets and their parent.

The remainder of this paper is organised as follows:

– Section 2 introduces the vending machine example that is used throughout this paper.
– Section 3 and Section 4 present the process of evaluating a test set using passive learning algorithms, and the genetic algorithm for efficiently searching the possible test subsets.
– The results of the process are evaluated in Section 5.
– Section 6 contains conclusions.

2   The Vending Machine Example

The example used throughout this paper is a simple vending machine simulation. The case study was implemented in Erlang[1] but the techniques developed operate on traces and are independent of the implementation language. The implementation consists of 60 lines of Erlang code. The module presents an interface with a number of functions that represent operations on the machine – `start`, `coin`, `choc`, `toffee` — some of which take parameters and all of which produce a return value.

The behaviour of the vending machine program can be best understood with reference to the state machine shown in Figure 2, which presents a convenient abstraction. The format for the transition labels is a triple with the name of the function, a list of arguments, and the expected return value. For example, `{coin,[2],ok}` represents a call to the `coin` function with the parameter 2 and the expected response `ok`. The machine is initialised with the `start` function, and can be re-initialised at any point, resetting it to the initial state. The machine

---

[1] Erlang is a concurrent, functional programming language developed by Ericsson and used extensively in the telecoms industry [2].

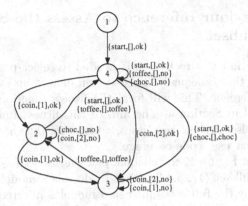

Fig. 2. The vending machine state machine

accepts 1p and 2p coins and charges 1p for `toffee` and 2p for `choc`. Since 2p is the most expensive item, the machine will reject coins that would take its stored value above 2p (this serves to make the machine's state space finite).

In the scenario in this example, a test set was generated randomly according to the following process. Elements of the trace alphabet were randomly selected and conjoined to produce traces. In this example the trace alphabet consists of the interface functions, combined with the valid arguments and valid responses for each function. These were then passed to a program that attempted to execute the generated sequence of function calls and checked that the returned values were consistent with those generated. Where there was an inconsistency — or where there was an exception thrown by the program — the trace was truncated at that point and marked as negative. If all elements of a trace completed successfully then it was marked as a positive trace. This forms a prefix-closed language describing the behaviour of the program.

```
+ {start,[],ok} {coin,[1],ok} {coin,[2],no} {coin,[1],ok}
+ {start,[],ok} {start,[],ok} {toffee,[],no} {choc,[],no}
- {start,[],ok} {coin,[2],ok} {toffee,[],no}
+ {start,[],ok} {coin,[2],ok} {toffee,[],toffee}
```

Fig. 3. Some example traces from the case study test set

A random test set was constructed by adding random traces to it until the set covered all the behaviour of the state machine inFigure 2. This produced a test set of 190 traces; some example traces are shown in Figure 3. The third trace is listed as negative because it expects the response `no` to the `toffee` call after giving the machine a 2p coin, when the implementation will instead respond `toffee`. This observed behaviour is listed in the fourth trace.

3   Using Behaviour Inference to Assess the Suitability of a Test Subset

As discussed in Section 1, a technique is needed to select possible test subsets and then evaluates their adequacy. This section defines an evaluation strategy using behaviour inference. This will form the fitness function for the selection technique presented in Section 4. The aim of this fitness function is to assess the *behaviour* exercised by the test cases, addressing the shortcomings present in previous work that uses code coverage.

In the example in Figure 1, the adequacy of the subset (1,4,5) must be evaluated against the full set (1,2,3,4,5,6,7,8). To do this a model is inferred of the behaviour covered by the full set, and then a model is inferred of the behaviour covered by the subset. These are then compared to assess the extent to which coverage has been maintained. This is particularly pertinent in the regression case where the only specification of correct behaviour is the log data of an existing system, so the model inferred from the complete set is the only available standard against which test set coverage can be measured.

3.1   Behaviour Inference

Behaviour inference builds finite state machine models from trace data using algorithms inspired by language learning models.

Passive learners aim to learn state machine language representations from partial data, usually a subset of the possible sequences of the language. Evidence driven state merging (EDSM) algorithms such as BlueFringe [11] operate on a set of positive and negative traces from a system or language and produce a state machine that accepts positive traces and rejects (in the form of a transition to a failure state) negative traces. It was shown to be highly effective in the "Abadingo One" [11] competition for learning algorithms.

We use the StateChum system [1], which was developed to implement an EDSM algorithm based on BlueFringe with the objective of reverse engineering state machine representations of software behaviour from software trace data [16]. The algorithm operates on prefix closed languages, which are a good model of software execution traces since traces cannot exist with failing prefixes. The supplied traces are merged into a Prefix Tree Automaton (PTA), which represents an accurate but excessively large FSM representation of the behaviour covered by the supplied traces. The algorithm proceeds by merging states to reduce the size of the state machine without altering the accepted language. The choice of states to merge is based on various *evidence*, such as similar outgoing traces, and the absence of explicit negative traces in the test set that would become accepted after the merge.

3.2   State Machine Comparison

A key component of the evaluation mechanism presented in this section is the comparison of inferred state machines. This paper will use what is called the

Balanced Classification Rate (BCR) measure to compare state machines, and thus compare the behaviour coverage of the test sets that produced them.

The BCR metric measures the accuracy of a state machine against a reference machine in terms of the correct classification of traces as either positive (accepted) or negative (rejected). Each of the possible traces of the reference machine are classified by the machine being measured and four sets are produced: true positives (TP), true negatives (TN), false positives (FP), and false negatives (FN). For machines with cycles the set of possible traces is infinite; this paper uses the W-Method [4] to produce a suitable set of traces that cover all of the behaviour in a finite set. For example, in Figure 4 the right hand FSM accepts traces that do not start with {start,[],ok}, whereas the correct model does not, so these form false positives.

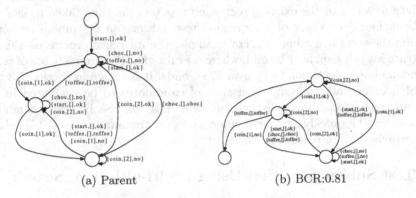

(a) Parent   (b) BCR:0.81

Fig. 4. The vending machine behaviour as inferred from the complete random trace set, and a behaviour model with a BCR score of 0.81 inferred from less than 4% of the trace set

These figures are used to compute two numbers, C_{plus} and C_{minus}, where $C_{plus} = TP/(TP + FN)$ and $C_{minus} = TN/(TN + FP)$. The BCR value is the harmonic mean between C_{plus} and C_{minus} and is defined as: $BCR = (2 * C_{plus} * C_{minus})/(C_{plus} + C_{minus})$. This produces a "score" between 0.0 and 1.0, where 1.0 represents correct classification of all traces, and smaller numbers represent decreasing levels of accuracy.

3.3 Subset Evaluation Metric

With these components in place, each candidate test subset can be compared to a reference model to produce a numeric adequacy value. The behaviour inference process is applied to the complete test suite and the inferred model forms the reference for all subset evaluations. This inference only needs to be conducted once, at the beginning of the process.

Each candidate test subset is compared to the reference set by inferring a model from the subset and then computing the BCR score (as described in

Section 3.2) of that model against the reference model. The BCR score gives a numeric metric to the accuracy of the model, and permits the user of the process to allow a trade-off between speed and accuracy. In cases where the optimal, completely accurate regression test still requires many hours to run it may be useful to produce a regression test that can be run in minutes and still find 80% of faults. This could serve as a quick regression test during the development program, that is supplemented by the full regression test at the conclusion of a development phase. By using a numeric metric of accuracy, such as BCR, this process allows quantitative decisions to be made about the appropriate accuracy/speed trade-off that would not be possible using less semantic measures such as code coverage.

Inferring a model from a set of recorded traces is much faster than actually performing tests themselves. Thus using recorded traces, either from in-service log data or a run of the existing regression test set, the time taken to evaluate the behavioural coverage of a regression test subset can be minimised versus running the tests to evaluate it. For example, the inference process on the 146 line trace set takes under 1 second, whereas evaluating the complete set of traces against an implementation takes over 50 seconds. It is shown in Section 5.3 that model inference allows many thousands of candidates to be evaluated in less than an hour. Model inference therefore provides a process by which candidate solutions can be quickly evaluated, allowing many thousands of possible subsets to be evaluated in a reasonable time.

4   Test Subset Selection Using Multi-objective Search

Having developed a suitable fitness function, the other component of the technique is the selection of candidate test subsets. This section presents a multi-objective search algorithm using the NSGA-II algorithm.

4.1   Genetic Algorithms

This paper uses genetic algorithms to approach the NP complete problem of selecting test subsets from a given test suite. The field of Search-Based Software Engineering [9] includes various techniques that provide general, meta-heuristic approaches to problems for which it is impossible or impractical to find perfect solutions. Genetic Algorithms (GAs) are one such technique that uses an evolutionary metaphor to direct and optimise a limited search of a very large search space. This makes them ideal for a task such as test suite optimisation where the search space is large, and while the best solution is desirable, there is a large space of sub-optimal, but still satisfactory solutions that a GA can discover.

The critical elements of a GA are: a representation of an individual candidate solution as a collection of "genes", and a "fitness function" that produces a numerical measure of the "correctness" of this candidate.

The search consists of the application of *operators* on a population comprised of a number of chromosomes, each of which containing one or more genes. The minimum operators required are selection, crossover and mutation.

The selection operator uses the fitness values of the chromosomes to determine which are selected in the next generation. Crossover and mutation are concerned with exploring the search space. Crossover models reproduction, where two individuals are mixed together to produce offspring. Crossover operators traditionally consist of a series of swap operations, however more complicated ones exist. The mutation operator serves to prevent the search from remaining in local optima by ensuring diversity in the population. It operates by randomly altering one or more genes in an individual to produce a new individual.

4.2   Chromosome Representation and Genetic Operators

The chromosome representation for a test set subset consists of a set of bits where each bit represents a trace or test from the original test set. Bits set to 1 represent that that trace is included in this subset, 0 represents that the trace is not included. Each bit is considered a gene by the implementation. The chromosome is therefore comprised of Tc bits, where Tc is the number of traces in the original set. Crossover is enacted by picking some n where $n < Tc$; the new chromosome is formed from bits 1 to n from one parent, and bits $n + 1$ to Tc from the other.

Random mutation of a bit would simply invert it. As the number of bits set to 1 or 0 decreases (i.e. the chromosome is "mostly 1s" or "mostly 0s") this becomes less effective, since inverting a random bit becomes decreasingly likely to further reduce the number of 0s or 1s. This is a significant issue for test set minimisation in cases where a significant optimisation is possible, or very little optimisation is possible, since the ideal solution may have very few traces included (1s) or very few traces excluded (0s).

This implementation uses two mutation operators: one that randomly "turns on" a bit, and one that randomly "turns off" a bit. This ensures that every generation contains some new solutions with more traces and some with fewer traces, even as the population tends towards one extreme or the other.

The binary nature of the individual genes also has a significant impact on the generation of the initial population for the search. If the initial chromosomes are simply generated randomly then they will all have approximately 50% of the bits set and approximately 50% unset. In theory the crossover and mutation will eventually correct for this, but it was found that producing a more even distribution of initial individuals allowed the search to focus more rapidly. Consequently, individuals for the initial population are created by first selecting a random number of bits to be set, and then a random distribution of those bits across the chromosome. This results in an even distribution of individuals from some with 0 bits set to some with Tc bits set.

4.3   Multi-objective Search Algorithms

The test set reduction problem involves optimising for both test speed and fault identification. In such instances where there are multiple, independent variables to optimise, this can be achieved by weighting the squares of each variable and using this as the fitness function for a conventional GA, however this has the possibility that a solution with a very high score for one objective will overpower solutions that have a more balanced profile. Consequently, this work uses a specialised multi-objective genetic algorithm, which has a more intricate selection process that seeks to avoid this drawback.

The search heuristic used in this paper is based on the "Non-dominated Sorting Genetic Algorithm II" (NSGA-II) [5], which has been demonstrated as effective in test set reduction by [19]. For each candidate solution the NSGA-II selection mechanism measures the number of other solutions that "dominate" this one, where dominance is defined as being superiour in all objectives. Those that are undominated represent the Pareto front of the currently explored solutions. These are retained as the population for the next generation.

Where there are many Pareto-optimal solutions it becomes necessary to select a subset. The subset is chosen to avoid clustering — that is, the selection mechanism attempts to distribute the chosen solutions evenly over the Pareto front. This distribution creates a much more effective basis for the next generation, since breeding solutions that excel in different objectives should produce offspring which posses both qualities. As an example: breeding a very accurate test set with a very fast one may produce offspring that retain most or all of the accuracy but are considerably quicker.

4.4 Fitness Evaluation

The minimisation process has two variables to be optimised: fault identification and cost.

Fault identification is estimated using the *BCR score* for the learned machine from a candidate individual as described in Section 3.3.

The "cost" of the test set may be defined as the time taken. For the purpose of the case study in this paper, uniform cost is assigned to all tests in a candidate subset, therefore the "cost" is a function of the size of the test set. In a more complex testing scenario it would be important to consider other costs, such as the execution time of each test. This may not be related to trace length, as some tests may include features such as external synchronisation that causes them to take arbitrarily long times. Wherever trace count (Tc) is used in the subsequent discussion this could be substituted for trace *cost*, which would be the sum of individual costs of tests in a test set. The *trace improvement* of a subset is defined as the number of test cases removed from the total set, (*i.e.* the number of 0 bits in the chromosome). This is expressed as a fraction of the total chromosome size: $Trace\ Improvement = \frac{Tc - Tc_{individual}}{Tc}$.

4.5 Selection

The two values, BCR score and Trace Improvement, measure the solution's fitness in each objective dimension. A solution's dominance is then measured by comparison to the other solutions in the current population. The selector proceeds by choosing undominated solutions. If the number of them exceeds a defined limit then it begins to reduce the set by measuring the "distance" between solutions. The distance is measured as the sum of the absolute difference between the accuracies and the trace improvements. Solutions with identical accuracy and trace improvement have a zero distance and one of the pair will be removed. If the size is still excessive then a threshold distance is established at 0.01 and steadily increased. Any solutions within the threshold distance are pruned and the threshold increased until the population size falls below the limit.

5   Evaluation

This evaluation seeks to assess the test set improvement that can be obtained using the multi-objective behavioural adequacy approach, as well as to validate the testing capability of the solutions it generates compared to that of the original test set. The research questions this evaluation answers are those defined in Section 1.

The evaluation was conducted on the vending machine example given in Section 2. A test was produced containing 190 randomly generated traces, which covered all behaviour in the program, such that running the EDSM algorithm (Section 3.1) on it will produce the state machine in Figure 2. The random nature of the test set means it is likely to contain duplication — traces that exercise the same behaviour, offering no value. The objective of the evaluation was to determine how much of this duplication the GA removed

5.1   RQ1: Reduction in Test Set Size

This research question is answered in terms of the *trace improvement* (as defined in Section 4.4) the search yields for test sets that exercise the same behaviour as an unoptimised test set.

The test set was optimised using the multiobjective genetic algorithm as detailed in Section 4.3. The individuals were assessed in terms of the constituent variables that make up their fitness (BCR and trace improvement).

The genetic algorithm used a 100% crossover rate, generating one extra individual for every pair of parents, a population size of 10 after each round of selection, and a mutation rate matched to the size of the trace set so that each individual in the population produces one mutant with one gene altered. Crossover and mutation were only applied to the surviving members of the previous fitness evaluation. Fitness values were recorded for all individuals evaluated as the search progressed. The search was repeated 30 times to ensure statistical significance.

The genetic algorithm was limited to 75 generations, which produced an average of 3500 evaluations of distinct individuals. A random set of 3500 individuals was generated and evaluated in the same way. This process was repeated 30 times to produce 30 sets of evaluations, each of a size that is comparable to a run of the GA.

5.2   Results

RQ1: Reduction in Test Size. The individual with the highest trace improvement and a 1.0 BCR was selected from each of the 30 sets of individuals

Table 1. Trace Improvement scores for the best individual with a 1.0 BCR score from each iteration for both search types

	Min	Max	Median	Mean	St. Dev.	N	p-value
GA	0.757	0.936	0.921	0.909	0.037	30	< 0.005
Random	0.710	0.873	0.808	0.806	0.028	30	

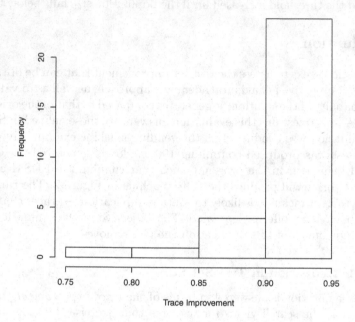

Fig. 5. Histogram of the trace improvement of the best individual with a 1.0 BCR score from each GA search

from the minimisation step. This was performed for both the genetic algorithm implementation as well as the random set. Statistics for the trace improvement values of these two samples are shown in Table 1 as well as visually for the GA in Figure 5.

The results demonstrate that a high reduction in test case size is achieved using the approach. Both search algorithms located reduced test sets with a high trace improvement, with the minimum being over 0.7. Consistency is demonstrated by the small standard deviation, which equates to a difference of 4% of the original test set size.

5.3   RQ2: Efficacy of the Behavioural Adequacy Metric

The validity of the behavioural adequacy metric as a measure of the fault identification of a test subset is assessed using mutation testing. Mutation testing [8] evaluates test sets by simulating faults in a software system and measuring the test set's ability to identify the faults.

Mutation testing modifies the software's source code to produce a "mutant". The mutant code is recompiled and then tested by the test suite. If the mutant fails the test suite it is referred to as "killed", if not then it is "alive". A large percentage of simple syntactic mutations result in code that does not compile; many of those that do compile have no functional change. Semantic mutation testing (SMT) [10] is intended to improve on this by applying mutation to a parsed form of the program. The *muTestErl* [7] system for Erlang semantic mutation testing was used in this evaluation.

To use mutation testing to evaluate BCR, the complete test set was first run on 4807 mutants. The complete set kills all but 386 of these mutants. These remaining mutants contain modifications that do not alter the observable behaviour of the program — many change the type of the internal representation of the stored coin value from integer to floating point, for example, but the Erlang implementation performs suitable implicit casting at each application of an arithmetic operator to allow all the updates and comparisons to continue to operate.

A selection of 288 randomly generated individuals were then subjected to mutation testing. Each of these individuals was a reduced test set, for which the BCR was calculated. The same set of mutants was then run on each of these reduced test sets, each killing some number of mutants. The result of these runs are shown in a scatterplot in Figure 6.

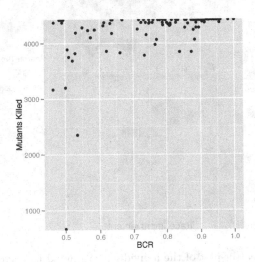

Fig. 6. Scatter-plot showing number of mutants killed against BCR for a selection of random test sets

The scatterplot shows that mutant killing power does not correlate highly with BCR (Pearson $r = 0.457$), however, it also shows that for particularly high values of BCR that the mutant killing power is as high as the original test set. In this evaluation BCR is observed to be prone to *false negatives*, but does not appear to suffer from false positives: of all the test sets with a BCR of 1.0, none killed fewer mutants.

These results suggest that BCR is likely to be too conservative, as smaller test sets with an equal mutant killing power will be discarded if they have a low BCR score. The multiobjective search used in this approach can mitigate this problem; adjacent solutions to test sets with a high trace improvement but low BCR score may still be explored, possibly yielding better adjacent solutions. This also has the implication that individuals on the Pareto front with sub-1.0 BCR scores (but better trace improvement) should not be rejected outright, as they are potentially more suitable minimisations of the test set.

RQ3: How Intelligently does the GA Search Use a Constrained Budget? The search space for an exhaustive approach for the case study is 2^{190}. The results for **RQ1** demonstrate the search reliably finds a test set that is significantly smaller than the original regression test set, despite only exploring a small fraction (30, 000 candidates) of the total search space.

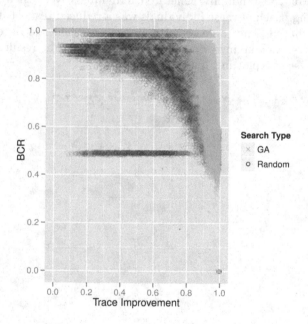

Fig. 7. Scatter-plot of the individuals evaluated by each search

Figure 7 shows a scatterplot of the trace improvement versus BCR score for each of the individuals selected by both the random and the genetic algorithm searches. Maximised values in both direction represent objectively better solutions. The plot clearly shows a Pareto front has been located by the genetic algorithm, which is beyond the region explored by the random searcher. Along this front are the best individuals found by the search. This front demonstrates the tradeoff between behavioural adequacy (BCR) and trace improvement. As

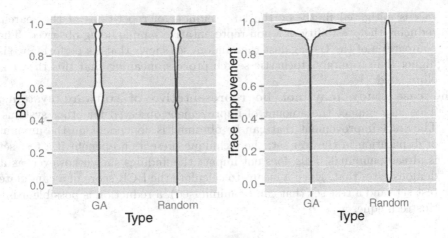

Fig. 8. Violin plots of BCR score and trace improvement of all individuals generated by each search

the findings for **RQ2** suggest that some solutions with sub 1.0 BCRs may be equally suitable as those with 1.0 BCR scores, the individuals to the right of the plot may actually be better overall.

The random search results exhibit a pattern where a large number of individuals with a widely varied trace improvement have the same BCR score. This is due to the common lack of a critical trace amongst this subset of the population and illustrates the difficulty of the selection problem, as well as demonstrating the benefit of intelligently searching the space, rather than randomly sampling it.

The "p-value" column of Table 1 gives the p-value for a one-sided Wilcoxon test. The p-value gives an indication of the likelihood that the null hypothesis (H_0) is true. In this case, H_0: median(GA) $\ngtr$ median(Random). As the p-value is small, the null hypothesis is rejected, indicating the difference in medians is statistically significant, demonstrating that the GA outperforms the random searcher.

Figure 8 shows a visualisation of the BCR scores and trace improvements of the solutions considered by both search algorithms. The higher density towards the higher BCR scores for the random searcher can be explained by the uniform distribution of trace improvement - solutions with more traces (*i.e* a lower trace improvement) are more likely to have a high BCR score. The genetic algorithm exhibits a more varied distribution of BCR scores, accounted for by the amount of solutions with higher trace improvement it considered; this corresponds to the Pareto front that is illustrated in Figure 7.

5.4   Threats to Validity

There are several factors that constitute potential threats to validity.

The performance of the GA may be due to chance. It is possible that the results of the genetic algorithm may be entirely due to random chance. This risk is mitigated firstly by the large number of repetitions of the search, reducing the possibility of a non-representative sample being observed. The comparison of the GA against the random set shows that its performance is higher than a purely stochastic search process, meaning that this threat is eliminated.

The case study may not be representative of software systems. This may impact the amount of improvement observed for other systems. The trace improvement that can be obtained is dependent on the amount of duplication in the test set; the technique presents no benefit if a test set is already minimal. This does not impact the findings shown however, as it demonstrates that, given a means to calculate the BCR score of a candidate test set (and a test set that can be minimised), a reduction is possible using this technique.

6   Conclusions and Future Work

This work presents an application of a genetic algorithm to the test suite minimisation problem. Although genetic algorithms have been used before, this is the first instance where the *behaviour* exercised by the tests has been used as a selection criterion. The evaluation demonstrates that the approach is able to locate high-quality minimised test sets using BCR to estimate the behaviour exercised by the tests, identifying a test set that exhibits the same behaviour, despite having 90% of the traces removed from it. This is validated in two aspects, comparison with a random algorithm, as well as the muation testing of the results to compare BCR accuracy.

The findings show this is a promising algorithm, however the survey only applies it to a small example. Real world performance is not likely to vary, however, as the learning process occurs separately from the software. GAs can handle large search spaces well, so larger test sets should be reduicible using this technique as well as smaller ones (albeit with a higher fitness evaluation budget). Immediate future work will seek to apply the minimisation process to larger and more varied case studies to test this hypothesis.

Although in this work BCR worked well, it is possible to utilise other comparison techniques [15,14] that aim to ensure that a less than perfect score corresponds to a small change in an inferred model. Whereas BCR is generally sensitive to transitions close to the initial state, these methods aim to ensure the measure of difference computed is relatively equally sensitive to a missing or added transition anywhere in an automaton. Future work could use these alternatives to improve the accuracy of the test adequacy measure, therefore allowing potentially better trace improvement scores to be reached.

References

1. StateChum, http://statechum.sourceforge.net/ (accessed March 14, 2012)

2. Armstrong, J., Virding, R., Wikström, C., Williams, M.: Concurrent Programming in ERLANG. Prentice Hall (1996)
3. Biswas, S., Mall, R., Satpathy, M., Sukumaran, S.: Regression Test Selection Techniques: A Survey. Informatica 35(3), 289–321 (2011)
4. Chow, T.S.: Testing Software Design Modeled by Finite-State Machines. IEEE Trans. Softw. Eng. 4(3), 178–187 (1978)
5. Deb, K., Agrawal, S., Pratap, A., Meyarivan, T.: A fast and elitist multiobjective genetic algorithm: NSGA-II. IEEE Transactions on Evolutionary Computation 6(2), 182–197 (2002)
6. Fraser, G., Walkinshaw, N.: Behaviourally Adequate Software Testing. In: Proceedings of the Fifth International Conference on Software Testing, Verification and Validation (ICST) (2012)
7. Guo, Q., Derrick, J., Taylor, R.: Mutation Testing of Erlang Distributed and Concurrent Applications. In: Automated Software Engineering (submitted, 2012)
8. Hamlet, R.G.: Testing programs with the aid of a compiler. IEEE Transactions on Software Engineering 3, 279–290 (1977)
9. Harman, M., Jones, B.F.: Search-based software engineering. Information & Software Technology 43(14), 833–839 (2001)
10. Clark, J.A., Dan, H., Hierons, R.M.: Semantic Mutation Testing. Science of Computer Programming (2011) (page under print)
11. Lang, K.J., Pearlmutter, B.A., Price, R.A.: Results of the Abbadingo One DFA Learning Competition and a New Evidence-Driven State Merging Algorithm. In: Honavar, V.G., Slutzki, G. (eds.) ICGI 1998. LNCS (LNAI), vol. 1433, pp. 1–12. Springer, Heidelberg (1998)
12. Lin, J.-W., Huang, C.-Y.: Analysis of test suite reduction with enhanced tie-breaking techniques. Information & Software Technology 51(4), 679–690 (2009)
13. Mansour, N., El-Fakih, K.: Simulated Annealing and Genetic Algorithms for Optimal Regression Testing. Journal of Software Maintenance 11(1), 19–34 (1999)
14. Pradel, M., Bichsel, P., Gross, T.R.: A framework for the evaluation of specification miners based on finite state machines. In: ICSM, pp. 1–10. IEEE Computer Society (2010)
15. Walkinshaw, N., Bogdanov, K.: Automated Comparison of State-Based Software Models in terms of their Language and Structure. ACM Transactions on Software Engineering and Methodology 22(2) (2012)
16. Walkinshaw, N., Bogdanov, K., Holcombe, M., Salahuddin, S.: Reverse engineering state machines by interactive grammar inference. In: Proceedings of the 14th Working Conference on Reverse Engineering (WCRE). IEEE (2007)
17. Weyuker, E.J.: Assessing Test Data Adequacy through Program Inference. ACM Transactions on Programming Languages and Systems 5(4), 641–655 (1983)
18. Xu, W., Huang, L., Fox, A., Patterson, D., Jordan, M.: Experience mining google's production console logs. In: Proceedings of the 2010 Workshop on Managing Systems via Log Analysis and Machine Learning Techniques, p. 5. USENIX Association (2010)
19. Yoo, S., Harman, M.: Using hybrid algorithm for Pareto efficient multi-objective test suite minimisation. Journal of Systems and Software 83(4), 689–701 (2010)

Machine Learning Approach in Mutation Testing

Joanna Strug[1] and Barbara Strug[2]

[1] Faculty of Electrical and Computer Engineering, Cracow University of Technology
ul. Warszawska 24, 31-155 Krakow, Poland
[2] Department of Physics, Astronomy and Applied Computer Science,
Jagiellonian University, Reymonta 4, 30-059 Krakow, Poland
pestrug@cyf-kr.edu.pl, barbara.strug@uj.edu.pl

Abstract. This paper deals with an approach based on the similarity of mutants. This similarity is used to reduce the number of mutants to be executed. In order to calculate such a similarity among mutants their structure is used. Each mutant is converted into a hierarchical graph, which represents the program's flow, variables and conditions. On the basis of this graph form a special graph kernel is defined to calculate similarity among programs. It is then used to predict whether a given test would detect a mutant or not. The prediction is carried out with the help of a classification algorithm. This approach should help to lower the number of mutants which have to be executed. An experimental validation of this approach is also presented in this paper. An example of a program used in experiments is described and the results obtained, especially classification errors, are presented.

Keywords: mutation testing, machine learning, graph distance, classification, test evaluation.

1   Introduction

Software testing is a very important part of building an application. It can be also described as a process aiming at checking if the application meets the starting requirements, works as expected and satisfies the needs of all involved in.

Software testing, depending on the testing method employed, can be applied at different stages of the application development process. Traditionally most of the testing happens during the coding process and after it has been completed, but there exist approaches (for example agile), where testing is on-going. Thus the methodology of testing depends on the software development approach selected. This paper deals with mutation testing, called also mutation analysis or program mutation - a method of software testing, which involves introducing small changes in the source code (or for some programming languages byte code) of programs. Then the mutants are executed and tested by collections of tests called test suites. A test suite which does not detect mutant(s) is considered defective. The mutants are generated by using a set of mutation operators which try to mimic typical programming errors. This method aims at helping the tester assess the quality and derive effective tests.

B. Nielsen and C. Weise (Eds.): ICTSS 2012, LNCS 7641, pp. 200–214, 2012.

One of the problems with mutation testing concerns the number of mutants generated for even a small program/method, what leads to the need of compiling and executing a large number of copies of the program. This problem with mutation testing had reduced its use in practice. Over the years many tools supporting mutation testing were proposed, but reducing the number of mutants is still important aspect of mutation testing and there is a lot of research in this domain, which is briefly reviewed in the next section.

In this paper an approach based on the similarity of mutants is used. This similarity is used to reduce the number of mutants to be executed. In order to calculate such a similarity among mutants their structure is used. Each mutant is converted into a hierarchical control flow graph, which represents the program's flow, variables and conditions. On the basis of this graph form a similarity is calculate among programs. It is then used to predict whether a given test would detect a mutant or not. The prediction is carried out with the help of a classification algorithm. This approach should help to lower the number of mutants which have to be executed and at the same time help to assess quality of test suits without the need of running them. This approach shows some proximity to mutant clustering approach [8,17] as it also attempts to measure similarity of mutants, but we represent mutants in a graph form and use graph based measure rather then converting them to a special space which allows for the use of Hamming distance. Graphs have been for a long time considered to have too high computational cost to be of practical use in many domains but recently there has be a large growth of research on them, which resulted in the development of many algorithms and theoretical frameworks. Much of this research, which is briefly reviewed in the next section, deals with bio- and chemoinformatics, but some other domains were also touched upon.

.The main contribution of this paper is a method to reduce the number of mutants that have to be executed in a dynamic way i.e. depending on the program for which they are generated rather than statically for a given language or the operator. Moreover this paper introduces a representation of programs that allows for comparing programs and it also proposes several measures of such a comparison. This approach was applied to two examples and the results seem to be encouraging.

The paper is organized in the following way, in the next section a related work concerning both the mutation testing and different approaches to graph analysis is briefly presented. Then, in section 3 some preliminary notion concerning classification, graphs, edit distance and graph kernels is presented, It is followed by a section 4, which presents fundamental components of our approach i.e. a hierarchical control flow graph and methods for calculating edit distance and kernel for such a graph. In section 5 experiments are presented, including the setup, and the results are discussed. Finally section 6 summarizes the paper by presenting conclusions drawn from the research presented here as well as some possible extensions, improvements and directions for future work.

2   Related Work

In this paper a number of issues from different domains is discussed. Thus in this review of related work several domains are taken into account, such as mutation testing and especially reduction approaches, different approaches to classification problem, graph analysis and, in particular, different approaches to calculating distances among graphs, (like edit distance and using kernel methods for graph data) and learning methods based on them.

Mutation testing goes back to the 70s [12] and it can be used at different stages of software development. It has also been applied to many programming languages including Java [9,10,21,22,23,24] (used in this paper). A lot of research work has also been concerned with defining mutation operators that would mimic typical errors [25]. As mentioned in the introduction one of the main problem of mutation testing is the cost of executing large number of mutants so there has been a great research effort concerning reduction costs. Two main approaches to reduction can be divided into two groups: the first containing methods attempting to reduce the number of mutants and the second - those aimed at reducing the execution costs.

One of the methods used to mutant number reduction is sampling. It was first proposed firstly by Acree [1] and Budd [6]. They still generate all possible mutants but then a percentage of these mutants is then selected randomly to be executed, and all other are discarded. Many studies of this approach were carried out, for example Wong and Mathurs [31,45] conducted an experiment using a random percentage of mutants 10% to 40% in steps of 5%.

Another approach to mutant number reduction used clustering [8,17]. It was proposed by Hussain [17] and instead of selecting mutants randomly, a subset is selected by a clustering algorithm. The process starts by generating all first order mutants, then clustering algorithm is used to put these mutants into clusters depending on the killable test cases. Mutants put into the same cluster are killed by a similar set of test cases, so a small selection of mutants is used from each cluster. All the other are then discarded.

Third approach to reduction was based on selective mutation, which consists in selecting only a subset of mutation operators thus producing smaller number of mutants [30,32]. A much wider survey of the domain of mutation testing, including approaches to reduction was carried out by Jia et al. [19].

The approach proposed in this paper is partially similar to the first two described above, as it also generates all mutants, but then only randomly selected number of them is executed and the test performance for others is assessed on the basis of their similarity to the executed mutants for which performance of test suites is thus known.

The similarity of mutants is measured using graph representation of each mutant. The use of graphs as a mean of object representation has been widely researched. They are used in engineering, system modeling and testing, bioinformatics, chemistry and other domains of science to represent objects and the relations between them or their parts. For use in computer aided design different types of graphs were researched, not only simple ones but also hierarchical graphs (called also nested graphs [7]).

In this paper a machine learning approach based on similarity is used to analyse graphs. The need to analyze and compare graph data appeared in many domains and thus there has been a significant amount of research in this direction. Three distinctive, although partially overlapping, approaches can be noticed in the literature.

The first one is mainly based on using standard graph algorithms, like finding a maximal subgraph or mining for frequently occurring subgraphs to compare or classify graphs. The frequent pattern mining approach to graph analysis has been researched mainly in the domain of bioinformatics and chemistry [2,15,18,46,47]. The main problem with this approach is its computational cost, and a huge number of frequent substructures usually found.

The second approach is based on transforming graphs into vectors by finding some descriptive features Among others Bunke and Riesen ([4,33,34,35,36]) have done a lot of research on vector space embedding of graphs, where as features different substructures of graphs are selected. Then their number is counted in each graph and these numerical values combined in a predefined order result in a vector that captures some of the characteristics of a graph it represents. Having a graph encoded in a vector a standard statistical learning algorithms can be applied. The main problem is in finding appropriate features/substructures and in enumerating them in each graph. It usually leads to problems similar to those in frequent pattern mining (which is often used to find features counted in vector representation). Nevertheless, this approach has successfully been applied in many domains like image recognition [5], and especially the recognition of handwritten texts [26,27].

The third direction, which was proposed, among others, by Kashima and Gartner ([13,20]), is based on the theory of positive defined kernels and kernel methods [40,41]. There has been a lot of research on different kernels for structured data, including tree and graph kernels [3,13,14,20]. Tree kernels were proposed by Collins and Duffy [11] and applied to natural language processing. The basic idea is to consider all subtrees of the tree, where a subtree is defined as a connected subgraph of a tree containing either all children of a vertex or none. This kernel is computable in $O(|V_1||V_2|)$, where $|V_i|$ is the number of nodes in the $i - th$ tree [14].

In case of graph kernels there is a choice of several different ones proposed so far. One of them is based on enumerating all subgraphs of graphs G_i and calculating the number of isomorphic ones. An all subgraph kernel was shown to be NP-hard by Gartner et al [13]. Although, taking into account that in case of labelled graphs the computational time is significantly lower such a kernel is feasible in design applications. Another interesting group of graph kernels is based on computing random walks on both graphs. It includes the product graph kernel [13] and the marginalized kernels [20]. In product graph kernel a number of common walks in two graphs is counted. The marginalized kernel on the other hand is defined as the expectation of a kernel over all pairs of label sequences from two graphs. These kernels are computable in polynomial time, $(O(n^6)$ [14]), although for small graphs it may be worse then 2^n, when the neglected constant factors contribute stronger.

The main research focus is on finding faster algorithms to compute kernels for simple graphs, mainly in bio- and chemoinformatics. Yet, to author's best knowledge, no research has been done in the area of defining and testing kernels for different types of graphs, such as hierarchical control flow graphs proposed in this paper..

3   Preliminaries

Classification is one of main tasks being part of machine learning. It consists in identifying to which of a given set of classes a new element (often called observation) belongs. This decision is based on a so called training set, which contains data about other elements (often called instances) whose class membership is known. The elements to be classified are analysed on the basis of their properties, called features. These features can be of different types (categorical, ordinal, integer-valued or real-valued), but some known algorithms work only if the data is real-valued or integer-valued based. An algorithm which implements classification is known as a classifier. In machine learning, classification task is considered to be a supervised learning algorithm, i.e. learning process uses a training set of elements classified correctly.

There is a number of known classification algorithms. One of them is $k - NN$ (k nearest neighbours, where k is a parameter), used in this paper. In $k - NN$ classifier training set consists of vectors in a multidimensional space, for which a class membership is known. Thus training stage of the classifier consists only in storing the vectors and class labels of the elements of the training set. Then, during the actual classification for elements of unknown class membership, a distance from the new element to all elements of the training set is calculated and it is assigned to the class which is most frequent among the k training examples nearest to that new one.

In majority of known classification algorithms, including $k - NN$ an instance to classify is described by a feature vector containing properties of this instance. As in this paper graphs are used, not vectors, to represent objects to classify a way of calculating distance between two graphs is needed. Two such methods, graph edit distance and graph kernel, are briefly presented in the following, together with some basic notions. Then, in the next section, we show how these concepts can be extended to deal with hierarchical flow graphs proposed in this paper.

3.1   Graphs

A simple graph G is a set of nodes (called also vertices) V and edges E, where $E \subset V^2$. Each node and edge can be labeled by a function ξ, which assigns labels to nodes and edges. A walk w of length $k - 1$ in a graph is a sequence of nodes $w = (v_1, v_2, \ldots, v_k)$ where $(v_i, v_j) \in E$ for $1 \leq i, j \leq k$. If $v_i \neq v_j$ for $i \neq j$ then a walk w is called a *path*.

Graph Edit Distance. A graph edit distance (GED) approach is based on the fact that a graph can be transformed to another one by performing a finite number of graph edit operations which may be defined in a different way, depending on algorithms. GED is then defined as the least-cost sequence of such edit operations. Typically edit operation sequences include node edge insertion,node and edge deletion, node and edge substitution (label change). A cost function has to be defined for each of the operations and the cost for the edit operation sequence is defined as the sum of costs for all operations present in a given sequence. It has to be noticed that the sequence of edit operations and thus the cost of the transformation of a graph into another one is not necessary unique, but the lowest cost is and it is used as GED. For any given domain of application the two main issues are thus the way in which the similarity of atoms (nodes and edges) is defined and what is the cost of each operation. For labelled graphs, thus having labels for nodes, edges, or both of them, the deletion/insertion/substitution costs in the GED computations may depend on these labels.

Graph Kernels. Another approach to use traditional classification algorithms for non vector data is based on the so called kernel trick, which consists in mapping elements from a given set A into an inner product space S (having a natural norm), without ever having to actually compute the mapping,i.e. graphs do not have to be mapped into some objects in space S, only the way of calculation the inner product in that space has to be well defined. Linear classifications in target space are then equivalent with classifications in source space A. The trick allowing to avoid the actual mapping consists in using the learning algorithms needing only inner products between the elements (vectors) in target space, and defining the mapping in such a way that these inner products can be computed on the objects in the source the original space by means of a kernel function. For the classifiers a kernel matrix K must be positive semi-definite (PSD), although there are empirical results showing that some kernels not satisfy this requirement may still do reasonably well, if a kernel well approximates the intuitive idea of similarity among given objects. Formally a positive definite kernel on a space X is a symmetric function $K : X^2 \to \mathbf{R}$, which satisfies $\sum_{i,j=1}^{n} a_i a_j K(x_i, x_j) \geq 0$, for any points $x_1, \ldots, x_n \in X$ and coefficients $a_1, \ldots, a_n \in \mathbf{R}$.

The first approach of defining kernels for graphs was based on comparing all subgraphs of two graphs. The value of such a kernel usually equals to the number of identical subgraphs. While this is a good similarity measure, the enumeration of all subgraphs is a costly process. Another approach is based on comparing all paths in both graphs. It was used by Kashima [20] who proposed the following equation:

$$K(G_1, G_2) = \sum_{path_1, path_2 \in V_1^* \times V_2^*} p_1(path_1)p_2(path_2)K_L(lab(path_1), lab(path_2)),$$

(1)

where p_i is a probability distribution on V_i^*, and K_L is a kernel on sequences of labels of nodes and edges along the path $path_i$. It is usually defined as a product of subsequent edge and node kernels. This equation can be seen as a marginalized kernel and thus is a positive defined kernel [43]. Although computing this kernel requires summing over an infinite number of paths it can be done efficiently by using the product graph and matrix inversion [13]. Another approach uses convolution kernels [16], which are a general method for structured data (and thus very usefull for graphs). Convolution kernels are based on the assumption that structured object can be decomposed into components, then kernels are defined for those components and the final kernel is calculated over all possible decompositions.

4   Data Preparation

To carry out an experiment a number of steps was needed to prepare the data. Firstly, two relatively simple, but nevertheless representative, examples were selected and mutants for them were generated by using Mujava tool [29]. One of the examples was a simple search presented in Fig. 1, For this example Mujava generated 38 mutants; for the second examples there were 87 mutants. The mutants were then converted into graph form described below.

```
public int search(int v){          public int search(int v){
int i;                             int i;
for(i=0;i<size;i=i+1)              for(i=0;++i<size;i=i+1)
if(values[i]==v) return i;         if(values[i]==v) return i;
return -1;                         return -1;
}                                  }
```

Fig. 1. A simple search method and one of its AOIS (Arithmetic Operator Insertion [29]) mutants

4.1   Hierarchical Control Flow Graphs

Although a well known method of representing programs or their components (methods) is a control flow diagram (CFD), it cannot be directly used to compare programs, as we need to compare each element of any expression or condition separately and a traditional CFD labels its elements by whole expressions. So in this paper a combination of CFD and hierarchical graphs is proposed. It adds a hierarchy to this diagram enabling us to represent each element of a program in a single node and thus making the graphs more adequate to comparison. An example of such a hierarchical control flow graph (HCFG) is depicted in Figs. 2a and b. It represents a method $Search(...)$ and its mutant depicted in Fig. 1a and b, respectively. It can be noticed that the insertion of $++$ into variable i in a for loop is represented by an appropriate expression tree replacing a simple node labelled i inside node labelled for.

Let for the rest of this paper R_V and R_E be the sets of node and edge labels, respectively. Let ϵ be a special symbol used for unlabelled edges. The set of node labels consists of the set of all possible keywords, names of variables, operators, numbers and some additional grouping labels (like for example *declare* or *array* shown in Fig. 2. The set of edge labels contains Y and N.

Definition 1. *(Labelled hierarchical control flow graph) A labelled hierarchical control flow graph HCFG is defined as a 5-tuple (V, E, ξ_V, ξ_E, ch) where:*

1. V *is a set of nodes,*
2. E *is a set of edges, $E \subset V \times V$,*
3. $\xi_V : V \to R_V$ *is a node labelling function,*
4. $\xi_E : E \to R_E \cup \{\epsilon\}$ *is an edge labelling function,*
5. $ch : V \to P(V)$ *is a function assigning to each node a set of its children, i.e. nodes directly nested in v.*

Let, for the rest of this paper, $ch(v)$ denotes the set of children of v, and $|ch(v)|$ the size of this set. Let anc be a function assigning to each node its ancestor and let λ be a special empty symbol (different from ϵ),$anc : V \to V \cup \{\lambda\}$, such that $anc(v) = w$ if $v \in ch(w)$ and λ otherwise.

4.2   Hierarchical Control Flow Graphs Distance

HCFG Edit Distance. To define edit cost for a particular graph a cost function for edit operations must be defined. In case of HCF graphs it was defined to mimic as much as possible the influence of a given operation over the similarity. Costs for changing labels were set separately for all pairs of possible keywords, variable names and operators. For example cost of changing the operator in a condition from $<$ into $<=$ is lower than changing $==$ into $!=$ as the perceived difference between them is higher. Changing the conditional expression into arbitrary *true* or *false* will be even higher, and it is well represented in the edit distance concept as replacing the expression tree with a single node requires significantly more delete/insert operations.

HCFG Kernel. The edit distance does not take into account the additional information contained in the hierarchical structure HCFG. To incorporate this information into similarity calculations a hierarchical substructure kernel K_{HCFG} is proposed in this paper. It takes into account the label of a given node, number of its children (and thus the internal complexity), the label of its hierarchical ancestor (and thus its position within the structure of the program), and the number and labels of edges connecting this node with its neighbourhood nodes (both incoming and outgoing edges are taken into account) This substructure kernel uses node, edge and tree kernels. The node and edge kernels are defined below. The tree kernel, used within the node one to compare expression trees, is a standard one [11].

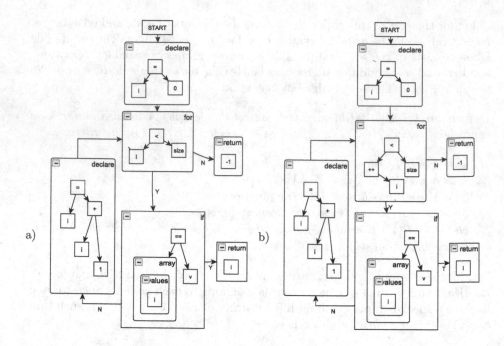

Fig. 2. Examples of flow graphs a) a graph for program from Fig. 1a, b) a flow graph for one of AOIS mutants (from Fig. 1b)

Definition 2. *A node kernel, denoted $k_V(v, w)$, where v, and w are nodes of a hierarchical control flow graph, is defined in the following way:*

$$k_V(v, w) = \begin{cases} 1 & : \xi_V(v) = \xi_V(w) \wedge |ch(v)| = |ch(w)| = 0 \\ k_V(ch(v), ch(w)) & : \xi_V(v) = \xi_V(w) \wedge |ch(v)| = |ch(w)| = 1 \\ K_T(ch(v), ch(w)) & : |ch(v)| > 1 \vee |ch(w)| > 1 \\ 0 & : \xi_V(v) \neq \xi_V(w). \end{cases}$$

It can be observed that for nodes having more than one child, thus containing an expression tree, a tree kernel K_T is used to compute the actual similarity. For nodes having different labels the kernel returns 0, while for nodes containing one children the node kernel is called recursively.

Definition 3. *An edge kernel, denoted $k_E(e_i, e_j)$, where e_i, and e_j are edges of a hierarchical flow graph, is defined in the following way:*

$$k_E(e_i, e_j) = \begin{cases} 1 : \xi_E(e_i) = \xi_E(e_j) \\ 0 : \xi_V(e_i) \neq \xi_V(e_j). \end{cases}$$

On the basis of the above kernel a similarity for HCFG is computed.

Definition 4.

$$K_{HCFG}(G_i, G_j) = \sum_{i=1}^{m} \sum_{j=1}^{n} K_S(S_i, S_j), \tag{2}$$

where m and n, is the number of hierarchical nodes in each graph and

$$K_S(S_i, S_j) = k_{node}(v_i, v_j) + k_{node}(anc(v_i), anc(v_j)) + \sum_{r=1}^{C_n}\sum_{t=1}^{C_m} k_{node}(c_r(v_i), c_t(v_j))$$

$$+ \sum_{w_j \in Nb(v_j)}\sum_{w_j \in Nb(v_j)} k_{edge}((v_i, w_i), (v_j, w_j)) k_{node}(w_i, w_j), \qquad (3)$$

where each S_i is a substructure of G_i consisting of node v_i, its direct ancestor anc(v_i), all its children ch(v_i) (where with C_n is the number of children and $c_n(v_i)$ - the $n-th$ child of v_i) , and its neighbourhood Nb(v_i).

This kernel is based on the decomposition of a graph into substructures according to the concept of $R - convolution$ kernels and thus is positive semidefinite [16], and so acceptable as a kernel function [40].

Remark on Computational Costs. Both edit distance and graph kernel are known to have a high computational cost, what was mentioned in sections 1 and 2. But in case of HCFG we have a special situation, i.e. as each graph represents a first order mutant, any two graphs can differ in at most two places. Moreover we know a priori where the change happened, and all the remaining elements of both graphs are identical. As a result the actual computation of both edit distance and HCFG kernel can be done much more efficiently than in general case of two arbitrarily chosen graphs.

5   Experiments and Results

For each set of mutants a k-NN classification algorithm was run using two different distance measures, an edit distance and a distance computed from HCFG kernel. For the first example three test suites were used and the set of mutants was randomly divided into three parts of similar size, the first was used as a training set and the other as instances to classify. The classification was then repeated using subsequent subsets as training sets. The whole process was repeated five times using different partitions of the set of mutants and the results obtained were averaged. Table 1 presents the results obtained for this example using HCFG edit distance to compute distances in $k - NN$ classifier. Parameter k was, after some experimental tuning, set to 5 for all experiments. The first column of the table shows the percentage of instances classified correctly. The results for mutants classified incorrectly are presented separately for those classified as detectable, while actually they are not (column labelled incorrect killed) and for those classified as not detected, while they actually are detected by a given test suite (column labelled incorrect not killed). Calculating these results separately was motivated by the meaning of these misclassifications. While classifying a mutant as not detected leads to overtesting, the misclassification of the second type can result in missing some errors in code, what is more dangerous. As the results are also used to evaluate the quality of test suites used, incorrectly classifying a mutant as not detected leads to giving a test suite lower score than actual one, why the second misclassification leads to overvaluation of a given test suite. Again, while the first situation is surely not desired, the second one poses more problems, especially as it may lead to a situation when a mutant not detected by any test suite would be labelled as detected, thus resulting in undetected errors in code.

It can be observed that the classification performed reasonably well for all test suits, with the exception of TS1. Deeper analysis of this case seems to suggest that it results from the random partition of the set of mutants for this test suite in which the training set contained unproportionally large number of undetectable mutants. This situation also suggests to perform the partition of mutants in a "smarter" way instead of random. One possible way to do it is to select proportional number of mutants of each type (generated by a given type of mutation operators). The results obtained with the use of HCFG kernel, presented in Table 2, are slightly better in general, especially the classification for TS1 improved significantly, although it may be due to better choice of training sets. It can be also noticed that, while the percentage of correctly classified mutants for test suite 3 is a bit lower, (but the difference is small), less mutants were incorrectly classified as detectable, although this gain happened at the expense if larger classification error in the last column. The results show that the classification improvements for the kernel method are not very significant, but more experiments are needed to decide whether this approach is worth its slightly higher computational cost.

Table 1. The classification of mutants of example 1 with the use of GED

	correct	incorrect killed	incorrect not killed
TS 1	65.2%	13.06%	21.74%
TS 2	78.25%	8.7%	13.5%
TS 3	82.6%	8.7%	8.7%

Table 2. The classification of mutants of example 1 with the use of kernel

	correct	incorrect killed	incorrect not killed
TS 1	75.55%	5.45%	19.00%
TS 2	84.1%	6.65%	9.25%
TS 3	82.2%	4.7%	12.7%

For the second example five test suites were used and, as there were more mutants, their set was divided into four parts of similar size, with, like in first example, the first part being used as a training set and the others as instances to classify. The classification was then repeated using subsequent subsets as training sets. The whole process was also repeated five times with different partitions of the set of mutants and the results obtained were averaged. Table 3 presents the results obtained with the use of edit distance and Table 4 - with the use of kernel based distance. Similarly to the first example the kernel based approach has produced slightly better results for correct classifications, with the exception of TS 2, where the error is slightly higher, but only by 0.2%. However a slightly higher improvement can be observed in having a lower percentage of mutants incorrectly classified as detectable. It can also be noticed that the results for TS 3 were visibly worse than for other suits. Closer inspection seems to suggest that this is also a problem with randomly partitioning set of mutants. As TS 2 detects only 22 out of 87 mutants there may occur an over representation of detectable mutants in the training set thus leading to incorrectly classifying many mutants as detectable. As in the first example it suggests replacing random partitioning by another one. Here a useful idea seems to be selecting into training set mutants in such a way that would preserve the proportion of both detectable and undetectable mutants close to the one in the whole set.

Table 3. The classification of mutants of example 2 with the use of GED

	correct	incorrect killed	incorrect not killed
TS 1	75.7%	12.1%	12.2%
TS 2	73.4%	6.5%	20.1%
TS 3	60.5%	26.2%	16.3%
TS 4	78.2%	10.3%	11.5%
TS 5	76.4%	11.3%	12.3%

Table 4. The classification of mutants of example 2 with the use of kernel

	correct	incorrect killed	incorrect not killed
TS 1	79.1%	6.3%	14.6%
TS 2	73.2%	4.5%	22.3%
TS 3	61.5%	22.6%	20.9%
TS 4	85.1%	4.6%	10.5%
TS 5	79.2%	9.53%	11.3%

6   Conclusions and Future Work

In this paper an approach to classification of mutants was proposed as a tool to reduce the number of mutants to be executed and to evaluate the quality of test suits without executing them against all possible mutants. This method deals with reducing the number of mutants that have to by executed in a dynamic way i.e. depending on the program for which they are generated rather than statically for a given language or the operator.The approach needs still more experiments to fully confirm its validity, but the results obtained so far are encouraging.

However, several problems were noticed during the experiment that require further research. Firstly, a random selection, although performing reasonably well, causes problems for some test suits. Possible solutions, as suggested in the discussion of results, include selecting mutants to assure they represent diversity of mutation operations thus avoiding selecting to the training set mutants generated by the same type of operations. The second solution is to select a number of detectable and undetectable mutants to preserve proportions from the full set. We plan to investigate both approaches to check whether they improve results in a significant way.

Another direction for future research is connected with the use of kernels. To make better use of them one of kernel based classifiers, for example support vector machines, could be used instead of $k - NN$. The kernel itself also offers some possibilities for improvements. The node kernel proposed in this paper is based on the label of the node independently form its position ("depth") in the hierarchy; adding some factor proportional to the depth of the node is also planned to be researched.

References

1. Acree, A.T.: On Mutation, PhD Thesis, Georgia Institute of Technology, Atlanta, Georgia (1980)
2. Agrawal, R., Imielinski, T., Swami, A.: Mining association rules between sets of items in large databases. In: Proc. 1993 ACM-SIGMOD Int. Conf. Management of Data (SIGMOD 1993), Washington, DC, pp. 207–216 (1993)
3. Borgwardt, K.M., Kriegel, H.P.: Shortest-path kernels on graphs. In: ICDM 2005, pp. 74–81 (2005)
4. Bunke, H., Riesen, K.: Improving vector space embedding of graphs through feature selection algorithms. Pattern Recognition 44(9), 1928–1940 (2011)
5. Bunke, H., Riesen, K.: Recent advances in graph-based pattern recognition with applications in document analysis. Pattern Recognition 44(5), 1057–1067 (2011)
6. Budd, T.A.: Mutation Analysis of Program Test Data. PhD Thesis. Yale University, New Haven, Connecticut (1980)
7. Chein, M., Mugnier, M.L., Simonet, G.: Nested Graphs: A Graph-based Knowledge Representation Model with FOL Semantics. In: Proceedings of the 6th International Conference "Principles of Knowledge Representation and Reasoning" (KR 1998), Trento, Italy, pp. 524–534. Morgan Kaufmann Publishers (June 1998)
8. Ji, C., Chen, Z., Xu, B., Zhao, Z.: A Novel Method of Mutation Clustering Based on Domain Analysis. In: Proceedings of the 21st International Conference on Software Engineering and Knowledge Engineering (SEKE 2009), July 1-3. Knowledge Systems Institute Graduate School, Boston (2009)
9. Chevalley, P.: Applying Mutation Analysis for Object-oriented Programs Using a Reflective Approach. In: Proceedings of the 8th Asia- Pacific Software Engineering Conference (APSEC 2001), Macau, China, December 4-7, p. 267 (2001)
10. Chevalley, P., Th'evenod-Fosse, P.: A Mutation Analysis Tool for Java Programs. International Journal on Software Tools for Technology Transfer 5(1), 90–103 (2002)
11. Collins, M., Duffy, N.: New Ranking Algorithms for Parsing and Tagging: Kernels over Discrete Structures, and the Voted Perceptron. In: Proceedings of ACL 2002 (2002)

12. DeMillo, R.A., Lipton, R.J., Sayward, F.G.: Hints on Test Data Selection: Help for the Practicing Programmer. Computer 11(4), 34–41 (1978)
13. Gartner, T.: A survey of kernels for structured data. SIGKDD Explorations 5(1), 49–58 (2003)
14. Gartner, T.: Kernels for structured data. Series in Machine Perception and Artificial Intelligence. World Scientific (2009)
15. Han, J., Pei, J., Yin, Y., Mao, R.: Mining Frequent Patterns without Candidate Generation: A Frequent-pattern Tree Approach. Data Mining and Knowledge Discovery: An International Journal 8(1), 53–87 (2004)
16. Haussler, D.: Convolutional kernels on discrete structures. Technical Report UCSC-CRL-99-10, Computer Science Department, UC Santa Cruz (1999)
17. Hussain, S.: Mutation Clustering, Masters Thesis. King's College London, Strand, London (2008)
18. Inokuchi, A., Washio, T., Motoda, H.: An Apriori-Based Algorithm for Mining Frequent Substructures from Graph Data. In: Zighed, D.A., Komorowski, J., Żytkow, J.M. (eds.) PKDD 2000. LNCS (LNAI), vol. 1910, pp. 13–23. Springer, Heidelberg (2000)
19. Jia, Y., Harman, M.: An Analysis and Survey of the Development of Mutation Testing. IEEE Trans. Software Eng., 649–678 (2011)
20. Kashima, H., Tsuda, K., Inokuchi, A.: Marginalized Kernels Between Labeled Graphs. In: ICML 2003, pp. 321–328 (2003)
21. Kim, S., Clark, J.A., McDermid, J.A.: Assessing Test Set Adequacy for Object Oriented Programs Using Class Mutation. In: Proceedings of the 3rd Symposium on Software Technology (SoST 1999), Buenos Aires, Argentina, September 8-9 (1999)
22. Kim, S., Clark, J.A., McDermid, J.A.: The Rigorous Generation of Java Mutation Operators Using HAZOP. In: Proceedings of the 12th International Cofference Software and Systems Engineering and their Applications (ICSSEA 1999), Paris, France, November 29-December 1 (1999)
23. Kim, S., Clark, J.A., McDermid, J.A.: Class Mutation: Mutation Testing for Object-oriented Programs. In: Proceedings of the Net. Object Days Conference on Object-Oriented Software Systems (2000)
24. Kim, S., Clark, J.A., McDermid, J.A.: Investigating the effectiveness of object-oriented testing strategies using the mutation method. In: Proceedings of the 1st Workshop on Mutation Analysis (MUTATION 2000), Published in Book Form, as Mutation Testing for the New Century, San Jose, California, October 6-7, pp. 207–225 (2001)
25. King, K.N., Offutt, A.J.: A Fortran Language System for Mutation- Based Software Testing. Software: Practice and Experience 21(7), 685–718 (1991)
26. Liwicki, M., Bunke, H., Pittman, J.A., Knerr, S.: Combining diverse systems for handwritten text line recognition. Mach. Vis. Appl. 22(1), 39–51 (2011)
27. Liwicki, M., Schlapbach, A., Bunke, H.: Automatic gender detection using on-line and off-line information. Pattern Anal. Appl. 14(1), 87–92 (2011)
28. Preller, A., Mugnier, M.-L., Chein, M.: Logic for Nested Graphs. Computational Intelligence 14(3), 335–357 (1998)
29. Ma, Y., Offutt, J., Kwon, Y.R.: MuJava: a mutation system for java. In: ICSE, pp. 827–830 (2006)
30. Mathur, A.P.: Performance, Effectiveness, and Reliability Issues in Software Testing. In: Proceedings of the 5th International Computer Software and Applications Conference (COMPSAC 1979), Tokyo, Japan, September 11-13, pp. 604–605 (1991)

31. Mathur, A.P., Wong, W.E.: An Empirical Comparison of Mutation and Data Flow Based Test Adequacy Criteria, Purdue University, West Lafayette, Indiana, Technique Report (1993)
32. Offutt, A.J., Rothermel, G., Zapf, C.: An Experimental Evaluation of Selective Mutation. In: Proceedings of the 15th International Conference on Software Engineering (ICSE 1993), pp. 100–107. IEEE Computer Society Press, Baltimore (1993)
33. Richiardi, J., Van De Ville, D., Riesen, K., Bunke, H.: Vector Space Embedding of Undirected Graphs with Fixed-cardinality Vertex Sequences for Classification. In: ICPR 2010, pp. 902–905 (2010)
34. Riesen, K., Bunke, H.: Cluster Ensembles Based on Vector Space Embeddings of Graphs. In: Benediktsson, J.A., Kittler, J., Roli, F. (eds.) MCS 2009. LNCS, vol. 5519, pp. 211–221. Springer, Heidelberg (2009)
35. Riesen, K., Bunke, H.: Dissimilarity Based Vector Space Embedding of Graphs Using Prototype Reduction Schemes. In: Perner, P. (ed.) MLDM 2009. LNCS, vol. 5632, pp. 617–631. Springer, Heidelberg (2009)
36. Riesen, K., Bunke, H.: Reducing the dimensionality of dissimilarity space embedding graph kernels. Eng. Appl. of AI 22(1), 48–56 (2009)
37. Rozenberg, G.: Handbook of Graph Grammars and Computing by Graph. Transformations. Fundations, vol. 1. World Scientific, London (1997)
38. Rozenberg, G.: Handbook of Graph Grammars and Computing by Graph. Transformations. Applications, Languages and Tools, vol. 2. World Scientific, London (1999)
39. Shawe-Taylor, J., Cristianini, N.: Kernel Methods for Pattern Analysis. 1-462 (2004)
40. Schölkopf, B., Smola, A.J.: A Short Introduction to Learning with Kernels. In: Mendelson, S., Smola, A.J. (eds.) Advanced Lectures on Machine Learning. LNCS (LNAI), vol. 2600, pp. 41–64. Springer, Heidelberg (2003)
41. Schölkopf, B., Smola, A.J.: Learning with kernels. MIT Press, Cambridge (2002)
42. Strug, B.: Using Kernels on Hierarchical Graphs in Automatic Classification of Designs. In: Jiang, X., Ferrer, M., Torsello, A. (eds.) GbRPR 2011. LNCS, vol. 6658, pp. 335–344. Springer, Heidelberg (2011)
43. Tsuda, K., Kin, T., Asai, K.: Marginalized kernels for biological sequences. Bioinformatics 18, 268–275
44. Vishwanathan, S.V.N., Borgwardt, K.M., Schraudolph, N.N.: Fast Computation of Graph Kernels. In: NIPS 2006, pp. 1449–1456 (2006)
45. Wong, W.E.: On Mutation and Data Flow. PhD Thesis, Purdue University, West Lafayette, Indiana (1993)
46. Yan, X., Yu, P.S., Han, J.: Substructure Similarity Search in Graph Databases. In: Proc. of 2005 Int. Conf. on Management of Data, SIGMOD 2005 (2005)
47. Yan, X., Yu, P.S., Han, J.: Graph Indexing: A Frequent Structure-based Approach. In: Proc. of 2004 Int. Conf. on Management of Data, SIGMOD 2004 (2004)

Lightweight Automatic Error Detection
by Monitoring Collar Variables

João Santos and Rui Abreu

Department of Informatics Engineering
Faculty of Engineering
University of Porto
Portugal
`joao.filipe.santos@fe.up.pt, rui@computer.org`

Abstract. Although proven to be an effective way for detecting errors, generic program invariants (also known as fault *screeners*) entail a considerable runtime overhead, rendering them not useful in practice. This paper studies the impact of using simple variable patterns to detect the so-called system's *collar variables* to reduce the number of variables to be monitored (instrumented). Two different patterns were investigated to determine which variables to monitor. The first pattern finds variables whose value increase or decrease at regular intervals and deems them not important to monitor. The other pattern verifies the range of a variable per (successful) execution. If the range is constant across executions, then the variable is not monitored. Experiments were conducted on three different real-world applications to evaluate the reduction achieved on the number of variables monitored and determine the quality of the error detection. Results show a reduction of 52.04% on average in the number of monitored variables, while still maintaining a good detection rate with only 3.21% of executions detecting non-existing errors (false positives) and 5.26% not detecting an existing error (false negatives).

Keywords: Error detection, program invariants, automatic oracles, dynamic execution.

1   Introduction

An application's *development phase* is usually restricted by the budget allowed for development and/or time-to-market. These restrictions provide a trade-off with the reliability of the system, which leads to an increase in defects that can lead to catastrophic results. In these cases proper *error detection* is vital in order to ensure the recognition and recovery from faults during the *deployment phase* as soon as possible [1]. One possible way of implementing error detection on a system is with the use of generic invariants, also known as *fault screeners*. They may present a higher rate of false positives (faults detected when none exist) and false negatives (the non detection of an error) when compared to hard coded error detection methods (such as asserts), due to the latter detecting anticipated faults. Despite this, generic invariants have the great benefit of being generated

B. Nielsen and C. Weise (Eds.): ICTSS 2012, LNCS 7641, pp. 215–230, 2012.

and intrumented *automatically* into the code. This along with the fact that (1) the invariants can be trained automatically during the *testing phase* and (2) hard coded solutions are cumbersome and time consuming to implement, might give an edge to generic invariants. Having generated automatically the invariants and trained them during the *testing phase*, they are ready for being used during the *deployment phase*, where the invariant detects deviations from the learned behaviour [2]. Generic invariants have been subject of study for many years, spawning various types like range screeners, bitmask screeners, and screeners that leverage Bloom filters [2,3]. They are mostly used for fault localization [4] and error detection [3].

Despite the benefits of generic invariants, their use on real-world, large software applications is currently impeded by the overhead that monitoring all the system's variables requires. However, monitoring every variable may not be required, as only a subset of variables, known as *collar variables*, truly affect the outcome of a system in a meaningful way [5]. Applications like TAR3 and TAR4.1 have some algorithms that already experiment on the detection of collar variables [6], but the use of these *collar variables* has not been applied on the reduction the number of generic invariants needed to monitor a system effectively.

To tackle this, two algorithms were devised to detect exectution patterns of variables both during executions and between them. These algorithms, called variable evolution pattern detectors in this paper, are executed during the training phase of the invariants and collect information from successful executions. During the operational phase, when the impact of the instrumentation overhead needs to be minimized, the data collected from the pattern detectors allows variables deemed unimportant to be ignored.

This paper makes the following contributions:

- Proposes two methods to detect variables that do not require monitoring (in other words, methods to detect the *collar variables* of the program under analysis).
- Investigates the reduction achieved on the number of used invariants on real world applications.
- Evaluates the quality of the *error detection* when comparing with the results obtained using the test suite of the applications.
- Reports the increase in execution time with the use of the invariants.

The paper is organized as follows. Section 2 gives a quick overwiew of how a fault screener works, along with a more detailed explanation of the used screener for the study, the dynamic range screener. In Sect. 3 explains the functioning of the two variable evolution pattern detectors. The experimental setup and results are shown in Sect. 4. Section 5 presents work related to this paper. Finally Sect. 6 gives some final thoughts and some insight on future work.

2   Fault Screeners

First used by Ernst et al. [7], fault screeners, also known as program invariants, are fault tolerance mechanisms that use historical data recovered from previous executions to determine the expected behaviour from a system's variables, issuing a warning when the expected behaviour is not met [2]. Hence, the use of fault sceeners is a possible way to achieve automatic error detecting by monitoring the system's variables. However, for the detection to be effective, a training phase is required. During this phase the spectrum of valid variable values is determined. This constitutes the expected behaviour for a variable that should raise a warning in case a value that does not fit the spectrum is detected [8]. Formally, screeners are not effective at detecting errors that involve the use of random values, or variables that store things like current timestamp.

There are various types of invariants, each with its own algorithms for training and error detecting. In this paper it is focused on the dynamic range invariants [2], due to its simplistic nature, reduced overhead, and known to work in practice [4]. The dynamic range invariant stores the bounds of valid variable values. During the training phase, when a new value is found, the range of values allowed by the screener is extended according to the following equations:

$$l := min(l, v) \tag{1}$$
$$u := max(u, v) \tag{2}$$

If the new value is lower than the lower bound l, the lower bound is updated. Likewise, if the value is greater than the upper bound u, that bound is updated. Table 1 shows an example of how the training works for the dynamic range screener. At first the invariant does not consider any value valid since no observation was made yet. After the first observation, in this case 5, both bounds need to be updated leading to a valid range of $[5, 5]$. The second observation is a 72. This value is greater then the upper bound of the range and not lower then the lower bound, so the upper bound is updated. With an updated range of $[5, 72]$, the new observed value 6 is compared to both bounds. It is between the upper bound and lower bound so no change is made. Lastly, the value 5004 is observed, again greater then the upper bound. This bound is updated leading to a final valid range of $[5, 5004]$.

Table 1. Dynamic Range Screener training

New Result Value	Range Point
5	$\emptyset$
72	$[5, 5]$
6	$[5, 72]$
5004	$[5, 72]$
	$[5, 5004]$

When on error detection phase, every observed value is checked against the range of values allowed by the invariant. If the value goes outside the range of permitted values, a violation to the expected behaviour is detected:

$$violation = \neg(l < v < u) \tag{3}$$

The dynamic range invariant can use a larger number of ranges in order to restrict the allowed spectrum [2]. While the concept is the same, additional ranges require more memory and more execution time. When using more then one range, the objective during the training phase is: when a new value is observed, the updated range is the one that increases the valid spectrum by the least amount of values. Table 2 shows an example of a dynamic range invariant with two ranges. The invariant begins with two empty ranges. Once it observes the value 5, one of the ranges becomes [5, 5]. On the second observed value, 72, since there is still one range that is empty, that range becomes, [72, 72]. Now that both ranges, when new values are observed, the invariant tries to make the ranges as short as possible to learn the least amount of unseen values. When 6 appears, there would be two range choices, [5, 6] and [72, 72] or [5, 5] and [6, 72]. Since the first has the smaller ranges, this is the selected option. The last value 5004 provides an interesting twist. At first glance it would seem that this update would lead to [5, 6] and [72, 5004], however that is not the case. The ranges are actually updated to [5, 72] and [5004, 5004]. This happens because the amount of values that is learnt is a lot smaller (from 6 to 72 compared to from 72 to 5004) and it still guarantees both the acceptance of the values from the values before the update and the new value observed. In this paper, the only version of the dynamic range invariant used is the single range one.

Table 2. Dynamic Range Screener training with two segments

New Result Value	Range Point 1	Range Point 2
5	∅	∅
72	[5, 5]	∅
6	[5, 5]	[72, 72]
5004	[5, 6]	[72, 72]
	[5, 72]	[5004, 5004]

One of the challenges for using generic invariants is the accuracy of the *error detection*, as the more training the invariants suffer, the number of false positives, errors detected that do not exist, tends to decrease, while the number of false negatives, the non detection of existing errors, increases [9]. This happens because of the increase of accepted values by the invariant.

Figure 1 displays a possible setup for a dynamic range invariant. During the *training phase* the invariant learnt that the values between −2 and 2 were the valid set of possible values. However the real case is that the values should be valid between −3 and −1, as 1 and 2, as well as between 3 and 4. This leads to some false positives and false negatives. Values observed that withing the ranges [−3, −2[or]3, 4] issue a detected error warning, hence they are false positives. Likewise, observations between −1 and 1 do not issue any warnings when they should.

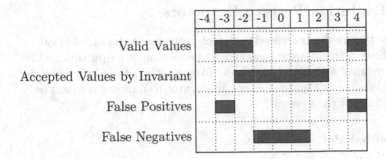

Fig. 1. False positive and false negative example

In the same scenario, if the invariant had been subject to more training, then more values would be added into the accepted range. On Fig. 2 the number 4 was such a value (even though 4 should not appear during executions if). This led to the values ranging from 3 to 4 to become valid, eliminating those false positives, but the ones from 2 to 3 also became valid, becoming new false negatives. In other words, there was an increase of false negatives and decrease of false positives. With more training the false positive rate tends to lead to 0 because the entire possibility of values become valid.

On the other side, the number of false negatives increases because since it accepts a lot more values then it should, it does not detect any values outside the huge accepted range.

Note that there are other types of invariants, each with their own behaviour regarding accuracy of error detection and performance [4]. Among them are bitmask invariants, which use a bitmask with the bits that were changed during the training when compared with the first observed value. Another one is the Bloom filter, an invariant that saves the entire history of values observed during the training phase. In this paper, the results were obtained by only using the dynamic range invariant. However the approach proposed is easily extensible to other invariant types.

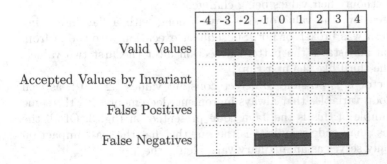

Fig. 2. False positive and false negative example with increased training

3   Variable Evolution Pattern Detectors

In this section, the two methods created to detect patterns on the variable values are presented. These patterns were designed to be as simple as possible, while still detecting constants and other variables, like counters. It is important to note that a variable is never classified as not important to monitor if it was only used on one execution of the system.

3.1   Delta Oriented Pattern Detector

The Delta Oriented Pattern Detector is the first of two algorithms created to detect *collar variables*. With this detector, the main objective is to discover variables that throughout its life cycle evolve in a constant fashion. These variables are then deemed not essencial since during every execution its value increases or decreases in the same manner, no matter what the input is, in other words variables with such detected pattern do not need to be monitored. This is accomplished by using a delta value (Δ), that is the difference between the last value observed and the current one:

$$\Delta := \text{current value} - \text{last value} \quad \text{if last value} \neq \emptyset \tag{4}$$

$$\Delta := 0 \quad \text{if last value} = \emptyset \tag{5}$$

Algorithm 1 demonstrates how this detector can determine which variables are important to monitor. Every variable in the system has a Δ associated to it. During the training phase, when the first value is observed, Δ is given the value 0 and the last value is updated to the observed one. On the next observation, Δ will be updated accordingly, using the current value and the last value, as seen in Line 8. After this, the pattern detection begins. With each observation, an updated Δ is generated (Δ_2) and is compared to the current Δ. If the new Δ is equal to the current one, the pattern detection continues as the evolution of the variable remains the same. In case the Δ is different, since the pattern is broken, a flag is stored indicating that this pattern does not exist for the variable being evaluated. There is, however, an exception to this. When the new Δ is 0, then it is not compared to the previous Δ (Line 12). This is done because variables can be accessed without their values being changed.

After each execution, the value of Δ is saved along with a flag indicating whether the pattern was broken or not. Subsequent executions use the Δ from the first execution and starts the pattern detection after the first two values, instead of after the third like the first run.

With this detector it is possible to detect constant values ($\Delta = 0$), as well as counters and loop variables that always increment/decrement with the same pace. A good example of this is the `Java` code presented on Fig. 3. Of all the variables from this small code sample, `j` is the one that has the least impact on the outcome. It only serves as an auxiliary variable for the loop.

Algorithm 1. Delta Oriented Pattern Detector

```
 1: pattern := true
 2: for all Execution ∧ pattern do
 3:     for all Observation ∧ pattern do
 4:         if first observation then
 5:             Δ := 0
 6:             LastValue := ObservedValue
 7:         else if second observation. ∧ nRuns = 0 then
 8:             Δ := ObservedValue − LastValue
 9:         else
10:             Δ₂ := ObservedValue − LastValue
11:             LastValue := ObservedValue
12:             if Δ ≠ Δ₂ ∧ Δ₂ ≠ 0 then
13:                 pattern := false
14:             end if
15:         end if
16:     end for
17:     nRuns + +
18: end for
```

The delta oriented pattern detector can be used to mark this variable as not essencial. It does not matter what the input of this function is, because j will always increment in the same manner. Δ will always be 1 (j always starts with the value 0 and increments by one on every access), so the pattern is never broken. Since this pattern is never broken, the variable will not be monitored during the error detection phase.

3.2   Range Oriented Pattern Detector

One of the main differences between this pattern and the previous one is that the range oriented pattern detector requires one full execution before it can determine a broken pattern. The basis of this detector is that if the range of values that a variable has between every run is the same, then it is not important to monitor. This is the reason why one full execution is required. The detector only has the range of the full execution at the end of it.

The functions of updating the bounds of the range are the same as the dynamic range invariant:

$$l := min(l, v) \tag{6}$$
$$u := max(u, v) \tag{7}$$

The main difference between the dynamic range invariant and the range oriented pattern detector is that the bounds of the detector are only updated on the first

```
public int funcExample(int i) {
    int accumulator = i;
    for(int j = 0; j < 3; j++) {
        if(accumulator == 1)
            break;
        accumulator *= accumulator;
    }
    int result = accumulator * 3;
    return result;
}
```

Fig. 3. Delta Detector code example

execution that a variable appears in. On the following executions, every time a new value is observed, it is determined if it is within the range of the first execution:

$$broken = \neg(l < v < u) \qquad (8)$$

Algorithm 2 shows how the detector works. During the first execution (Lines 4 and 5) the range is constantly updated with every observation of a given variable. Once the first execution is over, the pattern detector is ready to discover a pattern. Hence, on the following executions, each observed value is compared to the pattern detector range, as seen in Line 7. If the new value is not within the range determined by the first execution, then the pattern was broken. If this never happens then it is determined that there is a pattern in the execution and the variable will not be monitored during the error detection phase.

With this detector it is possible to detect variables that although do not evolve in a linear way that can be detected by the delta oriented pattern detector, are restricted in some way during the execution. This is the case of loop variables that are affected within the cycle. This can be seen in the example shown on the example shown on Fig. 4. In this case, variable j is not a very important variable to be monitored. Taking into account the previous, detector, it is easy to understand that it would not be marked as not essencial (as Δ can be both 1 or 2). However the range oriented detector can find a pattern. On every execution, despite what input is received, the range of values j takes is always $[0, 5]$. During the first execution, this range would be given to the pattern detector and the following runs would follow the pattern, so the variable would not be monitored.

Algorithm 2. Range Oriented Pattern Detector

```
1:  pattern := true
2:  for all Execution do
3:      for all Observation do
4:          if nRuns = 0 then
5:              updatePatternRange(ObservedValue)
6:          else
7:              if ObservedValue ∉ PatternRange then
8:                  pattern := false
9:              end if
10:         end if
11:     end for
12:     nRuns + +
13: end for
```

```java
public int funcExample(int i) {
    int accumulator = i;
    for(int j = 0; j < 5; j++) {
        if(accumulator == 1 && j < 3)
            j=j+2;
        accumulator *= accumulator;
    }
    int result = accumulator * 3;
    return result;
}
```

Fig. 4. Range Detector code example

4 Empirical Results

In this section the experimental setup is presented, along with the workflow of the experiments themselves. After that the experimental results are discussed.

4.1 Experimental Setup

Application Set. During the experimentation, three real world applications were used:

- NanoXML [1] - a XML parser.
- org.jacoco.report [2] - a report generator for the JaCoCo library.
- XML-Security - a XML signature and encryption library from the Apache Santuario [3] project.

In Table 3 some details of the applications used are shown. These details include the number of lines of code and the number of test cases.

---

[1] NanoXML – http://devkix.com/nanoxml.php
[2] JaCoCo – http://www.eclemma.org/jacoco/index.html
[3] Apache Santuario – http://santuario.apache.org/

Table 3. Application details

Subject	LOC	Test Cases
NanoXML	5393	9
org.jacoco.report	5979	235
XML-Security	60946	462

NanoXML is a free, easy to use and non-GUI based and non-validating XML parser for Java. It has three different components:

- NanoXML/Java, the main standard parser.
- NanoXML/SAX, an SAX adapter for the standard parser.
- NanoXML/Lite, an extremely small version of the parser with limited funcionality.

NanoXML is available under the zlib/libpng license, which is Open Source compliant.

JaCoCo is an open source code coverage library for Java, being developed by EclEmma. The current goal of JaCoCo is to provide a code coverage library that is able to provide coverage reports. To do this there is a bundle called org.jacoco.report. This bundle is able to provide reports in three formats:

- HTML, for end users.
- XML, to be processed by external tools.
- CSV, suitable for graph creation.

XML-Security is one of the libraries available on the Apache Santuario project, a project that aims at providing security standards for XML. It is distributed under the Apache Licence Version 2.0 which is compatible with other open source licenses. The XMLSecurity data format provides encryption and decryption XML payloads at different levels, namely Document, Element and Element Content. XPath can be used for multi-node encryption/decryption. There exist two versions of XML-Security: a Java one and a C++ one. The Java version is used for the experiments.

Workflow of Experiments. In order to determine if the pattern detectors were effective at reducing the number of instrumented points and if the error detection maintained a good quality, the system's variables is subject to training first. Each application is instrumented in order to train the fault screeners. This training is achieved by executing a random number of test case (roughly 50% of the tests in the original suite) of the target program. We did not use the complete suite in order not to influence the results positively.

Once the training of the fault screeners is complete, the error detection phase begins. To evaluate the quality of the error detection, each application is executed five times. On each execution a different bug is inserted into the code and the number of false positives and false negatives are collected. An additional execution is performed without any inserted bug to determine the execution time in a regular scenario.

Each application's test suite was executed without any instrumentation as well to determine the increase of time the instrumentation brings.

Figure 5 shows the different phases of the experiments. First, during the training phase, the test are executed with the instrumented code. Everytime a variable is used, the update function of the screener is called in order to update the accepted values. In addition, the screener uses the pattern detectors to detect broken patterns. At the end of the execution, both the invariant and the data collected from the detector are saved. On the operational phase the test cases are executed with the instrumented code once again. However, this time instead of monitoring every variable, only the variables that did not have a detected pattern are observed. On each observation the value is then validated by the screener using information gathered during the training.

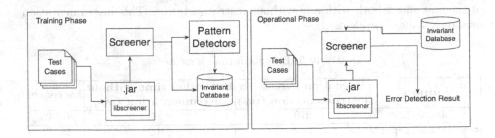

Fig. 5. Workflow of experiments

Injected bugs are of different types to guarantee a more varied input. Some examples of inserted bugs are:

- Change an operator when assigning values (i.e. change + to −).
- Change a random numeric value.
- Change comparation operator of a conditional clause (i.e. change a > to < on an `if` clause).
- Change the value of an argument of a function call.

With this setup the expected results are:

- Value of the reduction obtained in the number of used invariants.
- Comparison of execution times between executions with and without instrumentation.
- Accuracy of the error detection with the use of pattern detectors.

4.2   Results

Table 4 shows the number of variables that were trained and the number of variables that are considered *collar variables* by the pattern detectors. It is important to note that only numerical variables are subjected to training, in other words, only variables of the types `int`, `long`, `double` and `float`.

Table 4. Variable reduction

Subject	Variables trained	Collar Variables	Reduction
NanoXML	40	17	57.5%
org.jacoco.report	55	28	49.09%
XML-Security	325	164	49.54%

On average, a reduction of 52.04% is achieved with the use of the two pattern detectors. However the execution time of the program with instrumentation is also important to take into consideration. Table 5 presents the execution times of the test suites both with and without instrumentation. This instrumentation uses only *collar variables*.

Table 5. Execution time increase

Subject	Execution time with instrumentation (ms)	Execution time without instrumentation (ms)	Increase
NanoXML	270	827	206.3%
org.jacoco.report	3469	5162	48.8%
XML-Security	25005	63088	152.3%

The average increase in the execution time is 135.8%. Although this seems like a high value, it is greatly impacted by the increase noticed on `NanoXML` that is only a few miliseconds.

Having the data on the reduction of variables monitored and execution time increase, the quality of the error detection is what remains. To test the quality of the detection using these *collar variabes*, the number of false positives (N_{fp}) and false negatives (N_{fn}) was determined. A false positive is considered when the fault screener detects an error in the execution that does not exist. Likewise, a false negative is counted when a faulty execution has no objections raised from any fault screener.

The results shown on Table 6 were obtained by comparing the total number of false positives (N_{fp}) and false negatives (N_{fn}) with the number of tests on the test suite of the target program (N_t):

$$f_p := \frac{N_{fp}}{N_t} \tag{9}$$

$$f_n := \frac{N_{fn}}{N_t} \tag{10}$$

Table 6. False positive (f_p) and false negative rate (f_n)

Subject	Bug 1		Bug 2		Bug 3		Bug 4		Bug 5	
	f_p %	f_n %	f_p %	f_n %	f_p %	f_n %	f_p %	f_n %	f_p %	f_n %
NanoXML	0	0	0	0	0	0	0	66.67	0	0
org.jacoco.report	0	0	3.4	2.13	3.4	0	3.83	2.13	5.96	0
XML-Security	2.81	0.21	13.64	7.14	1.95	0.22	12.99	0.22	0.22	0.22

With an average of 3.21% rate of false positives and 5.26% rate of false negatives, the rate of these false results is considerably low, especially on the smaller applications. On the largest application, XML-Security, although having a higher rate of false results, the worst case scenario detected was a 13.64% f_p and 7.14% f_n.

In conclusion, with only the use of two pattern detectors, the decrease of used invariants is quite significant and the error detection quality remains very high, appart from some special cases. In terms of execution time, it may still not be enough to allow their use on real world markets, but perhaps the creation of even more detectors could be a solution.

4.3 Threats to Validity

The main threat to the validity of these results is the fact that only three test subjects were used during the experimentation. Despite these subjects being real world applications being diverse in both the size of the application (lines of code) and size of the test suite, the limited number of subjects implies that not all types of system's are tested. This means that a system with characteristics that are completly different might present different results.

Another threat is that the number of injected bugs is not enough to lead to accurate results, as these bugs might simply be "lucky bugs" that intercept a *collar variable*.

Naturally, there are also threats that are based on the implementation of the invariants, the instrumentation or the pattern detector algorithms themselves. The reduce these threats, additional testing was made prior to the experimentation to guarantee the quality of the experimental results in this regard.

5 Related Work

Since being introduced, generic invariants have been subject of study along the years with very different goals in mind. These goals range from study of program evolution [7,10], fault detection [2] and fault localization [3,11]. Invariants have also been used as an alternative way of error detection on a fault localization technique known as SFL [4,9].

Daikon [10] is a tool that reports likely invariants. It runs a program and then reports the properties observed during the executions. Besides storing pre-defined invariants like constants, range or linear relationships, it can be extended by the user with new invariant types. It is compatible with various programming languages, including C, C++, Java and Pearl.

Carrot [11] is a tool created with the purpose of using generic invariants for fault localization. It uses a smaller set of invariants than Daikon. The results obtained were negative which lead to the belief that invariants alone are insuficient as a means of debugging. However, in [9] the use of invariants for fault localization was successful when used as the input for the fault localization technique SFL.

DIDUCE [3] is yet another tool that uses dynamic bitmask invariants. Although the results appear to be good on four real world applications, the error that is detected is on a variable that is constant during the training phase and changed when it was on error detection mode (an error that is easily detected by a bitmask invariant, an invariant that detects differences on the allowed active bits of a variable value).

IODINE [12] is a framework for extracting dynamic invariants for hardware designs. It has been shown that accurate properties can be obtained from using dynamic invariants.

Zoltar [13] is a tool that applies a fault screener on every occurrence of a variable and tries to detect errors by finding perturbations on their behavior. In addition to detecting errors, Zoltar uses the errors detected to help debugging using SFL.

Another tool that works with fault screeners is PRECIS [14]. PRECIS introduces a different type of invariant based on pre- and post-conditions. The results obtained suggest the existance of some advantages over Daikon.

iSWAT [15] is a framework that uses invariants for error detection of a hardware level. It uses LLVM to instrument the source code to monitor the store values.

In [2] various invariants were subjected to performance evaluations. Among the tested invariants were dynamic range, bitmask, Bloom filters and TBL. Although the results show that bitmask outperforms Bloom filters and dynamic range, the errors used on the experimentation consisted of random bit switching, which is better suited for bitmask invariants and are not very common.

On the topic of *collar variables*, this term was used by Tim Menzies to describe the subset of variables that affect the output of an application in a meaninful way [5].

In [6] the algorithms of TAR3 and TAR4.1 are explained. These algorithms allow to obtain a ranking of "usefulness" of the different components of an application. TAR3 uses the concepts of *lift*, the change that a decision makes on a set of examples, and *support*. TAR4.1 uses Naive Bayes classifiers for the scoring heuristic in order to obtain an overall better performance in comparison to TAR3.1.

KEYS [16] is yet another algorithm that tries to discover the *collar variables*, called *keys* by the author. It is used to optimize requirement decisions and is faster then the TAR3 algorithm. In [17], an improved KEYS algorithm is shown called KEYS2. It outperforms the original version by four orders of magnitude in terms of speed.

In [18], the concept of *collar variable* is once again used, this time by the name of *back doors*. They were using these *back doors* to solve CSP/SAT search problems and suggest by formal analisys the potencial improvement of some hard problems from an exponential to polynomial time.

6   Conclusions and Future Work

In this paper two simple detectors were used to evaluate what were the *collar variables* in each of the systems. Experimenting on real world applications led to a more accurate take on the impact of the use of invariants for error detection. By only using two detectors, the reduction of number of invariants used was above 50% while still maintaining good quality detection. Still the increase in execution time might still be too severe for use and the inability of the detectors to view patterns on non numeric values is still an obstacle.

In this regard, for future work in order to reduce the overhead, a further decrease in the number of invariants used is necessary. The study of additional detectors that would filter even more variables would be a possibility to achieve such a decrease. Another option is the use of an algorithm similar to the one used on TAR4.1 [6] to make the decision of what variables to monitor. There are also plans to combine this method with static analysis in orther to try to achieve better results.

Futher work will also be invested in tackling one of the main issues of the current approach, the ability to only evaluate numeric variables. Efforts will be made to use invariants and create detectors that would evaluate patterns for other variable types like `String` or `char`. These variables may prove invaluable to increasing the effectiveness of this method.

Acknowledgements. This work is financed by the ERDF - European Regional Development Fund through the COMPETE Programme (operational programme for competitiveness) and by National Funds through the FCT - Fundação para a Ciência e a Tecnologia (Portuguese Foundation for Science and Technology) within project PTDC/EIA-CCO/116796/2010.

References

1. Patterson, D., Brown, A., Broadwell, P., Candea, G., Chen, M., Cutler, J., Enriquez, P., Fox, A., Kiciman, E., Merzbacher, M., Oppenheimer, D., Sastry, N., Tetzlaff, W., Traupman, J., Treuhaft, N.: Recovery-oriented computing (ROC): Motivation, definition, techniques, and case studies. Computer Science Technical Report UCB//CSD-02-1175, 1–16 (2002)
2. Racunas, P., Constantinides, K., Manne, S., Mukherjee, S.S.: Perturbation-based Fault Screening. In: Proceedings of HPCA 2007, pp. 169–180 (2007)
3. Hangal, S., Lam, M.S.: Tracking down software bugs using automatic anomaly detection. In: Proceedings of ICSE 2002, pp. 291–301 (2002)

4. Abreu, R., González, A., Zoeteweij, P., van Gemund, A.J.: Automatic software fault localization using generic program invariants. In: Proceedings of SAC 2008, pp. 712–717 (2008)
5. Menzies, T., Owen, D., Richardson, J.: The strangest thing about software. Computer 40(1), 54–60 (2007)
6. Gay, G., Menzies, T., Davies, M., Gundy-Burlet, K.: Automatically finding the control variables for complex system behavior. Automated Software Engineering 17(4), 439–468 (2010)
7. Ernst, M.D., Cockrell, J., Griswoldt, W.G., Notkin, D.: Dynamically Discovering Likely Program to Support Program Evolution Invariants. In: Proceedings of ICSE 1999, pp. 213–224 (1999)
8. Dimitrov, M., Zhou, H.: Anomaly-Based Bug Prediction, Isolation, and Validation: An Automated Approach for Software Debugging. In: Proceedings of ASPLOS 2009, vol. 44, pp. 61–72. ACM (2009)
9. Abreu, R., González, A., Zoeteweij, P., van Gemund, A.J.: Using Fault Screeners for Software Error Detection. In: Maciaszek, L.A., González-Pérez, C., Jablonski, S. (eds.) ENASE 2008/2009. CCIS, vol. 69, pp. 60–74. Springer, Heidelberg (2010)
10. Ernst, M.D., Perkins, J.H., Guo, P.J., McCamant, S., Pacheco, C., Tschantz, M.S., Xiao, C.: The Daikon system for dynamic detection of likely invariants. Science of Computer Programming 69(1-3), 35–45 (2007)
11. Pytlik, B., Renieris, M., Krishnamurthi, S., Reiss, S.P.: Automated Fault Localization Using Potential Invariants. In: Proceedings of AADEBUG 2003, pp. 273–276 (2003)
12. Hangal, S., Chandra, N., Narayanan, S., Chakravorty, S.: IODINE: A Tool to Automatically Infer Dynamic Invariants for Hardware Designs. In: Proceedings of DAC 2005, pp. 775–778 (2005)
13. Janssen, T., Abreu, R., van Gemund, A.J.: Zoltar: A Toolset for Automatic Fault Localization. In: Proceedings of ASE 2009, pp. 662–664 (2009)
14. Sagdeo, P., Athavale, V., Kowshik, S., Vasudevan, S.: PRECIS: Inferring invariants using program path guided clustering. In: Proceedings of ASE 2011, pp. 532–535 (2011)
15. Sahoo, S.K., Li, M.L., Ramachandran, P., Adve, S.V., Adve, V.S., Zhou, Y.: Using likely program invariants to detect hardware errors. In: Proceedings of DSN 2008, pp. 70–79 (June 2008)
16. Jalali, O., Menzies, T., Feather, M.: Optimizing Requirements Decisions with KEYS. In: Proceedings of PROMISE 2008 (ICSE), pp. 1–8 (2008)
17. Gay, G., Menzies, T., Jalali, O., Feather, M., Kiper, J.: Real-time Optimization of Requirements Models. Jet Propulsion, 1–33 (2008)
18. Williams, R., Gomes, C.P., Selman, B.: Backdoors To Typical Case Complexity. In: Proceedings of IJCAI 2003 (2003)

Protocol Testing and Performance Evaluation for MANETs with Non-uniform Node Density Distribution

Akihito Hiromori, Takaaki Umedu, Hirozumi Yamaguchi, and Teruo Higashino

Graduate School of Information Science and Technology, Osaka University
Yamadaoka 1-5, Suita, Osaka 565-0871, Japan
{hiromori,umedu,h-yamagu,higashino}@ist.osaka-u.ac.jp
http://www-higashi.ist.osaka-u.ac.jp/

Abstract. In this paper, we focus on Mobile Ad-hoc Networks (MANETs) with non-uniform node density distribution such as Vehicular Ad-hoc Networks (VANETs) and Delay Tolerant Networks (DTNs), and propose a technique for protocol testing and performance evaluation. In such MANETs, node density varies depending on locations and time, and it dynamically changes every moment. In the proposed method, we designate node density distributions and their dynamic variations in a target area. Then, we construct a graph called *TestEnvGraph* where all node density distributions are treated as its nodes and they are connected by edges whose weights denote differences of two node density distributions. We specify a set of edges to be tested in the graph, formulate a problem for efficiently reproducing all the given node density distributions and their dynamic variations as a rural postman problem, find its solution and use it as the order of reproduction of designated node density distributions and their variations. Protocol testing is carried out by reproducing node density distributions in the derived order. We have designed and developed a method and its tool for mobility generation on MANETs, which can reproduce any designated node density distribution and its dynamic variations in a target area. From our experiments for a VANET protocol, we have shown that our method can give a similar trend in network throughput and packet loss rates compared with realistic trace based protocol testing.

Keywords: Protocol testing, Performance evaluation, MANET, Mobility, VANET, DTN, Rural postman problem.

1 Introduction

With the advance of mobile wireless communication technology, recently several types of mobile wireless communication systems have been designed and developed. Smart phones and car navigation systems can be used for communicating neighboring people and vehicles, respectively. Mobile Ad-hoc Network (MANET) applications such as Vehicular Networks (VANETs) and Delay Tolerant Networks (DTNs) are becoming popular. VANET is the most promising MANET applications. Also, several DTN systems using smart phones and car

B. Nielsen and C. Weise (Eds.): ICTSS 2012, LNCS 7641, pp. 231–246, 2012.
© IFIP International Federation for Information Processing 2012

navigation systems have been proposed as emergency communication means in disaster situations. Those systems can be used as social systems and they require high reliability and sustainability. In general, sensor networks are stable and they are often used in areas with uniform node density distributions. However, unlike stable sensor networks, VANET and DTN applications are used under non-uniform node density distributions. Node density varies depending on locations and time, and it dynamically changes every moment. It is well-known that node mobility and density affect reliability and performance of MANET applications [2,18]. In order to improve reliability and performance of MANET applications, it is important to reproduce several types of node density distributions efficiently and carry out their testing in simulation using network simulators and/or emulation using real mobile devices (e.g. mobile robots).

In this paper, we propose a protocol testing method for such MANET protocols and applications. In the proposed method, first we designate a set of node density distributions and their dynamic variations for a target area for which we want to carry out protocol testing and performance evaluation. For example, in VANET applications, node densities near intersections might become high when their signals are red while they might become low when the signals become green. Here, we assume that protocol designers can designate such node density distributions and their variations for a target area through simulation and real trace data. Then, we construct a graph called *TestEnvGraph* where all node density distributions are treated as its nodes and they are connected by edges whose weights denote differences of two node density distributions. The graph *TestEnvGraph* represents a testing environment and its dynamic change of node density distributions to be tested. As shown in [2], it is known that it takes time to reproduce MANET with designated mobility and make it stable. Thus, it is desirable that we can reproduce all the designated node density distributions and their variations with a small cost. In this paper we formulate a problem for efficiently reproducing all the designated density distributions and their variations as a rural postman problem [12] of the graph *TestEnvGraph*, find its solution using a heuristic algorithm and use it as an efficient order to reproduce all the designated node density distributions and their variations.

On the other hand, in [20], we have proposed a method for generating a waypoint mobility model with designated node density distributions for a target area. In this paper, we slightly extend its method and use it to reproduce designated node density distributions and their dynamic variations mechanically. Fig. 1 denotes an example of a designated node density distribution and its mobility patterns. The dark gray cells in Fig. 1 (a) denote high node density while the light gray cells denote low node density. Fig. 1 (b) denotes example mobility patterns. Using a rural postman tour for the graph *TestEnvGraph*, we reproduce a testing environment which can treat any designated node density distributions and their dynamic variations with a small cost.

In order to show effectiveness of the proposed method, we have compared network throughput and packet loss rates of VANET applications in our approach with those obtained in real trace based (microscopic mobility based) approaches.

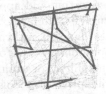

(a) node density distribution   (b) example mobility patterns

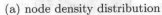

Fig. 1. Example of node density distribution and its mobility patterns

In ITS research communities, it is known that vehicular densities strongly affect the performance of vehicle-to-vehicle (V2V) communication. Therefore, trace based data and microscopic vehicular mobility models are often used. They are useful to reproduce typical traffic patterns. Here, we have generated vehicular mobility patterns using both the proposed method and a microscopic traffic simulator VISSIM [21], and compared their performance. We have generated typical 10 patterns of node density distributions and their dynamic variations near an intersection. Then, we have evaluated the performance of a protocol. The results are shown in Section 6. Our experiments have shown that the performance based on node density distributions and their dynamic variations derived using our proposed method and tool is rather close to that based on real trace based and microscopic vehicular mobility based traffic patterns.

Real traces and those obtained from microscopic traffic simulators can reproduce typical traffic patterns easily. However, it is difficult to reproduce peculiar traffic patterns using such methods. In general, it takes much time and costs to reproduce rare cases. On the other hand, the proposed method can designate any node density distribution and its variations. It can help to improve the performance and reliability of MANET protocols and applications. As far as the authors know, it is the first approach that we can designate any node density distributions and their variations and use them for protocol testing. By finding a rural postman tour for the graph *TestEnvGraph*, we minimize the cost for reproducing the designated node density distributions and their variations.

2   Related Work

It has been recognized that node mobility and density affect the performance of mobile wireless networks [15,23], and many mobility models have been proposed so far [3,18]. Random-based mobility models such as the Random Waypoint (RWP) model and the Random Direction (RD) model are often used, and some analytical researches have revealed their properties [5,14]. The results have shown that the node density distribution is not uniform; e.g. there is a high-density peak at the central point of the target area. There are several works for protocol testing of MANET. For example, Ref. [22] proposed a game theory based approach for formalizing testing of MANET routing protocols. Ref. [8] proposed a method for conformance testing and applied it to Dynamic Source Routing (DSR). For details, see a survey of Ref. [4].

On the other hand, if we want to design MANET applications for pedestrians with smart phones and/or running vehicles in urban districts, we need more realistic mobility. For example, in VANET application areas, Refs. [7] and [16] proposed adaptive protocols for efficient data dissemination from vehicles by considering neighboring vehicular density so that we can avoid the so-called broadcast storm problem. In [1], the authors proposed a method for estimation of vehicular density. Ref. [17] argued the need for combining a specific road traffic generator and a wireless network simulator. They need to be coupled bidirectionally when a target VANET protocol may influence the behavior of vehicles on streets. Recently, several microscopic vehicular mobilities are proposed as the means for reproducing realistic vehicular mobility [6,13,19,21]. A traffic simulator VISSIM [21] adopts a microscopic vehicular mobility. Ref. [19] also proposed a microscopic vehicular mobility which can reproduce a vehicular mobility close to real traffic traces obtained from aerial photographs of Google Earth.

MANET applications for pedestrians with smart phones have similar analysis. In [9], we have shown that there are large variations for performance and packet loss rates of multi-hop communications depending on node density distributions. In DTNs, it is known that node mobility and density strongly affect the reliability and performance of DTN applications (e.g. see [23]). Especially, if there are no rely nodes, in many DTN protocols, intermediate nodes store their received data and forward them to their preceding nodes when they are found. In order to show that proposed store-and-forward mechanisms can work well, we need to check sustainability for several types of node density distributions.

All the above research works show that reproduction of node mobility and density distributions is very important. However, there are very few works about testing of MANET protocols, which consider non-uniform node density distributions and their dynamic variations. This paper is motivated to give a solution for protocol testing on such a MANET.

3   MANETs with Non-uniform Node Density Distribution

In general, dissemination intervals of many VANET protocols are autonomously adjusted depending on observed node density so that we can reduce the probability of packet collisions. Many of DTN protocols have store-and-forward mechanisms so that packets can reach to their destinations even if node density for a part on their routes is very low for some period. Performance of such MANET applications cannot be evaluated by general random based mobility.

In Fig.2, we show node density distributions and average speeds of moving vehicles near an intersection where we divide a target road segment between intersections into three cells of 200 meters and show their node densities with three categories: "0(low)" (white cells), "1(middle)" (gray cells) and "2(high)" (black cells). In this figure, on the horizontal road, the densities of two cells close to the intersection are "high" and the other cells are very low, while the

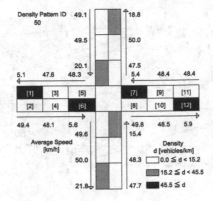

Fig. 2. Node density and average speed at an intersection in typical conditions

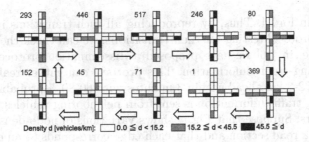

Fig. 3. Typical dynamic change of vehicular density distributions near an intersection

densities of the vertical road are "middle" or "low". It is a typical situation where vehicles on the horizontal road are stopping at the signal before the intersection and those on the vertical road run freely.

We have generated one hour's traffic trace data of 1 km² square area with 5×5 checked roads using the microscopic traffic simulator VISSIM [21], and analyzed their node density distributions (note that we have removed first 20 minutes' trace data in simulation since the simulated traffic has not been stable at first). In the analysis, we have made a density map like Fig. 2 at each intersection for every unit time period where the unit time period is 60 sec. Here, totally 1025 patterns of node density distributions are derived. In Fig. 3, we have shown typical 10 traffic patterns and their dynamic change representing a loop where an ID number is given for each pattern. We have classified the obtained patterns by density distribution patterns for horizontal roads, and found that the most emergent top 14 patterns can cover about 25 % of traffic situations.

Fig. 4 denotes the transitions among the top 14 typical patterns. When we execute typical VANET based dissemination protocols and multi-hop communications among running vehicles, the typical variations of their node density distributions correspond to transitions (sequences of edges) whose lengths are

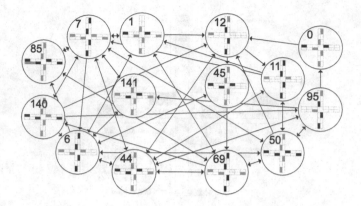

Fig. 4. Transitions among top 14 typical states

three or four in Fig. 4. Thus, by reproducing all such transitions in Fig. 4 and carrying out protocol testing for their transitions, we can check their reliability.

For example, in [16] we have proposed a dissemination protocol for propagating preceding traffic information. This protocol can gather real-time traffic information of 2-3 km ahead within 3 minutes with 60-80 % probability. Most of such preceding traffic information is sent from neighboring vehicles within a few hundred meters. Suppose that Fig. 4 shows variations of node density distributions for such a road section and that each edge corresponds to an one minute's variation of node density distributions. Then, each sequence of three edges from a state corresponds to dynamic change of node density distributions in the target road section for 3 minutes. Thus, by collecting all sequences of three edges from all states and by testing their performance, packet loss rates and buffer length, we can evaluate performance characteristic and reliability of the protocol. When we count the number of all sequences of three transitions from states corresponding to typical node density distributions, it becomes rather large. In Section 5, we will propose an efficient testing method.

We will give another example. In [10], we have proposed a protocol for realistic mobility aware information gathering in disaster areas where we combine the notion of store-and-forward mechanisms in DTNs and geographical routing on MANETs. In the proposed protocol, if intermediate nodes cannot relay safety information to its home cells by multi-hop communication, they hold it until they meet preceding nodes and re-transmit it as proxies. If shortest paths to home cells are not available, detours are autonomously found. However, in [10], we have only evaluated performance of DTN protocols for fixed disaster situations such as Fig. 5 (b) and (c) where the white cells and gray cells represent movable areas and obstacle areas, respectively. On the other hand, in an early stage in disaster, obstacle cells might be small like Fig. 5 (a), and they might become large like Fig. 5 (b) after time passes. It is desirable that we can reproduce such dynamic extension of obstacle cells (e.g. change from Fig. 5 (a) to Fig. 5 (b)), and carry out testing for a target DTN protocol.

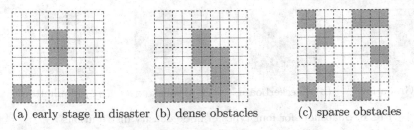

(a) early stage in disaster (b) dense obstacles   (c) sparse obstacles

Fig. 5. Expansion of obstacle cells in disaster

As we have discussed above, it is desirable that

(a) MANETs with designated node density distributions can be mechanically generated,
(b) dynamic variations (change) of node density distributions for a given MANET can be mechanically generated, and that
(c) if multiple dynamic variations (change) of node density distributions need to be tested, the total time necessary for testing should be minimized.

In the following sections, we will propose a testing method for considering those conditions.

4   Mobility Generation with Designated Node Density Distribution

In [20], we have proposed a method for generating a waypoint mobility model with designated node density distributions for a target area where each node repeats the process of (i) choosing a destination point in the target area, (ii) moving straightly toward the destination point with a constant velocity, and (iii) staying at the point for a certain time period. The goal of this work is to synthesize mobility patterns that can capture real (or intentional) node density distributions. Fig. 6 denotes typical node density distributions where dark and thin gray colors denote high and low node densities, respectively. A target area is divided into several subregions called *cells* and we can designate a favorite node density to each cell. In order to automatically generate natural mobility patterns realizing designated node density distributions, the method determines probabilities of choosing waypoints from those cells, satisfying given node density distributions. Fig. 7 denotes example mobility traces for the four types of node density distributions. The problem is formulated as an optimization problem of minimizing errors from designated node density distributions, and probabilities of choosing waypoints at each cell are determined. Since the problem has non-linear constraints, a heuristic algorithm generates near-optimal solutions.

Here, we extend the method in [20] so that we can treat variations of node density distributions. First, we give an outline of the method about how to determine the probabilities of choosing waypoints from each cell, satisfying given node density distributions. Assume that the target area is divided into $m \times n$

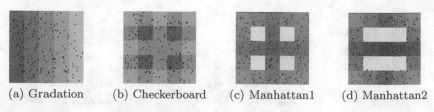

(a) Gradation   (b) Checkerboard   (c) Manhattan1   (d) Manhattan2

Fig. 6. Snapshots for four types of node density distributions

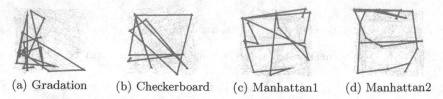

(a) Gradation   (b) Checkerboard   (c) Manhattan1   (d) Manhattan2

Fig. 7. Example traces for four types of node density distributions

square cells and these cells are numbered sequentially from top left (0) to bottom right ($m \cdot n - 1$) like Fig. 8 (a). Suppose that each node in cell i selects a destination cell (say j) with probability $p_{i,j}$ called *destination probability*. These probabilities need to satisfy the following equation.

$$\sum_{j=0}^{m \cdot n - 1} p_{i,j} = 1 \ (0 \leq i \leq m \cdot n - 1) \tag{1}$$

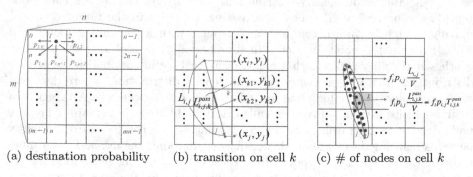

(a) destination probability   (b) transition on cell k (c) # of nodes on cell k

Fig. 8. Calculation of node transition probabilities

In a steady state, the number of nodes moving from an origin cell to a destination cell per unit time is constant. We call it as a *flow rate* and denote it as f_j. The flow rate f_j must satisfy the following equation.

$$f_j = \sum_{i=0}^{m \cdot n - 1} f_i \cdot p_{i,j} \ (0 \leq j \leq m \cdot n - 1) \tag{2}$$

Next, we define *cell transit time* representing time necessary for traveling from cell i to cell j and *cell transit number* representing the number of nodes moving through a cell (say, cell k). As shown in Fig. 8 (b), we denote an origin point in cell i and a destination point in cell j as (x_i, y_i) and (x_j, y_j), respectively. The average transit distance (denoted by $L_{i,j}$) between these two points is represented as $\sqrt{(x_j - x_i)^2 + (y_j - y_i)^2}$. Similarly, the transit distance on cell k (denoted $L_{i,j,k}^{pass}$) for nodes traveling from cell i to cell j is shown in Fig. 8 (b). Here, (x_{k1}, y_{k1}) and (x_{k2}, y_{k2}) denote the intersection points of the line segment between (x_i, y_i) and (x_j, y_j) on the two sides of cell k. Assume that all the nodes move at the same speed (denoted as V) and that they stop for the same pause time T^{pause} after arriving at their destination cells. Hereafter, $T_{i,j,k}^{pass}$ denotes the average cell transit time on cell k for nodes moving from cell i to cell j. $T_{i,j,k}^{pass}$ is represented by the following equation. Note that the value of $T_{i,j,k}^{pass}$ is zero if cell k has no intersection with the line segment (i.e. $L_{i,j,k}^{pass} = 0$).

$$T_{i,j,k}^{pass} = \begin{cases} \frac{L_{i,j,k}^{pass}}{V} & (j \neq k) \\ \frac{L_{i,j,k}^{pass}}{V} + T^{pause} & (j = k) \end{cases} \tag{3}$$

Hereafter, we show how to calculate the cell transit number by destination probabilities. The number of nodes moving from cell i to cell j per unit time can be represented as $f_i \cdot p_{i,j}$. The transit time for these nodes can be represented as $T_{i,j,k}^{pass}$. Thus the number of nodes passing cell k in the nodes moving from cell i to cell j is calculated as $f_i \cdot p_{i,j} \cdot T_{i,j,k}^{pass}$ (see Fig. 8 (c)). Since nodes might pass through cell k for different combinations of origin-destination cells, the total number of nodes at cell k (*cell transit number* d_k) can be represented as follows.

$$d_k = \sum_{i=0}^{m \cdot n - 1} \sum_{j=0}^{m \cdot n - 1} f_i \cdot p_{i,j} \cdot T_{i,j,k}^{pass} \tag{4}$$

Here, in order to treat the cell transit number for cell k as the node density for cell k, we assume that the number of all nodes is 1 as shown in Eq.(5). By applying f_i to Eq.(4), we can get the node density distribution obtained by $p_{i,j}$.

$$\sum_{k=0}^{m \cdot n - 1} d_k = 1 \tag{5}$$

Since the problem described above has non-linear constraints, we give a heuristic algorithm to derive a solution. A trivial solution satisfying the above constraints is that all nodes move only in the first assigned cells. In [20], we give a proof to show that for any node density distribution, we can generate the corresponding non-trivial waypoint mobility satisfying designated node density distributions like Fig. 7. For details about how to solve the problem with the above non-linear constraints, see [20].

In order to treat dynamic change of node density distributions, we give the following constraint when a new (next) node density distribution is generated from the current one. Let $\hat{p}_{i,j}$ and $p_{i,j}$ denote the destination probabilities from cell i to cell j at the current and next time slots, respectively. And, let $Diff$ denote the sum of the differences of destination probabilities at the current and next time slots for all cells. If we can minimize the value of $Diff$, the next node mobility can be generated relatively easily from the current node mobility. Then, when we find a solution satisfying the above constraints, we give the following objective function $Diff$ and find a solution minimizing the value of $Diff$. From our experiences, if the value of the objective function $Diff$ is small, time necessary to generate a steady next node density distribution becomes small. Thus, in this paper, from the obtained value of $Diff$, we will generate the next node density distribution by generating slightly different intermediate node density distributions sequentially from the current node density distribution. By using this method, we generate any dynamic variation of node density distributions.

$$Diff = \sum_{i=0}^{m \cdot n - 1} \sum_{j=0}^{m \cdot n - 1} \{p_{i,j} - \hat{p}_{i,j}\} \tag{6}$$

In Table 1, designated node density distributions and measured density distributions for the two mobilities are shown in the left side table and right side table, respectively. Although the derived mobility cannot reflect designated node density distributions perfectly, their errors are mostly within 0.1 % (there exist relatively larger errors for reproduction of empty node density distributions).

Table 1. Designated (left) and measured (right) density distributions (%)

3.00	4.00	3.00	4.00	3.00		3.01	3.92	2.94	4.00	3.00
4.00	6.00	4.00	6.00	4.00		4.14	6.04	4.07	6.07	4.03
3.00	4.00	3.00	4.00	3.00		2.98	3.99	3.94	4.01	2.92
4.00	6.00	4.00	6.00	4.00		3.94	5.99	4.02	6.01	3.91
3.00	4.00	3.00	4.00	3.00		3.01	3.99	3.01	4.00	3.00

(a) Checkerboard

4.00	4.50	5.00	4.50	4.00		3.95	4.41	4.96	4.41	3.95
4.50	0.00	5.50	0.00	4.50		4.39	0.41	5.34	0.41	4.39
5.00	5.50	6.00	5.50	5.00		5.00	5.43	5.92	5.43	5.00
4.50	0.00	5.50	0.00	4.50		4.39	0.41	5.34	0.41	4.39
4.00	4.50	5.00	4.50	4.00		3.95	4.41	4.96	4.41	3.95

(b) Manhattan1

5 Efficient Protocol Testing

In general, protocol testing is classified into two categories: simulation based testing and real machine based testing. Real machine based testing is not realistic for VANET applications. In such a case, using wireless network simulators and reproducing several node density distributions is one possibility. As far as the authors know, most of wireless network simulators can only reproduce random based and trace based mobility. On the other hand, our method can reproduce node density distributions corresponding to several types of vehicular mobility patterns and carry out the simulation based testing. The proposed method can be also used for real machine based testing. For example, if multiple mobile robots can follow the mobility patterns generated by the method described in the previous section, movement of such robots satisfies the designated node density distribution.

Here, we construct a graph *TestEnvGraph* for representing the testing environment in a target area. Let $T_{patterns}$ denote such typical dynamic transition patterns of node density distributions. For example, suppose that the node density distributions of three cells vary from "201" to "211" and "222" in turn where "0", "1" and "2" denote low, middle and high node densities, respectively. We want to carry out testing for variations of those node density distributions in this order. In such a case, we give a transition pattern ID "p_h" to this transition pattern "201 $\rightarrow$ 211 $\rightarrow$ 222" and make their pair $< p_h$, "201 $\rightarrow$ 211 $\rightarrow$ 222" $>$. We call this pair as the transition pattern with ID "p_h". Here, we assume that the set $T_{patterns}$ of transition patterns includes all the set of node density distributions and their variations for which we want to carry out testing.

Then, we construct the following graph $G = (V, E)$ where V denotes the set of all transition patterns with IDs where the node $< p_h, n_i > (1 \leq i \leq k)$ belongs to V if and only if a transition pattern $< p_h$, "$n_1 \rightarrow n_2 \rightarrow, ..., \rightarrow n_k$" $>$ is included in $T_{patterns}$, and the edge $< p_h, n_i > \rightarrow < p_h, n_{i+1} > (1 \leq i \leq k - 1)$ belongs to E if and only if $< p_h$, "$n_1 \rightarrow n_2 \rightarrow, ..., \rightarrow n_k$" $>$ is included in $T_{patterns}$. Here, we define *the difference of node density distributions*. For the transition pattern "201 $\rightarrow$ 211 $\rightarrow$ 222", we define that the difference of node density distributions between "201" to "211" is "1" since only low node density "0" of the second cell is changed to middle "1". On the other hand, the difference of node density distributions between "211" to "222" is "2" since the node densities of the second and third cells are changed from "1" to "2", and the sum of their differences is "2". We treat such a difference as the weight of the corresponding edge in E. Since only target transition patterns are represented as the graph $G = (V, E)$, $G = (V, E)$ is not always totally connected in general. Thus, we construct the graphs $G' = (V + V', E + E')$ and $G'' = (V + V' + V'', E + E' + E'')$ as follows.

For the graph $G' = (V + V', E + E')$, let V' denote the set of nodes where $< *, n_1 >$ and $< *, n_k >$ belong to V' if $< p_h$, "$n_1 \rightarrow n_2 \rightarrow, ..., \rightarrow n_k$" $>$ is included in $T_{patterns}$, and $< *, n_1 > \rightarrow < p_h, n_1 >$ and $< p_h, n_k > \rightarrow < *, n_k >$ belong to E' if $< p_h$, "$n_1 \rightarrow n_2 \rightarrow, ..., \rightarrow n_k$" $>$ is included in $T_{patterns}$. Here, we treat the weights for edges in E' as zero. Then, we construct the graph $G'' = (V + V' + V'', E + E' + E'')$ as follows, and treat it as the graph *TestEnvGraph* for representing the testing environment. For each pair of $< *, n_i >$ and $< *, n_j >$ whose difference of node density distributions is d, if there does not exist a path from $< *, n_i >$ to $< *, n_j >$ whose total sum of edges' weights is d in $G' = (V + V', E + E')$, we add $< *, n_{i_1} >, ..., < *, n_{i_{d-1}} >$ to the set of nodes V'', and add (i) edge $< *, n_i > \rightarrow < *, n_{i_1} >$, (ii) $< *, n_{i_p} > \rightarrow < *, n_{i_{p+1}} >$ $(1 \leq p \leq d - 2)$, and (iii) $< *, n_{i_{d-1}} > \rightarrow < *, n_j >$ to the set of edges E'' where

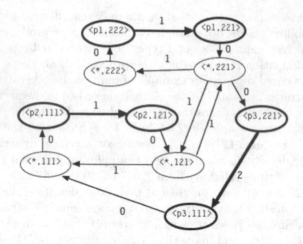

Fig. 9. Example *TestEnvGraph*

(i) the difference of node density distributions $< *, n_i >$ and $< *, n_{i_1} >$, (ii) that of $< *, i_p >$ and $< *, n_{i_{p+1}} > (1 \leq p \leq d - 2)$, and (iii) that of $< *, n_{i_{d-1}} >$ and $< *, n_j >$ are one. We treat the graph $G" = (V + V' + V", E + E' + E")$ as the graph *TestEnvGraph*. Note that there might be several choices for $< *, n_{i_p} > \rightarrow < *, n_{i_{p+1}} > (1 \leq p \leq d - 2)$. Here, any choice is acceptable as *TestEnvGraph*.

Fig. 9 denotes an example *TestEnvGraph*. Here, we assume $T_{patterns} = \{< p_1, \text{"222} \rightarrow 221" >, < p_2, \text{"111} \rightarrow 121" >, < p_3, \text{"221} \rightarrow 111" >\}$. In this example, there are three cells. The node density distribution "221" denotes that node density of the first two cells is "2" (high) and that of the third cell is "1" (middle). In $T_{patterns}$, three variations of node density distributions are required as those to be tested. The variation $<$ "222 $\rightarrow$ 221" $>$ requires that the node density distribution is changed from "222" to "221". In Fig.9, at first we construct the graph $G = (V, E)$. The nodes and edges with thick lines denote V and E, respectively. The value of each edge denotes its weight (the difference of node density distributions). The nodes and edges with fine lines denote those belonging to $V' + V"$ and $E' + E"$ of $TestEnvGraph = (V + V' + V", E + E' + E")$, respectively.

[*Property of TestEnvGraph*]

The graph *TestEnvGraph* holds the following properties.

(a) For each pair of $< *, n_i >$ and $< *, n_j >$ in $TestEnvGraph = (V + V' + V", E + E' + E")$ whose difference of node density distributions is d, there exists a path from $< *, n_i >$ to $< *, n_j >$ (also a path from $< *, n_j >$ to $< *, n_i >$) whose total sum of edges' weights is d in *TestEnvGraph*.

(b) If we carry out testing for all edges in E, then we can conclude that all the transition patterns representing the designated node density distributions and their variations in $T_{patterns}$ are tested.

[*Rural Postman Problem (RPP)*]

For a given directed graph $G = (V, E)$ and a subset $E' \subseteq E$ of edges (here, we call E' as the set of target edges to be traversed), Rural Postman Problem (RPP) is a problem to find the cheapest Hamiltonian cycle containing each of edges in the set E' of target edges to be traversed (and possibly others in E). The problem is shown to be NP-complete [12]. We call a cheapest Hamiltonian cycle as a rural postman tour for the graph.

Note that there are several heuristic algorithms for efficiently solving Rural Postman Problem (RPP) although such heuristic algorithms might not be able to find its optimal solution [12].

[Assumptions for protocol testing]

(a) We can generate a waypoint-based mobility model with any designated node density distribution using the method described in the previous section.
(b) It requires some cost (time) for generating the waypoint-based mobility model with a designated node density distribution.
(c) In order for changing a given node density distribution to another one whose difference of node density distributions is d, it requires some cost (time) in proportion to d.

[Problem to find the most efficient testing order for TestEnvGraph]

For a given $TestEnvGraph = (V + V' + V'', E + E' + E'')$ where E denotes the set of all the transition patterns of node density distributions and their variations belonging to $T_{patterns}$, if the above assumptions hold, then the problem to find the most efficient testing order for *TestEnvGraph* is formulated as a problem to find a rural postman tour for *TestEnvGraph* where E is treated as the set of target edges to be traversed.

In order for solving Rural Postman Problem (RPP), we have used a SA-based heuristic algorithm and found an efficient testing order for *TestEnvGraph*.

For *TestEnvGraph* shown in Fig. 9, suppose that we start testing from node $< *, \text{``111''} >$. Then, the rural postman tour (RPP) $< *, \text{``111''} > \rightarrow <$ $p2, \text{``111''} > \rightarrow < p2, \text{``121''} > \rightarrow < *, \text{``121''} > \rightarrow < *, \text{``221''} > \rightarrow < *, \text{``222''} > \rightarrow <$ $p1, \text{``222''} > \rightarrow < p1, \text{``221''} > \rightarrow < *, \text{``221''} > \rightarrow < p3, \text{``221''} > \rightarrow < p3, \text{``111''} > \rightarrow <$ $*, \text{``111''} >$ denotes a shortest tour for this testing and its total weights (the sum of the differences of node density distributions) is 6. If MANET designers generate variations of node density distributions in this order and carry out protocol testing, then they can carry out it with the minimum cost.

[Problem to find the most efficient testing order]

Let $V = \{n_1, n_2, ..., n_k\}$ denote the set of all designated node density distributions for which we want to carry out testing (and/or performance evaluation). Then, we designate $< p_i, \text{``}n_i \rightarrow n_i\text{''} > (1 \leq i \leq k)$ as $T_{patterns}$. Using the above algorithm, we construct *TestEnvGraph* and find a rural postman tour where $E = \{< p_i, \text{``}n_i \rightarrow n_i\text{''} > | 1 \leq i \leq k\}$ is treated as the set of target edges to be traversed. This modified rural postman problem (RPP) corresponds to the problem to find the most efficient testing order for carrying out tests of all designated node density distributions.

Table 2. The number of packet losses for trace data generated by VISSIM

Pattern	[1]	[2]	[3]	[4]	[5]	[6]	[7]	[8]	[9]	[10]	[11]	[12]	Total
293	0	0	0	3	0	1	0	0	0	0	0	1	5
446	0	0	0	0	0	1	0	0	0	0	1	0	2
517	0	0	0	2	0	0	1	0	0	0	1	0	4
246	1	1	0	2	0	1	0	0	0	1	2	9	17
80	0	0	0	0	0	0	0	0	0	0	6	7	13
369	0	1	0	0	0	0	0	0	0	1	7	4	13
1	0	1	0	0	0	0	0	0	0	0	4	6	11
71	0	0	0	0	0	0	1	1	0	0	0	2	4
45	1	0	0	0	0	1	1	1	0	0	1	1	6
152	0	1	0	1	0	1	1	0	0	0	3	3	10

Table 3. The number of packet losses for proposed method

Pattern	[1]	[2]	[3]	[4]	[5]	[6]	[7]	[8]	[9]	[10]	[11]	[12]	Total
293	0	0	0	2	0	2	0	0	0	0	0	2	6
446	0	0	0	0	0	1	0	0	0	0	0	0	1
517	0	0	0	2	0	0	0	0	0	0	1	0	3
246	0	0	0	2	0	1	0	0	0	1	3	8	15
80	0	0	0	0	0	0	0	0	0	0	7	6	13
369	0	0	0	0	0	0	0	0	0	0	6	6	12
1	0	0	0	0	0	0	0	0	0	0	4	6	10
71	0	0	0	0	0	0	1	1	0	0	0	2	4
45	0	0	0	0	0	1	1	1	0	0	1	1	5
152	0	0	0	1	0	1	1	0	0	0	3	3	9

6   Experimental Results and Analysis

Here, we show some experimental results and their analysis using a case study on VANET. Our method described in Section 4 can generate a similar node density distribution for a given traffic trace data. However, its mobility is not the same as that of real trace data. Therefore, we use the microscopic traffic simulator VISSIM and have measured node density distributions from the obtained typical trace data shown in Fig. 3. We have conducted a simulation for a trace composed of these 10 patterns to evaluate multi-hop communications by AODV protocol [11] over the intersection. We have transmitted packets from left to right through the intersection every 1 second. Table 2 shows the number of packet losses at each cell in Fig. 3 for the patterns. Each row [n] denotes the number of packet losses at the cell [n] on the horizontal road in Fig. 2. The routes by AODV protocol were usually constructed over cells on the horizontal road. Since the packets are transmitted from left to right and the vehicles on these cells also moved to the same direction. Thus, there are relatively few packet losses at the upside cells even though their densities are high.

We have also measured the node density distributions at those cells. Based on the obtained measured values, we have reproduced their node density distributions using the method described in Section 4 where "Manhattan1" mobility in Fig. 6 (c) is used for generating vehicular mobility. Then, we have evaluated the packet loss rates through network simulation. Table 3 shows the packet loss rates for the corresponding 10 patterns in Fig. 3. As shown in the two tables, although the results for Table 2 and Table 3 are not the same, they show that their similarity is rather high. Therefore, our proposed mobility model with designated node density distributions can expect a similar trend in network throughput/reliability that are related to how many packet losses occurred. Note that since the packet losses happen at different timing in the two methods, it might be difficult to reproduce and evaluate time sensitive protocols with our proposed method.

In general, trace based testing can represent realistic situations more accurately. Typical traffic patterns can be obtained easily. However, it is difficult to obtain unusual traffic patterns and it takes much time and costs. In order to improve reliability and sustainability of target protocols like VANET protocols, it is very important to reproduce not only typical traffic patterns but also unusual ones and evaluate the reliability and sustainability for those situations.

7 Conclusion

In this paper, we have proposed a method for efficiently carrying out protocol testing for a set of designated node density distributions and their variations. The method formulates the problem for finding the most efficiently testing order as the problem to find a rural postman tour for the graph called *TestEnvGraph*. The experimental results show that our method can easily reproduce node density distributions and their variations for VANET applications and their network throughput and packet loss rates are rather similar with those based on real trace based traffic data.

One of our future work is to collect several types of real trace data and evaluate the effectiveness and applicability of the proposed method.

References

1. Artimy, M.M., Robertson, W., Phillips, W.J.: Assignment of Dynamic Transmission Range Based on Estimation of Vehicle Density. In: Proc. of 2nd ACM Int. Workshop on Vehicular Ad Hoc Networks (VANET 2005), pp. 40–48 (2005)
2. Le Boudec, J.Y., Vojnovic, M.: Perfect Simulation and Stationarity of a Class of Mobility Models. In: Proc. of 24th Int. Conf. of the IEEE Computer and Communications Societies (INFOCOM 2005), pp. 2743–2754 (2005)
3. Camp, T., Boleng, J., Davies, V.: A Survey of Mobility Models for Ad Hoc Network Research. Wireless Comm. and Mobile Computing 2(5), 483–502 (2002)
4. Carneiro, A., Maag, S., Zaidi, F.: One Step Forward: Linking Wireless Self-Organizing Network Validation Techniques with Formal Testing Approaches. ACM Computing Surveys 43(2) (2011)

5. Chu, T., Nikolaidis, I.: Node Density and Connectivity Properties of the Random Waypoint Model. Computer Communications 27(10), 914–922 (2004)
6. Halati, A., Lieu, H., Walker, S.: CORSIM-corridor Traffic Simulation Model. In: Traffic Congestion and Traffic Safety in the 21st Century: Challenges, Innovations, and Opportunities, pp. 570–576 (1997)
7. Khelil, A., Becker, C., Tian, J., Rothermel, K.: An Epidemic Model for Information Diffusion in MANETs. In: Proc. of 5th ACM Int. Workshop on Modeling Analysis and Simulation of Wireless and Mobile Systems (MSWiM 2002), pp. 54–60 (2002)
8. Maag, S., Zaidi, F.: A Step-wise Validation Approach for a Wireless Routing Protocol. Posts, Telecomm. Inform. Tech. J. 1, 34–40 (2007)
9. Maeda, K., Uchiyama, A., Umedu, T., Yamaguchi, H., Yasumoto, K., Higashino, T.: Urban Pedestrian Mobility for Mobile Wireless Network Simulation. Ad Hoc Networks 7(1), 153–170 (2009)
10. Nakamura, M., Urabe, H., Uchiyama, A., Umedu, T., Higashino, T.: Realistic Mobility Aware Information Gathering in Disaster Areas. In: Proc. of IEEE Wireless Communications and Networking Conf. (WCNC 2008), pp. 3267–3272 (2008)
11. Perkins, C.E., Royer, E., Das, S.: Ad Hoc On-demand Distance Vector (AODV). Request for Comments 3561 (2003)
12. Pearn, W.L., Wu, T.C.: Algorithms for the Rural Postman Problem. Computers & Operations Research 22(8), 819–828 (1995)
13. Quadstone Paramics: Paramics, http://www.paramics-online.com/
14. Rojas, A., Branch, P., Armitage, G.: Experimental Validation of the Random Waypoint Mobility Model through a Real World Mobility Trace for Large Geographical Areas. In: Proc. of ACM/IEEE Int. Symp. on Modeling, Analysis and Simulation of Wireless and Mobile Systems (MSWiM 2005), pp. 174–177 (2005)
15. Royer, E.M., Melliar-Smith, P.M., Moser, L.E.: An Analysis of the Optimum Node Density for Ad Hoc Mobile Networks. In: Proc. of IEEE Int. Conf. on Communications (ICC 2001), pp. 857–861 (2001)
16. Saito, M., Tsukamoto, J., Umedu, T., Higashino, T.: Design and Evaluation of Inter-Vehicle Dissemination Protocol for Propagation of Preceding Traffic Information. IEEE Trans. on Intelligent Transportation Systems 8(3), 379–390 (2007)
17. Sommer, C., Dressler, F.: Progressing Towards Realistic Mobility Models in VANET Simulations. IEEE Comm. Magazine 46(11), 132–137 (2008)
18. Tracy, T., Jeff, B., Vanessa, D.: A Survey of Mobility Models for Ad Hoc Network Research. Wireless Comm. & Mobile Computing (WCMC) 2(5) (2002)
19. Umedu, T., Isu, K., Higashino, T., Toh, C.K.: An Inter-vehicular Communication Protocol for Distributed Detection of Dangerous Vehicles. IEEE Trans. on Vehicular Technology 59(2), 627–637 (2010)
20. Ueno, E., Hiromori, A., Yamaguchi, H., Higashino, T.: A Simple Mobility Model Realizing Designated Node Distributions and Natural Node Movement. In: Proc. of 8th IEEE Int. Conf. on Mobile Ad-hoc and Sensor Systems (MASS 2011), pp. 302–311 (2011)
21. PTV: VISSIM, http://www.ptv-vision.com/
22. Zakkuidin, I., Hawkins, T., Moffat, N.: Towards a Game Theoretic Understanding of Ad Hoc Routing. Electron. Notes Theoretical Computer Sciences 119(1), 67–92 (2005)
23. Zhang, X., Kurose, J., Levine, B.N., Towsley, D., Zhang, H.: Study of a Bus-based Disruption-Tolerant Network: Mobility Modeling and Impact on Routing. In: Proc. of ACM Int. Conf. on Mobile Computing and Networking (MobiCom 2007), pp. 195–206 (2007)

Parameterized GUI Tests

Stephan Arlt[1], Pedro Borromeo[1], Martin Schäf[2], and Andreas Podelski[1]

[1] Albert-Ludwigs-Universität Freiburg
[2] United Nations University Macau

Abstract. GUI testing is a form of system testing where test cases are based on user interactions. A user interaction may be encoded by a sequence of events (e.g., mouse clicks) together with input data (e.g., string values for text boxes). For selecting event sequences, one can use the black-box approach based on Event Flow Graphs. For selecting input data, one can use the white-box approach based on parameterized unit tests and symbolic execution. The contribution of this paper is an approach to make the principle of parameterized unit testing available to black-box GUI testing. The approach is based on the new notion of *parameterized GUI tests*. We have implemented the approach in a new tool. In order to evaluate whether parameterized GUI tests have the potential to achieve high code coverage, we apply the tool to four open source GUI applications. The results are encouraging.

1 Introduction

GUI testing is a form of system testing where test cases are based on user interactions. A user interaction may be encoded by a sequence of events (e.g., mouse clicks) together with input data (e.g., string values for text boxes). For selecting event sequences, one can use a black-box approach based, e.g., on EFGs (Event Flow Graphs, [9]). For selecting input data, one can use a white-box approach based, e.g., on parameterized unit tests [14] and dynamic symbolic execution [3].

Motivated by the established success of the black-box approach to GUI testing [2,9,16], we ask the question whether the black-box approach can be integrated with techniques from the white-box approach so that the resulting approach provides both, the selection of event sequences and the selection of input data.

Given the established success of parameterized unit testing [3,4,6,14,15], and given the apparent analogy between event handlers called in a GUI test and methods called in a parameterized unit test, it seems natural to ask whether we can obtain the desired integration by replacing method calls with event handler calls. At first sight, this approach is not possible: the assignment of the input data (e.g., the string value filled in by the user in a text box) cannot be found in any event handler called in a GUI test (the assignment is done, letter by letter, in the *message loop* of the GUI toolkit). There are other, more technical obstacles

B. Nielsen and C. Weise (Eds.): ICTSS 2012, LNCS 7641, pp. 247–262, 2012.
© IFIP International Federation for Information Processing 2012

(event handlers call native code of the GUI toolkit, event handlers hold a private access modifier which makes them unavailable for symbolic execution, etc.). I.e., the naive approach does not work.

The contribution of the work presented in this paper is an approach to make the principle of parameterized unit testing available to black-box GUI testing. The approach is embodied in a new tool, called *Gazoo*. Gazoo selects event sequences from the EFG of a GUI application and generates a set of *parameterized GUI tests*. Then, Gazoo applies Pex [3] in order to instantiate the parameterized GUI tests. Finally, Gazoo replays instantiated GUI tests on the GUI application.

In the terminology of the black-box/white-box dichotomy, Gazoo starts with a black-box approach (using the EFG in order to select executable test sequences), then moves on to a white-box approach (in order to generate parameterized GUI tests and instantiate them using Pex), and finally goes back to the black-box approach (using a replayer in order to execute the (instantiated) GUI tests on the GUI application). To establish the appropriate interface between the black-box approach and the white-box approach, we need to overcome a number of technical hurdles. In particular, we build an instrumented version of the GUI application in order to extract *sequential programs* as used in the parameterized unit test. We replace GUI widgets by *symbolic widgets* and inject *symbolic events* into the sequential programs in order to obtain what we call a *parameterized GUI test*. We evaluate Gazoo on four open source GUI applications. The experimental results indicate that parameterized GUI tests have the potential to achieve high code coverage.

2   Example

We illustrate how our approach tests GUI applications using an over-simplified example application given in Figure 1. The example application provides the functionality of an address book. The main window consists of two buttons that can add or remove a contact. When clicking the *add* button, a dialog window appears which provides two text boxes, for the first name and for the last name, and two buttons to store (OK) or discard (Cancel) the contact. In the following, we use the term *application* to refer to a *GUI application*.

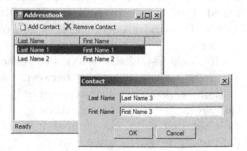

Fig. 1. Screen shot of the example application. The AddressBook application consists of two windows, a main window and a dialog. Clicking on `Add Contact` opens a new dialog and disables the events of the main window. Clicking on `OK` or `Cancel` closes the dialog and re-enables the events of the main window.

2.1   Selecting Test Sequences

When testing applications through its GUI there exist different possibilities in which order to interact with widgets. For example, one can first click the *remove* button and then the *add* button. However, the reverse order does not work as clicking the *add* button opens the dialog window, so *remove* cannot be clicked until the dialog window is closed. Thus, not all sequences of events are executable on the application. In order to avoid those non-executable event sequences, our approach incorporates a black-box model of the GUI, the Event Flow Graph (EFG) [9] depicted in Figure 2.

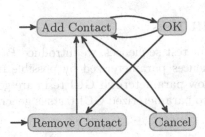

Fig. 2. Event Flow Graph of the example application. The events Add Contact and Remove Contact represent initial events that can be executed immediately after the application is launched. In contrast, the events OK and Cancel can be executed not until Add Contact is triggered.

An Event Flow Graph, $EFG = \langle E, I, \delta \rangle$, for an application is a directed graph. Each node $e \in E$ is an event of the GUI. Each event in $I \subseteq E$ is an initial event which can be executed immediately after the application is launched. An edge $(e, e') \in \delta$ between two events $e, e' \in E$ states that the event e' can be executed after the event e. If there is no edge between events e, e' then event e' cannot be executed after event e.

Using the EFG one can generate a set of *event flow sequences* of the application. An event flow sequence is a walk of a specific length in the EFG. Throughout this paper we generate event flow sequences of length 2, that is, neighbors of events. Event flow sequences do not necessarily start in an initial event, and thus, are not executable on the application. We expand event flow sequences to *test sequences* by inserting the shortest path from the first event of the event flow sequence to an initial event of the EFG. A test sequence $s = e_0, \ldots, e_n$ is a sequence of events, such that $e_0 \in I$ and $(e_i, e_{i+1}) \in \delta$ for all $0 \leq i < n$. Hence, a test sequence starts with an initial event and is executable on the application. Figure 3 shows all resulting test sequences of the example application obtained by event flow sequences of length 2 from the EFG. For the example application, our approach generates 6 test sequences in total.

The benefit of the EFG is the possibility to generate test sequences which are executable on the application. However, test sequences do not account for input data to widgets. When executing a test sequence on a GUI, recent efforts [9,17,18] insert random input data to widgets. We believe that the choice of input data is both vital to the coverage that can be achieved, and to the total number of executed tests. For example, choosing random values can result in low coverage.

Fig. 3. Test Sequences of the example application. The dark-colored events represent the events of the event flow sequence of length 2. The light-colored events represent intermediate events that make the event flow sequence executable on the GUI of the application.

$$t_1 = \langle\; \boxed{\text{Add Contact}},\; \boxed{\text{OK}}\; \rangle$$
$$t_2 = \langle\; \boxed{\text{Add Contact}},\; \boxed{\text{Cancel}}\; \rangle$$
$$t_3 = \langle\; \boxed{\text{Remove Contact}},\; \boxed{\text{Add Contact}}\; \rangle$$
$$t_4 = \langle\; \boxed{\text{Add Contact}},\; \boxed{\text{OK}},\; \boxed{\text{Add Contact}}\; \rangle$$
$$t_5 = \langle\; \boxed{\text{Add Contact}},\; \boxed{\text{OK}},\; \boxed{\text{Remove Contact}}\; \rangle$$
$$t_6 = \langle\; \boxed{\text{Add Contact}},\; \boxed{\text{Cancel}},\; \boxed{\text{Add Contact}}\; \rangle$$

Furthermore, multiple random values can result in a prohibitive large number of test cases (e.g., one randomly chosen value is integrated in one test case).

2.2   Generating Parameterized GUI Tests

To enable the generation of input data for test sequences, we introduce *Parameterized GUI Tests* which are test sequences parameterized by possible input data. In the following we first outline how parameterized GUI tests are generated. Then we describe how input data to parameterized GUI tests is generated in our approach.

```
1   class AddressBookWindow {
2       private ListView contacts;
3
4       // handler for event "Add Contact"
5       private void OnAddContact() {
6           ContactDialog dialog = new ContactDialog();
7           dialog.ShowDialog(this);
8       }
9
10   class ContactDialog {
11       private TextBox lastName;
12
13       // handler for event "OK"
14       private void OnOK() {
15           if ( 0 == lastName.Text.Length ) {
16               return;
17           }
18           if ( lastName.Text.Length > 255 ) {
19               throw new Exception("Text is too long.");
20           }
21           contacts.AddItem(lastName.Text);
22       }
23   }
24   }
```

Fig. 4. Excerpt of the source of the example application. The source code consists of two classes (AddressBookWindow and ContactDialog) and three event handlers (OnAddContact, OnRemoveContact, and OnOK). The event handler OnOK evaluates the text of the text box lastName. A new contact is only added, if the last name is not empty and contains less than 256 characters.

Figure 4 shows an excerpt of the underlying source code of the example application. The method OnAddContact represents the event handler which is

$$p_1 = \langle \boxed{\text{Add Contact}}, \boxed{\text{lastName}}, \boxed{\text{OK}} \rangle$$
$$p_2 = \langle \boxed{\text{Add Contact}}, \boxed{\text{Cancel}} \rangle$$
$$p_3 = \langle \boxed{\text{Remove Contact}}, \boxed{\text{Add Contact}} \rangle$$
$$p_4 = \langle \boxed{\text{Add Contact}}, \boxed{\text{lastName}}, \boxed{\text{OK}}, \boxed{\text{Add Contact}} \rangle$$
$$p_5 = \langle \boxed{\text{Add Contact}}, \boxed{\text{lastName}}, \boxed{\text{OK}}, \boxed{\text{Remove Contact}} \rangle$$
$$p_6 = \langle \boxed{\text{Add Contact}}, \boxed{\text{Cancel}}, \boxed{\text{Add Contact}} \rangle$$

Fig. 5. Parameterized GUI tests of the example application. In the PGT p_1, p_4, p_5, the event OnOK is prefixed with the parameter lastName. The PGTs s_2, s_3, s_6 do not need parameters.

$$t_{1a} = \langle \boxed{\text{AddContact}}, \boxed{\textit{empty string}}, \boxed{\text{OK}} \rangle$$
$$t_{1b} = \langle \boxed{\text{AddContact}}, \boxed{\textit{''a string with more than 255 characters''}}, \boxed{\text{OK}} \rangle$$
$$t_{1c} = \langle \boxed{\text{AddContact}}, \boxed{\textit{''Last Name 3''}}, \boxed{\text{OK}} \rangle$$

Fig. 6. Instantiated GUI tests of the parameterized GUI test p_1. The GUI test t_{1a} contains as input data an empty string; t_{1b} contains a string with a length greater than 255; and t_{1c} contains a string with a length lesser than 255.

executed once the corresponding button in the main window is clicked. The method OnOK is executed if the OK button in the dialog window is clicked. The event handler OnOK adds an element to the list of contacts (line 21), if the text of the text box lastName is not empty and contains less than 256 characters. If the text is empty, the event handler returns without adding a contact (line 16). If the text is too long, it returns with an exception (line 19).

Our approach detects that event handler OnOK evaluates the text of the text box lastName in the conditions (line 15 and line 18). That is, the event handler OnOK might need input data. We transform the test sequences from Figure 3 into parameterized GUI tests depicted in Figure 5. In particular, we prefix the event OnOK with the parameter lastName. The parameter lastName can adopt different values which can lead to different execution paths in the event handler OnOK. In our example application, only one text box is evaluated. If further text boxes are evaluated, we add parameters to the test sequence for each of them. Our approach does not only consider input data to text boxes, as described in Section 3.

Our approach instantiates each parameterized GUI test by an automatic computation of suitable input data. In this paper we incorporate Pex [3]. In general, input data can also be provided by alternative tools [15]. Pex uses dynamic symbolic execution to identify sets of input values that execute all control-flow paths of the program in the parameterized GUI test. E.g., for the parameterized GUI test $p_1 = \langle \boxed{\text{Add Contact}}, \boxed{\text{lastName}}, \boxed{\text{OK}} \rangle$, Pex identifies three distinct values of lastName that have to be tested as shown in Figure 6. With the valuations for lastName and the parameterized GUI test, we have all ingredients for a GUI test which can be executed using our replayer. The replayer accepts a set of GUI tests and mimics the events (user interactions) on the application. If a GUI test contains input data, this data is transferred to the corresponding widget. Furthermore, the replayer integrates an oracle that determines whether a GUI test passed or failed.

3   Approach and Implementation

In this section we present details of our approach and its implementation. As outlined in Section 1, there exist a bunch of issues in order to make the approach of parameterized GUI tests applicable to real world applications. Our approach depicted in Figure 7 consists of the following consecutive steps: (1) Event Flow Construction; (2) Symbolic Widget Injection; (3) Symbolic Event Injection; (4) Event Handler Elevation; (5) Generation of Parameterized GUI Tests, (6) Symbolic Execution, and (7) Replayer.

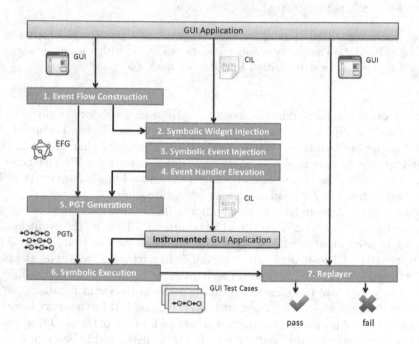

Fig. 7. Our approach, consisting of seven consecutive main steps. The input to our approach is a *GUI Application*. Input data is generated on the *Instrumented GUI Application*. GUI tests are replayed on the original *GUI Application*.

3.1   Event Flow Construction

The starting step of our approach is the *Event Flow Construction*. It takes the GUI of an application as input and outputs an Event Flow Graph. First, we execute the application and record its *GUI structure*. Second, we construct the EFG from the GUI structure. A GUI structure consists of widgets (e.g., windows, buttons, text boxes) and their corresponding properties (e.g., enabled or disabled). While executing the application, we enumerate all widgets of the GUI. This is done by calling specific functions provided by the GUI toolkit. For each found widget (e.g., a button) we trigger the assigned event (i.e., a click). If the click on the button opens a new window, we continue to record the GUI structure of the recently opened window and so on. The process stops if all found windows have been explored. Since a GUI represents a hierarchical structure, a depth-first search is performed. The obtained GUI structure is transformed into an Event Flow Graph. While the GUI structure contains information about widgets and their properties, the EFG represents an abstract view which only contains the events and their following events. The details of the EFG construction can be found in [10].

In our approach we enhance the EFG construction, such that, for each widget the event handler assigned to this widget is additionally stored in the GUI structure. This information is later needed during the generation of parameterized GUI tests and during the replaying of GUI tests.

3.2 Symbolic Widget Injection

In our approach we want to generate suitable input data, e.g., we want to reason about string values of text boxes. However, in order to perform a symbolic execution, we have to replace regular widgets by symbolic widgets. There are two main reasons: First, a change to a regular widget's property leads to a native call to the GUI toolkit. Including code of the GUI toolkit in the analysis is usually not feasible, as it would significantly increase the size of the code that has to be analyzed. Furthermore, in many cases, the code is in native format and thus not accessible by the analysis. Second, our approach focuses on validating the behavior of an application. In particular, we are not interested in validating the behavior of the GUI toolkit, i.e., validating whether a redraw of a widget was successful.

The step *Symbolic Widget Injection* takes the CIL[1] code of an application as input and replaces widgets by symbolic widgets. Figure 8 shows an excerpt of the symbolic representation of a text box. Gazoo uses Microsoft CCI[2] to modify the CIL code. By default, the main widgets included in the Windows Forms framework are considered, e.g., text boxes, check boxes, radio buttons etc. *Gazoo* is highly configurable: One can define further symbolic widgets for alternative GUI toolkits, such as Silverlight.

3.3 Symbolic Event Injection

In GUI applications, specific events do not have their own event handlers. For example, it is not likely to have an event handler which assigns a string value to a

---

[1] http://msdn.microsoft.com/en-us/netframework/aa569283.aspx
[2] http://ccimetadata.codeplex.com/

```
1  class TextBox {                        1  class SymbolicTextBox {
2                                         2
3    public string Text {                 3    string text;
4      get {                              4
5        // native call                   5    public string Text {
6        return GetWindowText();          6      get {
7      }                                  7        // a "getter"
8      set {                              8        return this.text;
9        // native call                   9      }
10       SetWindowText(value);           10      set {
11     }                                 11        // a "setter"
12   }                                   12        this.text = value;
13 }                                     13      }
                                         14    }
                                         15  }
```

Fig. 8. Comparison of regular widgets (left) and symbolic widgets (right). In symbolic widgets, native calls to the GUI toolkit are pruned (line 8 and line 12). A symbolic representative of the widget property (line 3), i.e., text, is injected. This property can be read and written by the get and set operations.

text box, once a user presses a key on the keyboard. This behavior is implemented in the GUI toolkit and does not exist in the application itself. In order to assign a string value, generated by the symbolic execution, to a text box, our approach injects symbolic events to the application. That is, we partially re-implement the event handlers of the GUI toolkit.

The step *Symbolic Event Injection* takes CIL code with symbolic widgets as input and returns a modified version of the CIL code, including symbolic widgets and symbolic events (see Figure 9). *Gazoo* visits the instructions of the CIL code. If it encounters an evaluation of a widget property, e.g., the Text property of a text box is evaluated, a symbolic event is added to the CIL code. A symbolic event is a *setter* method that takes one parameter representing the value to be assigned to the corresponding widget property. In our approach we separate the concerns of having both symbolic widgets and symbolic events: Symbolic widgets address the issue that properties of GUI widgets imply native calls. In contrast, symbolic events provide an interface that allows to assign a value to a widget property. Furthermore, in our setting we can assign values to widget properties. However, there exist widgets that prohibit the assignment of arbitrary property values. For example, the property Count which indicates the number of items in a *list widget*. In order to change the property Count, one has first to add an item to the list widget which increments the property Count. Those complex symbolic events are out the scope of this work and will be addressed in a future work.

3.4   Event Handler Elevation

Usually, in programming languages like C#, event handlers are implemented as *private* methods within classes. They are only visible to their surrounding class, and thus, cannot be called directly. In order to allow an exploration of the event handlers by the symbolic execution, we *elevate* event handlers. That is, for each method of the application we change their access modifiers from *private* to *public*; see Figure 9.

```
 1   // regular text box            1   // symbolic text box
 2   private TextBox lastName;       2   public SymbolicTextBox lastName;
 3                                   3
 4   // regular event handler       4   // elevated event handler
 5   private void OnOK() {           5   public void OnOK() {
 6     if (0 == lastName.Text.Length) 6    if (0 == lastName.Text.Length)
 7     {                             7     {
 8       // ...                      8       // ...
 9     }                             9     }
10   }                              10   }
                                    11
                                    12   // symbolic event
                                    13   public void SetLastNameText(string
                                             text) {
                                    14     lastName.Text = text;
                                    15   }
```

Fig. 9. Comparison of code from the original application (left), and the instrumented application (right). The instrumented application contains symbolic widgets (line 2), symbolic events (line 13), and elevated event handlers (line 5).

Gazoo visits the classes and methods of the executable. If it encounters a private class or a private method, it changes the access modifier and serializes all changes to the CIL code. Note that *Gazoo* also visits and modifies classes, in case they are not visible. The output of these steps is a *valid* executable. In particular, elevating classes and methods do not raise conflicts. For example, the access modifier does not influence the unique signature of a method.

3.5   Parameterized GUI Test Generation

Having obtained the EFG of a GUI (step 1) and built an instrumented version of the application (steps 2, 3, and 4), Gazoo generates a set of parameterized GUI tests. This step consists of two sub-steps:

First, Gazoo generates test sequences of a specific length from the EFG. Each test sequence represents a program that sequentially calls the event handlers of the events in the sequence. Second, for each event in the test sequence, Gazoo analyzes whether the event handlers rely on input data. For example, an event handler evaluates the property of a widget. If so, Gazoo transforms the test sequence into a parameterized GUI test. For each evaluated widget property, we add a new parameter to the parameterized GUI test. Furthermore, we prefix the event handler (that relies on input data) with a call to the symbolic event that assigns the input data. The idea is that the symbolic event writes the input data, while the selected event handler evaluates the input data. Figure 10 shows the difference between a test sequence and a parameterized GUI test.

3.6   Symbolic Execution

Having generated a set of parameterized GUI tests, our approach instantiates each parameterized GUI test by applying Pex. Pex takes as input a parameterized test and performs a dynamic symbolic execution on the instrumented

```
1  // a test sequence            1  // a parameterized GUI test
2  void TestSequence()           2  void PGT(string lastname)
3  {                             3  {
4    OnAddContact();             4    OnAddContact();
5    OnOK();                     5    SetLastNameText(lastName);
6  }                             6    OnOK();
                                 7  }
```

Fig. 10. Comparison of a test sequence (left) and a parameterized GUI test (right). In the parameterized GUI test, the call of event handler `OnOK` is prefixed with the symbolic event `SetLastNameText`. This symbolic event sets the parameter value `lastname` of the PGT to a text box.

application. The output of Pex is a set of concrete values of the parameters in the parameterized test. For each element in this set, we create an instantiated GUI test. An instantiated GUI test consists of the sequence of events from the parameterized GUI test, and the concrete parameter values for widget properties.

3.7   Replayer

The last step of our approach is the *Replayer.* The replayer takes as input a set of instantiated GUI tests and replays them on the original application. First, the replayer launches the application. Then, it executes the instantiated GUI test, consisting of an event sequence and its concrete parameter values for widget properties. After replaying a GUI test, the replayer closes the application. In our setting, the replayer uses a crash monitor as the oracle for each instantiated GUI test. However, the replayer is able to adopt further test oracles [11].

For each event handler in the GUI test, the replayer looks up the corresponding event in the EFG. Moreover, the replayer looks up the associated widget of the event in the GUI structure. Using this information, the replayer can find the widget on the GUI and can trigger its corresponding event. Gazoo incorporates *Ranorex*[3] to mimic user interactions, encoded as events, on the application.

For each parameter value in the GUI test, the replayer looks up the intended widget property. As described above, each parameter in the parameterized GUI tests is associated to one symbolic event. Moreover, each symbolic event writes a specific property of a widget. Like for the events in the GUI test, the replayer finds the widget on the GUI using the EFG and its GUI structure. Then, the replayer assigns the value of a parameter to the corresponding widget. This is done via *Reflection* and *Memory-mapped files*[4] in order to send data across processes (i.e., the replayer and the application under test). In Section 5 we discuss the implication of using reflection and memory-mapped files in GUI testing.

---

[3] http://www.ranorex.com/

[4] http://msdn.microsoft.com/en-us/magazine/cc163617.aspx

	AddressBook	OpenImage	Handbrake	FareCalculator
LOC	2778	2347	520	298
Classes	98	87	30	22
Methods	163	109	19	14
Events	45	13	7	3

Fig. 11. Statistical data of the AUTs used in our experiments

4   Experiments

In this section we evaluate our approach. We compare how our approach performs, (a) when the computation of input data is replaced by the use of random values, and (b) when the Event Flow Graph is not considered for event sequence generation. We first present the setup of the experiments. Then we discuss the results of the experiments. We define the following two research questions:

- **Q1**: Is it reasonable to use Pex-generated values instead of random values for widgets? A priori, this is not clear, for two reasons: (1) In GUI applications, events that evaluate input data might be simple, that is, they only check whether an input is entered or not. Then, one can achieve a reasonable coverage by providing arbitrary input (or no input). (2) Events might evaluate input data in complex ways, that is, checking whether a specific string is entered or not. Then, one cannot achieve a reasonable coverage due to limitations of the symbolic execution (wrt. to the underlying constraint solver).
- **Q2**: Is it reasonable to incorporate the Event Flow Graph in order to generate parameterized GUI Tests? In principle, the idea of selecting event sequences of an application is related to the generation of method calls of a library. In libraries, one can call each method at any time. Hence, there exist no order, in which library methods are allowed to call. In GUI applications one can call an event handler at any time as well. However, a call of an event handler may not be allowed, e.g., when the window of an event handler is not yet displayed. This leads to GUI tests that are not executable on the GUI.

4.1   Setup of the Experiments

We evaluate our approach on four C# open source applications: *AddressBook* manages contacts; *OpenImage* downloads images from websites; *HandBrake Encoder* converts video files; *FareCalculator* calculates ticket prices for trains. Except for FareCalculator [5], all other applications are fetched from CodePlex[5]. It is important to observe that we use stable versions where bugs are rarely found. We choose various applications to cover different code styles. Figure 11 shows some statistics of each AUT (Application Under Test).

Our experiments consists of the three configurations **A**, **B**, **C**. The configuration **A** generates event sequences of length 2 from the EFG, and uses Pex to

---

[5] http://www.codeplex.com/

generate input values for the event sequences. The choice of the parameter 2 is motivated by previous empirical studies on bugs in GUI applications [17]. The configuration **B** generates event sequences of length 2 from the EFG, but uses random values as input data. In order to have statistical confidence, we choose random values using 10 different seeds. Thus, each parameterized GUI tests is instantiated 10 times containing different input data. The configuration **C** generates all sequences of events of length 2. That is, it does not use the EFG, and thus, might select non-executable event sequences. By comparing configuration A and B, we investigate the coverage that our approach can achieve. By comparing configuration A and C, we investigate the number of non-executable GUI tests that our approach discards.

As a precondition of all GUI tests we define that all user settings of an AUT have to be deleted before executing the GUI test. As a postcondition of all GUI tests we use a crash monitor. In particular, we record any exception occurred during test case execution, and we automatically observe if a test case is executable on the GUI. For a discussion of alternative oracles we refer to [4,11].

The GUI tests are executed on 10 virtual Windows machines with 2.0 GHz CPU, 2 GB RAM, 500 GB HDD. In order to mitigate the effect of randomness, the configurations A, B and C are executed three times. The total number of executed test cases amounts to 24,063.

4.2   Results of the Experiments

Figure 12 shows the results of the experiments. We answer **Q1** with **Yes**: We find that it is reasonable to use Pex-generated input values instead of random input values. In all AUTs, the configuration A achieves a higher line and a higher branch coverage than the configuration B. For OpenImage, the improvement of the line coverage amounts to 19%, for AddressBook 41%, and for HandBrake 45%. FareCalculator is an outlier; the line coverage improvement is 76%. The reason is that FareCalculator consists of event handlers that need specific input data. Pex is able to generate this input data, while random values do not suffice. It is unlikely to achieve 100% line and branch coverage in an application, as the applications may also need input data that cannot be generated automatically. For example, if an application requires a valid URL to download an image from the web, Pex cannot generate such a valid URL. In this case, the application depends on external test data that must be specified by a test engineer.

We answer **Q2** with **Yes**: We find that it is reasonable to incorporate the Event Flow Graph in order to generate parameterized GUI Tests. For AddressBook, the configuration A generates 319 PGTs which leads to 349 instantiated GUI tests. In comparison, the configuration C generates 2025 PGTs which leads to 2352 instantiated GUI tests. Thus, 2003 out of 2352 GUI tests, that is 85%, are not executable on the application. For OpenImage, 17% of the GUI tests are not executable on its GUI. The reason is that in AddressBook and OpenImage it is not allowed to execute an arbitrary event at any time. For the AUTs HandBrake and FareCalculator, the configuration C generates the identical set of PGTs as configuration A. In these applications, the EFG is fully-connected, and each

AUT / Configuration	A	B	C
AddressBook			
Line Coverage (%)	74	43	74
Branch Coverage (%)	65	38	65
# PGTs	319	319	2025
# GUI Tests	349	3190	2352
Generation Time (s)	407	255	2739
Execution Time (m)	93	850	730
# Non-executable GUI Tests	-	-	2003
OpenImage			
Line Coverage (%)	63	51	63
Branch Coverage (%)	59	29	59
# PGTs	139	139	169
# GUI Tests	148	1390	179
Generation Time (s)	278	222	336
Execution Time (m)	38	359	46
# Non-executable GUI Tests	-	-	31
HandBrake			
Line Coverage (%)	88	48	88
Branch Coverage (%)	84	44	84
# PGTs	49	49	49
# GUI Tests	73	490	73
Generation Time (s)	71	42	71
Execution Time (m)	17	116	17
# Non-executable GUI Tests	-	-	-
FareCalculator			
Line Coverage (%)	93	22	93
Branch Coverage (%)	91	19	91
# PGTs	9	9	9
# GUI Tests	39	90	39
Generation Time (s)	49	34	49
Execution Time (m)	8	20	8
# Non-executable GUI Tests	-	-	-

Fig. 12. Results of the experiments.

event is also an initial event. We believe that is reasonable to incorporate the EFG by default: For large applications, our approach generates a subset of event sequences of the GUI. The event sequences in this subset are actually executable on the GUI. For small applications, our approach generates the same set of event sequences which would be generated without considering the EFG.

4.3   Threats to Validity

Beyond the selection bias due to the limited availability of open source C# applications, we report one threat to external validity: We evaluated four C# open source applications which incorporate the Windows Forms toolkit for building the GUI. Alternative programming languages and GUI toolkits, e.g., Java Swing, follow different paradigms of building graphical user interfaces. For example, it might be not possible to obtain event handlers during the construction of the

EFG. Thus, the construction of the EFG, the generation of parameterized GUI tests, and the symbolic execution must be adapted to the corresponding environment. In principle, there is no reason to believe that our approach is not applicable to other environments.

5   Discussion

Why a Black-Box Model?. In this paper we use a black-box model to represent events and their corresponding event flow. An EFG is constructed by executing the application and observing the behavior of its GUI. In principle it is also possible to use a white-box model of the application. For example, this white-box model might be constructed by techniques from static analysis. Since GUI code is written in many ways, a static analysis technique must be tailored to comprehend how a GUI is built. The use of a black-box model is justified by the reasonable trade-off between applicability and precision. The constructed EFG in our approach represents an approximation of the actual event flow of the application. Thus, our approach cannot guarantee to find all events of the application. For example, the application itself might be hostile or even faulty.

Why a Replayer?. One can argue it is not necessary to replay instantiated GUI tests on the original application. For example, one can execute GUI tests in a fashion of unit testing by simply calling the event handlers, and without mimic user interactions on the application. We believe it is mandatory to replay instantiated GUI tests on the application in order to comply with the idea of system testing. For example, timing problems can only be detected when executing the GUI test on the application itself. E.g., the replayer tries to execute an event on a window, but this window is not yet displayed.

The replayer assigns values, e.g., a string value to a text box, by reflection and memory-mapped files. In principle, this may violate an invariant of the application. For example, it may not be allowed to access a certain text box, since the text box is currently disabled. In our approach we use the EFG and its corresponding GUI structure to guess that a widget is accessible. However, since the EFG represents an approximation, it cannot be guaranteed that a widget is actually accessible. A possible alternative is to add annotations to the source code, stating that a value to a widget may only be assigned under specific conditions.

6   Related Work

In [13], Symbolic Java PathFinder is used to generate test cases. The symbolic execution is performed on unit level and combines concrete execution on system level. The use of Pex on a parameterized GUI test can be seen as symbolic execution on unit level. However, in our approach concrete execution on system level takes place when replaying instantiated GUI tests. Further, testing on system level eliminates the problem of executing infeasible sequences [7].

The approach presented in [5] generates test cases for GUI applications using symbolic execution. Our work differs in three main aspects: First, we incorporate a black-box model (an Event Flow Graph) of the GUI in order to select event sequences that are actually executable on the GUI. Second, we generate parameterized GUI tests which can also be used with other techniques than symbolic execution. Third, our approach is able to replay instantiated GUI tests in a black-box fashion on the application.

The work in [8] is related to our work on an abstract level in that it combines black-box and white-box testing. Concretely, however, the underlying technical issues to be solved are incomparable due to the different settings (unit testing vs. system testing, method calls vs. event handlers).

The focus in [1] (with shared co-authors) is to generate test sequences that are at the same time executable and justifiably relevant. Random values for widgets are used, as opposed to generated values as in this paper. We have to use different sets of benchmarks for the experiments, corresponding to the different programming environments (Java vs. C#). The migration of the work in [1] to C# is in progress.

7   Conclusion and Future Work

In this paper we have proposed a novel approach to the generation of GUI tests, implemented in a new tool called *Gazoo*. Gazoo selects event sequences from the EFG of an application and generates a set of *Parameterized GUI tests*. Then, Gazoo applies Pex in order to instantiate parameterized GUI tests. Finally, Gazoo replays instantiated GUI tests on the application. In the terminology of the black-box/white-box dichotomy, Gazoo starts with a black-box approach (using the EFG in order to select executable test sequences), then moves on to a white-box approach (in order to generate parameterized GUI tests and instantiate them using Pex), and finally goes back to the black-box approach (using a replayer in order to execute the (instantiated) GUI tests on the application). As shown in the paper, we needed to overcome a number of non-trivial technical hurdles in order to establish the appropriate interface between the black-box approach and the white-box approach.

The scope of this paper was to show that our approach can achieve high code coverage. Usually one expects that high code coverage translates to high bug detection rate. For future work, we need to evaluate that this holds true in our setting. This evaluation requires its own series of experiments where one applies statistical methods to fault-seeded versions of AUTs, following, e.g., [11,18].

Our work opens an interesting perspective for future research because the general scheme behind our approach goes well beyond a specific tool, here Gazoo. We need to explore different alternatives such as, e.g., [2,16] and, e.g., [12,19] for going back and forth between the black-box approach and the white-box approach in the sense described above.

Acknowledgments. This work is partially supported by the research projects EVGUI, ARV, and SAFEHR funded by the Macau Science and Technology Development Fund and the Chinese NSFC No. 61103013.

References

1. Arlt, S., Podelski, A., Bertolini, C., Schäf, M., Banerjee, I., Memon, A.M.: Lightweight Static Analysis for GUI Testing. In: ISSRE (2012)
2. Belli, F.: Finite-State Testing and Analysis of Graphical User Interfaces. In: ISSRE, pp. 34–43 (2001)
3. de Halleux, J., Tillmann, N.: Parameterized Unit Testing with Pex. In: Beckert, B., Hähnle, R. (eds.) TAP 2008. LNCS, vol. 4966, pp. 171–181. Springer, Heidelberg (2008)
4. Fraser, G., Zeller, A.: Generating parameterized unit tests. In: ISSTA, pp. 364–374 (2011)
5. Ganov, S.R., Killmar, C., Khurshid, S., Perry, D.E.: Event Listener Analysis and Symbolic Execution for Testing GUI Applications. In: Breitman, K., Cavalcanti, A. (eds.) ICFEM 2009. LNCS, vol. 5885, pp. 69–87. Springer, Heidelberg (2009)
6. Godefroid, P., Klarlund, N., Sen, K.: DART: directed automated random testing. In: PLDI, pp. 213–223 (2005)
7. Gross, F., Fraser, G., Zeller, A.: EXSYST: Search-based GUI testing. In: ICSE, pp. 1423–1426 (2012)
8. Kicillof, N., Grieskamp, W., Tillmann, N., Braberman, V.A.: Achieving both model and code coverage with automated gray-box testing. In: A-MOST, pp. 1–11 (2007)
9. Memon, A.M.: An event-flow model of GUI-based applications for testing. Softw. Test., Verif. Reliab. 17(3), 137–157 (2007)
10. Memon, A.M., Banerjee, I., Nagarajan, A.: GUI Ripping: Reverse Engineering of Graphical User Interfaces for Testing. In: WCRE, pp. 260–269 (2003)
11. Memon, A.M., Banerjee, I., Nagarajan, A.: What Test Oracle Should I Use for Effective GUI Testing? In: ASE, pp. 164–173 (2003)
12. Pacheco, C., Lahiri, S.K., Ernst, M.D., Ball, T.: Feedback-Directed Random Test Generation. In: ICSE, pp. 75–84 (2007)
13. Pasareanu, C.S., Mehlitz, P.C., Bushnell, D.H., Gundy-Burlet, K., Lowry, M.R., Person, S., Pape, M.: Combining unit-level symbolic execution and system-level concrete execution for testing NASA software. In: ISSTA, pp. 15–26 (2008)
14. Tillmann, N., Schulte, W.: Parameterized unit tests. In: ESEC/SIGSOFT FSE, pp. 253–262 (2005)
15. Visser, W., Pasareanu, C.S., Khurshid, S.: Test input generation with java PathFinder. In: ISSTA, pp. 97–107 (2004)
16. White, L.J., Almezen, H., Alzeidi, N.: User-Based Testing of GUI Sequences and Their Interactions. In: ISSRE, pp. 54–65 (2001)
17. Yuan, X., Cohen, M.B., Memon, A.M.: Covering array sampling of input event sequences for automated gui testing. In: ASE, pp. 405–408 (2007)
18. Yuan, X., Memon, A.M.: Using GUI Run-Time State as Feedback to Generate Test Cases. In: ICSE, pp. 396–405 (2007)
19. Zhang, S., Saff, D., Bu, Y., Ernst, M.D.: Combined static and dynamic automated test generation. In: ISSTA, pp. 353–363 (2011)

Author Index